Principles of Succession, Wills&Probate

Cavendish
Publishing
Limited

London • Sydney

Principles of Succession, Wills & Probate

Caroline Sawyer, BA (Hons), MA, Solicitor
Lecturer in Law
Bristol University

Cavendish
Publishing
Limited

London • Sydney

First published in Great Britain 1995 by Cavendish Publishing Limited
The Glass House, Wharton Street, London WC1X 9PX, United Kingdom.
Telephone: +44 (0) 171 278 8000   Facsimile: +44 (0) 171 278 8080
e-mail: info@cavendishpublishing.com
Visit our Home Page on http://www.cavendishpublishing.com

This title was previously published under the Lecture Notes series.

© Sawyer, C 1998
First edition 1995
Second edition 1998

British Library Cataloguing in Publication Data

Sawyer, Caroline
Principles of succession, wills and probate – 2nd ed – (Principles Series)
1. Inheritance and succession – England 2. Inheritance and succession – Wales
I. Title II. The law of succession III. Succession, wills & probate
346.4'2'052

ISBN 1 85941 386 2

Printed and bound in Great Britain by
Biddles Ltd, Guildford and King's Lynn

PREFACE

The law of succession involves many areas of life, some of it real life and some of it the more tortuous inadequacies of the law. It provides numerous examples of the problems of language which are the foundation of so many of the problems of law and practice, as well as being closer to the cutting edge of debates on the meaning and morality of private property than is sometimes immediately apparent. There is no viable alternative to succession law so long as private property exists and the individuals who own it keep dying; however total the control allowed them by the state during their lifetime, they cannot exercise it once they have died. How far and in what manner the state, in the shape of the law, will allow them to delegate their power is the stuff of succession law and practice.

This book is intended as a comprehensive introduction to the law of succession and the practice of wills and probate. It is recommended that it be used in conjunction with a statute book, with the precise words of the relevant parts of legislation being used to orientate the explanation of the application of the law in each chapter.

Readers will note that the deceased is referred to almost throughout as 'he'; the writer offers the excuse that succession is largely concerned with property and most property tends to be owned by men – at least until they die leaving some of it (for tax reasons) to their more long-lived wives.

I wish to thank Chris Willmore and Emily Sawyer for all their help.

Caroline Sawyer
March 1998

CONTENTS

Contents

Contents

Contents

Contents

Contents

Contents

Contents

Contents

Contents

Contents

Contents

TABLE OF CASES

TABLE OF STATUTES AND STATUTORY INSTRUMENTS

TABLE OF ABBREVIATIONS

A & M Trusts	Accumulation and maintenance settlements
AEA	Administration of Estates Act 1925
AJA	Administration of Justice Act 1982
CGT	Capital Gains Tax
IHT	Inheritance Tax
IHTA	Inheritance Tax Act 1984
I(PFD)A	Inheritance (Provision for Family and Dependants) Act
LPA	Law of Property Act 1925
LR(S)A	Law Reform (Succession) Act 1995
NAA	National Assistance Act 1948
NCPR	Non-Contentious Probate Rules
PET	Potentially exempt transfer
SLA	Settled Land Act 1925
TA	Trustee Act 1925
TCGA	Taxation of Chargeable Gains Act 1992

INTRODUCTION

The subject of succession is not always appreciated for the lively arena that it is. The provisions of the law of succession are an attempt to deal with a fundamental problem of the acquisition of individual wealth; you cannot take it with you when you go. Ownership of property represents success and achievement; it also represents security and power. In today's climate of individualism based on the importance of the ownership of property, succession law offers a construction of the property without the individual.

Contemplating the making of a will involves, for the individual, facing not only the fact of mortality but the passing of security, power and the control represented by wealth. For a society as a whole, succession law involves deciding how far and in what way the state will intervene in the individual's disposal of his property on death. It bites just where the freedom to be responsible for oneself meets the consequences of irresponsibility. The most ardent supporter of private property and testamentary freedom will usually hesitate to suggest that a man with a wife and several small children should be entitled to make no provision for them at all but to leave his property elsewhere; to have them left destitute by him offends the sense of family responsibility, and to have them supported by the state also offends the taxpayer's pocket.

The complexity of the formalities for the making of a valid will are often criticised, but suggestions for altering them have to be considered along with any risk of giving increased scope for fraud to unscrupulous relatives, or wider discretion to courts which might result in extra, hopeful litigation. Other jurisdictions, in this area as in others, have much to tell us about what the alternatives may be and what their advantages and disadvantages are.

Times change, and so does the law and its operation. The construction put by the courts on certain words or phrases has much to reveal about the working of the law as well as the minds of judges in particular, and the study of the errors of others offers much to the person who wishes to improve his practical drafting skills as well as his ability to identify pitfalls in whatever situation he may meet in practice.

The practical, concrete side of dealing with wills is one fraught with the conflicting structures of the past and the future. The law of succession essentially changes only slowly, often insufficiently slowly to deal with the fast-changing world it interacts with every day. It can impose on a modern world the assumptions and functions of a world that has passed by. Succession is, at least as much as other areas of law, one which involves looking at how other fields, such as how equity, or the rules of evidence, might affect the outcome in any given situation. However, because it deals with the future arrangements for property in the real world, incorporating such wide variables as the future births or deaths of family members, or the possible future of the testator's business enterprises, it also involves looking at the uncertainties of the world outside. Succession law involves the whole person and all areas of his life, so that each person must deal with both property and personal considerations in the same context, and do so in an attempt to predict how best to integrate the two in an uncertain future.

The ownership of real property has spread enormously – many more people own their own home than was the case a few decades ago. Factors such as the spread of divorce have meant more women owning property alone than might have previously been predicted. More people feel the need to have a will to deal with the property they own, and they also need to consider giving away their property during their lifetime in order to minimise tax liabilities.

The move towards intangible property such as pension entitlements and security of housing tenancy or employment that was observed during the 1970s has been replaced by the ever-increasing withdrawal of state systems. The retreat from state-enforced security in housing and employment, and moves towards temporary employment contracts, low wages and self-employment combine with the concerns over the reliability of private pension and insurance arrangements to produce a different attitude to the future of the sort of security that property provides, and thus a different attitude to the giving away of that property.

There may have been a move towards very concrete property in the shape of home ownership, but other changes have made the meaning of that form of property more elusive. Changes in social security legislation and practice mean that the risks and advantages of giving away property before death have altered considerably. Elderly people who have nothing to live on may find themselves at the mercy of a much reduced state system; but those who retain their property may simply find it rapidly depleted by nursing home charges, leaving them still dependent on the state system after a comparatively short time, with nothing to leave to their families. The potential for growth in the insurance industry overshadowed by revelations about the selling methods of many companies and the question marks over some private pension schemes. Planning for old age, especially now that so many people live so long after (often early) retirement, raises huge questions as to the future of state provision or regulation of insurance; the results of privatisation may be a considerable increase in unwillingness to take the risk of giving away anything during life, which may thus have unexpected consequences for the law and practice of succession.

The individual who is considering making his will does not necessarily want to know any more than how to order his affairs in a sensible, reliable and tax-efficient manner. The student of succession law needs to learn how to advise him to do that. But the student also has the opportunity to consider the broader picture – how the operation of the provisions fits into the wider context of changing patterns of property and family relationships and of the involvement of the state, both law-makers and judiciary, in an intensely personal area of the lives of individuals. And the practitioner, working in a field sometimes unaccountably neglected, will wish to know of current developments and especially of those areas which appear to be a minefield of potential negligence actions.

CHAPTER 1

HISTORY

1.1   Why study the history of the law?

The issues in succession law today all have roots in the depths of history. Just as with institutions such as government or education, the study of the history of the law may provide explanations of how particular principles arose, and once the roots of the current law are clear, that law itself becomes more apparently logical.

1.2   The old solutions may be the best ones

Live issues in succession today include, for example, the division of the deceased's property on intestacy, something which has been governed by rules since the first laws of this country were made in Anglo-Saxon times, and the use of the law to override a testator's will and restrict his testamentary freedom. The effects of the family provision legislation of today look very like the reintroduction of the ancient principles whereby a person could dispose only of a part of his personal property; the extension of the rules of family provision to the estates of intestates by the Intestates' Estates Act of 1952 echoes the proclamations of King Canute.

1.3   Some things are gone forever

Some things, on the other hand, have changed considerably. The rules of inheritance of land and personalty have been aligned. The rise of commerce and the increasing use of credit brought about changes in the role of a deceased person's personal representatives and their obligations to deal with his debts as well as his property. These basic changes are most unlikely to be reversed.

1.4   Land and personalty

Historically, the division between land and personalty was fundamental. The inheritance of each has a separate history: they devolved under different rules of intestacy in England until 1926, and indeed the difference persisted in the Scottish law of intestacy until 1964. Generally, it is said that the common law dealt with the devolution of land, and the ecclesiastical courts had jurisdiction over personalty; it has been suggested that the roots of the division do, however, lie further back, in Germanic laws which show the same dichotomy. The law governing the devolution of land was itself divided; various strands of law might combine to act differently on different parcels of land so that they did not all devolve alike, but varied in accordance with the tenure of the land, the prevailing customary law and the nature of the deceased's family relationships.

1.5 Land

Before the Norman Conquest of 1066, land was in most parts of England divided equally amongst the sons on the father's death. It was not permissible for a father to give more of his land to one son than another. In theory this did not stop him giving property outside the family, but rules grew up to prevent this. In the years following the Conquest, after a brief period during which realty was devisable by will and despite the reputed statement of William the Conqueror that 'I will that every child be his father's heir', the rule of primogeniture ('the first-born') began to hold sway. This held that the eldest son took all his father's land to the exclusion of any younger brothers (and, of course, all sisters). The Anglo-Saxon rules determining who took a division of the inheritance were replaced by new rules for determining who the heir was who would inherit realty. The right to inherit never ascended lineally – parents could not inherit – but descended to the issue of the last person seised of the land. Male issue had priority over female issue, and where there was more than one male, the eldest took alone, though females took together. Thus, if there was a son, or an eldest son, he took all his father's real property. The landowner's ancestor was represented by his lineal descendants; if this line failed, there was procedure for ascertaining the collateral heir.

Once the demand of maintaining equality amongst the sons had gone, the reason for restricting alienation went too, so that by 1200 land had become freely alienable during a man's lifetime. There were also more lenient rules governing the passing of land that had been purchased rather than inherited. By the 13th century, the courts were resisting attempts to disguise heirs as purchasers in order to avoid the rules against the alienation of land. It was not until the Inheritance Act of 1833, however, that ascendants as well as descendants were allowed to inherit. That Act replaced the old rules for ascertaining the heir with a simpler system, based on descendants, parents, siblings and their issue, grandparents and lastly the siblings of parents and more remote collaterals. The roots of the 1925 legislation, with its emphasis on the exclusion of inalienable interests in land, can be clearly seen in the history of the devolution of land.

1.6   Personalty

It was traditional for the personal property of a man who left a widow and children to be divided into three (or two, where the deceased left only a widow or only children), with his widow and children taking their parts and the remaining 'dead's part' being for him to distribute as he wished. This custom of the dead's part may even originate in the pagan custom of burying part – often a third – of the deceased's property with him to smooth his way in the underworld; reinterpreted under Christianity, this way of ensuring the safety of the soul of the deceased became construed as the making of charitable gifts on death.

By the 13th century, the church had assumed jurisdiction over the inheritance of chattels, and the making of a will expressing charitable gifts was regarded as an important religious duty almost equivalent to making a final confession of sins. There were customary rules as to the division of the chattels, a common scheme being the 'tripartite division' mentioned above, which persisted in London, Wales and Yorkshire until as late as the 18th century, and is perhaps echoed in the 20th century judge-made 'rule' for the distribution of property between husband and wife on divorce. The 'dead man's part' might be considered the origin of testamentary freedom, which has a more limited history than is sometimes supposed.

1.7   Wills

Wills of a sort were made in the Anglo-Saxon period, but they were irrevocable and, probably, not ambulatory. Thus, once the testator had by his 'last words' made a will, he could not retract it and was probably also obliged to carry it out immediately, rather than retaining the property until death. He might, however, make a so-called 'post-obit gift', or an immediate gift of personalty but with the retention of the use of the chattels until death. Wills of land were not usually possible at all; in any case, it was considered proper for land to devolve in accordance with the customary rules of inheritance. Gradually, wills in writing evolved, stating what the testator considered would be his last words when the time came; the church did not insist on any formalities, given that the potential for technical defects could only open the way to sinful intestacies.

After the Norman Conquest, the Anglo-Saxon forms of written wills disappeared, though the 'last words' remained. A century and a half later, however, a new form of written will appeared, owing much to the rediscovery of Roman law at the dawn of the middle ages. The ecclesiastical courts favoured testation rights in respect of both land and personalty, and would recognise and enforce wills of either, but the common law courts of the king did not accept devises of land which devolved in accordance with a system which protected the rights of the feudal barons. The common law courts began to oust the jurisdiction of the ecclesiastical courts in respect of land, save in certain parts of the country where particular privileges operated, for example Kent and the City of London.

1.8   Uses

In the centuries following the Norman Conquest, 'uses' developed to avoid the difficulties with the Crown's refusal to accept devises of land. Uses were a device by which the landowner passed the legal ownership of his land to grantees, retaining the use of the land during his lifetime and giving directions by will as to the use of it thereafter, thus bypassing the control of the common law courts over the inheritance of land. These directions would be enforced after his death by the Court of Chancery, until the Statute of Uses 1535 abolished uses altogether. This proved very unpopular, leading to the 'Pilgrimage of Grace', and in 1540 the Statute of Wills allowed certain forms of land tenures to be devised; in 1542 the scope of the Statute was widened by an Act Concerning the Explanation of Wills, and a further development of 1660 meant that estates in fee simple could be devised without restriction.

1.9   Formalities

The Statute of Wills 1540 brought in a requirement of writing, but only for wills of land. The formalities were made stricter by the Statute of Frauds of 1677, which required wills of land to be signed by the testator and witnessed by three credible witnesses. A beneficiary under the will was not a credible witness and could therefore cause the will to fail if he attested – the current position, where a witness-beneficiary's gift, rather than the will, fails dates from 1752. Nuncupative (oral) wills of personalty, unless the estate was worth no more than £30, had to be made in the testator's last illness in the house where he had lived for the previous 10 days, witnessed by three witnesses and committed to writing within six days unless proved within six months.

The requirements as to formalities varied with the nature of the property disposed of in the will, and were not always easily understood. This was one of the principal reasons for the passing of the Wills Act of 1837, which, with various amendments, remains in force today. It still reflects the exclusion from the provisions relating to formalities for soldiers and sailors which existed in the earlier legislation.

1.10   Married women

After 1660, when a man became fully able to devise his real property, that freedom was nevertheless restricted by his wife's right of dower. This gave her one-third of his freehold property. However, by the Dower Act of 1833, the husband was enabled to defeat the right of dower by alienation or by declaring in a deed or a will that he overrode the right. A married woman could not devise realty, and could dispose of her personalty only with the continuing consent of her husband and in certain other limited circumstances; the restrictions on her under the Statute of Frauds 1677 were continued under the Wills Act 1837 and not removed until the Married Women's Property Acts of 1882 and 1893. The Acts also gave the wife a right to defeat her husband's right of courtesy, which was his equivalent of dower; his entitlement was to a life interest in all her real property, subject to certain conditions.

1.11   Executors

The church, which encouraged charitable giving, viewed the appointment of an executor as a religious duty almost as important as the making of the will itself. The history of the executor began with the role of the person to whom the testator gave his 'dead's part' for distribution. In the absence of an executor, the heir at common law could obtain the deceased's property without any obligation to make charitable gifts; the church would have to rely on its powers of persuasion over him. From the 13th century, the ecclesiastical courts had jurisdiction over the validity of wills and required the testator's will to be proved immediately on his death. The courts acted in the person of the bishop, or 'ordinary', to whom the property of an intestate also passed.

1.12   Intestacy

The traditional division of property amongst a deceased's family customarily applied on intestacy, but was subject to competing claims from the church and the King. Intestacy is first mentioned under King Canute, in laws which appear to uphold the customary distribution of the intestate's property amongst his widow and children. William the Conqueror appears to have confirmed that the King would not lay claim to the chattels of an intestate, though there is doubt as to whether this promise was adhered to. The intestate's property was often regarded as forfeit. By the time of Magna Carta (1215), however, the barons had given up their claim to the property of the intestate and it was distributed amongst the deceased's family by the church. The ecclesiastical courts thus oversaw the distribution of personalty on intestacy as well as succession to personalty by will.

1.13   Administrators

By a law of 1285, the same obligation was imposed on the ordinary in respect of an intestate's debts as on an executor for the debts of a testator. Problems arose, however, where the estate of an intestate was administered by his family, for example, rather than the ordinary, who merely oversaw the administration. Creditors had no way of enforcing payment of the deceased's debts against the family members. In 1357, the ordinary became obliged to appoint administrators and they were in turn obliged to deal with the debts of the estate. The administrators were also empowered to sue on behalf of the intestate's estate. However, the common law courts so obstructed the overseeing of the administration by the church that eventually there was no enforceable obligation on the administrators to make a proper distribution once the debts had been met, until parliament endeavoured to remedy the situation by the Statute of Distributions of 1670.

The Statute of Distributions prescribed the distribution of personalty of an intestate, setting out a different scheme of ascertaining the entitled beneficiaries from that operating for realty. The heir could be included in the list of next of kin, who took a share unless the deceased left both widow and children. In that case, the widow took one-third and the children two-thirds; if the deceased left only children, they took the whole estate, and if a widow only, then she took half, with the other half going to the next of kin. The medieval London rule of hotchpot was incorporated into the Statute of Distributions and its remains were buried only in this decade.

1.14 Lay courts

The Court of Probate was established in 1857. It was a lay court to which the jurisdiction over probate and administration was transferred from the ecclesiastical courts. In the 1870s, the Supreme Court of Judicature Acts transferred jurisdiction over all testamentary matters to the Probate, Divorce and Admiralty Division of the High Court. A century later, this was abolished, when the High Court was re-established with its three divisions of Queen's Bench, Chancery and Family. The Family Division retains jurisdiction over probate matters; contentious matters of construction are assigned to the Chancery Division.

HISTORY

All societies with even the most rudimentary form of individual property must have some way for their members' property to be dealt with when they die. That involves questions about the nature of individual property and the nature of the claims of different persons on that property. The rules of any society – its laws and customs – will prescribe when and how far a person can control his property, and sometimes, with it, other people, from beyond the grave.

Many systems do not allow testamentary freedom. Often in ancient societies the deceased's property was automatically divided amongst his family, subject to a certain amount which was reserved for spiritual purposes. For example in certain ancient cultures it was buried with him, or under Christianity in Europe was supposed to be left for charitable purposes. With the beginnings of the separation of church and state the part left to charity became the part a person could leave as he wished. In many systems of law the ability to leave your property as you wish is still curtailed by law, particularly by the demand that parts of it are divided amongst the family. In England however in theory there are no such demands, though this is much more recent than many people think.

The devolution of property was historically different according to whether it was land or personal property that was being dealt with. The systems were, in broad terms, governed and administered by the crown and church respectively. The administration of the deceased's personal estate was originally carried out by the church, but it passed gradually into the hands of the deceased's family, being overseen at first by the church and then by the lay court.

The system of making wills and setting out what the deceased wanted to happen to his property evolved from the Anglo-Saxon spoken word to the formalities laid down by the Statute of Frauds of 1677, which required a will, in most circumstances, to be in writing. However, the formalities required for wills differed according to the type of property involved until they were unified under the Wills Act 1837, which remains the basis for the current law. All restrictions on testamentary freedom were gradually removed by the end of the 19th century, when such freedom did exist until it was limited by the introduction of family provision legislation just before the Second World War.

CHAPTER 2

WILL SUBSTITUTES

A person may not wish to leave all his property by will. An important reason for not doing so, for many people, is the tax implications. Inheritance tax is charged on the total value of the property the deceased owned at the moment before his death, with certain exemptions, so keeping the property until then, given that the deceased cannot take it with him, often means giving at least part of it to the Inland Revenue.

There are various ways in which a person may pass on his property without leaving it by will. The obvious method is give it away during his lifetime; this, if done sufficiently long before death, will have tax advantages. Death may effectively perfect an imperfect gift made during the deceased's lifetime. Property held on a beneficial joint tenancy will pass automatically to the other joint tenant or tenants; for the deceased's interest under a beneficial joint tenancy to pass under his will or intestacy, that joint tenancy must have been severed by one of the various methods available during the lifetime of the deceased, as it cannot be severed by will. A person may make a 'deathbed gift' of property or he may nominate it to another during his lifetime or deal with it through pension or life assurance arrangements. He may also contract to leave his property by will; such a contract may be enforceable.

2.1   Lifetime gifts

Lifetime gifts differ from gifts on death in respects other than that they are made whilst the donor is still alive. The transfer of ownership requires different formalities when it is made *inter vivos* (between living persons) from when it is made by means of a will. A gift of a chattel is made *inter vivos* by physical delivery of the chattel with the intention of making a gift. A gift of land *inter vivos* must generally be made by deed to be effective at law (s 52 of the Law of Property Act 1925), and for the requirements for registration to be complied with.

2.1.1   Capacity and intention

The transferor must have the appropriate capacity and intention to make the gift. In *Re Beaney* (1978), the transferor in question was the mother of three children, namely Valerie, Peter and Gillian. The mother became ill and Valerie returned home to look after her. She looked after her mother for two years before the mother executed a deed making over her house to her. A fortnight later, the mother was admitted to a hospital for the mentally ill, where she eventually died intestate about a year later. The gift of the house was challenged in the courts by Peter and Gillian, and the court held that the mother had not had the necessary capacity to make the gift, so it fell into her estate and was shared between the three children equally.

2.1.2 Undue influence and lifetime gifts

If a person has used undue influence to obtain a gift from another, that will negate the gift. A presumption of undue influence may arise in certain circumstances, which will give rise to a resulting trust in favour of the donor where there might otherwise have appeared to be a gift. This situation may arise 'where two persons stand in such a relation that ... confidence is necessarily reposed by one, and the influence which naturally grows out of that confidence is possessed by the one, and this confidence is abused ...' (*per* Lord Chelmsford LC in *Tate v Williamson* (1886)). In such a situation, the recipient cannot be allowed to retain their advantage. In *Allcard v Skinner* (1887), a nun had left her personal fortune to her convent. She had been under a duty of obedience to her Mother Superior, and in the circumstances of the case the court held that the Mother Superior had had undue influence over her. That finding of undue influence would have negated the gift had the plaintiff not left it so long before bringing her claim that the court also held her claim barred by the equitable doctrine of laches.

Undue influence may arise in respect of a lifetime gift even where there is no presumption, if it can be shown by evidence. In *Re Craig, Meneces v Middleton* (1971), where a man of gentle disposition in his 80s took on a secretary of somewhat stronger character and gave her £28,000 of his estate of £40,000 during his last five years of life, the court found that the gifts had been the result of her undue influence over him and set them aside.

Undue influence is, however, something quite specific, and different from showing that a person's liking for his donee is (at least in the eyes of the disappointed relatives) unaccountable. In *In the Estate of Brocklehurst* (1978), the Court of Appeal considered the grant by an autocratic landowner of a 99-year lease to a small garage proprietor with whom he had been on good terms. The grant was made after the date of the landowner's last will, made when he was 87 years old, and some six months before his death. The court held that the gift might be eccentric, but that a person of sound mind is entitled to make eccentric gifts, and it did not find that there had been any undue influence.

There is no presumption of undue influence in respect of gifts by will, but undue influence may be found on the facts (see 4.8).

2.1.3 Presumption of advancement

The effect of the presumption of advancement is that certain transactions are taken to be gifts rather than giving rise to a resulting trust in favour of the donor if they are between certain categories of persons, including, in particular, gifts from husband to wife (but not wife to husband), or father (but not mother) to child. In *Shephard v Cartwright* (1955), a father bought shares in the names of his children in 1929. During the 1930s, he sold them, and put the proceeds into the children's bank accounts. He subsequently withdrew the money and did not account for it. It was held by the court that he could not rebut the presumption of advancement of a gift by a father to his children because that would contravene the rule that statements of conduct on the part of the transferor after the transfer are inadmissible unless the transferor was speaking or acting against his own interest.

The continued existence of this presumption is in some doubt. It was decried in *Pettitt v Pettitt* (1970), and in *Falconer v Falconer* (1970) Lord Denning described the presumption of advancement as having 'no place, or, at any rate, very little place, in our law today'. The Law Commission in its Report No 175 *Matrimonial Property* recommended that the presumption be abolished by Parliament so as to reflect 'the modern legislative approach of treating men and women equally'. Nevertheless, the presumption can be revived when it is useful; it was applied, for example, in the case of *Harwood v Harwood* (1991), a matrimonial matter, in order to explain the decision of the court in that case.

2.2 Formalities

The formalities required to make a lifetime gift are very different from those required for a gift by will.

2.2.1 Delivery of personalty

A gift of most forms of personal property may be, and usually is, effected by delivery of the property. Where, however, some symbol of the property is given – for example, the key to a box – that will suffice. This rule appears to originate in practical considerations. The court in *Chaplin v Rogers* (1800) said: 'When goods are ponderous, and incapable ... of being handed over from one to another, there need not be an actual delivery; but it may be done by that which is tantamount, such the delivery of the key ... or by delivery of other indicia of property.' It appears, however, that whether or not property is capable of physical delivery, symbolic delivery will suffice, but that there must be some unequivocal delivery. The claim of a bankrupt's wife in *Re Cole* (1963) to the furniture she had been told was now hers failed because the Court of Appeal held the property still belonged to her husband. He had not made a deed nor sold the furniture to her, and when they were living together in the house it could not be said that the furniture had been delivered to her. The rules for *inter vivos* gifts could be compared to those for the making of *donationes mortis causa* (see 2.6).

2.2.2 Transfer of particular kinds of personalty

Certain sorts of personal property need to be dealt with in accordance with particular rules.

2.2.3 Cheques

Cheques must have gone through the bank account of the person who drew the cheque before the gift can be said to be complete. In *Re Swinburne* (1926), the Court of Appeal, categorising a cheque as an order for the delivery of money, held that it did not constitute an assignment of the money in the hands of the banker but only an authorisation for the cheque-holder to obtain the money from the bank.

2.2.4 Stocks and shares

Securities are usually transferred by using a form of stock transfer prescribed by statute. The usual stock transfer form requires a signature only, the Stock Transfer Act 1963 stating specifically at s 1(2) that a stock transfer need not be attested. The completion of the transfer is governed by the Companies Act 1985, which states at s 183 that a company may only register a transfer of shares in it if a proper instrument of transfer has been delivered to it. The transfer is therefore not complete until the transferee has sent both the signed transfer form and the share certificate to the company and the transaction has been registered.

2.2.5 Transfer of equitable interests

A transfer of an equitable interest is governed by s 53(1)(c) of the Law of Property Act 1925, which states that a disposition of an existing equitable interest must be in writing. The rationale behind this is that otherwise, if oral transactions were allowed, trustees could not be sure who was the real beneficiary. The only situation in which this does not apply is where the trust is a bare trust; the rationale for the requirement is irrelevant where the beneficiary can control the legal interest as well as the beneficial interest (*Vandervell v Inland Revenue Commissioners* (1967)).

2.2.6 Creation and disposition of equitable interests in land

Dealings with equitable interests in land are governed by s 53(1) of the Law of Property Act 1925. This states that dealings with equitable interests in real property must be in writing and signed, or made by will. It is expressly stated in s 53(2) that this rule does not affect the creation or operation of resulting, implied or constructive trusts.

2.2.7   Transfer of a legal estate or interest in land

A deed is generally required to deal with a legal estate or legal interest in real property (s 52 of the Law of Property Act 1925). The formalities required for deeds have changed a good deal over time, even though they may appear to be the essence of legal transactions. Before 1926, the making of deed called for the deed to be in writing on paper or parchment, sealed by each of the parties and then delivered. The 1925 legislation added the requirement that the deed be signed. 'Signed, sealed and delivered' became a well-known phrase, but the Law of Property (Miscellaneous Provisions) Act 1989 s 1 implemented the recommendations of the Law Commission in its Working Paper No 93 *Transfers of Land: Formalities for Deeds and Escrows* by abolishing the need for sealing, and requiring the intention to make a deed to be apparent from its face. The phrase 'signed as a deed' therefore replaced both the recitation of 'signed, sealed and delivered' and the sticky red discs to which the seal had been reduced (save for companies). Attestation (witnessing), which was compulsory in registered conveyancing and common practice for all deeds, also became compulsory, though only one signature is usually required.

2.2.8   Gifts not properly made

The general rule is that where the gift is not properly made, it will not be perfected in equity, because equity will not assist a volunteer. However, in certain situations, death itself may finally effect a gift (see *donatio mortis causa* at 2.6 below and the rule in *Strong v Bird* (1874) at 2.7).

2.3   Nominations

A person may make a written nomination of property which operates only at his death even though it is not a will. The nomination directs the person holding the relevant funds on his behalf to pay the funds to a named person on his death.

The original scheme was intended to avoid the need for those with little property to incur the expense of making a will. As the court in *Eccles Provident Industrial Cooperative Society Ltd v Griffiths* (1912) explained, it worked by giving the nominee a right to claim the relevant money from, in that case, the society, if the nominator died without having revoked the nomination.

Nominations may be non-statutory, which will usually mean those operating under pension schemes, or they may be statutory. Statutory nominations may be of sums not exceeding £5,000 payable by Friendly Societies or Trade Unions. It is no longer (since 1 May 1981) possible to make unlimited nominations of National Savings.

2.3.1 Ambulatory in nature

A statutory nomination is ambulatory, like a will. The nominator may therefore deal with the property as he likes during his lifetime. If the donee predeceases him then the nomination will fail.

Where nominations are required to be executed in the same manner as a will, they have been held to be testamentary; the designation of nominations as testamentary has also allowed the courts to apply the doctrine of lapse (see 10.6) where the nominee dies before the nominator. In *Re Barnes* (1940), the court held that 'this nomination has all the elements of a testamentary disposition and is, therefore, governed, so far as the question of lapse is concerned, by the ordinary rule in regard to a testamentary disposition'. So far as the formalities are concerned, in *Pearman v Charlton* (1928), the nomination failed when it was discovered that the person signing as 'witness' to the nominator's signature had not actually seen him sign.

2.3.2 Other jurisdictions

The rules relating to nominations within other common law jurisdictions are not standard. In Canada, for example, non-statutory nominations are viewed as testamentary documents and therefore void if they are not executed in accordance with the requirements for a will, whereas in the US the Uniform Probate Code provides that such dispositions are deemed to be non-testamentary by virtue of s 6-201.

2.3.3 Differences between nominations and wills

A nomination is unlike a will in three ways:

(a) firstly, it can be made by a person over 16. A formal will, however, requires a person to have reached the age of majority;

(b) secondly, the formalities required differ. Provision is made in each statute for what is required for each kind of nomination; non-statutory nominations were discussed in the *Danish Bacon* case (see below);

(c) thirdly, to revoke the nomination, the nominator will have to comply with the formalities laid down in the relevant statute, as a nomination cannot be revoked by a will or codicil. This last point can often be overlooked when the nominator later forgets that he has made the nomination.

2.3.4 The case against execution

If a nomination is executed like a will, it can be admitted to probate provided that it is also proved that the person executing it intended it to take effect only at his death. A statutory nomination, however, takes effect under the relevant statute, which will provide for the necessary formalities. It was argued in *Re Danish Bacon Co Ltd Staff Pension Fund Trusts* (1971) that a non-statutory nomination should be ineffective unless executed and witnessed like a will, because it was essentially testamentary. The court held however that although the nomination had certain testamentary characteristics, it was not a testamentary disposition as such and did not require execution in accordance with the Wills Act 1837. The court regarded it as a contractual arrangement outside the deceased's estate and not as a disposition by the deceased.

The deceased in *Baird v Baird* (1990) had worked for an oil company which provided a contributory pension scheme for its employees, certain benefits of which could be passed to others if he was still in the company's employment when he died. The deceased nominated his brother by signing the company's form. Five years later, he married, and two years after that he died. His widow claimed that the benefit should go to her, but the company claimed it should go to the brother. The widow eventually appealed to the Privy Council on the grounds that the benefit was an ambulatory disposition valid only if it was executed with the formalities required for a will. The court held that the power under a contributory pension scheme to appoint a non-assignable 'death-in-employment' benefit subject to the prior approval of the trustees of the scheme was in essence no different from any other power of appointment and did not dispose of any property, and therefore did not have to be executed as if it were a will.

2.4   Life insurance

Life insurance benefits may pass outside the estate if the policy has been taken out for the benefit of other persons. If nothing is done to direct the proceeds of a policy, those proceeds will fall into the estate of the deceased and pass in accordance with his will or intestacy. As, however, they are never going to be of any practical use to him, the deceased will usually ensure they pass directly to the ultimate recipient. If he directs that the policy proceeds should be held for his spouse or his children, then a trust in their favour will arise under s 11 of the Married Women's Property Act 1882. The policyholder may also divest himself of the benefit under the policy by making a declaration of trust or by assigning the legal and beneficial interest to the insurance company who will then pay to the intended beneficiary on death. This can be a very tax-efficient way of providing for dependants, since the gift thus made does not fall to be calculated with the rest of the estate for inheritance tax purposes; although the premiums paid will qualify for assessment to lifetime inheritance tax, they will usually be exempt under the provision allowing for normal gifts out of income or fall within the annual personal allowances.

2.5   Contracts to make a will or leave property by will

A person may contract to make a will. If the testator then makes a will as anticipated by the other party to the contract, there is no difficulty, but there is no guarantee for the other party that it will remain valid until the death of the testator. It may be revoked by the testator deliberately, or by operation of law.

Alternatively, he may make a contract to pass his property to someone on his death. There is no guarantee that the testator will retain the property which is the subject of the contract in his ownership until death so that it falls into the estate and can pass to the other contracting party.

2.5.1   Requirements for establishing a contract

A contract to make, or leave property in a will is valid if it complies with the usual requirements of a contract. A contract not to revoke a gift in an existing will is similarly valid. The validity of the contract does not necessarily mean that it can be enforced.

2.5.2   Effect of the contract on the making of wills or gifts by will

The existence of a valid contract does not mean that the testator can be forced to make a will with the necessary provisions. Nor does it mean that the testator, if he makes the will, cannot revoke it, if he so wishes. The testator retains full testamentary freedom in that he may still make his will in whatever terms he requires and he may freely revoke his will whenever he wishes. The existence of the contract also has no effect on the general provisions for the revocation of wills by operation of law on marriage.

2.5.3   If the contract is breached

If the testator has contracted simply to make a will, the contract will be fulfilled by the making of the will, although the testator will not be prevented from revoking the will afterwards.

If the testator has contracted to leave property by will and he breaches that contract by leaving the property elsewhere, a remedy may be obtained for the breach. This was established in the early case of *Hammersley v De Biel* (1845), where a father covenanted to his proposed son-in-law that he would settle £10,000 on his daughter, on the basis of which the marriage took place. The father left no such gift in his will, however, and the House of Lords affirmed that in such a situation 'a Court of Equity will take care that he is not disappointed, and will give effect' to the contract.

2.5.4 Breach by marriage

Where the will the testator contracted to make is revoked by his marriage, however, there will be no breach of contract because, as was confirmed in *Re Marsland* (1939), public policy does not allow constraints on marriage. A purported prohibition on automatic revocation by marriage is considered to operate in restraint of marriage and thus to be void on grounds of public policy.

It was established in *Robinson v Ommanney* (1883), however, that the fact that a contract may be breached by marriage, and that a breach of this kind would not be recognised as such by the law because of the rules against restraint on marriage, does not mean that the contract is therefore invalid of itself. The court will look to see why the contract was apparently breached before deciding whether or not to remedy the breach.

2.5.5 Breach of contract

If, however, the testator alienates the property during his lifetime, in breach of contract, the contractor may sue immediately for damages for the breach, subject probably to a reduction for the possibility of his dying before the testator. This construction does not square with the line of English authority which suggests that benefits passing by will in fulfilment of a contract may fail by the doctrine of lapse, but it is suggested particularly from the American authorities that the doctrine does not apply to contracts to leave property by will.

If the testator's estate turns out to be insolvent, the contractor will not have any advantage over other creditors merely because of the breach of contract. In *Graham v Wickham* (1863), it was argued that the claimant should be paid out of the assets applicable to legacies; the court held that what had been created was a specialty debt.

2.5.6 Contract to leave estate or part of estate

Any contract to leave the whole or a specified share of an estate to the contractor relates to the extent of the estate at death. Thus, if the testator who has made an agreement in those terms disposes of all his property during his lifetime, there will be no breach.

2.5.7 Contract to leave specific property

However, if the contract concerns specific property, the situation is different. In *Synge v Synge* (1894), a man had persuaded a woman to marry him by telling her (in a letter) that he would leave her a life interest in his house if she did so. After she had married him, he contracted to sell the house elsewhere, and she immediately became entitled to proceed against him for damages for breach of contract.

2.5.8 Enforceability of contracts

Whether and how the contract can be enforced depends on whether what the contracting party is trying to enforce is the making of a will or the passing of property. The former is unenforceable, whereas the latter may be dealt with by the court. Thus, a court will not oblige a testator who has contracted to leave a person his house to make a will in those terms, but it will either enforce a claim by that person against the estate for the house if the testator does not make the gift of it by will, or award that person damages if the testator alienates the property during his lifetime.

2.5.9 Effect on contract property of claims against the estate

If a valid contract is established, it was held in the Privy Council case of *Schaefer v Schuhmann* (1972) (see 15.35) that the property so contracted to be left is not available for distribution on a claim under the family provision legislation.

2.6 *Donationes mortis causa*

Donatio mortis causa is a Latin phrase meaning 'a gift because of death'. The plural of *donatio* is *donationes*. They are sometimes called 'deathbed gifts', although that may be misleading as the donor does not have to be quite on his deathbed. Although the gift is made by the testator during his lifetime, it differs from an ordinary lifetime gift in that it is made in expectation of an imminent death and operates only if that death comes to pass. *Donationes mortis causa* are, however, unlike gifts by will because, although they are dependent on death and operate only at death, anyone, not just a person entitled to make a privileged will (see 6.5), may make a *donatio mortis causa* without the need for writing or the other formalities required for wills.

2.6.1 Origins of the *donatio mortis causa*

The phrase is Latin and the concept comes from Roman law. In Roman law, a gift was not originally treated as a way of acquiring property so much as a reason for requiring its delivery; it was the delivery itself which transferred the ownership. When under the Emperor Justinian the law was extensively codified, however, '*donatio*' was treated as a mode of acquisition which passed ownership, divided into '*donationes inter vivos*' and '*donationes mortis causa*'. A *donatio mortis causa* was revocable at any time before death, unlike a *donatio inter vivos*, which could not be revoked. Unlike a legacy, however, a *donatio mortis causa* required no formalities and involved immediate possession. The *donatio mortis causa* of modern English law is a direct descendant of the Roman *donatio*, and 'dominion' (see below) a descendant of the Roman concept of *dominium*.

Donationes mortis causa appeared in English law at the beginning of the 18th century, following the introduction by the Statute of Frauds of 1677 of the requirement for writing in the making of wills. In *Hedges v Hedges* (1708), the court defined a valid gift of this kind as one which a man makes when he believes he is in his last illness and fears he will die before he has a chance to make a proper will. He then 'gives with his own hand his goods to his friends about him: this, if he dies, shall operate as a legacy; but if he recovers, then does the property thereof revert to him'.

Two centuries later, however, the nature of a *donatio mortis causa* was still giving rise to conceptual difficulties. The court in *Re Beaumont* (1902) thought it neither fish nor fowl, calling it 'of an amphibious nature ... neither entirely *inter vivos* nor testamentary'. The difficulty lies in that the gift is not an *inter vivos* gift, because it is dependent on the death of the donor, but neither is it testamentary; not only can the gift be made without the need for the usual formalities required for gifts by will, but 'if the donor dies the title becomes absolute and not under but as against his executor'.

2.6.2 Essentials of a *donatio mortis causa*

To be valid as a *donatio mortis causa*, the gift must be made:

(a) in contemplation of death; and

(b) conditionally on death; and

(c) by parting with dominion over the gift.

2.6.3 In contemplation of death

Donationes mortis causa, under Roman law, were essentially a way of avoiding the formalities required for the making of wills. The Roman *donatio mortis causa* did not have to be made in contemplation of death; this has been described as a 'peculiar requirement' and 'home-grown English law' (Kerridge, R, *Parry & Clark's Law of Succession*, 1996, 10th edn, p 23).

The death that must be contemplated is not the eventual death that will come to everyone but an imminent death within the near future. The death must be expected 'within the near future ... impending' (*Re Craven* (1937)).

2.6.4 Mistake as to cause of death

If a gift purporting to be a *donatio mortis causa* is made in contemplation of fairly imminent death from one cause and death subsequently results from another, the *donatio mortis causa* may still be valid. In *Wilkes v Allington* (1931), the donor had cancer and believed he would soon die from it. He made a *donatio mortis causa* in contemplation of that death. However, a month later he died of pneumonia which developed after he caught a chill on a bus journey. The court held the *donatio mortis causa* valid nevertheless.

2.6.5 Mistaken belief in imminent death

It is probable that a donor who genuinely but mistakenly believes he is danger of imminent death can make a valid *donatio mortis causa*. Clearly, the *donatio* will not take effect unless the donor's parting with dominion over the property is followed by his death. There is no reason of logic why death from a cause the donor did not expect should render a *donatio* invalid where the cause of death he did expect could not have materialised, when, as in *Wilkes v Allington* (1931), it does not affect the validity of the *donatio* if the expected cause of death could have materialised but did not do so. However, an authority on the point is awaited.

2.6.6 Death by suicide

There is no recent English case on the validity of a *donatio mortis causa* where the donor's contemplated or actual death occurs by suicide. Suicide used to be illegal, before it was decriminalised by the Suicide Act 1961. As one would expect, no-one was ever convicted of suicide. However, it remained an offence, as did attempting suicide.

The cases on *donationes mortis causa* and suicide predate the legalisation of suicide. The court in the Irish case of *Agnew v Belfast Banking Co* (1896) was explicit in its refusal to find a *donatio* valid when the death contemplated was one by suicide and therefore 'so purely voluntary as to be criminal in its origin'. The decision in that case was followed without analysis or discussion in the English case of *Re Dudman* (1925) but that again predates the 1961 Act. In another Irish case, *Mills v Shields and Kelly* (1948), the deceased had given property as a *donatio mortis causa* to a priest in contemplation of an imminent death from illness. On the way to Dublin for treatment, he left the train and killed himself. The *donatio mortis causa* was held valid by the court.

2.6.7 Conditional on death

The gift is revocable until death. Thus, if the donor finds he was mistaken about his imminent death, he can have the property back. Moreover, the *donatio* is always ineffective if the donee dies before the donor. The intention that the gift should be conditional on death does not need to be express; it may be inferred. In *Gardner v Parker* (1818), the donor was seriously ill when he gave the donee a bond for £1,800 and said, 'There, take that and keep it'.

Two days later, he died. The court inferred that the gift was intended to be conditional on the donor's death and therefore held that it was a valid *donatio mortis causa*.

The intention to make an immediate gift *inter vivos*, or the intention to make a gift by will, invalidates a gift as a *donatio mortis causa*, because the intention to do either of these things is incompatible with the necessary intention required for making a valid *donatio mortis causa*.

In *Edwards v Jones* (1836), the assignee of a bond signed a memorandum, not under seal, some five days before her death. This memorandum was indorsed on a bond purporting to be an assignment bond, without consideration. It was delivered to the donee but the language of the assignment was held to exclude the possibility of treating the attempted gift as a *donatio mortis causa*. It was therefore held to be an incomplete gift which equity would not perfect because there was no consideration.

2.6.8 Knowledge not fear of death

There have been suggestions that there can be no *donatio mortis causa* where the donor does not so much fear an imminent death as know that it is inevitable. Such an argument was raised in *Re Lillingston* (1952) (below), where it was suggested that donor, from her references to 'when I am gone' knew that she could not recover from her last heart attack. The argument is that a person who knows they are about to die cannot sensibly be found to have made a gift carrying a condition that it will be returned if they recover, since they know they will not recover. The court in *Re Lillingston* however, despite her words 'keep the key; it is now yours', construed the donor's words to mean that she would require the return of her property, both jewellery and keys, if she were to recover.

This point was, however, successfully argued in the case of *Lord Advocate v M'Court* (1893). The court was asked to construe a gift made by a donor who knew he was terminally ill. It held that the donor who knew he would not recover could not make a *donatio mortis causa* because the conditional element of the gift was lacking. However, it is submitted that this is one of those cases in which the court's view of the law may have been influenced by the preferred outcome of the case. At the time of this case, tax was payable on gifts passing on death, including *donationes mortis causa*, but not on lifetime gifts. The decision that it was a lifetime gift relieved the estate of a potential tax burden.

2.6.9 Parting with dominion

There is a difference between merely giving someone else physical possession of property and parting with dominion over it to them. For the requirements of a *donatio mortis causa* to be satisfied, there must be not only a parting with the goods – delivery of them to the donee – but also an intention existing at the time of delivery to part with control of them. Only once the two requirements of delivery and transfer of control have coincided will there be a parting with dominion sufficient to establish a *donatio mortis causa*.

In *Reddel v Dobree* (1834), the donor was ill when he gave a locked cash box to the donee telling her that the box had money in for her but that, while he lived, the donor wanted to see the box every three months. At his death, the donee was to go to the donor's son to get the key to the box. The court held that there was no valid *donatio mortis causa* because the donor had retained control over the property and had not parted with dominion it to the donee.

It was demonstrated in *Cain v Moon* (1896), however, that the delivery and the intention to part with control over the gift do not need to occur together, provided they are both present before the donor dies. In that case, the deceased had asked her mother to take possession of a deposit note, not with the intention of giving it to her, but merely for the purposes of safe keeping. When she fell ill, her mother still had the deposit note, and she said 'the bank note is yours if I die'. The earlier physical delivery of the deposit note, taken together with the later intention to part with control over it conditionally upon the donor's expected death, was held to be sufficient parting with dominion to establish a valid *donatio mortis causa*.

It follows that the donor must deliver the property to the donee during his lifetime. The donor in *Bunn v Markham* (1816) believed he was dying and directed that the words 'For Mrs and Miss C' be written on sealed parcels containing money and securities. The donor then declared that the parcels were to be kept in his locked iron chest until his death, following which they were to be delivered to the addressees. This clearly was not an *inter vivos* gift since the purported donor had retained the property during his lifetime. It did not fulfil the requirements for a gift by will. However, it also failed to fulfil the requirements for a *donatio mortis causa*, since the donor had not delivered the property with the intention of parting with dominion.

In *Treasury Solicitor v Lewis* (1900), the purported donee said that the elderly Mrs Dash had given him all her property subject to his settling her affairs, seeing about her funeral and making certain gifts to charity. She delivered to him a deposit note and share certificate saying, 'Take charge of them. If I get better you will bring them back; if not, you will know what to do with them'. Later she told him where he would find gold and notes, but she gave no further directions. The court held that she had reserved dominion over the property during her life and therefore there was no *donatio mortis causa*.

2.6.10 Parting with dominion does not necessarily mean giving a beneficial interest to the donee

A donor may part with dominion over the property he gives to the donee even though there is a trust imposed on the donee in respect of the property. Thus, in *Hills v Hills* (1841), the donee took the property on the basis that he would meet the expenses of the donor's forthcoming funeral and this was held to be a valid *donatio mortis causa*.

2.6.11 Agents of the parties

The delivery may be made by the use of agents, but they must be the agents of the relevant parties. This means that it will be sufficient for the donor to deliver to the donee's agent. It is not sufficient for the donor to deliver only to his own agent, even with instructions that the property be passed to the donee, because that is not equivalent to delivery to the donee.

2.6.12 Parting with dominion over the means of obtaining physical possession of the property

If the property is a chattel, it has long been settled that the chattel itself or else the means of obtaining it can be delivered. In *Re Craven* (1937), the donor's delivery of the keys to a box containing the gift was held to be sufficient delivery of the gift itself. Those were, however, the only keys. In *Trimmer v Danby* (1856), however, the donor's attempted gift to his housekeeper failed as a *donatio mortis causa*. He put 10 Austrian bonds in a box and wrote a note indicating that 'the first five numbers of those Austrian bonds belong to and are Hannah Danby's property'. He then delivered the keys to the box to her. However, it was held that he had not parted with dominion over the property because the housekeeper, being the servant of the donor, was presumed to be the agent of the donor, and he was held not to have parted with dominion over the property by giving her the keys.

2.6.13 Parting with total dominion over the means ...

In *Sen v Headley* (1991) (below), the court heard a claim by the deceased's housekeeper that the deceased had given her his house by *donatio mortis causa* by delivering to her the keys and the deeds to the property. However, the housekeeper made no claim that the deceased had also given her the contents of the house by the same means, because he had kept a separate set of keys to the property.

2.6.14 ... or over the means to obtaining the means

In *Re Lillingston* (1952), the donor gave the donee a parcel of jewellery and the keys to a trunk. She told the donee that the trunk contained the key to her safe deposit at Harrods, which in turn contained the key to her city safe deposit. She said she wished the donee to have the jewellery in the safe deposits as well, which the donee could go and get 'when I am gone'. The donee put the parcel of jewellery in the trunk and the donor then said 'keep the key: it is now yours'. The court held that there had been a valid *donatio mortis causa* of all the jewellery in both safes as well as the trunk.

2.6.15 Subject matter of the gift

The law of succession usually changes only slowly, but there has, in recent years, been a great change in the law relating to *donationes mortis causa* of real property. It used to be thought that the requirement for delivery, although much hedged about in the cases of such property as building society accounts (see 2.6.17 below), could not be effected even symbolically in the case of land, but this is no longer true (see 2.6.23).

2.6.16 Choses in action

Many items which are the subjects of *donationes mortis causa* are assets which are not really capable of delivery, but *donationes mortis causa*, as has been mentioned above, are an anomalous form of gift and the usual rules for the passing of title do not apply to them in the same way as to normal gifts. Some choses in action are clearly capable of delivery, for example, banknotes, or bearer securities such as cheques payable to 'the bearer' (these are less common now that most cheque books are automatically issued crossed 'account payee'). Bills of exchange, cheques and promissory notes payable to the donor have been held capable of passing by *donatio mortis causa* even though unendorsed and not capable of passing by delivery.

The deceased in *Re Mead* (1880) had held a banker's deposit note for £2,700. He had filled in a form requiring seven days' notice in order to give £500 of this to his wife, but died before the seven days were up. He had also signed a note saying 'pay self or bearer £500' and given this to his wife, as well as two bills of exchange payable to himself, not indorsed by him and falling due after his death. It was held that the orders not payable until after death could not form the subject matter of a *donatio mortis causa*.

In *Clement v Cheesman* (1884), the donor had given his son a cheque payable to the donor or order. The court, applying the case of *Veal v Veal* (1859) held that it operated as a promissory note or a bill of exchange and that therefore it had passed by *donatio mortis causa*. *Veal v Veal* appears to be the origin of the present law on *donationes mortis causa* of choses in action.

2.6.17 Essential *indicia* of title

A chose in action which is not capable of delivery may become the subject of a *donatio mortis causa*, provided the 'essential *indicia* or evidence of title, possession or production of which entitles the possessor to the money or property purported to be given' is delivered to the donee.

The definition of the essential *indicia* of title which are needed for a chose in action to pass by *donatio mortis causa* is taken from the judgment in *Birch v Treasury Solicitor* (1951). In that case, the donee handed over various post office and bank account books, intending the money to pass in the event of her contemplated death. The Court of Appeal held this amounted to a transfer sufficient to pass the money in the bank accounts by *donatio mortis causa*.

2.6.18 Need for *indicium* of title to be essential

The only accounts which may be transferred in this way are those which require the possession or production of a passbook. Obviously, the mere possession of a passbook does not entitle a person to the contents of the account in the normal way; a person finding a passbook in the street does not thus obtain entitlement to take the money from the account. The delivery by the donor of the passbook is simply the way in which he may fulfil the requirements of a *donatio mortis causa* for an account which otherwise cannot be 'delivered'.

Most accounts, however, cannot be delivered at all, even for the purposes of *donationes mortis causa*. These are those which do not have passbooks which must be produced in order for money to be taken out. The money in those accounts cannot be the subject matter of a *donatio mortis causa*.

2.6.19 Cheques made out to the donor

Cheques and promissory notes do not operate quite like most personal property. The donor of a lifetime gift of this kind of property (that is, a person making a gift of a cheque made out to himself by someone else) would have to endorse it in order to make the gift valid; where the cheque was drawn by someone other than the donor it can, however, form the subject matter of a valid *donatio mortis causa* because the donor could have used it to enforce by action the debt it represents.

2.6.20 Cheques drawn by the donor

Where, however, a cheque is drawn by the donor of the *donatio* himself, it is not enforceable as a *donatio mortis causa*. A cheque does not constitute entitlement to property of the sum drawn on it but is an order to the drawer's bank to pay that sum. The judgment in *Re Beaumont* (1902) made it clear that the order to the bank represented by the cheque is revoked by the donor's death, so the rule corresponds with that for lifetime gifts.

2.6.21 Real property

Until (in succession terms) very recently, it was thought that land generally could not pass by *donatio mortis causa*, although it had been held by the House of Lords that a mortgage could. The House of Lords in *Duffield v Elwes* (1827) held that a mortgage could be the subject of a *donatio mortis causa* by delivery of the mortgage deed. What passed was held to be the debt; the mortgage, being the security for the loan, then passed with it in a manner analogous to that of other securities and choses in action. The House of Lords went on to declare in that case that land as such could not be the subject of a *donatio mortis causa*.

2.6.22 *Sen v Headley* (1990) (High Court) – the last of the old rule

Mummery J at first instance in *Sen v Headley* (1990) followed the accepted rule that land cannot pass by *donatio mortis causa*. The plaintiff, Mrs Sen, had remained a close friend of the deceased after living with him for many years, and had visited him in hospital during what they both knew to be his final illness. He had given her the keys to his house, of which there were duplicates, and to a locked box, which had no other key and which contained the title deeds to the property. It was not in dispute that the deceased had given Mrs Sen the keys in contemplation of death and with the intention that the property should pass to her only on his death. The question was whether the title deeds could be regarded as the essential indicia of title necessary for property incapable of delivery to pass by *donatio mortis causa*; Mummery J held that this construction of a *donatio* could not be applied to land.

2.6.23 *Sen v Headley* (1991) (Court of Appeal) – the watershed

However, Mrs Sen appealed and won. The Court of Appeal in *Sen v Headley* (1991) held that the whole system of *donationes mortis causa* was an anomaly, and that the different rules relating to the *inter vivos* transfer of land did not justify making exceptions from the rule that were themselves anomalous. An exception for land was anomalous because the same rules ought to apply to it as to choses in action and mortgages. The court found that it was insufficient to suggest that the requirements of the Law of Property Act 1925 meant that land could not pass by *donatio*, because those formalities represented the same kind of obstacle, albeit a larger one, as the obstacles to the transmission by *donatio* of choses in action and mortgages.

The Court of Appeal did not consider itself bound by the statement of the House of Lords in *Duffield v Elwes* (above), because that had been *obiter*. It stated that if the point under consideration had been the subject of decision, then it would have 'loyally followed it', but 'we cannot decide a case in 1991 as the House of Lords would have decided it, but did not decide it, in 1827'.

2.6.24 Unregistered and registered land

Sen v Headley (1991) concerned unregistered land. Title to unregistered land is proved by production of the deeds to the land; the deceased had passed dominion over the deeds to the plaintiff. There is no decision as yet on whether the extension of the potential for *donationes mortis causa* to unregistered land covers registered land as well. The nearest equivalent to deeds in the case of registered land is the land certificate, but this is not really analogous as the title to the land is properly to be proved only through inspection of the current records of the land registry, of which the land certificate may not be an up to date representation.

Although in theory the introduction of the system of registration of title was a conveyancing matter and was not intended to alter substantive law, it is clear that the operation of the registered system has led to substantive differences in the law relating to the two systems. However, if the *donationes mortis causa* principle extends to choses in action, despite the particular rules which apply to their transfer, and to mortgages and unregistered land, despite the provisions of the Law of Property Act 1925, there is no reason why a court could not extend them to registered land as well.

A *donatio mortis causa* is an exception to the rules about the passing of property. As the Court of Appeal said in *Sen v Headley* itself: 'A *donatio mortis causa* of land is neither more nor less anomalous than any other. Every such gift is a circumvention of the Wills Act 1837. Why should the additional statutory formalities for the creation and transmission of interests in land be regarded as some larger obstacle? The only step which has to be taken is to extend the application of the implied or constructive trust arising on the donor's death from the conditional to the absolute estate.'

2.7   Imperfect gifts/ incompletely constituted trusts

Equity will not assist a volunteer, nor will it perfect an imperfect gift; however, the rule in *Strong v Bird* (1874) may assist someone who has been the object of an ineffective attempt at the making of a gift. It might also be possible to save an ineffective attempt to make a *donatio mortis causa* by use of the rule, although the intention required to make a lifetime gift and that required to make a *donatio mortis causa* are arguably too different from each other.

2.7.1   The rule in *Strong v Bird* (1874)

The rule in *Strong v Bird* (1874) comes into operation where the donor had the necessary intention to make the gift but did not pass the title to the property, and on his subsequent death the purported donee becomes his executor. Because the executor has the legal title to the property in the estate, his appointment to that office will perfect the gift. (The potential for perfecting an imperfect gift might be one reason why a person would be keen to take a grant (see 12.4).)

The case of *Strong v Bird* concerned the forgiveness of a debt. Mr Bird was the stepson of the deceased. The stepmother was living in his house and paying him for board when Mr Bird borrowed a large sum from her, which it was agreed should be repaid as a deduction of £100 from her next 11 quarterly payments for board. After two quarters of deductions, the stepmother forgave the debt expressly but not under seal or for consideration and thus not at law.

The stepmother died appointing Mr Bird as her executor. His debt was thus owed to her estate at law, but he was executor and could not sue himself. Thus, at common law, Mr Bird was no longer liable for the debt, and equity would not compel payment of it because the stepmother had intended to forgive it.

2.7.2   Imperfect gifts of property

The operation of the rule in *Strong v Bird* was extended to an imperfect gift of property. In *In Re Stewart* (1908), Neville J commented that '... where a testator has expressed the intention of making a gift of personal estate belonging to him to one who upon his death becomes his executor, the intention continuing unchanged, the executor is entitled to hold the property for his own benefit'. He held that the vesting of the property in the executor completed the imperfect gift and that the testator's continuing intention to make the gift prevailed over the gifts in the will, once the legal estate was vested in the executor.

However, in *Re Freeland* (1952) an imperfect gift of a car which was not delivered to the purported donee failed. The deceased had told one of her executrices that she intended to give her the car; she then lent it to a third party, which the Court of Appeal held was fatal to the claim that she had intended to make an immediate gift, even though the purported donee had consented to the loan.

Re Stewart was followed in *Re James* (1935), where the court, in upholding an imperfect gift of a house, stated that the rule applied to administrators as well as executors. Although this point was followed in *Re Gonin* (1977), where a daughter who had cared for her parents understood that she was to be given her mother's house when they died, the court doubted that it was correct. The mother died intestate and the daughter took out letters of administration of her estate, claiming this perfected the imperfect gift to her. The court disagreed strongly with the authority of *Re James* in respect of administrators and described the principle that a person taking the legal estate by operation of law, rather than under the deceased's will, should thereby be able to perfect an imperfect gift as 'in the nature of a lottery', doubting that equity was 'so undiscriminating'. In *Re Ralli* (1964), however, Buckley J said: 'In my judgment the circumstance that the plaintiff holds the fund because he was appointed trustee of the will is irrelevant. He is at law the owner of the fund. The question is: For whom ... does he hold the fund in equity?'

2.7.3 Incompletely constituted trusts

The area of gifts only partially made also requires consideration of the cases on incompletely constituted trusts. These often involve the transfer of company shares; see 2.2.4 for the formalities.

In *Milroy v Lord* (1862), a settlor purported to transfer certain bank shares to trustees on trust for the plaintiff. The legal transfer required entry in the bank's books. The intended trustee held the share certificates as well as a power of attorney from the settlor which would have enabled the trustee to apply to the bank for completion of the transfer. However, under the terms of the power the trustee could only act as agent for the settlor. No entry in the bank's books had been made at the time of the settlor's death, and the court held firstly that the trust was not completely constituted and that the shares belonged therefore both in law and in equity to the settlor's estate, and secondly that it could not be said that the settlor had put it out of his power to recall the gift as the terms of the power of attorney equated the trustee with the settlor.

This case was applied in the case of *Richards v Delbridge* (1874), where the attempting donor had tried to make over a lease of a business property together with the stock-in-trade by writing and signing on the deed. Because the gift was not made by deed it was ineffective, and the court, applying *Milroy v Lord*, declined to treat it as a declaration of trust, as this had not been intended by the would-be donor. Regarding it as such would amount to converting an imperfect gift into a perfect trust, and equity coming to the assistance of a volunteer.

In *Re Rose* (1952), the deceased had executed a share transfer but the legal title could not pass until entry had been made in the company register, which could be refused at the discretion of the directors. The transfer was executed in March 1943 and the entry was made in June 1943. The transferor died in 1947. The court held, for the purpose of estate duty computation, that the beneficial interest had left the deceased in March 1943, since from that date it lay within the power of the transferee to apply for registration. *Milroy v Lord* was distinguished on the ground that the power of attorney in that case was limited as described above. The court held that the deceased was in the position of a trustee of the legal title in the shares for the transferees. It distinguished the position of the transferee as regards the company from that of the transferee as regards the transferor. In *Milroy v Lord*, though the transfer form had been fully completed and the transfer and certificate delivered to him, the transferee had no rights as against the company until he was placed on the register; in *Re Rose*, the transferee became the beneficial owner because the transferor had done everything necessary to transfer his legal and beneficial interest in the shares. The case of *Re Rose* may be contrasted with, for example, that of *Re Fry* (1946), where the facts were similar but the transfer required Treasury consent because of the operation of exchange controls on foreign shares such as those concerned in that case.

2.8 Joint tenancies

If property is jointly owned in equity, then it will pass on the death of one joint owner to the other. It is very common for a matrimonial home to be owned jointly in equity as well as at law. It was confirmed in *Kecksemeti v Rubens Rabin & Co* (1992) that a solicitor who fails to advise a client of the effects of the right of survivorship on property held on a joint tenancy will be liable to an intended beneficiary who is thereby disappointed. In that case, the testator intended to benefit the plaintiff but his gift was ineffective because he held the property on a joint tenancy with his wife, and it therefore passed automatically to her instead. Joint tenancies of bank or building society accounts are also popular. In the case of a joint tenancy, two or more persons hold the property as if they were one person, and each of them is entitled to the whole of the property.

2.8.1 Creation of a joint tenancy

The joint tenancy will come into existence where property is conveyed or bequeathed to two or more persons and there are no words to show that they are to take separate and distinct shares and there is no presumption of a tenancy in common.

2.8.2 Joint tenancy at law and in equity

Since the Law of Property Act 1925, all co-owners of land must be joint tenants at law, whether they are joint tenants or tenants in common in equity.

There are three requirements for a joint tenancy to exist in equity:

(a) the four unities must be observed;

(b) there must be no words of severance;

(c) it must not be one of the instances where equity presumes a tenancy in common.

2.8.3 The four unities

The four unities are as follows:

(a) Possession:

Each co-owner has the right to the enjoyment or possession of the whole of the property. This also applies where there is a tenancy in common.

(b) Interest:

The nature and duration of each co-owner's interest must be the same.

(c) Title:

Each co-owner must derive his title from the same instrument as all the others.

(d) Vesting:

Each joint tenant's interest should vest at the same time as the others' interest.

2.8.4 Words of severance

Words of severance include 'in equal shares', 'equally', 'between', 'amongst' – all words which show that each co-owner is to take a distinct share in the property. If there are no words of severance in the relevant instrument and the four unities are satisfied, then the presumption of a joint tenancy will arise unless equity presumes otherwise.

2.8.5 Equitable presumption of tenancy in common

Equity presumes a tenancy in common in three situations:

(a) Purchase of partnership property:

It is presumed that the holding of business property is inconsistent with the right of survivorship, which is more appropriate to family situations.

(b) Joint mortgagees of land:

Where money is lent by two or more persons on a mortgage, the mortgage is held by them as tenants in common.

(c) Purchase money provided in unequal shares:

Co-owners who provide purchase money in unequal shares are presumed to hold the property as beneficial tenants in common in the same proportion to their contributions. If there is, however, a declaration of trust stating that the beneficial interests are to be held jointly, that will rebut the presumption. (This principle is rarely applied in practice, however, where the joint tenants are spouses.)

2.8.6   Tenancy in common

Where there is a tenancy in common, the co-owners have a right to a distinct share in the property but it is not physically divided between them. Tenants in common are said to hold the property in undivided shares.

2.8.7   Effect of death

On the death of one joint tenant, his interest automatically accrues to the surviving joint tenant by the right of survivorship or *jus accrescendi*. It cannot be left elsewhere by will.

The right of survivorship does not apply to tenants in common. A tenant in common's share on death devolves to his personal representatives and then, if it is not needed to meet debts or expenses, to the beneficiary entitled under his will or on his intestacy.

2.8.8   Severance and purported severance of a joint tenancy

A joint tenancy is easily severed, by notice to the other party or parties, or by other method such as the homicide of one joint tenant by another (see 10.10), but it cannot be severed by will. Thus, if a beneficial joint owner purports to leave his 'share' of the jointly owned matrimonial home to someone in his will, the gift will simply be ineffective. In respect of severance occasioned by the bankruptcy of one joint tenant, it was confirmed in *Re Dennis* (1995) that severance occurs on the act of bankruptcy, not on the later adjudication of bankruptcy itself.

2.9   Secret trusts

Where property is transferred by will to someone who has previously agreed to hold that property on trust for a third party, equity will enforce that trust, which operates outside the will and therefore does not conflict with the rule that wills must be in writing (s 9 of the Wills Act 1837 – see *Re Snowden (deceased)* (1979)). Clearly, however, there may be difficulties of evidence in establishing the trust.

2.10   Statutory succession

A person may have a right to succeed to a residential or agricultural tenancy held by the deceased. Such rights are limited to those created by the relevant statute (for example, s 17 of the Housing Act 1988, Pt IV of the Agricultural Holdings Act 1986) (see *Fitzpatrick v Sterling HA* (1998)).

WILL SUBSTITUTES

There are ways of disposing of property other than leaving it by will on death.

Lifetime gifts are an obvious solution; the formalities for making a successful lifetime gift are different from those for making a gift by will. All gifts by will are made in the same way, whereas the formalities for lifetime gifts differ depending on the type of property. The lifetime donor must have sufficient mental capacity to make the gift. A presumption of undue influence will be raised if the relationship with the donee falls into certain categories. If the gift is not successfully made, the property will remain with the donor and fall into his estate on death if not otherwise disposed of in the meantime.

Certain property, for example under a pension scheme, may be nominated during lifetime to be paid out to a named person on death; this is not the same as leaving it by will. The necessary formalities are those which apply to the particular form of nomination, not those which apply under the Wills Act 1837.

One may provide for others by taking out a life insurance policy on one's own life. The premiums on the policy will not usually give rise to any charge to tax and the proceeds, if in trust for the donee, will not form part of the insured's estate for tax purposes after his death. Because the policy is comparatively worthless during the insured's life, the emotional difficulty of parting with property during one's life does not arise.

Contracts to leave property by will are valid if they fulfil the usual conditions for contracts, but enforcing them may be difficult. A person cannot be obliged to make a will or to make one in any particular terms; nor can they be prevented from revoking a will once it has been made. If the contract is not carefully phrased, just making the will may fulfil it, and revoking it will not give rise to any cause of action. However, if a contract is breached then that will give rise to an action for damages against the estate. But if a contract is breached when a will is revoked by marriage, the law will not remedy that breach, because to recognise it would constitute a restraint on marriage and would thus be against public policy.

A *donatio mortis causa* is a particular form of gift whereby the donor makes a gift in contemplation of a particular and imminent death, conditionally on that death, and parts with dominion over the property to the donee during his lifetime. All these conditions must be fulfilled for there to be a valid *donatio*. If the donor then does not die, the property reverts to him. Parting with dominion usually means handing the property over, but where it is property incapable of being handed over then passing the essential *indicia* of title – for example, a building society passbook – is sufficient. It is now possible to pass land by *donatio mortis causa* by parting with dominion over the title deeds.

There is a general rule that equity will not assist a volunteer, so that if a person unsuccessfully attempts to make a gift, the donee cannot appeal to equity to perfect the gift. However, the rule in *Strong v Bird* is an apparent exception to this. It says that where the person who obtains the legal title to the deceased's property by virtue of being his personal representative after death also has the equitable claim on the property, the gift is thus perfected. This may be compared with the rules concerning incompletely constituted trusts. Equity will perfect a gift incompletely made only if the settlor or donor had so put the property out of his own control that he had become the trustee of the property.

If the deceased held property on a joint tenancy then it will automatically pass to any surviving joint tenant(s) at his death. Leaving a share of a joint tenancy by will is not possible; the joint tenancy must be severed before death. Once this is done, the property held by a person as tenant in common will pass in accordance with his will or intestacy.

Certain relatives of tenants of land may be entitled by statute to succeed to their tenancies and it should not be forgotten that equity will recognise a secret trust, where it can be proved.

CHAPTER 3

NATURE AND CHARACTERISTICS OF A WILL

3.1   Meaning of 'will'

The testator's will, in the sense of the means of making his testamentary dispositions, is the document or documents in which he has expressed what he wishes and intends to become of his property at his death. It should embody his will in the sense of his volition. If the testator has not had a will, in the sense of a volition, to make testamentary gifts of his property, then even if he makes and executes a document which states on the face of it that it is the testator's will and which complies with all the formalities laid down by statute, the lack of intention to make a will means that the document does not operate as such.

The will, to be valid, must comply with all the necessary formalities and be intended to take effect at the testator's death, disposing of his property or making other appointments; if it complies with all the requirements it will be the testator's will even if he did not know at the time that he was making a will.

Anything which is propounded as the testator's will must have all the necessary characteristics of a will and also comply with the formalities. If both these general conditions are satisfied, then the will is valid; whether or not it describes itself specifically as a will is not important.

3.1.1   Will is ambulatory

A will is ambulatory. This means that it is of no effect until the testator dies. The will may also be changed at any time. A declaration by a testator in his will that it is irrevocable is of no effect. He may revoke the will, including the clause stating that the will cannot be revoked, if he wishes. The beneficiary named in the will obtains no interest or rights until the testator's death.

Before 1926, wills were not ambulatory as regards real property. This meant that the real property to which a will could refer was fixed at the date the will was made. If the testator made a gift of 'all my real property', it would not include any real property acquired after the date of the will. Moreover, the formalities for realty and personalty were different before 1837. This is no longer the case; the same formalities now apply to real and personal property, so far as wills are concerned. This might be compared to the provisions for passing property *inter vivos* (between living persons), when common law and statute lay down different requirements for the passing of land and personalty (see 2.2).

3.1.2   How many documents?

Although the word 'will' is usually thought of as meaning – and is usually used to mean – a single document in which the testator sets out his intended testamentary dispositions, it is important to remember that, properly speaking, the testator's will is the embodiment of all his testamentary dispositions as whole in a form the law recognises as valid after his death. Thus, the testator has, strictly speaking, only one will, but it may be made up of many testamentary documents. The Privy Council considered this question in *Douglas-Menzies v Umphelby* (1908), saying: 'It is the aggregate or the net result that constitutes his will, or, in other words, the expression of his testamentary wishes. The law, on a man's death, finds out what are the instruments which express his last will ... In this sense, it is inaccurate to speak of a man leaving two wills; he does leave, and can leave, but one will.'

3.2   Intention to make a will

Although a will may, in the appropriate circumstances, be found in various and perhaps unexpected forms, no-one can ever make a will accidentally. It is one of the indispensable requirements of a valid will, of whatever kind, that the testator should have *animus testandi* (the intention of making a will) when the will is executed. Lack of testamentary intention renders a purported will invalid. The question of intention should not arise with a professionally-drawn will; the testator will have consulted his solicitor specifically to have a will drawn and there can be no doubt as to what he intended. Home-made wills, however, may be in the form of a letter, so that the true intention of the writer has to be inferred after his death from the words he uses, and the privileged (or informal) wills of soldiers and sailors may be made orally (see Chapter 6), so that even establishing what was said, let alone the intention behind it, can present difficulties. Nevertheless, the intention to make a testamentary disposition must be established if the will, or codicil, is to be admitted to probate. Admission to probate is vital to allow the personal representatives to give effect to the wishes contained in a document; they have no entitlement to carry out wishes expressed in a way which does not amount to a will just because they sincerely believe they represent the deceased's intention.

A recent case confirmed that testamentary intention must coincide with the execution of the will. In *Corbett v Newey* (1996), the deceased, Miss Tresawna, had owned two farms which were occupied by relatives and which she had originally intended to leave to them by will, with the residue of her estate to the same persons equally. She then decided to make *inter vivos* gifts of the farms to their occupiers and leave the residue to two great-nephews, and instructed her solicitors accordingly. The will was ready in September, before the deeds of gift of the farms, and Miss Tresawna, realising that if she died having made the will but not the deeds, the farms would pass to the great-nephews, executed but did not date the will. She and her solicitor were under the incorrect impression that the will would become valid only when dated; however, a date is not a formal requirement (see s 19). In December, the *inter vivos* gifts were made and Miss Tresawna dated her will. After her death, her niece claimed that the will was invalid because, when she executed it in September, Miss Tresawna had no immediate testamentary intention. In the first instance she lost, as the court found the will made in September valid as a conditional will. The Court of Appeal, however, found for the niece on the basis that the will was not conditional on the face of it and no extrinsic evidence was admissible to make it so; therefore, the question was simply whether it had been duly executed with testamentary intention and, clearly, it had not.

3.2.1 Presumption of intention

It is questionable how far proof of the necessary intention or *animus testandi* is required, or whether it will be presumed if the document appears to be intended to operate as a will. Certainly, however, any such presumption is subject, like any presumption, to being rebutted by evidence, as it was in *Corbett v Newey* (above). In *Nichols v Nichols* (1814), the deceased was a solicitor who, after a meal at which alcohol was drunk and the verbosity of lawyers criticised, made a document reading: 'I leave my property between my children; I hope they will be virtuous and independent; that they will worship God, and not black coats.' He wrote out his purported will with little apparent care and left it with his friend who later attested the signature. There was evidence that the deceased died believing that he had no will and stating that his property would devolve quite satisfactorily on intestacy; the court accepted that the purported will had been a demonstration of how brief the deceased could make a will – it was based on the will of his friend, but much shorter – and perhaps even a joke. The will therefore failed for want of testamentary intention.

Note that the state of mind of a testator is also relevant to his revocation of a will.

3.2.2 Document not made of testator's free volition

The testator may appear to have made a will freely and of his own volition, but appearances may be misleading. Even if the document contains dispositions which are exactly what the testator could be expected to make, it may be shown that the testator was pushed into making the document itself through the undue influence of another person, or that he did not know of the contents of the document and approve them before he executed the document. The details of other circumstances in which a will which is properly executed may yet fail for want of satisfaction of other mental requirements are dealt with below, in Chapter 4.

3.3 Conditional wills

A will may be conditional on certain events. For instance, it may be made expressly to take effect only if the testator should die on a particular voyage. If he survived the voyage, the will would then be of no effect. This is what occurred in *In the Goods of Robinson* (1870), where the will was expressed to be made 'in case anything should happen to me during the remainder of the voyage from here to Sicily and back to London'. He survived that voyage but died without making another will. The court held that the will was valid only if he died on the voyage specified.

Whether the will is conditional in such a way depends on the wording in each case; the precise meaning of the words used by the testator is a recurrent theme in the cases about wills. By the time the question arises, it is inevitably too late to ask the one person whose answer might be most useful. If the testator's intention was to make a conditional will, it will have to be established what the conditions were and whether or not they have been satisfied.

Thus, resort may have to be had to a court as the final arbiter of not only what words mean but also what a testator meant when he used them. In *In the Goods of Spratt* (1897), a soldier on campaign who expressed himself as writing to his sister because '... the chances are in favour of more of us being killed and as I may not have another opportunity of saying what I wish to be done with any little money I may possess in case of an accident, I wish to make everything I possess over to you ...'. He was held to have shown the necessary intention to make an unconditional will.

3.4 Testator may do other things by will than dispose of property

As well as doing what one would conventionally think of as the purpose of a will, namely disposing of his property, the testator may do other things by will. He may appoint testamentary guardians, though the formalities for this are less strict since the Children Act 1989 came into force (on 14 October 1991) and such appointments may be made in ordinary writing. The position is governed by ss 5 (appointment) and 6 (revocation and disclaimer) of the 1989 Act. By virtue of s 4 of the Law Reform (Succession) Act 1995, if there is a divorce or nullity recognisable under the Family Law Act 1986, the appointment of a spouse as guardian will cease to be effective unless the contrary intention appears.

The testator may also exercise powers of appointment by will – note that if he does so in another document which fulfils all the requirements of a will, including that it should take effect only on death, then the court may admit that document to probate too.

3.4.1 Testator may not dispose of his body by will

The testator may not, however, dispose of his own body by will, though attempts to do so are regularly made. The entitlement to possession of the body resides in his executors, who generally have the duty of disposing of it in accordance with regulations about public health. The executors do not, however, have any rights of ownership in the body. Private property in humans or parts of them is not recognised in English law. No doubt it often appears effective for testators to make directions as to the disposal of their bodies by will, but such directions are effective only insofar as their executors choose to abide by them. It can thus be an extremely bad idea to rely on putting one's wishes as to the disposal of one's body only into one's will. The grieving relatives will undoubtedly return from the crematorium to find, too late, that the deceased wished to leave his body to medical science. If a person wishes to dispose of his body in any particular way, he should make sure his relatives are aware of it and that he has signed any necessary, more relevant papers, such as kidney donor cards, and that they will be easily discoverable in the event that they are needed – for example, donor cards might be kept, signed, with the testator's driving licence.

3.5 When is a will valid?

A will is valid to pass any property the deceased has at his death if it made with the necessary mental capacity and intention and is executed in accordance with formalities laid down by the Wills Act 1837. The same applies to a codicil, which is a document amending a will but otherwise fulfilling all the same functions and conditions.

3.5.1 Presumption of will where document fulfils requirements

Although a will usually does describe itself as such, it is not necessary for it to do so. Lord Penzance in *Cock v Cooke* (1866) said: 'It is undoubted law that whatever may be the form of a duly executed instrument, if the person executing it intends that it shall not take effect until after his death, and it is dependent upon his death for its vigour and effect, it is testamentary.' If a document appears to be testamentary, a presumption will arise that the deceased intended it to take effect only at his death. This presumption may arise if the document complies with the formalities prescribed by the Wills Act 1837.

In *Re Morgan* (1866), the deceased had executed during his lifetime three deeds of gift conveying property to trustees for the benefit of his children. Each deed of gift contained a clause directing that it was not to take effect until after his death. The court looked at all the deeds and held that, taking them all together, they contained the deceased's will. They had been signed and witnessed in accordance with the formalities required for wills and they made dispositions which were to take effect on death. The court therefore granted probate of the deeds of gift as the deceased's will. In *Miles v Foden* (1890), the testatrix had executed a power of appointment over property by making revocable deeds which would take effect on her death. The court held that the deeds fulfilled all the requirements of a will and therefore admitted them to probate.

In a much more recent case, that of *Re Berger* (1989), the court granted probate of a Jewish religious will as an English will because it was shown that the testator had fulfilled all the mental and formal requirements for an English will and had intended the document to take effect in all essential ways just as he would have done had he intended it as an English will.

3.5.2 Requirements

The court in *Re Berger* (1989) held that, to be a valid provable will, an instrument must:

(a) make a revocable disposition of the testator's property;

(b) be in accordance with the formalities laid down in the Wills Act 1837;

(c) be intended to take effect on death.

However, the testator need not have intended the document and its contents to be admissible to probate as an English will or even have addressed his mind to that point.

3.6 Provisions must be certain to be valid

The testator must not only have intended to make a will and have executed it with whatever formalities are necessary, but must also have made provisions which do not fall foul of the law – for example, contravening the rule against perpetuities. In particular, his gifts must be sufficiently certain.

3.6.1 Delegation of testamentary powers

It is a principle that a testator may not delegate his testamentary power. This means that he may not pass it on to another on the basis that that person is entitled not to the property itself but to choose who will take it. The basis of this was expressed by Lord Haldane in the cases of *Houston v Burns* (1918) and *AG v National Provincial and Union Bank of England* (1924). In the former, he said: 'A testator can defeat the claim of those entitled by law in the absence of a valid will to succeed to the beneficial interest in his estate only if he has made a complete disposition of that beneficial interest. He cannot leave it to another person to make such a disposition for him unless he has passed the beneficial interest to that person to dispose of as his own.'

More succinctly, in the later case he said: '... a man cannot disinherit his heir by giving away his property unless he really gives it away.'

3.6.2 Powers of appointment

This may appear to be somewhat contradicted by the possibility that a power of appointment may be conferred on, for instance, the trustees of a will. The testator in *Re Park* (1932) gave his residuary estate in trust, the income to be paid to such person (other than his sister Jane) or charitable institution as his sister Jane should direct in writing. The court referred to the principle that a testator may confer a general or a special power on any person by will and held that this was an 'intermediate' power and thus valid. The testatrix in *Re Carville* (1937), however, left £100 to each of her executors, with the residue to be disposed of 'as my executors shall think fit'. The court held that the disposition relating to the residue gave powers to the executors which were too wide and held that the residue went on intestacy because the gift failed. The essence of the rule is that a power given to trustees to appoint beneficiaries will be valid if the testator draws the class of beneficiaries from whom they may choose. This includes a class subject to a 'hybrid' power, like that in *Re Park* (above), where certain named individuals may be excluded.

3.6.3 Gifts to charity

The rule about the delegation of testamentary powers does not apply in the case of gifts to charities, since charity is considered to be a whole. However, if a gift infringes the rule against delegation and is not truly, but only potentially, charitable, it will not be saved. In *Chichester Diocesan Fund and Board of Finance v Simpson* (1944), the testator had directed his executors to apply his residuary estate for such 'charitable or benevolent' objects in England as they might in their absolute discretion select. The House of Lords held that the gift failed for uncertainty because it was not confined to charitable objects. Lord Simonds said: 'It is a cardinal rule ... that a man may not delegate his testamentary power. To him the law gives the right to dispose of his estate in favour of ascertained or ascertainable persons. He does not exercise the right if in effect he empowers his executors to say what persons or objects are to be his beneficiaries. To this salutary rule there is a single exception. A testator may validly leave it to his executors to determine what charitable objects shall benefit, so long as charitable and no other objects may benefit.' Where, however, the gift was not truly and exclusively charitable, that exception could not apply.

3.6.4 Other jurisdictions

It is worth noting that English law is particularly relaxed about the principle of delegation of testamentary power. The situation is different, for example, in

Australia, where several types of powers of appointment were rejected by Fullagan J in the case of *Tatham v Huxtable* (1950), including the 'hybrid' type of appointment mentioned in Re Park above, where the choice amongst a class is restricted in respect of certain named individuals. It was also held in *Re Lutheran Church of Australia* (1970) that a power of appointment in favour of a range of benefits consisting of one object will fail, and in *Re Nevil Shute Norway* (1963), that a power given for trustees to encroach on a gift to another beneficiary is likewise invalid. In the latter case the trustees were given the power to make further provision for the testator's wife from gifts left to other people, after balancing the interests of all parties. The desired effect might have been obtained if the power had been expressed to give the trustees power to appoint the property to certain named persons, with a gift to the wife in default of such appointment. This only demonstrates how important careful drafting is.

3.6.5 Certainty or delegation?

In the English jurisdiction, the principle that there should be no delegation of testamentary power has become indistinguishable in practice from the principle that gifts must be certain if they are not to be void for uncertainty, and any court asked to make a decision on the former point would probably be referred mostly to decisions on the latter.

3.7 Contents of wills

This book is not concerned with how to draft a will, but it is often useful to consider the outline of a basic will at the outset in order to see what shape it takes and how the clauses of the will fit together. Knowing what structure a will should have often makes it easier to see how problems and ambiguities have arisen. The essential structure of a will is what is contained on a printed will form of the sort obtainable from newsagents, but in the individual situation of each testator it is likely that several clauses may require particular consideration and explanation if the clause is to be drafted to suit that testator precisely. A large part of the art of giving appropriate legal advice in matters of succession (as in other matters) consists in identifying potential difficulties or potential outcomes which the untrained layman will often not see, because he does not regard his estate with a legal eye. Often he will think that legal advice is an unnecessary expense, ignoring perhaps the potential difficulties and legal costs for his family if there is any dispute or even uncertainty. Home-made wills, including those made using forms from newsagents (which have their own particular pitfalls), provide much material for the study of the law of succession and how a court operates when asked to deal with something out of the ordinary, as well as a substantial amount of work for practising litigators.

3.7.1 How a will is usually set out

Most professionally drawn wills much resemble each other, at least in structure, the usual form being a logical order even if each firm of solicitors or even each individual solicitor has a particular way of dealing with each item. The basic parts of the structure might be categorised as follows:

(a) Setting the scene
  - testator's name and address
  - recitation that this is a will

(b) Preliminaries
  - revocation of previous wills
  - appointment of executors and trustees

(c) Dispositions – giving away the property
  - provisions for payments of debts and expenses
  - particular gifts to individuals
  - provision as to from where legacies should be paid
  - gifts of what remains (residue)
  - substitutional gifts in case certain gifts fail

(d) Administrative powers for executors and trustees in addition to their powers under statute

(e) Execution
  - testimonium (recitation that the testator signs to validate his will)
  - attestation clause (reciting the presence of the testator and witnesses on signature by the testator)
  - signatures of testator and witnesses

A form of will might look like this:

3.7.2 Example of will

This is the last will of me John Bonaparte of 13 Napoleon Street Bethnal Green

1. I revoke all testamentary dispositions previously made by me

2. I appoint my wife Josephine Bonaparte of 13 Napoleon Street Bethnal Green and Peter Alexander solicitor of 24 Moscow Avenue Chiswick to be the executors and trustees of this my will and I declare that the expression 'my trustees' used in this my will or in any codicil hereto shall mean the executors or trustees for the time being of this my will

3. I give the following specific legacies free of inheritance tax:

   (a) To my wife Josephine Bonaparte my yacht *Warfarer*

   (b) To my grandson Jasper Palmerston my collection of the novels of Charles Dickens bound in leather

4. I give the following pecuniary legacies free of inheritance tax:

   (a) To Ann Marengo-Brown the sum of £30,000 (thirty thousand pounds)

   (b) To Ethel Wellington-Smith the sum of £25,000 (twenty-five thousand pounds)

5. I give the whole residue of my estate (out of which shall be paid my funeral and testamentary expenses my debts and legacies and all inheritance tax payable in respect of the property passing under this will or arising on my death in respect of any gift made by me in my lifetime) to my trustees on trust:

   (a) For my wife Josephine Bonaparte absolutely if she survives me for the period of one calendar month and subject thereto

   (b) for such of my children living at my death as attain the age of twenty-one years and if more than one in equal shares but if any child of mine dies before attaining a vested interest but leaving a child or children alive at or born after my own death who attain the age of twenty-one such child or children shall take absolutely and if more than one in equal shares such whole or part of the trust fund as that child of mine would have taken had such child lived to attain a vested interest

   (c) In the event of the failure of the trusts hereinbefore declared my trustees shall hold the trust fund for Oxfam absolutely (registered charity No ...)

6. I declare that if under this will any money shall become payable to a beneficiary under the age of eighteen years then the receipt of the parent or guardian of such beneficiary shall be a sufficient discharge to my trustees

7. My trustees shall have the following powers in addition to their powers under the general law:

   (a) To exercise the power contained in s 31 of the Trustee Act 1925 in relation to any contingent gifts hereinbefore declared but as if the words 'the trustees may in their absolute discretion think fit' had been substituted for 'may in all the circumstances be reasonable' in paragraph (i) of sub-section (1) and as if the proviso at the end of sub-section (1) had been omitted

(b) To exercise the power of advancement contained in s 32 of the Trustee Act 1925 but as if proviso (a) to sub-section (1) were omitted provided that whenever s 71 of the Inheritance Tax Act 1984 or any enactment amending or replacing the same applies or would apply in respect of the whole or any part of the trust fund the said power shall not be capable of being exercised in any way which whether such exercise were carried out or were possible would prevent the said section from applying as aforesaid except and insofar as one or more 'beneficiaries' as defined in sub-section (1)(a) of the said section would if such section ceased to apply become entitled to or to an interest in possession in the advanced part of the trust fund

(c) To invest trust money and transpose investments with unrestricted freedom in their choice of investment as if they were absolutely entitled and to purchase retain maintain or improve a freehold or leasehold house or other dwelling in any part of the world including any for use by my beneficiaries as a dwelling-house

(d) All the powers of a beneficial owner including power to borrow on the security of all or any part of my estate or otherwise and for any purpose

8. Any executor or trustee of this my will who is a solicitor or other professional may charge and be paid all usual fees for work done by him or his firm in proving my will and carrying out its trusts including work outside the usual course of his profession which he could or should have done personally had he not been a professional person

9. In the execution of the trusts and powers hereof or of any statutory power my trustees shall not be liable for any loss in respect of any property for the time being comprised in the trust fund arising by reason of any improper investment made in good faith or for the negligence or fraud of any agent employed in good faith by any of the trustees or by reason of any mistake or omission made in good faith by a trustee or by reason of any other matter save individual fraud or wrongdoing by the trustee who is sought to be made liable

AS WITNESS my hand this first day of October One thousand nine hundred and ninety-four

SIGNED by the testator John   )

Bonaparte in our joint   )

presence and then by us in his   )

The recital at the top of the document makes it easy to see what the document is but is not a technical requirement.

(1) Revocation clause

The revocation clause revokes all previous dispositions by will or codicil. Revocation may occur by other means, as discussed in Chapter 7, but revocation of all previous dispositions when making a will is standard, and good, practice. Revocation clauses are included in will forms, though their operation is sometimes misunderstood.

(2) Appointment of executors and trustees

Executors and trustees are appointed in the next clause. Here, two persons are appointed, which is usual except when there is a sole beneficiary of full age. The appointment of executors is dealt with in Chapter 12. Personal representatives are the people who take the place of the deceased and deal with his property after his death.

The executors will carry out the terms of the will, getting in the money and property belonging to the estate, paying the debts of the estate and the expenses involved in the administration and distributing the remaining property in accordance with the terms of the will and the general law. Executors and trustees should be people the testator trusts to deal with the estate efficiently, and, especially if they are given any discretion, they should be people whom the testator trusts to know what he would have wanted. They should be people in whom the testator has complete confidence, even if they are expected to hand the paperwork over to a solicitor. If there is property in the estate which will not vest in the appropriate beneficiary immediately – where there is a contingent gift (for example, one dependent on the beneficiary attaining a certain age), or where someone does not have an absolute interest (for instance, where a life interest arises), then trustees will be needed to administer the property involved.

Note that as the trust property includes land, the powers in the Trusts of Land and Appointment of Trustees Act 1996 will cover all the property in it, including the personalty, by virtue of s 1 of that Act as repeated in the amended s 39 of the Administration of Estates Act 1925. If there is any chance of a trust of personalty only, wider trust powers must be given expressly (see Chapter 13).

(3)–(5) Dispositive provisions

Only at this point does a will in its usual structure begin the dispositive provisions – so called because they involve the disposal of the testator's property which many people think of as being the sole aim of a will.

The first dispositive provisions are usually specific gifts – gifts of a particular piece of property. These are usually followed by pecuniary and general legacies, which are gifts of money or of items which are not special parts of the testator's estate. The order in which these are mentioned in a will is not technically important because it is the type of gift which governs how it will be classified, not where it appears in the document. How each sort of gift is classified can be very important when it comes to deciding whether a legatee will get all of their gift. The distinctions between the different sorts of gifts are dealt with below in Chapter 10.

(5) Dealing with failure

Different things happen to different sorts of legacies and their subject matter when they fail. There are some standard ways of dealing with the practical effects of failure of gifts, one of which is to provide an alternative gift should the original beneficiary not survive for a certain period. This 'survivorship clause' deals with the situation where the testator's chosen beneficiary would not be able to enjoy the property because the two died at the same, or almost the same, time. For more on what happens when two people die together, see references to 'commorientes'.

The dispositive provisions should always include a 'gift over' of residue, even in the simplest of wills, or even where it appears that a testator has made sufficient substitutional provisions to deal with a major family disaster. The well-drawn will should always deal with the total catastrophe situation in which the testator's nearest and dearest are all wiped out and he too dies before updating the will further. If there is no provision by will to dispose of a deceased's property, he is said to be intestate, and the general law governs where his property goes (see Chapter 9). The deceased intestate will have lost the opportunity of choosing what becomes of his property, and of maximising tax advantages and making the administration of his estate easier and more efficient. If only part of the testator's property is not disposed of by will, the deceased is said to be partially intestate, so the general law deals with the undisposed-of part of his property. The provisions of the law for the administration of partially intestate estates are particularly cumbersome, although some of the Law Commission's recommendations for improvement have recently been implemented. A gift over to charity will solve such difficulties since gifts to charity will never fail (provided they are exclusively charitable). It is helpful, but not vital, to include a charity's registered number, which can readily be obtained from the charity itself. If there is difficulty in obtaining a number, it may be the case that the organisation is not, in fact, a charity.

(6)–(9) Administrative powers

Specifying who is to deal with the estate and the beneficiaries to whom they are to pass the assets is not enough; the general law does not provide adequate powers for personal representatives and trustees to deal efficiently with a testator's property, especially where there are potential difficulties such as trusts for minor children or where property – for example a business – cannot simply be held in an inert state before being passed to a beneficiary of full age and able therefore to give a good receipt.

The possibility of having administrative clauses giving such powers is a very important reason for having a will. Powers which are commonly needed are those of investment, insurance, appropriation without consent, carrying on of any business, widened powers of maintenance and advancement and the power to take a receipt from a child under 18 or his parent or guardian. Why such clauses are needed can be seen below in Chapter 13. Whilst the effects of the Trusts of Land and Appointment of Trustees Act 1996 may make some common trust powers redundant, especial care should be taken where a trust may turn out not to contain land.

Execution

The will ends with the 'testimonium' – a recitation that the testator signs to execute his will, leaving no room for doubt about the matter – and an attestation clause and the signatures of the testator and witnesses. Though the inclusion of the clause itself is not necessary as a technical matter, it makes the paperwork easier. The testimonium and attestation clause will give rise to a presumption that the testator had testamentary intention and that the will was properly attested. The formalities for signing and witnessing are dealt with in Chapter 5; thorough knowledge of the formalities for wills is fundamental to the study and practice of this area of the law.

3.7.3 Other matters

This is by no means an exhaustive outline of what may be found in a fairly ordinary will. A testator may wish to make (unenforceable and perhaps unhelpful) statements about how he wishes his body to be disposed of, or he may wish to set up more complex trusts or to make provisions about how the will should be treated in relation to other wills he has which deal with foreign property. He may need to impose other powers or to make his provisions dependent on the precise operation of the Inheritance Tax regulations at his death. Nevertheless, a professionally-drawn will always follows the same basic structure.

NATURE AND CHARACTERISTICS OF A WILL

The testator's will is the expression of his wishes of what will become of his property at death, made in a way the law recognises as enforceable.

A will is of no effect until the testator's death and may be revoked at any time before then.

The testator must have the mental capacity to make the will and must also have testamentary intention. However, these will usually be presumed. A document which fulfils all the requirements for a will may be admitted to probate whether or not it describes itself as a will and whether or not the testator thought he was making a will as such. A will may be expressly conditional on certain events or may be found to have been conditional.

The testator must make his gifts sufficiently certain, because otherwise they will fail, and he must not delegate his testamentary power – his ability to give away his property – to anyone else. The will should also make provision for where the testator's property should go if his original choice of gifts fails; for example, if a beneficiary predeceases him.

A professionally-drawn will in particular may do many things as well as dispose of property. It will appoint executors to deal with the administration of the estate and will usually give them powers over and above those given by the general law. That applies particularly where there is a fund which continues to need to be administered after the winding up of the estate itself. In that case, the testator will generally appoint trustees and give them a wide discretion to administer the fund. In relation to estates arising after 1996, personal representatives and trustees have wide powers under the general law where the estate includes land.

There is no property in the body of the deceased, but his wishes as to its disposal will normally be carried out. He should, however, make them clear to his family or friends before his death, or at least readily accessible.

CHAPTER 4

CAPACITY TO MAKE A WILL

4.1 Need for testamentary capacity, free will and knowledge and approval

A person may make a valid will under English law provided that (save in the case of privileged wills) they are over the age of majority and they comply with the prescribed formalities and (in all cases) provided that the necessary mental elements are present. The testator must have the mental capacity to make a will and he must not be unduly influenced by any other person. The will must be truly his, that is, he must know and approve of all parts of it that are to be admitted to probate. This last point can give rise to difficulties where the testator knew and approved of the words in the will but was mistaken as to their meaning. The documentary will should give expression to the testator's true 'will' about what should become of his property; this is not a coincidence in terms, but a different use of a single word.

4.1.1 Age

Section 7 of the Wills Act 1837 provides that no will made by a minor shall be valid. When the 1837 Act was originally passed, that meant a person under 21. However, the recommendations made in 1967 by the Latey Committee on the Age of Majority that the age of majority be lowered to 18 were implemented by the Family Law Reform Act 1969. Thus, with effect from January 1970 the age of majority has been 18.

The provisions of s 7 are part of the formalities from which soldiers and sailors are excluded (see the subject of privileged wills, at 6.5). Soldiers and sailors under 21 or 18 have always been able to make wills provided they come within the meaning of s 11 of the 1837 Act.

The attitude of the legislature to when a child becomes an adult varies depending on the topic under consideration. A person who is under the age for making a will may not own realty but may still marry, for instance. In New Zealand the rule is mitigated by a provision allowing a person to make a will under the age of majority if they have married, or if they are at least 16 and have the approval of the Public Trustee or a magistrates' court.

The Latey Committee felt that the age of majority needed lowering in respect of the making of wills because young adults often had responsibilities, including families of their own, which they needed to be able to deal with in the event of their death. The emphasis of the committee's reasoning was on the practical arrangements for the deceased's property rather than any consideration of the right of a person of the age of 18 to deal with their own affairs in full.

4.1.2   Other ways to challenge a will

The capacity to make a will is usually thought of in terms of mental capacity. It is noticeable that the number of wills challenged on the grounds that the testator lacked mental capacity has reduced greatly since family provision legislation was introduced in 1938. It is no longer necessary for disappointed relatives to prove that the testator was mentally incapable as the court may provide for them anyway by overriding the valid dispositions of the testator (see Chapter 15).

4.1.3   Other ways to make a will

It has also been possible since the amendment of the Mental Health Act 1959 by the Administration of Justice Act 1969, now superseded by the 1983 Mental Health Act, for the Court of Protection to make a will for a person who had become incapable. (For more on this point, see the subject of statutory wills at 6.1.) This may also have contributed to the reduction in cases concerning testamentary capacity since it provides a procedure whereby a will may be validly made if not by then at least on behalf of an incapable person, so that it cannot be challenged on the grounds of that person's lack of capacity.

4.1.4   Courts will define testamentary capacity

A testator must have the mental capacity to make a will in order for it to be valid. Lack of testamentary capacity is not the same as mental disorder under the Mental Health Act 1983, though evidence that the testator was a patient within the meaning of the Act will mean that any presumption of capacity will fail to arise, even if the will itself appears rational.

If there is a dispute over whether the testator had the necessary mental capacity, the court will consider the case on its own facts. This means that the standard of mental capacity will depend on a legal definition of mental incapacity, not a medical one, although medical evidence may be crucial to the court's decision.

The courts are bound to apply the principles discernible from previous decisions, many of which were reached in the 19th century, but they will inevitably do so in the light cast on the facts of each particular case by developments in the understanding of mental capacity in general. However, as the number of mental capacity cases has fallen since the introduction of the family provision legislation (see Chapter 15), there has been comparatively little opportunity for the courts to develop their ideas of testamentary capacity.

4.2 Assessing testamentary capacity

What has to be decided is whether, at the time of making the will, the testator had the necessary mental capacity. In theory, testamentary capacity has to be proved by the propounder of the will in every case in which a grant is sought; in practice, unless something arises to disturb the position, it will be presumed. Sir JL Knight-Bruce VC in *Waters v Waters* (1848) said: 'The questions will be these: whether ... the testator had a mind undiseased at the time, and of sufficient memory and understanding to know *generally* the state of his property ... if he is disposing of his property, he ought to know generally the state of his property and what it consists of, and he ought to have knowledge, memory and understanding of his relations in life.'

4.2.1 Court's test of mental capacity

The essential test of mental capacity that a court will apply in assessing whether or not a testator was capable of making a will was stated by Cockburn CJ in *Banks v Goodfellow* (1870). He said: 'It is essential ... that a testator shall understand the nature of the act and its effects; shall understand the extent of the property of which he is disposing; shall be able to comprehend and appreciate the claims to which he ought to give effect; and, with a view to the latter object, that no disorder of the mind shall poison his affections, pervert his sense of right, or prevent the exercise of his natural faculties – that no insane delusion shall influence his will in disposing of his property and bring about a disposal of it which, if the mind had been sound, would not have been made.'

Sir J Hannen in *Boughton v Knight* (1873) thought, in explaining what state the testator should have been in, that '... *sound mind* covers the whole subject, but emphasis is laid upon two particular functions of the mind, which must be sound in order to create a capacity for making a will; there must be a memory to recall the several persons who may be fitting objects of the testator's bounty, and an understanding to comprehend their relationship to himself and their claims upon him'.

4.2.2 Issues of proof when capacity is questioned

Where a question arises as to whether a person had the mental capacity to make a will at the relevant time, the burden of proof of testamentary capacity lies on the person propounding the will. This was confirmed in *Barry v Butlin* (1838). In that case, an elderly man executed a will at the house of his attorney. The attorney had prepared the will, under which he took one quarter of the estate. The will excluded the son and other family members. There was much to excite the suspicion of the court (see below on preparation of the will by a beneficiary) but the court heard evidence from the witnesses, whom it found good, and found that there were no suspicious circumstances, and it held that the will was valid. It confirmed, however, that the *onus probandi* (burden of proof) lies in every case upon the propounder of a will to satisfy the court that it is the last will of a free and capable testator.

4.2.3 Presumptions and rebuttals

There are, however, presumptions that a will which looks rational on the face of it is so (*omnia praesumuntur rite esse acta* – everything is presumed to be okay which looks okay), and, conversely, that any serious mental illness from which the testator suffered for a period prior to execution of the will was continuing at the time of execution and negated the testator's testamentary capacity. These are only presumptions and are liable to be rebutted by evidence produced by one party or another.

4.2.4 Reliance on presumptions

Lord Brougham discussed the burden of proof and the raising of presumptions as to capacity in *Waring v Waring* (1848). In that case, the deceased was a widow who died without issue, leaving considerable real and personal property. She had made a will in 1834 and later was found lunatic by inquisition (a phrase used under the law which preceded the Mental Health Acts of today). It was thus established that she had been insane by 1838. The question for Lord Brougham – in the days before the courts were discriminating as to the degrees of incapacity – was whether she had had testamentary capacity in 1834. He said: 'The burden of the proof often shifts about in the process of the cause, accordingly as the successive steps of the inquiry, by leading to inferences decisive, until rebutted, casts on one or the other party the necessity of protecting himself from such inferences; nor can anything be less profitable as a guide to our ultimate judgment, than the assertion which all parties are so ready to put forward in their behalf severally, that, in the question under consideration, the proof is on the opposing side.'

4.2.5 Presumption of capacity from rationality on the face of the will

If the will is rational on its face, making reasonable dispositions, the presumption of capacity may arise, but it is by no means conclusive. The testatrix's will in *Cartwright v Cartwright* (1793) was clear and rational, but she had been declared insane six months before making it and remained so until death, so her will failed. The testator in *Harwood v Baker* (1840) made gifts to his wife to the exclusion of the rest of his family; his will was held to be invalid, although those dispositions might appear to be, in themselves, rational.

4.2.6 Irrational will raises no presumption of capacity

If the will is, however, irrational on its face – if the testator states that he makes the will in his capacity as King of Ruritania, or, sometimes, even if he leaves his estate for the payment of the National Debt (as Sir Joseph Jekyll, a former Master of the Rolls, did; the court found this as rational as attempting to stop the middle arch of Blackfriars bridge with a full-bottomed wig and concluded that the testator lacked testamentary capacity), then that presumption may not arise. Note that it is not the case that a presumption of no capacity arises as such – it was always the business of the propounder to prove capacity, so the starting point is that there is no presumption as to whether the testator was mentally capable and, in the absence of any presumption or evidence of capacity, the will fails.

4.2.7 Shifting the burden of proof

The evidential burden of proof may move from one party to the other during the case, as Lord Brougham observed in *Waring v Waring* (1848) (above). He commented on the way it is easily presumed that a testator was of sound and disposing mind. He said that the propounder of a will must prove the testator's capacity: 'But very slight proof of this, where the *factum* is regular, will suffice; they who impeach the instrument must produce their proofs, should ... the party propounding choose to rest satisfied with his *prima facie* case, after an issue tendered against him.'

If the slight proof necessary for a rational will is produced, 'the proof has shifted to the impugner; but his case may easily shift it back again'.

4.2.8 Presumption displaced by evidence that testator was not rational

The example given by Lord Brougham of a situation in which, at the outset of a case, grave suspicion as to the testator's mental capacity would arise, was that in which the testator was shown to have made his will in a lunatic asylum. In that case (which he said he had known to happen), '... the burden of proving, and very satisfactorily proving, the testator's sanity would be so clearly on the propounding party, that no further proof would be required to impugn it'.

4.3 Testamentary and general capacity

The capacity to make a will is not necessarily the same as the capacity to do other things.

4.3.1 Type and degree of capacity

The mental capacity required to make a will is not the same as, for instance, the mental capacity required to contract a valid marriage. In *Re Park* (1953), a wealthy man whose wife had died made a will in favour of his step-nephew. Later he suffered a stroke from which he never really recovered. Medical evidence showed that he was sometimes lucid and sometimes confused. He then married one morning, made a fairly complex will in the afternoon in favour of his new wife and died that evening. The step-nephew argued that the marriage and the will were both invalid by reason of the testator's mental incapacity. The court of first instance held that 'a lesser degree of capacity is required to marry than to make a will'; the marriage was valid, but the testator did not have the mental capacity to make the second will. The Court of Appeal disagreed with the remarks of the court below about the capacity required respectively to conclude a marriage and to make a will, finding it better to say that the would-be testator lacked the capacity only to make a complicated will. It agreed, however, that he had the capacity to marry. The first will having been revoked by the valid marriage and the complicated second will being invalid, the testator's property passed on intestacy to the new wife.

4.3.2 Is mental incapacity the same as testamentary incapacity?

Once the court has assessed the testator's state of mind, it will have to decide whether it thinks that state of mind constitutes one of testamentary incapacity or not. The court in *Mudway v Croft* (1843) said that eccentricity in one person may be mental incapacity in another; the eccentric behaviour must be tested against the whole life and habits of the testator.

It is not relevant how the testator came to be mentally impaired.

4.3.3 Delusions which deprive a testator of testamentary capacity

If the testator suffered delusions, they invalidate his will if they satisfy certain conditions. The definition for these purposes of a delusion which deprives the testator of testamentary capacity is one which:

(a) no rational person could hold and which reasoning with him cannot eradicate from his mind; and

(b) which is capable of influencing the provisions of his will.

4.3.4 Showing general mental incapacity is not conclusive

A testator may be, for other purposes, substantially mentally incapable without lacking testamentary capacity. Thus, although a person who is challenging the will on the grounds that the testator lacked testamentary capacity will be greatly assisted by being able to show that the testator was, for general purposes, not sane, he will not have made out a conclusive case. (What he will have done is put the propounder of the will in the position of having actively to prove the testator's capacity to make the will; there will no longer be any presumption of capacity.)

4.3.5   Not conclusive in respect of a particular will

Even if a testator's general incapacity is shown to be such that it would necessarily negate testamentary capacity, it may be possible to show that the will was made during a lucid interval. It may also be possible to show that even a high level of general incapacity may not have impinged on testamentary capacity.

4.3.6   Lucid intervals

In *Chambers and Yatman v Queen's Proctor* (1840), the testator had been suffering insane delusions for the three days previous to the execution of the will. Two days after the making of the will, the delusions returned and the testator killed himself. However, the court was satisfied that the deceased had been in a lucid interval when he made the will and it held the will to be valid.

The provisions which allow the Court of Protection to make a statutory will for a person who has become mentally incapable (see 6.1) do so by attributing to the testator a notional interval of lucidity.

4.3.7   Delusions must relate to the provisions of the will

In many cases, any delusions the deceased can be shown to have had will be highly relevant to his testamentary capacity, because they will often concern members of his family – exactly those who might have expected to benefit from his will.

The person wishing to allege lack of capacity is commonly a disappointed relative who, because of a family relationship with the deceased, would benefit more from the application of the intestacy rules or, sometimes, from an earlier will being valid. The challenge to the will in *Dew v Clark* (1826) came from the testator's daughter. Her father had not provided for her in his will, which did not necessarily of itself raise any presumption of lack of capacity. However, the court heard that he had had an irrational aversion to her, believing her to be evil, though the court found as a matter of fact that she was 'charming and religious'. In the circumstances, the court found his aversion insane; he was found to be a lunatic by inquisition (an old procedure for establishing general mental incapacity) somewhat after the making of the will. His lack of capacity had influenced the provisions in his will and the court therefore found that he lacked testamentary capacity and that the will was invalid.

The testatrix in *In the Estate of Walker* (1912) was obsessionally insane, but took an intelligent interest in her affairs. When not under delusions, she made a will which was admitted to probate, the three doctors who witnessed it having certified that she was capable.

Situations can arise, however, which are much less clear, and in which it is difficult to draw a distinction between, say, a very strong aversion to a relative and an irrational and deluded one. Today, the daughter might well be advised to seek relief under the family provision legislation, where she might be able to feel more certain at the outset of establishing a good case and winning her action.

4.3.8 What has to be proved

The more recent case of *Re Nightingale* (1974) shows the difficult questions that can arise where the court is asked to infer the testator's state of mind from the provisions on the face of his will and the information available to it about the circumstances surrounding the making of the will. In that case, the testator was a widower in his last illness. He had made a will benefiting his son, but shortly afterwards made another cutting out his son, based on his belief that his son's treatment of him in the crises of his illness constituted attempts to kill him. There was no evidence of any general incapacity on the part of the testator, but clearly there was some reason, which the court had to hear about, why the testator had made the particular provisions he did. The view was that the provisions of the later will would be reasonable only if the testator was right in believing that his son had tried to kill him. The court held that, in order to establish that the testator had capacity to make the later will, its propounders had to establish in this case that the son had tried to murder the testator. This they could not do, so the later will was declared invalid and the son proved the earlier will.

4.3.9 Irrational and insane delusions do not equate with testamentary incapacity

Irrational delusions which do not affect the provisions of the will do not affect testamentary capacity. A testator may, therefore, be insane for many purposes but still capable of making a will.

The testator in *Banks v Goodfellow* (1870), above, suffered from delusions throughout his life and had spent a short period in an asylum. He managed his own affairs and he could cope with daily life, but he believed that he was haunted by evil spirits. In particular, he believed that he was persecuted by a man called Featherstone Alexander who was in fact dead. He made a will in favour of his niece. After his death in 1865, the will was challenged by another relative, who would have been entitled on his intestacy. It was admitted that the testator was generally capable in his everyday life, so it was a question of fact whether the testator had lacked testamentary capacity at the time of making the will in favour of the niece. The court held that he had had *testamentary* capacity and the niece would take.

4.4 Supervening mental incapacity

If the testator has testamentary capacity when he executes the will, that is sufficient. If he subsequently becomes incapable, that does not affect the will. Once the testator has lost the capacity to make a will, the only way in which any previous testamentary dispositions he has made (or failed to make, since the same applies to his intestacy) can be changed is by the making of a will for him by the Court of Protection under the provisions of the Mental Health Act 1983 (see 6.1).

4.4.1 Loss of capacity between instructions and execution – the rule in *Parker v Felgate*

There is, however, a possibility of saving a will where it can be shown that the testator, although lacking testamentary capacity to give instructions for a will at the time when he executed the will, did still have the capacity to understand that he was executing a will for which he had earlier given instructions. If the testator instructed a solicitor to prepare a will when he still had capacity, and, the solicitor having prepared the will in accordance with the instructions, he loses his testamentary capacity but knows on the later execution of the will that he is executing his will for which he has earlier given instructions, that suffices to establish testamentary capacity. In *Parker v Felgate* (1883), the testatrix gave instructions for a new will and then went into a coma. When the will came to be executed, the testatrix realised that she was signing her will, but no longer had any real recollection of what it contained. It was held that the will was valid and could be admitted to probate.

4.4.2 Rationale for the rule in *Parker v Felgate*

The rule in *Parker v Felgate* appears to be a somewhat irregular creation of courts particularly anxious to save certain wills. It may, of course, be particularly helpful given that people often make their wills when they realise that they are terminally ill, and the situation may therefore arise comparatively frequently that, by the time the will is formally prepared, their condition has deteriorated further and they have arguably lost the capacity to deal with the provisions in the will even though they still have the capacity to execute it.

4.4.3 When the rule in *Parker v Felgate* will not apply

The rule in *Parker v Felgate* will not be available to save a will where the testator had not given his instructions to the solicitor direct, but had done so through an intermediary. This is a situation which the court always regards as raising doubts about the accuracy of the transmission of the testator's instructions (see *Battan Singh v Amirchand* (1948) below).

The rule will also be applied only to cases where the testator still had the necessary capacity to understand the execution of the will at the relevant time. In *Re Flynn* (1982), the capacity was questionable and the rule did not save the will.

4.5 An alternative approach?

The courts may, however, take a different approach to the question of what to do with the will of a person alleged to be mentally disordered. The testator in *In the Estate of Bohrmann* (1938) made a will which included gifts to certain English charities. Later, he developed a delusion that he was being persecuted by the London County Council. After this delusion had set in, he executed a codicil by which he declared, *inter alia*, that the relevant clause of his will should be read as if the words 'United States of America' were substituted for the word 'England'. The court upheld the codicil with the exception of that part of it.

This is the only instance of a court holding that a testator had the capacity to make part, but not all, of a will or codicil. The alternative reasoning, namely that it rested on the practice of deleting parts of instruments not brought to the knowledge and approval of the testator, is doubted, given the facts of the case and the surrounding circumstances. It is suggested that the particular decision in this case is unlikely to be followed.

4.6 The infirm client

If there appears at the time of execution of a will to be a possibility that queries may arise later about the testator's mental capacity, arrangements should be made for a medical practitioner to confirm in writing the testator's capacity and understanding. It was the witnessing doctors that saved the wills of the arguably insane testatrix in *In the Estate of Walker* (1912) (see 4.3.7). In *Kenward v Adams* (1975), the court referred to the 'golden, if tactless, rule' of having a medical practitioner as witness to the will of such a client, and that he should make an examination of the client and record its results. These recommendations were confirmed in *Re Simpson* (1977). Requests to witness wills in this way or make such examinations rarely meet with enthusiasm from doctors, but compliance can save a great deal of potential difficulty and litigation. The Law Society has produced jointly with the British Medical Association a booklet of guidance, *Assessment of Mental Capacity*, for the use of practitioners.

4.7   Judges or doctors?

The question of capacity to perform particular legal transactions still remains a legal, rather than medical, decision, as was confirmed in *Richmond v Richmond* (1914). This must be at least partly because it rests in large part on the nature of the legal transaction. In *Gibbons v Wright* (1954), the court said: 'The mental capacity required by the law in respect of any instrument is relative to the particular transaction which is being effected by the instrument, and may be described as the capacity to understand the nature of that transaction when it is explained', thus entailing different criteria of competence for different transactions.

Practitioners should be careful that examination related to the particular transaction is capable of testing the right issues. The court may consider that the provisions of the will provide some evidence as to whether or not the testator had mental capacity, but this should not be relied upon. In *Re Beaney* (1978) (an *inter vivos* case – see 2.1.1), the solicitor had asked the client relevant questions, but as they were all answerable by 'yes or no' answers, the court was not convinced she had really understood, even though the relevant dispositions were in no way unusual.

Note that if a matter may become a Court of Protection case, that court has, by s 94(2) of the Mental Health Act 1983 and Court of Protection Rules 1994 r 36, to consider medical evidence before making a decision, and that in that case, there is a requirement that the evidence be given by a registered medical practitioner, a term which does not necessarily include a clinical psychologist. Given this, as Sir JL Knight-Bruce VC said in *Waters v Waters* (1848) (see 4.2): 'There can be no doubt that an intelligent and honest medical man is the very best witness you could have to speak to the competency of a party as to making his will.' It has been suggested that, although the heavy reliance of courts on medical evidence in this area, as in others, is understandable, such reliance may call into question to what extent the judge is making his own decision and to what extent it is being made by the doctor.

4.8   Undue influence

If there is shown to have been undue influence on the testator at the time of the making of the will, then it will not be valid, the undue influence having overcome the testator's own 'will', in the sense of volition. It is difficult to discharge the burden of proof of undue influence, since, though the standard of proof is the balance of probabilities, as is usual in civil proceedings, a finding of undue influence tends to impute some immoral action on the part of the influencer, an imputation which courts may be unwilling to find.

4.8.1 No presumption of undue influence

In the making of wills, unlike the situation with gifts or contracts, there is no presumption of undue influence whatever the relationship between the testator and the person alleged to have influenced them – this is precisely the area in which gifts to persons with a close relationship are regarded as normal, and not liable to excite any suspicion. If there were any such presumption of undue influence, it would also mean a great number of wills having to be proved in a formal manner, which would be inconvenient and expensive.

An example of a more unusual relationship which did not give rise to a finding of undue influence is that of testatrix and priest which arose in *Parfitt v Lawless* (1872), which in the particular circumstances might be usefully compared with the *inter vivos* case of *Allcard v Skinner* (1887), discussed at 2.1.1. The testatrix in *Parfitt v Lawless* left all her property to a Roman Catholic priest who had spent much time with her and her husband and acted as chaplain to them during the last years of her life. The will was challenged on the grounds of his alleged undue influence, but it was held that there was no evidence of it and that the relationship did not raise any presumption of it which needed to be disproved before a jury (nowadays, this would be just a judge). Accordingly, the will was valid.

4.8.2 Reasons why undue influence is viewed differently *inter vivos* and on testation

The court in *Parfitt v Lawless* explicitly discussed the differences between the rules relating to undue influence in transactions *inter vivos* and on death. Lord Penzance said that *inter vivos* it is considered by the courts of equity that the natural influence which certain relationships involve is an undue influence, but '[t]he law regarding wills is very different from this. The natural influence of the parent or guardian over the child, or the husband over the wife, or the attorney over the client, may lawfully be exerted to obtain a will or legacy, so long as the testator thoroughly understands what he is doing and is a free agent ... No amount of persuasion or advice, whether founded on feelings of regard or religious sentiment, would ... set aside this will, so long as the free volition of the testatrix to accept or reject that advice was not invaded'.

4.8.3 Reasons why undue influence should be more readily found on testation?

It was suggested by the Justice Committee in 1971 that Parliament should act to bring in a statutory presumption of undue influence where an elderly testator was found to have made a will giving a substantial benefit to a person on whom they were physically dependent. To exclude from the presumption those who cared for elderly relatives (that is, the allegation of undue influence could still be made, but the presumption of undue influence would not arise automatically) the provision was to be limited to those who cared for the elderly person under the terms of a contract. Thus it would include a carer in a residential home but exclude for instance a daughter who devoted her life, or even some of it, to her parents. The Justice Committee thought the presumption should apply where the testator was over the age of 60. However, Parliament has not shown the will to implement legislation of this kind.

4.8.4   Undue influence or reasonable persuasion?

It is difficult to draw the line between the reasonable persuasion of a testator, which is quite permissible, and the sort of persuasion which goes so far as to be coercion. There is no need for there to have been any use or threat of force for undue influence to be shown. It is not easy to elucidate the principles which will be applied by a court in deciding which side of the line behaviour in any particular case may lie, but the words of Sir JP Wilde in *Hall v Hall* (1868) may be considered. He said that persuasion '... appeals to the affections or ties of kindred, to a sentiment of gratitude for past services, or pity for future destitution ... On the other hand, pressure of whatever character, whether acting on the fears or the hopes, if so exerted as to overpower the volition without convincing the judgment, is a species of restraint under which no valid will can be made ... In a word, a testator may be led but not driven; and his will must be the offspring of his own volition, and not the record of someone else's'.

4.8.5   The record of someone else's mind

It was said in *Smith v Smith* (1866) that the question of undue influence is often mixed with that of the capacity of the person under pressure from the influencer to resist.

In *Moneypenny v Brown* (1711), the deceased had made his will on his deathbed, with his wife importuning him and guiding his hand in making his signature. The will was held to be invalid for her undue influence. In *Mynn v Robinson* (1828), a woman who was dying of cancer made a will nine days before her death appointing her husband sole executor and leaving him all her property. A few months earlier, she had made a completely different will. The court held that she had been under the marital authority and undue influence of her husband.

A more recent example of a situation in which undue influence was found is the case of *Re Harden* (1959). In that case, the testatrix had developed an interest in spiritualism after her husband's death. In the course of pursuing that interest, she met a man who rapidly trained as a spiritualist medium and thereafter held seances with Mrs Harden during which he apparently relayed messages from beyond about what provisions should be inserted in her will. Mrs Harden made two wills under which the new medium took substantial benefits. The court was quick to find that there had been undue influence on his part; he had not only taken over her mind, but had set out to do so, and what he had done went beyond permissible persuasion.

4.9   Knowledge and approval

The testator must know and approve of the contents of his will at the time of execution, unless the rule in *Parker v Felgate* can save the will on the grounds that, at the time of execution, the testator knew he was executing a document for which he had earlier given instructions to his solicitor.

The rule in *Parker v Felgate* was applied in the case of *In the Estate of Wallace* (1952). The testator was seriously ill when he wrote and signed a document headed 'Last wish', stating that he wished two named persons to have all his possessions. He then instructed a solicitor to prepare a will which gave effect to this document, the contents of which he knew and had approved. The testator executed the will without reading it or having it read to him on the day before he died. He knew, however, that he was executing a will for which he had given instructions. The court followed *Parker v Felgate* and held the will to be valid.

4.9.1   Presumption of knowledge and approval where capacity is not in issue

There will usually be a rebuttable presumption that the testator knew and approved the contents at the time of execution, once the propounder of the will has discharged the burden of proof that the testator had mental capacity. If someone wishes to challenge the will, they have the evidential burden of rebutting that presumption. If they succeed, the burden of proving the will will pass back to the person propounding it.

4.9.2   No presumption of knowledge and approval where testator is blind or illiterate

There will be no presumption of knowledge and approval if the testator was blind or illiterate, unless the attestation clause of the will is so worded as to constitute *prima facie* evidence for the Probate Registry that the testator did know and approve the contents of the will (see 5.16.1 below).

4.9.3   Reading the will out to the testator is not conclusive

There used to be a rule, set out in *Atter v Atkinson* (1869), that the testator was conclusively taken to have known and approved of the will, save in the case of fraud, if he had read it or had it read over to him. That is no longer the case, but evidence of it, albeit no longer conclusive, is of course weighty. It did not dispel the suspicions of the court in *Re Ticehurst* (1973), however. The testatrix, though elderly, was fully alert when she changed her will and left three houses to relatives rather than, as previously, to their tenants. The will was prepared by a solicitor after correspondence with the testatrix, but that correspondence had to be conducted by the testatrix through an amanuensis because her eyesight was very poor; the amanuensis was the wife of one of the testatrix's nephews. The nephew was also one of the relatives who benefited under the new will. The court's suspicions were raised by such close involvement of someone so near to the donee with the preparation of the will, and although it was shown that the will had been read out to the testatrix before she executed it, the court found on the facts that those suspicions had not been allayed and the will failed.

4.9.4   Other circumstances in which there is no presumption of knowledge and approval

The presumption of knowledge and approval will also fail to arise where the will has been signed by someone else on the testator's behalf, although again a *prima facie* case may be raised by an appropriate attestation clause. There may also be other suspicious circumstances which will raise queries and mean that the testator's knowledge and approval has to be proved. Those suspicious circumstances include where there is a substantial gift to the person who prepared the will, especially if they are the main beneficiary, or where instructions for the will were conveyed through an intermediary.

4.9.5   Preparation of the will by a beneficiary

Where the will has been prepared by someone who receives a substantial benefit under it and those circumstances are brought to the attention of a court, the court will consider that there are suspicious circumstances which may rebut, or prevent from arising, any presumption of the testator's knowledge and approval of the contents of his will. This was stated in *Barry v Butlin* (1838), where the court said 'If a party writes or prepares a will under which he takes a benefit, that is a circumstance that ought really to excite the suspicion of the court'. It was confirmed in *Fulton v Andrew* (1875) that such a state of affairs will arouse the court's suspicions and put a heavy burden of proving that knowledge and approval on the person propounding the will.

4.9.6 Heavy but not impossible burden

In *Harmes v Hinkson* (1946) (a Privy Council case from Canada), a dying man had his will drawn up by the principal beneficiary. It was subsequently disputed by the next of kin on the grounds that the testator lacked mental capacity, had no knowledge and approval and suffered undue influence from the principal beneficiary. The court was, however, satisfied that the will represented the free intention of the testator and it was upheld.

4.9.7 Benefit to solicitor who prepares the will

There is no particular provision of law that prevents a solicitor who draws up a will from obtaining a benefit under it in a way that does not apply to anyone else. Solicitors are, of course, generally more likely than other people to draw up wills, and it does happen that their clients do wish to give them something over and above their professional fees.

The most celebrated case on knowledge and approval is that of *Wintle v Nye* (1959). The defendant was a solicitor (since he eventually lost, this may in part explain the popularity of the case). He had been concerned with an elderly testatrix who had recently lost her brother and who wanted to make a will. Mr Nye, the solicitor, and the testatrix had a long series of interviews. The first draft of the will made Mr Nye and the Bank the executors, with the estate going to charity. In the second draft, Mr Nye was the sole executor; there were legacies to charity and some annuities, and the residue to Mr Nye. The testatrix executed the second draft, and subsequently made codicils which reduced the amounts of the annuities, thus increasing the residue. On the death of the testatrix, her friend Colonel Wintle, after a physical attack on Mr Nye, bought a small interest under the will from one of the beneficiaries and, thus armed with *locus standi*, started court proceedings against him.

The court, too, was unhappy to hear about a will substantially benefiting the person who had prepared it, though it was not concerned that Mr Nye was a solicitor on principle. Mr Nye's explanation of the large gift to him was that the testatrix wanted to benefit her sister Mildred, but she was a Roman Catholic and the testatrix had not wanted the property to end up with the church. Thus, Mr Nye was to hold the money and gradually pay it over to Mildred. The court did not find this completely convincing. The matter went to the House of Lords, which found that the court's suspicions were not dispelled and that all the gifts in the will to Mr Nye should fail. It said, in the words of Parke B in *Barry v Butlin* (1838) (above), that the court must be 'vigilant and jealous' where a will had been prepared by someone who benefited substantially by it, and that such a person trying to show that a will had the knowledge and approval of the testator has a very heavy burden to discharge.

4.9.8 Solicitors' professional rules relating to benefits under wills they draft

However, the position of a solicitor is also governed by the rules of professional conduct laid down by the Law Society, breach of which is a serious matter for the solicitor and can lead to penalties which include being struck off the roll of solicitors. The rules of professional conduct relating to solicitors drawing up wills containing gifts to themselves are much stricter than the general law. They state that a solicitor may not accept a gift which is more than a token gift. That is defined as being one which is large neither in itself nor in relation to the size of the estate or having regard to other claims on the testator's bounty. Contravening this rule, now part of the solicitors' disciplinary rules, may result in professional disciplinary proceedings, as it did in the case of *Re A Solicitor* (1975).

4.9.9 Benefit of close relative

The same suspicions arise where the benefit is not for the person who prepared the will but for a close relative of that person. There is no presumption of knowledge and approval and the propounder of the will has a heavy burden to discharge in showing that the testator did know and approve the contents of the will. This situation arose in *Thomas v Jones* (1928), where the testatrix appointed her solicitor as executor of her will and made substantial gifts to his daughter; the will failed.

In *Tyrrell v Painton* (1894), for example, the testatrix was ill when she made a will in favour of her cousin, the plaintiff. Two days later, the defendant's son brought to her another will, prepared by himself and in favour of his father. The testatrix executed this will in the presence of the son and a young friend of his. No-one else was present and the existence of the will was kept secret until the testatrix died a fortnight later. The Court of Appeal held that the circumstances raised a well-grounded suspicion and that the defendant had failed to remove that suspicion and to prove affirmatively that the testatrix knew and approved of the contents of the will in favour of the defendant.

4.9.10 Instructions through an intermediary

The testator may give instructions to his solicitor for the preparation of his will through an intermediary. This will however raise a query in the mind of the court as to the reliability of the provisions in the will and whether the testator truly knew and approved of them. The test in a situation such as this is quite strict. The testator in *Battan Singh v Amirchand* (1948) had made a series of wills, all of which benefited his nephews, until the last, which he made in the last stages of terminal illness. The testator stated that he had no relatives, and left all his property to two creditors. The will failed partly because, the nephews being still alive, the testator clearly did not know what he was doing when he stated that he had no relatives, but partly because the will was prepared through an intermediary, raising suspicion in the mind of the court. The House of Lords said that 'the opportunities for error in transmission and of misunderstanding and of deception in such a situation are obvious, and the court ought to be strictly satisfied that there is no ground for suspicion, and that the instructions given to the intermediary were unambiguous and clearly understood, faithfully reported by him and rightly apprehended by the solicitor'. The involvement of the intermediary in *Re Ticehurst* (1973), above, also raised suspicions in a case which was perhaps less clear-cut, which were not dispelled by the evidence before the court about the precise circumstances in which the will was prepared and executed.

4.10 Lack of knowledge and approval or undue influence?

Where a person seeks to challenge a will on the basis that the testator was persuaded into making and executing it by someone else, as a matter of practicalities they are far more likely to succeed if the case is presented as one of a lack of knowledge and approval rather than one of undue influence. This is because a finding of lack of knowledge and approval, even where it arises because of the involvement of another person, in no way reflects on the morality of the conduct of that other person, whereas a finding of undue influence involves some condemnation of what the other person has done and the courts are for that reason very unwilling to reach such a conclusion. The distaste with which the courts regard charges of fraud and undue influence was apparent from the judgment of Harman J in *Re Fuld* (1965), who expressed the hope that cases would, after *Wintle v Nye* (1959), be pleaded on the basis of lack of knowledge and approval.

4.11 Mistake

The testator may have been mistaken about his will in various ways. He may have been mistaken as to the contents of it, so that it says something which, if he had considered it more carefully, he would not have included in the will at all, or it may contain some words which he mistakenly considered to embody what he wanted whereas their meaning and effect, in law, is quite different. He may also have been completely mistaken about the document he was executing, so that it was not his will at all.

4.11.1 Mistake about the whole document

If the testator was mistaken about the whole document, because it was not his will, it will not be admitted to probate. In the situation where the document is something completely different from what the supposed testator expected, it is usual to say that he was mistaken about the whole document, and that therefore it is not admissible to probate as his will. It might also be said, again, that the testator does not have the necessary knowledge and approval of the document.

4.11.2 Mistake about the whole document, or mistake about part of it?

Cases of mistake about a whole document have been decided in opposite ways on very similar facts in England and elsewhere. In the English case of *Re Meyer* (1908), two sisters instructed their solicitor to prepare wills in similar terms save for the names in each. Unfortunately, they then executed each other's documents, so that the references made in them to the other sister by name made no sense because they appeared to refer to themselves. The court refused to make any grant of probate, on the basis that the supposed testatrix did not know and approve the contents of the document. On similar facts, however, the New Zealand court in *Guardian Trust & Executors v Inwood* (1946) and the Canadian court in *Re Brander* (1952) admitted the documents to probate as wills by the expedient of omitting the names, those being the parts which the testatrices did not know and approve, leaving the references to 'my sister', with which the wills still made sense. The court in *Inwood* held that 'the testatrix did really know and approve of the effective provisions' which were the principal part of the document she executed.

4.11.3 Mistake about the document or lack of testamentary intention?

The situation where someone is in error about the will should be distinguished from that of the person who never intends the document as his will; in that case, the supposed testator lacks testamentary intention and the document is, for that reason, not his will. Mistake arises where the testator intends to make a will, but the document he executes does not have the wording or the effect he expected.

4.11.4 Mistake as to legal effect of words

Where there has been a mistake as to the legal effect of words used in a will, those words will still be admitted to probate. It makes no difference whether the mistake arose through the wrong advice of a solicitor or a lay person (a surprising number of people take legal advice from lay persons) as to the effect of the words used. This touches on matters of construction; where a testator uses technical language, it is construed technically, even if he has clearly done so in error because he does not understand what it means (see 11.2.3). The court will look at the words used and whether or not the testator knew and approved of the words; if it is satisfied that the testator knew and approved of the words, it will then go on to establish their meaning. In taking that first decision as to whether or not the testator knew and approved of the words, it will not examine whether he understood their technical meaning.

In *Collins v Elstone* (1893), the testatrix was making a home-made will dealing with an insurance policy. She was wrongly advised as to the effect of the printed revocation clause, being told that it would revoke her earlier will only as regarded the policy. The court nevertheless admitted the words of general revocation to probate, because the testatrix had intended those words to remain in the will. She knew and approved of the words, even though they did not have the legal effect she expected. The previous will was therefore revoked.

Problems over revocation clauses also occurred in *Re Howard* (1944) and *Re Phelan* (1972). In the former case, the would-be testator executed two wills on the same day, both of which contained revocation clauses. The wills were irreconcilable and the court held them invalid, save that they showed sufficient intention to revoke a previous will, leaving the deceased intestate.

4.11.5 Proper construction of the will may overcome the problem

In the later case of *Re Phelan*, however, the court was able to construe the wills so as to avoid the problem. The testator executed a home-made will in favour of his landlady and her husband. He had three holdings in unit trusts and conceived (wrongly) the idea that they each had to be disposed of by further, separate wills. He executed three more wills in favour of the landlady and her husband, each one on a pre-printed will form. He did not delete the printed revocation clause on any of the forms, all of which he executed on the same day. The court was faced with four will documents, of which only the last would be valid, as each one would have revoked any that came before it. As they were all executed on the same day, however, there was no way of telling which was the last. The court managed to admit all four wills to probate, with the revocation clause deleted from the last three on the grounds that the testator did not know and approve of it.

4.11.6 Two types of mistake identified

The difference between the mistaken inclusion of the revocation clauses in *Collins v Elstone* and *Re Phelan* might be said to be that in the latter case the testator did not address his mind to the words used at all and so could be said not really to know and approve the words themselves, whereas in the former the testatrix addressed her mind directly to the relevant words but came to the wrong conclusion about them. As to the difference between *Re Howard* and *Re*

Phelan, the court was able to construe the wills together in the latter to make sense of all of them, whereas in *Re Howard* this was impossible since they were inconsistent.

4.11.7 Mistake as to the contents of the will

Testators generally manage to make mistakes in their wills, especially as to the legal effect of the words they use (and more particularly where those words come from printed will forms) without the assistance of solicitors. In the case of clerical errors, however, the involvement of a solicitor is perhaps more likely to produce a mistake. In *Re Horrocks* (1939), the testator's solicitor, drafting the words of the gift of residue, used the words 'charitable or benevolent' rather than 'charitable and benevolent'. The argument that it was a typing error failed because the two phrases had different meanings and change would affect the meaning of the rest of the will. 'The insertion of words would run counter to the provisions of the Wills Act', stated Greene MR.

4.11.8 Dealing with clerical error

A typing error or error of a drafter may mean that words are inserted into a document without the knowledge and approval of the testator. They can then be omitted from probate for that reason, provided that the meaning of the rest of the will is not affected.

4.11.9 Omission of words of which the testator did not know and approve

The omission of words which the testator intended to be in the will and without which the will's meaning is changed from that which the testator intended, however, operates differently. In *Re Morris* (1970), the testatrix made various gifts by will and then intended to revoke by codicil certain clauses of the will, namely clauses 2 and 7(iv). The (iv) was omitted from the codicil, so it appeared to revoke clauses 2 and also 7, both in their entirety. The court held that it could not insert the (iv) but it could omit the 7, so the revocation read 'clauses 2 and '. The testatrix's intentions were clear to Latey J from the extrinsic evidence brought to his notice, but he could not admit that evidence because it would be admissible only in the case of a latent ambiguity, not a patent one, as here.

4.11.10 Lack of power to insert words

The lack of a power to rectify by inserting words was also regretted by the court in *Re Reynette-James* (1975), where the typographical omission of a clause meant that a share of the estate devolved as capital to the testatrix's son instead of his receiving the income as she had wished. 'Any document other than a will could be rectified by inserting the words which the secretary omitted, but in this respect the court is enslaved by the Wills Act 1837,' complained the court.

4.11.11 Law Reform Committee 19th Report

The case of *Re Morris* (above) prompted much comment. In 1973, the Law Reform Committee published its findings on proposals to change the powers of the court of construction so as to allow it to rectify a will to accord with the testator's intentions. It recommended that the court should have the power to insert words to achieve this, and also that the evidence admissible to the court of the intentions of the testator should not be restricted either by reference to the giving of instructions for the will or by time. It did not, however, suggest any solution to the problem which arises when the testator is reasonably felt to have intended something different from what he has said but has known what words were used and approved them, that is, where he has been mistaken as to the meaning the courts would put on his words or the effects they have in law.

4.11.12 Rectification and the Administration of Justice Act 1982, s 20

The recommendations of the Law Reform Committee as to powers of rectification were accepted and put into effect in s 20 of the Administration of Justice Act 1982. This allowed the court to rectify a will so as to carry out the testator's intentions if the difficulty was caused by either a clerical error or a failure to understand instructions. In such circumstances, the court may add words to the will as well as omit them.

In *Wordingham v Royal Exchange Trust Co* (1992), the problem was an error in the recording of the testatrix' intentions. She had made a will in 1975 exercising a power of appointment of income from her father's estate to the plaintiff. In 1979 she redrafted her provisions and made a new will. Unfortunately, when she did the same in 1989, the exercise of the power of appointment was inadvertently omitted. The court held, however, that such an 'inadvertent error made in the process of recording' the testatrix' intentions could be rectified under s 20(1)(a) of the Administration of Justice Act 1982 by the insertion of the missing clause.

The court in *In re Segelman* (1996) had to consider a similar question. The testator had executed the final draft of a fairly complex will which contained a class gift, the operation of which depended on a proviso which, it was claimed, had been included in error. ChadwickJ held that: '... the probability that a will which a testator has executed in circumstances of some formality reflects his intentions is usually of such weight that convincing evidence to the contrary is necessary.' However, in this case the burden was quite easily discharged, given the difficulty of construction the proviso presented: 'It is artificial to assume that a testator must know what he is doing if he uses language, the effect of which cannot be ascertained without a decision of the court.' The inclusion of the proviso was a clerical error within the meaning of s 20(1)(a) of the Administration of Justice Act 1982, and was thus capable of rectification by the court.

4.11.13 Limits of rectification under s 20

If, however, the mistake arises from any cause other than a clerical error or a failure to understand instructions, the court cannot use its powers under this section. Consequently the court cannot add words, only omit them as before, on the basis that the testator did not know and approve of them. The Scottish Law Commission suggested that any equivalent provision to s 20 in Scotland should include a power to rectify an 'error' caused by deliberate disobedience of the testator's instructions, which is not within the section of the Administration of Justice Act 1982 as it stands.

4.11.14 Applications for rectification

An application for rectification must be made within six months of a grant of representation unless the court gives leave for an extension of time. The application should be supported by an affidavit setting out the details of the application including the grounds on which it is based and evidence of the testator's mistake and true intention.

4.12 What to do where the will is wrong – an overview

The court has three limited powers to alter the words in a will:

(a) omission for want of knowledge and approval by a court of probate;

(b) rectification in equity under s 20 of the Administration of Justice Act 1982 (where the testator died after 1982);

(c) rectification by a court of construction where the will on the face of it can be construed as containing an error and showing what the true intention was (rare in practice).

4.12.1 Omission of words in probate for want of knowledge and approval

Words can be omitted in probate if the testator did not know and approve of them. The court had no power to add words to a will if the testator died before 1983, because that would have contravened the Wills Act 1837. A court of probate could only omit, and then only if it did not alter the sense of the rest of the will. This was the reasoning, set out by Latey J, behind the decision in *Re Morris*; the method of all those available which produced the result the nearest to the testatrix's true intention.

4.12.2 Construction

A court of construction can construe the will as if certain words were inserted, omitted or changed, if it is clear from the will itself first that an error has been made in the wording and secondly what the substance of the intended wording was. This is difficult to show in practice.

CAPACITY TO MAKE A WILL

As well as complying with the formalities for making a will, the testator must be shown to have had testamentary capacity. For a formal will, the testator must be over the age of majority, though this does not apply in the case of a privileged will. For any kind of will, privileged or formal, the testator must be shown to have had mental capacity.

Testamentary capacity is not the same as general mental capacity and there is no necessary direct correspondence between lack of testamentary capacity and incapacity under the Mental Health Acts. However, the latter raises a presumption of the former. This may however be rebutted if it can be shown that the testator made the will during a lucid interval. More capacity is needed to make a complicated will than a simple one; the mental capacity required to make a simple will is not greater than that required to marry.

The time at which testamentary capacity has to be present is that of execution of the will. However, if the testator had previously given instructions to a solicitor and then lost testamentary capacity before executing a will prepared in accordance with those instructions, the will might still be saved under the rule in *Parker v Felgate* provided that the testator still had the capacity to understand, at the time of execution, that he was executing a will for which he had previously given instructions, even if he could not then recall the contents of the will.

The contents of the will must also reflect the free volition of the testator. There is no presumption of undue influence in respect of gifts by will, but it may be shown on the facts.

The testator must know and approve the contents of the will. This means that anything in the will document which he can be shown not to have intended to be there will not be admitted to probate even if the document is properly executed. There is a presumption, but no longer a rule, that if the will was read over to the testator before execution, he knew and approved of it. The court will also be suspicious where the will has been prepared by a beneficiary, or by a close relative of the beneficiary. This is a matter of general law and thus completely separate from the professional rules which disqualify solicitors from drawing up wills containing gifts to themselves, on pain of disciplinary proceedings from The Law Society. The courts are also suspicious where the instructions for the will are relayed through an intermediary.

If the testator made a mistake about the document he executed, there may be various ways of dealing with that after his death. If he did not know and approve of part of it, that part can be omitted. If he was mistaken about the whole document, he may have lacked testamentary intention and thus not made a will at all. However, where he was aware of the words being used in his will but mistaken as to their legal effect, that cannot be cured. Since 1982, it has been possible under s 20 of the Administration of Justice Act of that year to add words to a will as well as omit them if this is required because there was a clerical error or a failure to understand the testator's instructions.

CHAPTER 5

FORMALITIES FOR THE EXECUTION OF WILLS

5.1 Why have formalities?

If a person can leave instructions about the disposition of his property after his death, clearly at the point where those instructions are dealt with he cannot be asked about any queries that arise. This gives rise to problems both of construction – how the words he has used are to be interpreted – and of being sure that the will documents truly represent the testamentary wishes and intentions of the deceased. He cannot be asked to confirm that the will is definitely his own, rather than forged, or that it was his considered opinion rather than something he wrote in the heat of anger. The purpose of the prescription of formalities is to provide a safeguard against forgery and undue influence and also against dispositions in the heat of the moment.

5.1.1 History of current provisions

That a will must be attested by two witnesses is one of the better-known provisions of the law. Historically, however, the need for attestation varied according to the amount and nature of property in the estate. By the early 19th century, the multiplicity of provisions was felt to be not only anachronistic but also unnecessary and positively harmful. There was even then a general belief, mentioned by the Real Property Commissioners, that a will which required attestation called for only two witnesses, although this was insufficient if the will purported to dispose of freehold realty. The varied provisions and the widespread failure to understand them (and, worse, the failure to appreciate that they were not understood) meant that testators could and did make wills which were valid as to some of their dispositions and invalid as to others, which created grave difficulties. When the Real Property Commissioners presented their Fourth Report in 1833, they recommended that there be only one set of provisions for the attestation of wills, whatever the nature or quantity of property they disposed of. They justified this not only by the importance of the execution of wills being easily and generally understood but also by pointing out that the purpose of formalities is to prevent forgery and fraud, the danger of which is the same whatever the nature of the property dealt with by the will.

5.1.2 Purpose of the formalities

The idea is that the formalities of the Wills Act 1837 make it difficult to forge a will or to pressurise the testator into making any particular provisions, because of its requirement that two people who are not beneficiaries of the will witness its signature. The very unwieldiness of the formalities makes it less likely that a testator would be able to make a valid will in the heat of the moment which he might later regret.

5.1.3 Problems with formalities

Of course, the disadvantage of having formal requirements is that they may in many cases mean that a will fails because it falls foul of those requirements, when in fact it was a true representation of the testator's testamentary intentions and, in that sense, a genuine will. This is a particular risk with those wills which are made without the benefit of legal advice, a situation in which the testator's estate and his disappointed beneficiaries are also unable to take redress against anyone.

5.1.4 A possible solution?

Other jurisdictions have provisions in their laws which allow courts to validate a will that does not comply with all the formal requirements if it largely complies with them and the court is satisfied that the will is a genuine representation of the testator's intentions and was intended by him to be his will. This is usually called the doctrine of 'substantial compliance'. A provision often cited as setting out the way such a doctrine should operate in law is that of s 12(2) of the Wills Act 1936–75 of South Australia. This provides that a document purporting to embody the testamentary intentions of a deceased person shall, notwithstanding that it has not been executed with the formalities required elsewhere in the Act, be deemed to be a will of the deceased person if the Supreme Court, upon application for probate, is satisfied that there can be no reasonable doubt that the deceased intended the document to constitute his will. The Law Reform Committee, in its 22nd Report *The Making and Revocation of Wills,* invited consideration of whether a 'general dispensing power' should be given to the court to allow probate of a will which it was satisfied was genuine even where it was technically invalid.

5.1.5 Problems with this solution

There are, however, potential objections to the inclusion of such provisions within the law. One is that the formalities do serve a purpose. Such formalities as the requirement for the 'publication' of a will (the testator stating that it is his will) and for the signature to be at the end of the will, which caused some undoubtedly genuine wills to fail without apparently giving any real advantage, have been abolished. The provisions for signature and attestation which remain arguably do provide protection against forgery and undue influence. Another potential difficulty is that where rules are not hard and fast, uncertainty is raised as to whether something is valid or not which can be resolved only by litigation. In the context of the declaring valid of a defectively executed will, it is not even the case that the litigation can be settled without going to court, because it is precisely a declaration of the court that is required.

Legislators are very unwilling to pass any laws which might lead to uncertainty as to how the law applies to any given situation, because of the increased risk of litigation. There may also be an objection of principle in giving the final decision on whether a will is valid or not to a court. It is not an uncommon view that the courts are have too much discretionary power in general, and also that their involvement in people's daily lives should be kept to a minimum.

5.1.6   Other jurisdictions

Some other, continental, jurisdictions, operating under civil rather than common law, have formalities which might be described as stricter rather than more lax. They require that a will be notarised, which means that there is a necessary involvement of a professional, in order to be valid.

5.1.7   Law Reform Committee 22nd Report *The Making and Revocation of Wills*

In 1980, the Law Reform Committee presented its 22nd Report, which discussed certain specific difficulties with the formalities as they then stood. It referred in particular to the case of *Re Colling* (1972), where a will which was plainly 'genuine' – that is, it represented the testator's true intentions – failed for want of compliance with the requirement for the simultaneous presence of two witnesses. It had also transpired that when the Probate Registry investigated home-made wills on which a printed attestation clause had been left to refer to the testator as 'him/her' it found that it appeared commonplace for that requirement to be breached, though normally the Probate Registry would not make sufficient enquiries ever to find that out. It seemed likely that this requirement was regularly breached without consequence. The Committee queried whether there was a need for the requirement for the presence of witnesses at the time of the testator's own signature (there is no such requirement in Scotland).

The Law Reform Committee's 22nd Report also encompassed some other ideas. It suggested the possibility that nuncupative (oral) wills, which are otherwise valid only if made by a privileged testator (see 6.5), might be valid for small estates. This had indeed been the position after the Statute of Frauds 1677, one of the exceptions to the requirement for writing being in respect of estates under £30. It also considered the suggestions that English law might bring in provisions relating to notarial wills and holograph wills.

5.1.8 Notarial wills

Some legal systems make attestation by a notary compulsory, the testator either having the notary draw up the will or else making a formal declaration to him that the document he gives him is his will. The Law Reform Committee did not think it would change the current system much unless it were compulsory, since the problems now tend to arise where someone has attempted to deal with their own will without the assistance of a legal professional. They were not keen to see such provisions introduced compulsorily, and indeed the Law Commission in its 1966 Working Paper *Should English Wills be Registrable?* had said that '... although we are very conscious of the risks run by the testators who are not well advised, we apprehend that public opinion would not tolerate any change in the law which would compel testators to have resort to a solicitor'. There would also be some difficulties in aligning the English system with the continental notarial system stemming from the difference between solicitors and notaries; most English solicitors are not qualified as notaries and do not have their powers.

5.1.9 Holograph wills

A holograph will is one made by the testator in his own handwriting. These are valid in some jurisdictions without the need for attestation, on the grounds that, being handwritten, they are proof against forgery anyway. They do, however, have their own problems – a letter may contain terms which look like those of a will, but the question of whether the letter was made with testamentary intention may arise much more easily than with a more formal will, and already arises under English law in the similar situation of privileged wills. In jurisdictions which do have more informal provisions for holograph wills, the question of testamentary intention may fall to be decided by a court.

In the Canadian province of Ontario, for example, holograph wills are permitted by the Succession Law Reform Act (RSO 1980), s 6, which says that: 'A testator may make a valid will wholly by his own handwriting and signature, without formalities, and without the presence attestation or signature of a witness.'

The Canadian courts have, however, had to adjudicate in order to establish testamentary intention. They have evolved the requirement of a 'deliberate, fixed and final expression' of the testator's wishes for the disposal of his property at death. In *Bennett v Gray* (1958), however, the court had to consider letters of instruction written to the solicitor Mr Dysart from the purported testatrix Mary Gray; it held that, in their context, the letters expressed no testamentary intention as such and that therefore they were not valid as a will. In *Canada Permanent Trust Co v Bowman* (1962) the testator's words 'I would like Laura to have this property ...' were, however, considered sufficient.

Canadian statute requires the holograph will to be made fully in the testator's handwriting, but Scottish law, which also admits holograph wills, allows for the adoption of a typewritten will provided the words of adoption are themselves handwritten (save in the case of an ill testator who always used a typewriter and who was allowed to type his own words of adoption (*McBeath's Trustees v McBeath* (1935))). Where adoption of a typewritten will as holograph is allowed, there is the further question over whether it is prudent to allow the holograph will in principle at all, as it becomes much easier to forge.

English law has no particular provisions relating to holograph wills.

5.1.10 Administration of Justice Act 1982

The Administration of Justice Act (AJA) 1982 made certain provisions relating to the formalities required for wills. Firstly, s 17 of the 1982 Act allowed the testator to sign anywhere on the will so that his signature would still be valid, provided that it appeared that he intended by his signature to give effect to the will. Secondly, it provided that witnesses could acknowledge their previous signatures. This meant that the acknowledgment by a witness of his previous signature has the same effect as his actual signature, so if one or both witnesses sign the will, the testator makes or acknowledges his signature in their simultaneous presence, and each witness either attests and signs the will or acknowledges his previous signature in the presence of the testator, the execution will be valid. If *Re Colling* (1972) (below) had been decided under the new rules following the implementation of the 1982 Act, it would have had the opposite conclusion. The Act applies to those testators who die after 1982.

5.2   Current provisions as to formalities

Section 7 of the Wills Act 1837 provides that no will made by a minor shall be valid; at the time of the original Act, that meant a person under 21 but, since the coming into force of the Family Law Reform Act 1969 in 1970, it means a person under 18.

The provisions which have to be formally complied with for a will to be valid are contained in s 9 of the Wills Act 1837, as amended by the Wills Act Amendment Act 1852 and by the AJA 1982 for those dying after 1982. Section 9 applies to all English internal wills except privileged wills and statutory wills. Privileged wills are those which are made by soldiers or seamen and which do not have to comply with the formalities under s 9; they are sometimes called informal wills. Statutory wills are those made for the mentally incapable under the provisions of the Mental Health Act 1983. (These should not be confused with the Statutory Will Forms originally prescribed by the Lord Chancellor in 1925, which consist of a number of provisions which can be incorporated by express reference into any will; these have been very little used.) For details of these, see 6.1.

5.2.1 Wills Act 1837, s 9

Section 9 of the Wills Act 1837 should be considered in close detail. Each part of it has been subject to interpretation in cases decided under the Act, but in considering whether or not any particular will is valid, usually more than one part of the section is involved.

5.2.2 How the formalities operate in practice

It is important, as a matter of practice, to bear in mind that, although all the formalities must have been complied with for a will to be valid, it is only in a very few cases that any enquiry is made specifically about whether the requirements were complied with, provided that the will on the face of it appears to have been properly made. The principle operating is usually expressed in Latin as *omnia praesumuntur rite esse acta* – everything which looks okay is presumed to be okay. Note, however, that this is only a presumption, and where there is evidence before a court that the appearance of compliance with the rules was misleading, the court will not overlook that evidence, but will find the presumption rebutted. In *In the Estate of Bercovitz* (1962), the court was invited to apply the maxim after it had heard that the particular signature the witnesses had attested had not been the one that would have been valid; the court declined to ignore that evidence in order to save the will and it was held invalid.

Where no questions arise about the validity of a will, it is dealt with under the Non-Contentious Probate Rules, currently those of 1987, which set out precisely how a probate registry should deal with an application for probate in an ordinary case. To have a full enquiry about every will would take a great deal of time and therefore be extremely expensive, and it would very probably serve little purpose, since there is no difficulty with most wills.

In saying this, however, one might bear in mind the experience of the Probate Registry as reported in the Law Reform Committee's 22nd Report *The Making and Revocation of Wills*, mentioned above. The Registry began raising queries about the attestation of home-made wills and found that a high proportion of them had not been properly witnessed and therefore were not valid. No doubt this had always been the case, but they had not previously enquired. This discovery tends to suggest that the formalities may not be serving the purpose they are supposed to, or at least not very efficiently, if only because they are not being complied with and, perhaps, most of the time no-one notices.

5.3   The formalities – s 9 itself

Section 9 of the Wills Act 1837, as amended, lays down that:

No will shall be valid unless:

(a) it is in writing, and signed by the testator, or by some other person in his presence and by his direction; and

(b) it appears that the testator intended by his signature to give effect to the will; and

(c) the signature is made or acknowledged by the testator in the presence of two or more witnesses present at the same time; and

(d) each witness either:

(i) attests and signs the will; or

(ii) acknowledges his signature,

in the presence of the testator (but not necessarily in the presence of any other witness)

but no form of attestation shall be necessary.

Each of these provisions will be considered in turn.

5.4   In writing

The will must be in writing, but the interpretation given to that statutory requirement has been very wide. There is no difference in the English jurisdiction between the formalities prescribed for handwritten wills and those prescribed for other wills, as there is, for example, in Scotland. The will may be typed or handwritten or printed, or any combination of the same.

The cases show that the interpretation of 'in writing' is wide as to both the vital aspects of writing, namely the materials used and the language. Most wills are, obviously, typed or printed in English on paper, but the law allows for other methods.

5.4.1   Materials

In *Re Barnes* (1926), the court held valid a will which had been written on an egg-shell. No doubt the same would apply today, although it is possible that queries might be raised in the mind of the probate registrar about the testator's mental capacity. Clearly, where someone does not use ordinary paper for their will, it will be administratively more difficult to deal with. However, the Non-Contentious Probate Rules 1987, which govern the administrative side of proving a will, provide specifically for the difficulties created when people use non-standard materials – which might include an unusual size of paper. Rule 11 allows the court to require an engrossment (a fair copy, typed or printed) for the purposes of record, and provides how it should be set out.

Pencil may be used to write the whole will. If, however, there is writing in ink as well, it is generally stated on the basis of the decision in *In the Goods of Adams* (1872) that it will be assumed that the pencil writing was a draft only unless there is evidence to the contrary. However, in that case, which concerned a will written on a printed form, the pencil words were plainly written in draft, as they were partly obscured by other writing, and the will read sensibly if they were excluded and only the ink words included.

5.4.2 Language

There is also a very wide range of language which may be used. In *Whiting v Turner* (1903), a will written in French was held valid. The use of a code was also held not to invalidate a will in the case of *Kell v Charmer* (1856), where the deceased was a jeweller whose codes were those used in a jeweller's business and could be deciphered by reference to extrinsic evidence as to his business practices.

5.5 Signed by the testator

Anyone executing their will under the guidance of their solicitor will be asked to sign the will using their normal signature, or, sometimes, to sign with their full name. The courts have, however, had to look at various cases of somewhat less regular versions of signatures and to decide what the essential elements of a valid signature are.

5.5.1 What is a signature?

The decisions have elicited the principle that a testator may make any kind of mark which is intended to be his signature and it will be valid for the purposes of execution of the will. This has involved some decisions which may appear to be stretching the meaning of 'signature' to its limits. In *In the Goods of Savory* (1851), initials were a valid signature. A stamped signature was held to be valid in *In the Goods of Jenkins* (1863). An illiterate person may sign by means of a mark; this may be their usual signature and will then be valid as such. The 'signature' of the testator in *In the Estate of Finn* (1935) was not so much a thumb-mark as 'merely a blot' as his thumb slipped and made a smudge. Nevertheless, it was held to be a valid signature, because the testator had intended it as such.

The testator's signature, whilst usually in his own name, may be in a form which is not his usual name or any name at all, provided that it was intended as his signature. In *Re Cook* (1960), the testatrix signed her will 'your loving mother'; this was held to be a valid signature for the purposes of executing the will. The court reviewed many cases on what constituted a signature, especially those of *Baker v Dening* (1838), where the court had in mind the provisions of the Statute of Frauds of 1677, which provided that the making of a mark was sufficient signature for a will of realty, and *Hindmarsh v Charlton* (1861), where the court had said that a signature was 'either the name or some mark which is intended to represent the name'. It concluded that the testatrix had meant 'your loving mother' as her signature.

5.5.2 Signature must be complete

However, the signature must be exactly what the testator intended, and in particular it must be complete. The testatrix in *In the Goods of Chalcraft* (1948) began to sign her codicil, but could not complete the signature because of her physical state. All she managed to write was 'E. Chal' before she became too weak to continue. It was held that 'E. Chal' was sufficient because, in the circumstances, it was intended by her as the whole of her signature.

5.5.3 Completeness as a matter of intention

The principle that a wide interpretation will be given to what constitutes a valid signature provided that it is what the testator intended as his signature was reinforced by the decision in *Re Colling* (1972). The testator was signing his will whist ill in hospital. One of the witnesses was a fellow-patient and one was a nurse. The nurse was called away while his signature was still incomplete, and then returned afterwards and signed as a witness. The will was held not to have been validly attested. The partial signature at which the witnesses had both been present did not count as a valid signature for execution, because it was not all the testator intended.

5.6 Signature on the testator's behalf

Someone else may sign on behalf of the testator, provided that the signature is made in the presence of the testator and by his direction. This means he must be physically present and directly requesting that the other person sign on his behalf at the time of the signature. If either of these conditions is not satisfied, the signature will not be valid. In *Smith v Harris* (1845), it was confirmed that the person signing on the testator's behalf may be one of the attesting witnesses. The person signing for the testator may sign his own name rather than that of the testator, as was held in *In the Goods of Clark* (1839).

5.7 Signature of the whole will

The whole will needs to be regarded as having been executed. The testator may leave various different documents – wills and codicils – which must each be properly executed if they are to be valid. However, it is not necessary to execute each page of a will. If only the last page of the will is executed, any other pages ought to be attached to it at the time of execution (or incorporated by reference; see below). The question of how firmly they had to be attached has been addressed by the courts. The court in *Lewis v Lewis* (1908) held that, in the absence of proper securing at the time of execution, the pages being pressed together by the testator's finger and thumb will suffice. In *In the Estate of Little* (1960), the testator's pressing the pages together on a table with his hand was also considered sufficient.

In an Irish case, *In the Goods of Tiernan* (1942), and a case under the Northern Irish jurisdiction, *Sterling v Bruce* (1973), it sufficed that all the parts of a will which were shown to have been in the same room at the time of execution, even though they were not attached to each other physically. This rule might be followed in a similar English case.

The testator in *Wood v Smith* (1992) (below) 'signed' his will before writing out the dispositive provisions. He clearly intended his name in the heading 'My will by Percy Winterbone' to be his signature, as he said he had already signed the will at the top, and the Court of Appeal agreed that, as he had written the will as one action, the testator had effectively signed it (though he was found lacking in testamentary capacity, so the will failed anyway). The distinction between writing all the will as one action and writing the signature substantially in advance was considered by the court in *Re White, Barker v Gribble* (1990).

5.7.1 Signature at the bottom of the will?

Under the original provisions of the Wills Act 1837, a will had to be signed at its foot or end. This led to some unsatisfactory decisions. In *Smee v Bryer* (1848), for example, the testatrix signed on the following page because there was less than an inch left at the bottom of the last page of her will. It was held that missing this space meant her will was invalid.

5.7.2 Amendments to the original rules

The testator's signature originally had to be at the very bottom of the will but this was amended by the Wills Act Amendment Act 1852 so that the signature could be somewhere about the end. This applied even if there were a blank space between the end of the will, and the signature could even be on a separate page from the text of the will. It could also be in or under the attestation clause and signatures of the witnesses. The essential element of signing at the end to prevent fraudulent insertion of anything further (*Re Stalman* (1931)) remained, however. It trapped the testator in *In the Estate of Bercovitz* (1962) (above), who had failed to have the signature at the bottom of his will properly witnessed and found that the signature at the top, which the witnesses had seen, would not do.

The Administration of Justice Act 1982 provided that the testator could sign anywhere on the will and the signature would still be valid, provided that the testator intended by it to give effect to the will and provided that the will complied with all the other necessary formalities. There are, therefore, no longer any current rules relating specifically to where on the will the testator has to place his signature. However, the old rules still apply where the deceased died before 1983.

Over-confidence in the re-amended provision almost trapped the testator in *Wood v Smith* (1992) (above), who signed his will at the top – before writing the rest of its provisions. In such a case, one should note that the upholding of a will after a contested court case may be a pyrrhic victory; its gifts may have been rendered irrelevant by legal costs.

5.8 Intention to give effect to the will by the signature

Note the difference between intending to give effect to the will by the signature and having testamentary intention; the latter means that the testator intended the document to operate as his will, whereas the former means that he intended that the document should, by his writing his signature on it and the other necessary formalities being completed, be executed so as to comply with the rules as to validity of wills.

5.8.1 Signing something other than the will

In *Re Mann* (1942), the testatrix signed not the paper on which the provisions of her will were written but the envelope into which that paper was put. She wrote on the envelope 'Last Will and Testament of JC Mann' and then signed the envelope and had her signature duly witnessed. The court found that the paper with the provisions of the will on it together with the envelope which was duly executed constituted her will and that it was therefore valid.

In *In the Estate of Bean* (1944), however, the deceased again did not sign his will, but put it in an envelope. On this he wrote his name and address. The court found that this writing was intended not as a signature of the will but for the purpose of identifying the contents and that therefore the will was invalid for lack of a signature. Similarly, the testatrix in *Re Beadle* (1974) was held to have signed an envelope in order to identify its contents, rather than with the intention of giving effect to her will, when she wrote on the front of it 'My last will and testament, EA Beadle, to Charley and Maisy' and had those two friends write 'We certify that the contents of this letter was written in the presence of ourselves' on the back and then sign. The testatrix had believed the will was already properly executed, because she had signed the contents of the envelope, but her signature was witnessed only by Charley and so the document was not properly executed.

5.8.2 Establishing the intention

The intention to give effect to the will must, according to the 1852 Act, be apparent from the face of the will. However, s 21 of the Administration of Justice Act 1982 may be available in dubious cases. That section applies *inter alia* where the language used in any part of the will is ambiguous on the face of it, and it allows the introduction of extrinsic evidence (evidence from outside the will), including evidence of the testator's intention, to be admitted to assist in the interpretation of the will.

5.8.3 Time of the intention

A more recent case about (as is often the situation) a home-made will, established that the testator may sign his will before it is written and his signature may still be valid for the purposes of execution. The testator in *Wood v Smith* (1992) made a holograph (handwritten) will which he began 'My will by Percy Winterbone'; after writing out the provisions underneath, he asked two other persons to sign as witnesses, assuring them that he had already signed at the top of the document and that he could sign anywhere on the will. It was held in the Chancery Division that the testator could not have intended, at the point when he signed, to give effect to a will as, there being no dispositive provisions (those relating to how his property was to be disposed of), there was no will to which effect could be intended to be given. The Court of Appeal, however, regarding the writing out of the will and its execution as one operation, held the will validly executed (but note that it ultimately failed by reason of the testator's lack of mental capacity). It doubted however that if the will had not been completed on the one occasion it would have come to the same conclusion.

5.9 Signature or acknowledgment in the presence of witnesses

The signature of the testator must be either made or acknowledged by him in the presence of two witnesses present at the same time. This provision often appears to cause much difficulty, but in reality falls into two separate areas. Firstly, if the testator does not write his signature in the witnesses' presence as one would expect, it must be established whether what he does do constitutes acknowledgment for the purposes of the formalities. Secondly, it must be clear that both the witnesses were present when the testator's signature is made or acknowledged by him, whether or not they are both then present while they are each signing.

The Statute of Frauds of 1677 did not require the three witnesses demanded for a will of freehold realty to be present at the same time. In *Ellis v Smith* (1754), the court held good a will witnessed separately by the three witnesses, but was reluctant. Willes CJ said: 'I think the cases admitting the attestation at three different times have gone too far ... I have known one man swear that he did not see the testator sign and the other two swear that he signed it before the three ... an inlet is made for great frauds and impositions. But when they attest it *simul et semel* they are a check on each other and prevent such frauds.'

The courts were supported in their belief that the separate presence of witnesses could lead to fraud by the Ecclesiastical Commission in its General Report of 1832 and the Real Property Commissioners in their Fourth Report of 1833. The present requirement for them to be present together was therefore enacted in the Wills Act of 1837. Lord Brougham described it (in *Casement v Fulton* (1845)) as 'a most wholesome addition' to the law, saying that 'if one witness may be present one day and another a different day, perhaps at an interval of years, how can we say that both attest the same fact ...?'. This judgment reflected that the witnesses were to attest not only the making of the signature but the mental capacity of the testator to make the will.

5.10 Acknowledgment of signature

A signature may be validated later by acknowledgment. It can be elicited from the case law that three conditions must be satisfied for an acknowledgment to be valid:

(a) the will must have been signed before the acknowledgment;

(b) the signature must be visible at the time of the acknowledgment;

(c) the signature must have been acknowledged by words or conduct.

If the will has not already been signed when the testator makes an acknowledgment, there is clearly nothing for him to acknowledge.

The second requirement above has been established by case law, but again it would be difficult to read a requirement for the acknowledgment of a signature to be witnessed as sensibly countenancing a situation in which the witness does not have the means of seeing for himself that the signature exists. In *Re Groffman* (1969), only one of the testator's two proposed witnesses was present when he produced the will and showed the signature on it. It was held that, as the will had not been produced to the second witness so that the signature was visible to him, that signature had therefore not been acknowledged to both witnesses, and the will failed for lack of due execution.

The courts have evolved a very wide interpretation of the physical meaning of acknowledgment mentioned in the third point above. Not only are no particular words of acknowledgment required, but words are not necessarily needed at all. In the early case of *Keigwin v Keigwin* (1843), it was said that it was sufficient if it clearly appeared that the testatrix's signature was existent on the will when she produced it to the witnesses and was seen by the witnesses when they subscribed the will at her request. This was applied in *Daintree v Butcher*

(1888), where the testatrix showed a witness a codicil, saying she had something requiring two witnesses. The second witness then came into the room and it was clear that someone had requested them to sign and that the testatrix's signature was present when they both signed. Although they did not know that the document was a testamentary paper, the will was held validly attested. Because the signature was so placed that they could see it, whether they actually did see it or not, her request that they witness her signature amounted to an acknowledgment of it. In *In the Goods of Davies* (1850), the testator's acknowledgment of his signature by gestures was held to be sufficient for the purposes of due execution.

Note that since the Administration of Justice Act 1982 a witness may also acknowledge his signature (see 5.14.1).

5.11 Presence

The essence of a person being in another's presence, in the context of wills, is that they are visible to the other person.

5.11.1 Simultaneous presence of testator and both witnesses on testator's signature

The witnesses have to be present both at the same time while the testator makes his signature, or else the testator must acknowledge his signature in their simultaneous presence. Therefore, when concentrating on the question of whether a will has been validly executed, the question of the validity of the testator's signature requires it to be established that both witnesses were present at the moment when the testator either wrote his signature or else when he acknowledged that it was his signature, by whatever method. This would mean that, in either case, the testator and his signature were visible to them, though whether they looked carefully or not will not be examined since the cases show that to be present means, in the context of the simultaneous presence of testators and witnesses, being in the line of sight of the other person.

5.11.2 Old cases – presence and the line of sight

The old cases often involved careful consideration of whether it was physically possible for the testator and witnesses to have seen each other had they looked. In *Shires v Glascock* (1688), the court considered the purpose of the Statute of Frauds: 'The Statute required attesting in his presence, to prevent obtruding another will in place of the true one. It is enough if the testator might see, it is not necessary that he should actually see them signing ...'

In *Casson v Dade* (1781), the testatrix had signed her will and was outside in her carriage when the witnesses in her attorney's office made their signatures. However, the court accepted on the facts that she could have seen them through the windows and so they were in her presence; the attestation was therefore held to be valid. The later case of *Norton v Bazett* (1856) looked at witnesses signing in the next room to the testator (the report includes a site plan). The court commented that, '... where the witnesses subscribe in a different room to that in which the testator is, they must be shown to have subscribed in a position visible to the testator' or the court is unable to find a constructive presence.

5.11.3 Later cases – lack of attendance

The more usual situation arose in *Wyatt v Berry* (1893), where, the first witness having signed, the second came in and was told by the testator, 'It is a bit of ordering of my affairs'. He signed, as requested, what was clearly a genuine will, but it failed for lack of simultaneous presence. Something similar occurred in *Re Davies* (1951), where the testator made his mark in the presence of one witness, who was writing his signature when the second witness came into the room. The testator acknowledged his mark to the second witness, who then signed. The will was held invalid because the testator should have signed or acknowledged in the presence of both witnesses at the same time. (Note that the possible solutions to this situation have widened since the Administration of Justice Act allowed for acknowledgment by witnesses as well as testators.)

5.11.4 Lack of attention?

A slightly more interesting case on 'presence' was that of *Brown v Skirrow* (1902) where the testatrix had her will witnessed during business hours by two shop assistants. It was held that the will must fail because the second assistant would have been unable to see even had he looked up; as it was, he was paying no attention. It is submitted, however, that the requirement for some mental 'presence of mind' as well as a physical presence is unlikely to cause difficulties save in the most unusual circumstances.

5.12 Simultaneous presence of testator and each witness on that witness' signature

Whilst the witnesses need not sign in the presence of each other, they must sign, or acknowledge, in the presence of the testator. The difference between the requirement for the witnesses both to be present when the testator signs or acknowledges and the requirement for the testator – but not necessarily the other witness – to be present when a witness signs, is a frequent cause of some confusion. It demonstrates why it is the usual practice for solicitors to insist that all three, testator and two witnesses, remain together in the same room and each sign in the presence of both of the others, and the presence of the testator and both witnesses throughout the procedure is usually recorded in the attestation clause. This avoids any unnecessary error, even if it goes further than that which the law strictly requires, and it makes it more likely that the witnesses will be able to recall the details necessary to show due execution. The requirements of the law would, for example, be satisfied by the situation in which the testator, having signed his will previously, acknowledges his signature to both his witnesses in their joint presence and then remains in the room while one witness leaves and the other signs, and then the other returns and signs the will after the first witness has left.

5.13   Acknowledgment by a witness

The validity of an acknowledgment by a witness of his signature was one of the changes to s 9 of the Wills Act 1837 brought in by s 17 of the Administration of Justice Act 1982, in accordance with a recommendation made by the Law Reform Committee in its 22nd Report *The Making and Revocation of Wills*.

5.14   What the witnesses need to know

The witnesses do not need to know that the document is a will, still less to read it and be aware of its contents. What they are really witnessing is not the will but the testator's signature. In practice, however, although it is unusual for witnesses to be invited to read a will, a solicitor dealing with one will tell them what sort of document is being executed; most testators proceeding without the benefit of a solicitor will do the same. One of the functions of a witness is to be available after the testator's death so they can be asked about the circumstances of the execution of the will. If they did not know that they were attesting a will, they are much less likely to be able to remember the occasion at all, still less the details of what occurred.

What the witnesses do have to know is that the testator is making his signature. They must therefore be aware that he is writing and they must, to accord with the rules, be present together throughout the making of the signature. In *Smith v Smith* (1866), the attestation clause was handwritten. The testatrix held blotting paper over her signature while the witnesses signed. It was held that where the testatrix signed the will in the presence of the attesting witnesses, who saw her writing, then the attestation was good even though they did not see her signature and it was not acknowledged by her (though where the signature was covered by blotting paper in the case of *Re Gunstan* (1882), the will failed for that reason). A testatrix may also acknowledge her signature as, since the coming into force of the Administration of Justice Act 1982, may the witnesses.

5.14.1 *Couser v Couser* (1996)

Couser v Couser (1996) is an unusual case turning on the acknowledgment of a signature by a witness. The late Mr Couser, when in his seventies, had made a home-made will with clear dispositions, to which it appears, however, that his son, John, objected. John sought to have the grant of probate made to his step-mother revoked on the basis that the will had not been properly executed and was therefore invalid. He claimed that the deceased's signature had not been acknowledged in the presence of two or more witnesses present at the same time, and further, or alternatively, that the witness did not subscribe the will after the deceased acknowledged his signature on it. The court's view was that where there was nothing amiss on the face of the will, the burden of establishing that it had not been properly executed was a heavy one, and that John had failed to discharge it. Mr Couser had signed the will first, acknowledging the signature in the presence of both witnesses. The first witness then signed. However, she mistakenly believed that the will, which Mr Couser had drawn up himself on a printed form, would not be valid and she was some ten feet away on the other side of the room, protesting that the execution in progress was invalid, when the second witness signed. The court considered the old cases on testators' presence and remarked that what was important was not that a person had been looking but that they were able to see what was going on. It held that the testator and witnesses had all been present in the same room and were discussing the will when it was executed, that the necessary signatures and acknowledgments were made and that the will was therefore valid.

5.15 Capacity to be a witness

Anyone may be a witness, though clearly some persons will be more appropriate than others. Section 14 of the Wills Act 1837 specifically provides that if a witness turns out to have been incompetent to be admitted as a witness at the time of execution or at any time thereafter, the will will not be invalid for that reason. However, it is clearly best to choose as witnesses persons who are likely to be both available to give, and capable of giving, evidence of the circumstances of the attestation. Therefore, they should be, if possible, reasonably competent adults who are not too much older than the testator and in reasonable health, and therefore not too likely to predecease him.

5.15.1 Blind witnesses

In *Re Gibson* (1949), the court held that a blind person was incapable of being a witness to a will because it could not be signed in his 'presence' and he could not be a 'witness' to the visible act of signing for the purposes of s 9. However, the court did leave open the possibility of a blind witness to a will written and signed in braille if the testator acknowledged his signature to the witness.

5.15.2 Compare blind testators

This is different from the situation for a blind testator – clearly if the testator's position were the same as for witnesses, it would be difficult or impossible for a blind person to make a will, which would be unacceptable (see attestation clauses at 5.16.1 below). The testator, however, merely signs the will, which is equally possible for a blind testator; he is, according to *Re Piercy* (1845), attributed with notional vision as far as the witnesses being in his presence is concerned. The witnesses' role is to witness the testator's signature, so if they cannot see the signature itself, they cannot perform their essential function.

5.15.3 Witnesses' evidence as to due execution

If a witness is called, after the testator's death and on an attempt to prove his will, to give evidence as to the circumstances of the execution, he does so as a witness of the court. Where a witness is called in most proceedings, the party calling them may not cross-examine them; only the opposing party may do that. The effect of the witness being a witness of the court is that representatives of any party may cross-examine him. If no witness is available to give evidence as to the due execution of the will, the court may take evidence from other persons, as for instance in *Re Phibbs* (1917), where the will, after the testator's death, was lost in the post on the way to the testator's solicitor in Dublin. However, the two persons who had posted the will had read it before doing so and were able to give sufficient evidence as to its apparent execution to satisfy the court (fortunately, as one of them was the principal beneficiary).

An attesting witness who is a beneficiary or the spouse of a beneficiary loses any gift under the will (see s 15 of the Wills Act 1837 below), but will still be a valid witness and may give evidence as to its execution.

5.15.4 Signatures of witnesses

The witnesses must attest and sign the will, or else acknowledge their signatures, in the presence of the testator. They do not, however, have to be in the presence of each other, even though they must both be present when the testator himself signs or acknowledges. Thus the re-amended provision might not assist in a situation like that in *Bercovitz*.

5.15.5 Which signature?

If there is more than one signature by the testator, the signature the witnesses see must be the operative one. The testator in *In the Estate of Bercovitz* (1962) signed his will at the top and also at the bottom. The witnesses saw the top signature but not the bottom one, which was covered by blotting paper. The will was held to be invalid due to lack of due execution, since at that time (before s 17 of the Administration of Justice Act 1982 re-amended s 9 of the Wills Act) the testator's signature had to be somewhere around the bottom of the will, as provided by s 9 of the Wills Act 1837 after the amendments of the Wills Amendment Act 1852. The testator's signature which was at the bottom of the will had not been properly witnessed because the witnesses had not seen it.

The operative signature since the further amendment to s 9 of the Wills Act 1837 by s 17 of the Administration of Justice Act 1982 is the one by which it appears that the testator intended to give effect to the will.

5.15.6 Witnesses' state of mind

The witnesses must intend by their signatures to attest the due execution of the will by the testator. This requirement was particularly useful before the comparatively recent amendments to the law relating to the taking of benefits under the will by superfluous witnesses made by the Wills Act 1968. Three people witnessed the testator's signature in *In the Goods of Sharman* (1869), two attesting and one signing as residuary legatee. The third signature was excluded from probate.

5.15.7 Witnesses' signatures

As with testators, the witnesses may sign by means other than their names. Where one of the witnesses who attested the testator's signature used a description of himself rather than his name, it was held that because he intended the description to operate as his signature, then it did so. He signed as 'Servant to Mr Sperling'; the court on considering the will of Mr Sperling (*In the Goods of Sperling* (1863)) found that sufficient signature for valid attestation.

5.15.8 Witnesses must sign by their own hands

However, the witness must sign himself, even if his own hand is guided by another witness or a third person. There is no provision which allows for the signature of another person on the witness' behalf, whether in his presence and at his direction or not. This would be unnecessary in the case of a witness where it is not in the case of a testator; one can find another witness, but testators are not interchangeable.

5.15.9 Place of witness' signature

The witnesses' signatures may be anywhere on the will, so long as they intended them to attest the testator's operative signature and so long as they are on the same paper or paper physically attached to the paper on which the will appears. Obviously it will be clearer, and may save potential queries, if the signatures of the witnesses are just by the testator's signature, so that it appears clearly from the face of the will that the persons making the signatures will have had in mind the purpose of their signatures and thus their intention to attest will be quite apparent.

5.16 Attestation clause

Although the witnesses do not have to be in the presence of each other when they sign, it is usual for that to be the case, and likewise, although the Act states that no attestation clause is necessary, one is usual. The former procedure may not make any difference at all, or may be done to make it very easy for any witnesses asked years later what went on at the execution and who was in whose presence to remember that everyone was present all the time. The latter practice, of appending an attestation clause reciting the way in which the will was executed, has a definite reason behind it.

5.16.1 Example of an attestation clause

Precise forms of attestation clause differ from solicitor to solicitor or, perhaps as accurately, from secretary to secretary. In essence they recite that the terms of s 9 of the Wills Act 1837 were complied with. For example, the clause may read:

> Signed as her last will by the above named testatrix in our joint presence and then by us in hers

or:

> Signed by the testator in the joint presence of both of us together who at his request and in his presence have hereunto subscribed our names as witnesses

An attestation clause may be worded so as to raise the appropriate presumption of knowledge and approval in the case of a testator who is unable to read the will over or sign for himself. Examples of such clauses may be found in precedent books.

5.16.2 Purpose of an attestation clause

The granting of probate of a will is usually a fairly simple procedure. Provided that everything is in order, it can be done through the post with the only required evidence being an affidavit by the proposed personal representatives (people who will administer the estate) which is made in a prescribed form – indeed on a form, since the oath is so similar in each case that printed forms are available which require only details to be filled in (alternatively, many firms of solicitors keep the form set up on a word-processor and produce their own with the necessary details for each case). The rules by which probate is granted in simple cases are set out in the Non-Contentious Probate Rules, currently those of 1987, of which r 12 relates to attestation clauses.

Only in the case of there being no attestation clause, or a defective clause, is the probate registrar obliged to require the due execution of the will to be established by affidavit evidence before granting common form (simple non-contentious) probate, because the attestation clause will raise a strong presumption that the will was executed as stated in the clause. It is particularly important to have an attestation clause where witnesses cannot give evidence of due execution after the death of the testator, if, for example, they are both dead themselves or cannot be found, but no-one administering an estate would wish to have the extra expense and paperwork involved in establishing due execution in any case when such problems can so simply be avoided.

Harris v Knight (1890) concerned a will without an attestation clause. The witnesses could not be called to give evidence as they had both died. In that case, the court fell back on the presumption *omnia praesumuntur rite esse acta* in order to find that, there being nothing else amiss, the will could be presumed to have been duly executed.

5.17 Beneficiary as witness

Section 15 of the Wills Act 1837 provides that, if a witness is also a beneficiary, he will lose his benefit under the will. It now also provides that this rule will not apply if the beneficiary-witness in question can somehow be excluded as a witness without affecting the validity of the will; this essentially means that if a witness has a benefit under the will, he may still keep it if there were in fact at least three witnesses, so that the exclusion of the one who is also a beneficiary still leaves sufficient witnesses to validate the will.

If a gift fails because of contravention of s 15, that section will be applied after the gifts under the will have been ascertained, not before. In *Aplin v Stone* (1904), the testator gave his property to his wife for her life, with remainder to his two daughters Harriet and Ellen. The will was witnessed by Ellen's husband. The court held that, rather than Ellen's share going automatically to Harriet, it went on intestacy.

5.17.1 Solicitors' charging clauses

There is also a separate rule, not confined to s 15 of the Wills Act 1837, which prohibits executors and trustees from obtaining any benefit from their office without specific authority to do so. In most cases, solicitors would not take on the job of executor or trustee if they could not charge for their work, and of course where a lay executor is appointed he will usually instruct a solicitor to deal with the estate and do exactly the same work that a solicitor-executor would do, save that in that case the legal fees are expenses of the administration and therefore payable from the estate. Therefore, if solicitors are to be appointed executors of the will, they will put a charging clause in it allowing them to charge for their professional work in executing the will and administering the estate. The charges they make constitute a benefit under the will, however, and so they must not also be witnesses to the execution of the will.

The Law Commission, in its Consultation Paper No 146 *Trustees' Powers and Duties* (1997), suggests that, save where there is a direction to the contrary in the will, or where the personal representative or trustee obtains some other benefit or remuneration under the will or trust, there should be a charging clause implied by statute. Such a proposal was disapproved by the Law Reform Committee in its 23rd Report, and it remains to be seen whether legislation will follow.

5.17.2 Section 15 before the Wills Act 1968 amendments (*Re Bravda* (1968))

The change in the rules, allowing supernumerary witnesses to be excluded in this way in order to save gifts to them, was brought about by the case of *Re Bravda* (1968). This was an extremely sad tale of how the application of strict rules designed to prevent fraud on the testator defeated his intentions completely. Mr Bravda had been married twice when he died. He had purported to make a will in favour of the two daughters of his first marriage, Sarah and Rachel, but that will was contested after his death by his second wife, from whom he was judicially separated and who had previously accepted a lump sum in settlement of her future maintenance claims. The purported will was a home-made item drawn up by Mr Bravda himself. It was executed in the presence of two neighbours whom Mr Bravda sent out for specifically for the purpose of executing the will, saying of them 'he can be a witness' and 'she can be the other witness', which was accepted as indicating that he knew the will required witnessing by two independent persons. However, after they had signed their names and added their addresses, Mr Bravda asked Sarah and Rachel to sign 'to make it stronger', and they did so, under the word 'witnessed', though they did not put their addresses.

5.17.3 Strictness of the pre-1968 rules

The courts had often striven to save gifts which might have fallen foul of s 15. In *Gurney v Gurney* (1855), the court had held that where the beneficiaries under the original will had witnessed codicils, the gifts were not lost because for the purposes of s 15 the will and codicil would be treated as two separate documents. This goes against the idea that a testator leaves but one will, even if in several documents, but it saved the gifts to the intended beneficiaries. In *In the Estate of Crannis* (1978), the testatrix made a will in 1948 leaving everything to her sister, who was also her executrix. In 1958, she made a codicil with a gift over to her niece should the sister predecease. In 1960, the sister did die, and in 1962 the testatrix made a new will leaving all her property to the niece and appointing her executrix. The will was witnessed by the niece's husband. The court held that the 1962 will would be read together with that of 1948 and the codicil of 1958 to save the gift to the niece.

In *Re Bravda*, the daughters sought to propound the will with the omission of their signatures, and at first instance Cairns J allowed them to do so, saying he was satisfied that the signatures of the daughters had been appended not to indicate that they were witnesses but to please their father. This was an argument essentially to show that the witnesses had not signed the will with the necessary intention to attest to the due execution of the will, by showing that there was some other reason. The widow appealed to the Court of Appeal, relying on the signatures and the description of them within the document as 'witnesses'. The Court of Appeal disagreed with Cairns J, saying that it was clear on the facts that the daughters were witnesses and that this invalidated their claims under the will. Although no-one had suggested to the court that, where two witnesses had validly attested, any others could simply be excluded if necessary to save a gift, the court brought the subject up itself, saying that the words of the Wills Act were too clear and that it was too late after 130 years to put a new construction on the 'well-known words' of the relevant section.

5.17.4 Consequences of *Re Bravda* – the Wills Act 1968 amendments to s 15 of the Wills Act 1837

The court in *Re Bravda* regarded the effects of its decision as 'monstrously unfair to the testator and his daughters'. Nevertheless, the signatures of the daughters under the word 'witnessed' had raised a presumption that they were indeed witnesses which they had not been able to rebut. The lack of their addresses did not assist. The court therefore allowed the widow's appeal, but recommended that the Wills Act 1837 should be amended. As a direct result of this case, the Wills Act 1968 was passed, and with astonishing speed. Section 1 of the 1968 Act amended s 15 of the Wills Act 1837 to read that any superfluous witnesses may be ignored. Thus, the sisters would have taken, given that without their signatures the will was still duly attested. Unfortunately, for them it was too late.

However, if a situation arises where there are three witnesses of whom two are also beneficiaries, then the gifts to them cannot be saved by using the rule separately in each case. In that situation, both witness-beneficiaries lose their gifts.

5.17.5 Spouse of a witness as beneficiary

The same rules about a witness losing a benefit under a will apply to benefits to a spouse of a witness. If there is a gift in a will to the spouse of a witness, the gift will be lost unless the witness can be excluded under the amended s 15 of the Wills Act 1837. Persons who are beneficiaries under the will and who marry a witness after the execution of the will are not caught by these rules and may still take the benefit under the will whether or not the spouse-witness is supernumerary. The rule does not apply, however, where the spouse-beneficiary marries the witness after the execution of the will (see, also, 10.8).

5.17.6 Implications for solicitors' practice of the witness-beneficiary rules

A solicitor who fails to ensure that no-one falls foul of the rule against witnesses or their spouses taking a benefit under the will will be liable to the disappointed beneficiary in negligence. An important case on this is *Ross v Caunters* (1979). The testator had instructed a solicitor to draw up a will which included gifts to a Mrs Ross. The solicitor drew up the will and at the testator's request sent it to him for signing. At the time, the testator was staying at the Rosses' house, where the solicitor addressed the will to him. A covering letter was sent about how to execute the will, but it did not mention the provisions of s 15. The will was witnessed by Mr Ross. After the testator's death, the mistake came to light. Mrs Ross lost her benefit and sued. The solicitor argued that he owed a duty only to the testator and could not be liable to Mrs Ross as a third party. He also argued that there were reasons of public policy against holding him liable. It was held, however, that the solicitor owed a duty of care to the third party intended to benefit under the will.

5.18 Liability in tort to a prospective beneficiary

A solicitor has a contractual duty to his client; the courts have found over recent years that he also owes his client a duty of care in tort. The decision in *Ross v Caunters* held that a solicitor also owes a duty of care to a beneficiary under a will, a person the solicitor may never have met, and that the relationship between the solicitor and the beneficiary is sufficiently proximate for the purposes of a claim for economic loss, which is what a claim relating to the loss of a benefit under a will amounts to.

5.18.1 Limits of a solicitor's liability to a beneficiary

Once *Ross v Caunters* had established that a solicitor owed a duty to the prospective beneficiaries under a will which he was instructed to prepare, it was inevitable that there would be further claims by disappointed beneficiaries. The case of *Clark v Bruce Lance* (1988), however, established that there are limits on this duty. In that case, the solicitor drew up a will for the testator under which he made a gift of a petrol station. Subsequently he assisted the testator in his grant of an option to purchase the petrol station. The option was exercisable after the death of the testator and his wife. When the option was exercised, the beneficiary was deprived of his benefit and he sued the solicitor, alleging that in acting for the testator in the grant of the option he had breached his duty to the beneficiary who would lose his benefit if the option were exercised. The court held that the solicitor owed the beneficiary no duty of care in the later transaction, because to impose such a duty would entail 'a liability in an indeterminate amount for an indeterminate time to an indeterminate class'.

Such a line of argument would also have other implications. A will has no effect until death, and the testator's freedom to deal with his property is unaffected by the making of the will. There seems no good reason at all why a person's solicitor should be precluded from advising that person further on dealing with their property just because a will has already been made; that would preclude the altering of the will as well. A solicitor's duty cannot logically be to protect the beneficiaries' interests against a change of mind or heart by the testator, since the testator is fully entitled to change his will if he wishes. The situation may require careful explanation by the solicitor of the consequences where the testator, rather than merely revoking gifts, is in breach of contract in doing so (see 2.5), or where, for example, the anomalous rule in *Lawes v Bennett* (1795) may produce an effect the testator did not expect when granting an option (see 10.7.6).

5.18.2 Why tort liability to beneficiaries?

A solicitor's negligence, if there is any, will come to light only once the testator has died and it is too late for anything practical to be done about the error. The testator's estate will probably not have lost anything, so the personal representatives will be unable to show the loss necessary to bring an action against the solicitor. Applying the usual basic rules for bringing an action in negligence, they will be able to establish that the solicitor owed the testator a duty of care which he breached, but unable to establish any loss arising from the breach. Therefore, they would have no action. Before *Ross v Caunters*, it would have been thought that the beneficiary who does have a loss arising from the breach of duty of the solicitor could not establish that the solicitor owed him a duty of care, so he would not have had an action either.

5.18.3 How far does solicitors' liability to beneficiaries go?

The area of solicitors' liability to beneficiaries developed considerably in the 1990s and remains likely to continue to do so. The plaintiffs in the case of *White v Jones* (1995) were the daughters of the testator, who had intended them to benefit under a new will. He had already instructed his solicitors, but they had not yet drawn up the new will when he died. At first instance, the court held that the liability of solicitors in negligence did not apply to an omission to draw up a will, as opposed to the *Ross v Caunters* situation, where the will was drawn up, but negligently. However, in the Court of Appeal the plaintiff daughters won on the basis that they were identifiable to the negligent legal executive who had failed to deal with the new will during the several weeks between the testator's instructions and his death.

The solicitors appealed to the House of Lords, who upheld their liability on a majority, but on different principles. Instead of applying *Ross v Caunters*, they applied the negligent misrepresentation case of *Hedley Byrne & Co Ltd v Heller & Partners Ltd* (1964). This appears to continue the Court of Appeal's point that the plaintiff daughters were identifiable to the solicitors, but to do so by different means. The basis of *Hedley Byrne* liability is that a person has taken on a responsibility and knows that someone specific is relying on their carrying it out. The House of Lords was, however, unclear about how a potential beneficiary comes into the necessary relationship with the solicitor to have a right to sue if the solicitor fails to fulfil his responsibilities. In *White v Jones*, one of the plaintiff daughters had been in personal contact with the solicitors' firm, but it appears that the class of beneficiaries who can sue may be much wider, potentially including anyone whom the testator intends to benefit. It remains for courts dealing with future cases to decide whether, and if so, how far, that class is limited.

5.19 Date

It is not essential to include the date on the will, but it is sensible. The omission of the date does not of itself render the will invalid, because the date is not one of the required formalities (see *Corbett v Newey* (1996) at 3.2). However, if the will is not dated it may make it very difficult to establish whether it is valid or has been revoked, in whole or in part. A testator may make or have made other wills, and probably each will will have a general revocation clause revoking all previous wills. The wills may, alternatively, deal with the same property, so that the provisions of later wills override those of earlier wills. If any of the wills is not dated, it will be difficult to establish which of them or which provisions in any of them are valid. It may also be difficult to establish what a particular provision means if it makes a specific gift of a particular item of property, because the will speaks of the subject matter of a specific gift at the date of execution of the will; if it is difficult or impossible to establish that date, it may likewise be difficult or impossible to establish whether the gift is valid or not. Moreover, if the date of the will is uncertain there may also be problems in ascertaining the relevant beneficiaries (see 11.19–11.21).

5.20 Doctrine of incorporation by reference

The basic rule is that if a document is not properly executed in accordance with the formalities laid down by the Wills Act 1837, it will not be, or form part of, the testator's will. However, if it complies with the rules relating to the doctrine of incorporation by reference, a document which has not been duly executed by the testator may be incorporated into a will which has been so executed.

For the doctrine of incorporation by reference to apply, three conditions must be satisfied:

(a) the document must already be in existence when the will is executed;

(b) the will must expressly refer to the document to be incorporated as being in existence;

(c) the document must be identified clearly in the will.

In *Palin v Ponting* (1930), it was held that 'see other side for completion' written on a page of the will was sufficient to incorporate the later page by reference (when it would otherwise have failed as wills then had to be signed at or about the bottom).

5.20.1 Document must already be in existence

The document must already be in existence when the will is executed; this rule was stated in *Singleton v Tomlinson* (1878). It is for the person who is alleging that the document has been incorporated to prove this; it will not be presumed. If, however, the document is not in existence when the will is made, but comes into existence subsequently and the will is later republished or confirmed (see 8.2), that is sufficient to comply with this rule. The relevant date for the execution of the will becomes that of the execution of the codicil, so that where the document to be incorporated is in existence by that date, it is deemed to comply with the rule in *Singleton v Tomlinson*. A document referred to in the will but expressly excluded will not be incorporated.

5.20.2 The will must expressly refer to the document as being already in existence

The will must expressly refer to the document as being in existence. References to existing documents which, however, include the possibility of substitution by non-existent documents will be invalid. If a will erroneously refers to a document as being in existence, and that document comes into existence before republication of the will, it will thus be incorporated. If the reference in the will is not, however, clearly a reference to a document that is already in existence, the fact of the document's existence at the time of republication or confirmation will not save it. All that republication of the will does is shift the relevant date; it does not remove the requirement for a definite reference to the document as already existing.

The testatrix in *Re Smart* (1902) directed her trustees to give certain articles 'to such of my friends as I may designate in a book or memorandum that will be found with this will'. The memorandum did not exist at the time of execution of the will and so could not be incorporated because it did not comply with the first rule for the doctrine of incorporation by reference to work. The testatrix later made the memorandum; this of itself made no difference to its validity and incorporation in the will. She then republished the will by codicil. This shifted the operative date to that of the execution of the codicil. However, the gifts still failed, because the reference was not worded in terms of a document which already existed.

A similar reason caused the failure of a substantial gift to the College in *University College of North Wales v Taylor* (1908), where the testator directed the income from the gift to be used for scholarships in accordance with 'any memorandum found with my papers'. It was held that here was insufficient reference to a document that was in existence; this could equally have been a reference to documents made after the date of the will. The gift therefore failed. Note that the difficulty is not that the relevant document did not exist at the time of the execution of the will – it might well have done – but that the will did not sufficiently refer to it as doing so. A similar problem arose in *Re Jones* (1942), where the testator referred to the terms of a deed of trust bearing the same date as the will but left open the possibility that it might be substituted with another at a later date; that possibility meant that the incorporation failed to operate.

5.20.3 Document must be identified in the will

The document to be incorporated must be identified in the will. In *Croker v Marquis of Hertford* (1844), the court described identification as of the very essence of incorporation. If the identification is too vague, it will be invalid, and, however clear it is as to what the testator meant, if there is no actual reference to the document, it and its contents will not, or should not, be incorporated. However, the decisions on this point do show that a court may interpret this requirement quite widely.

In *Re Saxton* (1939), the testator left, separately from his will, lists of names which began with the statement that the testator intended them to benefit from his estate. The court managed to hold that a reference in the lists that he wished to leave 'the following amounts' corresponded sufficiently to the reference in his will that he wished to leave legacies to 'the following persons'. This decision appears perhaps to have been an attempt by the court more to save apparently genuine gifts than to apply the law as such. The testatrix in *Re Mardon* (1944) referred to the document to be incorporated as 'the schedule hereto'; this too was held to be sufficient.

5.20.4 Effects of incorporation

An incorporated document is admissible to probate and operates as part of the will. This means it will form part of the probate documents which are a matter of public record. The doctrine of incorporation by reference is therefore of no use to someone who wishes to keep his affairs secret.

The only circumstances in which a document incorporated by reference may not be included in the probate is where it is too large and inconvenient; such circumstances are exceptional but they did occur in *Re Balme* (1897), where the testator validly incorporated a large library catalogue. Note that even a document which is not included in the probate is a valid testamentary document and must be construed with the will as such.

5.20.5 Republication or incorporation?

The possibility is discussed in Chapter 8 of a will being republished (or, in more modern terms, confirmed) by codicil, so that the operative date for any references to existing documents is shifted to that of the later codicil. There is, however, a different situation in which a codicil may validate gifts in an earlier will; rather than republishing a valid will containing an ineffective incorporation, thus making the attempted incorporation in that will valid, it may incorporate the will as a document so that the provisions of the earlier will, which may have been wholly invalid, become valid provisions under the codicil. The testatrix in *In the Goods of Heathcote* (1881) had made just such an invalid will. Later she duly executed a codicil describing itself as 'a codicil to the last will and testament of me ...'. It was shown that she had made no other will. The court held that the invalid will was sufficiently described in the codicil and would be incorporated and admitted to probate.

5.21 Deposit and Registration

The Law Commission in its 1966 Working Paper *Should English Wills be Registrable?* expressed grave concern that '... although an English will is a document of the greatest importance, the law does little to protect it from the very real danger ... that it will be suppressed or simply overlooked after the death'. Because of the lack of registration, much time and money is spent ensuring that when a grant of representation is taken out, it is taken out in respect of the last valid will or correctly on intestacy; nevertheless, the Law Commission found that about 100 grants were revoked each year, most because of the subsequent discovery of a further will.

Provisions for deposit were contained in s 91 of the Court of Probate Act 1857 and re-enacted by s 172 of the Supreme Court of Judicature (Consolidation) Act 1925. The High Court provided 'safe and convenient repositories for the custody of the wills of living persons' on the executors attending personally at a Probate Registry to be sworn and on payment of a fee. These provisions are hardly used at all; they are governed by the Wills (Deposit for Safe Custody) Regulations 1978.

The Public Trustee often holds wills for safe keeping, if appointed a trustee under them, and in New Zealand, the Public Trustee there was found by the Law Commission to be frequently used as a depository for the safekeeping of wills. A registry set up in British Columbia in 1945 to record particulars of wills was also much used; this, though voluntary, was free. In Holland, however, compulsory registration and deposit of wills was brought in in 1918, which was apparently completely successful in preventing disputes about the authenticity or date of Dutch wills.

The Law Commission was keen that some compulsory system, which it thought would operate at nominal fees and be self-financing, should be brought in (in contrast with its views on the suggestion that consulting a lawyer should be compulsory, see above). It thought registration should be applied for within two months of the date of the making of the will; where solicitors were guilty of failing to do this, it recommended that they should be liable to the beneficiaries who thus lost out – in this respect, developments in tort law have since rendered that unnecessary (see above).

A testator may lodge his will in a sealed envelope at a probate registry for a fee of £1; he will be given a certificate of deposit and his will will be held at the Principal Registry. The testator will need leave from the court to obtain the will back again; the proposed propounder of the will may obtain it on production of the death certificate.

However, the system of registration of wills set out in ss 23–25 of the Administration of Justice Act is not yet in force. Moreover, the deposit system is a matter of safe-keeping only; the testator may still revoke and thus render invalid the will which is kept at the Principal Registry.

FORMALITIES FOR THE EXECUTION OF WILLS

The purpose of formalities is to ensure that the will is truly the one the testator intended to make – that it is not a forgery nor something made in the heat of the moment. Formalities achieve their object largely by making the process of executing a valid will more awkward, and thus they also catch out many people who are attempting to make a genuine will but who fail to observe a particular requirement. Some jurisdictions allow a court to investigate in those circumstances, and to find that a will should be proved despite failing to comply with the formalities. In England however there is no such provision, though the formalities are less strict than they were.

The formalities are laid down in s 9 of the Wills Act 1837, which states that a will must be in writing and signed by the testator or by some other person in his presence and by his direction. It must appear that the testator intended, by his signature, to give effect to the will. The signature must be made or acknowledged by the testator in the presence of two or more witnesses present at the same time, and each of them must either attest and sign the will or acknowledge his signature in the presence of the testator. However, it does not matter whether the other witness is present when he does this. No form of attestation is necessary.

Writing is interpreted widely, both as to materials and as to language. A signature is likewise essentially any mark the testator intended to be his signature, though it must be complete. The whole will must be signed and the witnesses must attest the operative signature which gives effect to it. Section 9 as amended provides that the testator may sign anywhere on the will provided that it is apparent he intended to give effect to the will by the signature; the intention must be present at the time of the signature, but the writing of the will and the signature may be considered to be one act if they are both carried out on the same occasion. Acknowledgment, like writing or signing, is interpreted widely. It may be effected by words or gestures. There is no formal requirement for the will to be dated.

The old cases show that being present means being in the line of sight, so that the witnesses could have seen the testator had they looked. The witnesses must know and be able to see that the testator is signing, but they do not need to know that he signing a will, or to read the will. It follows that a blind person may not be a witness.

Because a beneficiary who is also a witness loses his gift under s 15 of the Wills Act 1837, as does his spouse, care must be taken not to infringe this rule. If it is infringed however, the gift may be saved if there are more than two witnesses, either by showing that the beneficiary did not sign as a witness but for some other reason, or by excluding supernumerary witnesses provided that sufficient witnesses remain who are not beneficiaries to validate the will.

If certain conditions are satisfied then a document which has not been executed may nevertheless be incorporated into the will and admitted to probate. For the doctrine of incorporation by reference to work, the document must already be in existence when the will is executed, the will must expressly refer to the document as being in existence and the document must be identified clearly in the will.

A will may be formally deposited but usually is not.

CHAPTER 6

SPECIAL WILLS

There are certain kinds of wills which differ from the usual kind of wills in that they have different requirements as to the formalities for validity or operate differently from ordinary wills. These include wills made under the statutory provisions relating to the making of wills for the mentally incapable, privileged or informal wills, which are made by soldiers and sailors, and mutual wills, which are governed by particular principles of equity.

6.1   Statutory wills

Wills made for a person who is mentally disordered are called statutory wills. The provisions do not have any necessary correlation with those for assessing whether or not a person had testamentary capacity at the time of making his will, but a person who is a patient within the meaning of the Mental Health Act 1983 will usually not have the mental capacity to make a will. If there were no statutory provisions entitling a will to be made for them, then the intestacy provisions would apply in the case of anyone who had never had the capacity to make a will, and in the case of someone who lost capacity, their dispositions would remain as they were when the capacity was lost. This could mean irremediable intestacy, or could involve a will which would become outdated with changing circumstances in the testator's life and family.

6.1.1   When the power to make a statutory will arises

The power to make a statutory will is available when an adult person is considered by the Court of Protection, which looks after the affairs of the mentally infirm, to be incapable of making a valid will for himself. It is a power which arises under statute and did not exist before the Mental Health Act 1959 was amended by ss 17–19 of the Administration of Justice Act 1969 to include it. Earlier, the High Court had used its inherent jurisdiction to make settlements with life interests for incapable settlors, as, for example, in *Re WJGL* (1965).

6.1.2   Mental Health Act 1983

The power for the Court of Protection to make and execute a will for the patient is contained in s 96 of the Mental Health Act 1983. The will may contain any provision which the patient could have made were he not mentally disordered. The Court of Protection will order the dispositions in the patient's will as it thinks proper, and an appeal may lie to the court if there is dispute. Sections 95–98 deal with the detailed powers of the court.

6.1.3 Court of Protection orders the will as the patient would have done

If the patient had previously had testamentary capacity and had made a will which has become outdated because of events, the Court of Protection may seek to draw up a new will reflecting the spirit of the old one and thus the perceptible testamentary wishes of the patient before the loss of capacity. In *Re D(J)* (1982), the patient, a widow with five children, had previously made a will leaving her house to one of her daughters, the gift being adeemed when she sold the house and moved in with that daughter. The residue was to be split between her five children equally. The patient's children all agreed that the daughter who was caring for the patient was entitled by virtue of that care to a greater share of the patient's estate, though they were not agreed as to how much she should have. The court therefore took that decision and a statutory will was then made accordingly.

6.1.4 Taking account of the actual patient

The court held in *Re D(J)* that it should order execution of such a statutory will as the actual, rather than a hypothetical, patient might make, so it ordered a provision that the daughter be given a legacy to replace the adeemed gift of the patient's old house, before the residue was split between all the children equally. Megarry VC said: 'I think that the court must take the patient as he or she was before losing testamentary capacity ... the court must seek to make the will which the actual patient, acting reasonably, would have made if notionally restored to full mental capacity, memory and foresight.'

6.1.5 Where the patient has never been capable of making decisions about her property

In *Re C (a patient)* (1991), the case concerned an elderly woman of considerable personal wealth who had never been mentally capable and had lived in institutions since the age of 10. If no will were to be made for her, she would die intestate, survived by four first cousins. No member of her family ever visited her; however, they did not appear to know she existed. The court was invited to make provision for gifts to charity and to family members. The court referred to the judgment in *Re D(J)* (above) and recognised the difficulty in forming a view of what might have been expected from a person who has never enjoyed a rational mind, as in this case.

6.1.6 The normal, decent mentally incapable testator

Hoffman J went on to say: 'But I think that in those circumstances the court must assume that she would have been a normal decent person, acting in accordance with contemporary standards of morality.' The court felt that as her fortune was derived from her family and she had been cared for in practical senses by charity, she would wish to benefit both. It held that it had power to order some immediate distributions and did so partly for reasons of avoiding Inheritance Tax.

Cases of this kind might be seen as an example of courts not only exercising a wide discretion, but also justifying it by reference to moral standards which *are stated* as absolutes but in which judges of the Chancery Division might in fact differ from other people. However, in the case of a mentally incapable person who has never had the capacity to form rational ideas about the disposition of their property, either the law of intestacy must take its course – in which case the estates of the patients in *Re C* and *Re S* (below) would not have benefited the charities and persons who had looked after the patients – or someone must have the power to alter those provisions. The court may be considered a better arbiter than the interested relatives, and clearly it must be given powers which are wide enough allow it to deal with any particular case which may arise, and it must have some basis for its decision. It is submitted that what the court perceives as contemporary standards of morality may be as good a guideline as can be obtained.

It was said in *Re S (gifts by mental patient)* (1997) that the judgment in *Re C* should not be taken as a firm model. Ferris J said: 'This is not an area in which judicial precedent really has any weight ...' However, the reference is essentially to the calculation of the proportions in which charities, carers and family members should benefit, rather than to the more general principles behind such calculations.

6.1.7 Effect of will

The will is irrevocable after the patient's death.

6.1.8 Formalities for a statutory will

The formalities necessary for a statutory will are set out in s 97 of the Mental Health Act 1983. It must be:

(a) expressed to be signed by the patient acting by the person authorised by the Court of Protection to execute the will for the patient; and

(b) signed by the authorised person with the name of the patient and with his own name, in the presence of two or more witnesses present at the same time; and

(c) attested and subscribed by those witnesses in the presence of the authorised person; and

(d) sealed with the official seal of the Court of Protection.

In *Re HMF* (1975), the testatrix had made a will in 1960 giving her estate equally between two charities. By 1975, when she had been under the Court of Protection for some six years, she was expressing the wish to make a will in favour of her two nephews. They applied to the Court of Protection for a fresh will to be made and the court joined the two charities in the action to satisfy itself that the testatrix would have made such provisions had she been mentally capable, and in order to balance the claims of the parties.

The court subsequently issued a Practice Note (1983) directing that 'all persons materially affected by proposals' should be parties. Practice Notes are rules of procedure issued by the court itself, rather than by the legislature, which are enforceable. Failure to comply with them may mean that the court will refuse to hear a matter further. They are thus as effective in practice as legislation, if not more so.

This point had been raised in *Re Davey* (1980), where the patient, not expected to live long, was found to have undergone a clandestine marriage to a man who worked at the home where she lived. The marriage was voidable for want of her mental capacity, but a voidable marriage revokes earlier wills, as was held in *Re Roberts* (1978). The court therefore made a new will for the patient as a matter of urgency, referring on the complaint of Mr Davey to its powers under the Mental Health Act to do so.

6.1.9   The Public Trustee and the Court of Protection

In 1994, the Public Trust Office became an executive agency within the Lord Chancellor's Department, and new rules were made to clarify its interrelationship with the Court of Protection. The Court of Protection Rules 1994 confer on the Public Trustee most of the functions of the judge under Pt VII of the Mental Health Act 1983. However, certain functions remain with the Court of Protection, including the making of orders to execute statutory wills. Other functions remaining with the Court of Protection are those of giving directions relating to the execution of a will by a patient with testamentary capacity, of making orders settling a substantial gift of a patient's property (see 6.1.6) and of giving directions to sever a joint tenancy.

6.2   Enduring Powers of Attorney and living wills

Neither an Enduring Power of Attorney nor a 'living will' is a will. Neither has anything to do with the Wills Act 1837 or the Administration of Estates Act 1925 or any of the other machinery of succession. They operate, insofar as they do, whilst the relevant person is still alive, the former pertaining to property and the latter to the person. Nevertheless, it is helpful to consider them in the context of succession law and practice because they relate to the giving over of personal powers after the loss of capacity, though the physical body subsists. They therefore deal with the period of limited personal capacity which arises before, and is often related to, death. Some of the same issues arise as with wills – whom to appoint, how to do it, what provisions to make, how to ensure it will be enforceable. Students of succession often query the nature of 'living wills' in particular, and indeed some of the concerns of a person seeking to make a will may be better answered by reference to documents of this kind.

6.2.1   Reform?

More people are living longer; many of them lose mental capacity before their death. There is increasing public consciousness of the difficulties of the issues surrounding the care and treatment of those who no longer have the capacity to consent to or refuse medical treatment. Many people would not wish their life to be artificially prolonged if the quality of that life were minimal, and such prolongation, especially in the days of formidable medical technology, can be expensive as well as potentially against the wishes, or even interests, of the patient. Moreover, medical treatment aside, there remains the question of how the incapacitated person's property is to be dealt with. Following the Law Commission's investigations of these questions in its consultation papers *Mentally Incapacitated Adults and Decision Making* (Nos 119, 1991 and 128 and 129, 1993), and its proposals in its Report No 231 *Mentally Incapacitated Adults* (1995), the Lord Chancellor's Department issued a Consultation Paper *Who Decides?* in December 1997 inviting comments on various potentially far-reaching proposals. These include suggestions that persons over 16, rather than 18 as at present, should be entitled to make a new form of Continuing Power of Attorney, and that such powers should cover health care as well as property matters. Questions such as whether certification by a solicitor or doctor should be required, and what should be done to ensure the rights to such powers of those with reading difficulties or those whose understanding of English is limited, were also broached. The results of these enquiries are awaited.

6.3   Enduring Powers of Attorney

An ordinary power of attorney, under the Powers of Attorney Act 1971, is a deed by which a person grants another authority to deal with his property during his lifetime. It may be limited as to time or as to the property it refers to; it will be revoked automatically by operation of law on the donor's death, when any valid will he has comes into operation, or on the donor's loss of mental capacity. Therefore, an Enduring Power of Attorney is needed to deal with this situation.

6.3.1 Dealing with an incapable person's affairs: the Court of Protection

The inherent jurisdiction of the High Court to deal with the affairs of a person who has lost mental capacity has effectively been replaced under statute. A person who has lost his mental capacity to manage his own property and affairs may be dealt with by the appointment of a receiver under the Mental Health Act 1983. Under that Act, the Court of Protection will use the powers delegated to it by the Chancery Division to manage the patient's affairs. However, calling in the Court of Protection can be slow and cumbersome, and it is also expensive.

6.3.2 Recommendations for change in 1983

The Law Commission published its Report No 122 *The Incapacitated Principal* in 1983. It said that, given that ordinary powers of attorney lapse just when they become most useful – when the donor, though still living, can no longer exercise his powers himself – they often continued to be used, improperly, in order to avoid the need for invoking receivership and the Mental Health Acts. The Law Commission recommended the creation of a power of attorney which would operate after the loss of capacity.

6.3.3 Enduring Powers of Attorney Act 1985

The recommendation was accepted and put into practice as the Enduring Powers of Attorney Act 1985, which came into force in March 1986. It allows a person appointed in the correct manner to retain their authority after the loss of capacity of the donor of the power.

6.3.4 Making and activating an Enduring Power of Attorney

The form of appointment is prescribed by regulations; it is wordy and requires little to be written in beyond the details of the donor and the attorney. Once the donor has lost capacity, there is a duty on the attorney to register the Enduring Power if they then wish to act under it. The application is made to the court on notice to the donor and to specified relatives, so they have a chance to object.

6.3.5 Capacity to make an Enduring Power of Attorney

The Enduring Power has to be made while the donor still has capacity, but it would appear from the cases that the amount of capacity required to give such a Power is quite low, so that a person may be both capable of granting a Power and incapable of managing their affairs (and thus liable to have any power they make registered immediately). Many Powers are indeed registered within a remarkably short time of being made, and there has been an instance of a Power being refused registration, only to be re-made by the apparently incapable donor – and accepted by the court.

The court in *Re K; Re F (Enduring Powers of Attorney)* (1988) said that it was questionable how much capacity was needed to execute such a Power but that it could not be equated directly with the power to make an *inter vivos* gift. The court said: 'The power does not amount to an outright disposal of assets like a gift, settlement or will. It is fiduciary and further limited as to gifts and payments to the attorney himself ... the court has its supervisory powers ...'

However, there is some suggestion from those who are closely involved in Enduring Powers – the solicitors who deal with them – that the exercise of the courts' supervisory powers is open to frustration. Some solicitors believe that there is, however, considerable danger in allowing the execution of an Enduring Power during a 'lucid interval', since the nature of the power may not be fully appreciated. Enduring Powers of Attorney are still quite new and are not widely understood by the general public as are wills. Thus, a person who is very ill may still retain an understanding of what a will is but be incapable of validly executing one, whilst not understand what an Enduring Power of Attorney is but be able to make one.

However, the standard of capacity required for making an Enduring Power remains arguably lower than that for a will, and the Powers can provide a useful practical solution to the difficulties of dealing with the property of a person who can no longer deal with his affairs himself.

6.3.6   Whose power?

The Law Society's Mental Health and Disability Sub-Committee has recently produced guidelines for solicitors advising clients on Enduring Powers of Attorney. These stress that the solicitor's client is the donor of the Enduring Power, not his relatives or those who will be the attorneys in the event of the donor's loss of mental capacity. That such guidelines are required is indicative of the extent to which a person may be prematurely or inappropriately deprived of autonomy as old age and infirmity are foreseen.

6.3.7 The Public Trust Office

The Court of Protection (Enduring Powers of Attorney) Rules 1994 give the Public Trustee the functions of registering, or refusing to register, Enduring Powers of Attorney on grounds of formalities or lack of capacity other than mental capacity, and set out the time limits and other formalities for the process of registration.

6.4   Living wills

The subject of living wills is an area much under debate at present and one in which the law is in the process of change. The law of what are usually termed 'living wills' operates in a similar area to that of wills and succession, but one should be clear that a so-called 'living will' is not a will at all. The Law Commission and the courts sometimes call them 'advance directives' or (perhaps more helpfully) 'enforceable advance directives'.

The Law Commission has looked at this area in some depth during the last few years and the Lord Chancellor's Department is now inviting public comment (see 6.2.1). This is a fraught area, which, when looked at more widely, overlaps with that of euthanasia and involves questions of economics as well as medical ethics.

6.4.1   Issues involved

The questions of consent to and refusal of medical treatment have been lively issues of debate, in respect both of children's competence (for example, *Gillick* (1985) and *Re R* (1991)) and of adults', when, though of age, they are incapable through some form of illness. It arises where a doctor wishes to carry out a particular course of treatment, including ceasing treatment, and the patient is not competent either to consent or refuse. Various questions may be involved, including those of medical ethics and the criminal law, as were discussed, for example, in the case of *Airedale NHS Trust v Bland* (1993). This was the case in which a young man had been left in a Persistent Vegetative State following crushing at the Hillsborough football stadium disaster, and the House of Lords eventually authorised his doctors to terminate his treatment and nourishment and thus his life.

In theory, similar questions may arise each time a decision is taken to switch off a life support machine or discontinue treatment which would prolong life. The doctor's ethical duty is to treat the patient, and the law may impose duties to do so by the law of torts or the criminal law. A competent patient may, in theory at least, refuse treatment which a doctor might wish to continue. Living wills are most often concerned with a future patient recording, in advance of the loss of the mental capacity to refuse treatment, the point at which they would refuse medical treatment if they were competent to do so. The question is whether there is any provision of law under which such wishes can be enforced.

6.4.2   Current practice

The practice of taking note of the wishes of the incompetent patient varies. Lord Donaldson in *Re T* (1992) recommended that doctors should ask the patients' relatives what his wishes were. It is submitted, however, that this is a questionable approach. There is a chance that relatives may have their own agenda; at best, they may have misunderstood what the patient has said to them and any information they can offer is hearsay. If doctors are to take note of patients' wishes, it is arguably better for there to be an accepted system of patients recording those wishes rather than relying on their being relayed as hearsay.

6.4.3 Statutory provisions allowing advance directives

Enduring Powers of Attorney operate only for a patient's property, not for his person. There is no current provision of statute in England equivalent to the Enduring Powers of Attorney Act 1985 but referable to the person. In the US, such a provision was first introduced at state level by California in its 1976 Natural Death Act; it is now contained in, for example, that state's Durable Powers of Attorney Health Care Act 1983. (A recent referendum in California on proposals to widen the powers of individuals from refusing treatment designed to prolong life to include being able to seek euthanasia, designed to end life, failed.)

6.4.4 Provisions suggested

There is, however, widespread belief that an advance directive should be enforceable, and very recent authority to suggest that this may already be so. The questions that are not entirely settled are the form such advance directives should take and what they should cover. There is also the question of what capacity should be required to make an enforceable advance directive, and whether the person may appoint a proxy to give consent for them relating to particular questions as they arise, as is possible in Australia, for instance.

6.4.5 Recommendations and support

The Law Commission in its 1995 Report (see 6.2.1) suggested the form that advance directives ought to take and posited a basic level of nursing care which could not be refused (even, possibly, by the otherwise competent). It pursued its suggestion that it should be possible to nominate a health care proxy to take decisions once the patient had lost capacity. The report contains a draft bill, one of the purposes of which is to introduce at Part I Chapter III a 'Continuing Power of Attorney' which will operate rather like an Enduring Power of Attorney but relating to the incapacitated person's health and welfare as well as their property and affairs. Shortly after publication, the then Government said that it did not intend to put the draft bill forward but to consult further. This is currently being pursued by means of the Lord Chancellor's Department's 1997 consultation paper *Who Decides?*

6.4.6 Enforceability in case law

The view that advance directives are enforceable in law was confirmed by the case of *Re C* (1994). This concerned a man who was a patient in Broadmoor and wished to refuse the amputation of a gangrenous foot. The court was asked to declare whether or not he was competent to refuse, and, using the definition of competence to refuse treatment suggested by the Law Commission in its Report No 129, it declared that he had. It then went on to state that the refusal would hold good even after Mr C lost competence, thus creating an enforceable advance directive. The British Medical Association has declared its support for the principle of advance directives and forms are available (for example, from the Terrence Higgins Trust for use particularly by those suffering from HIV or AIDS).

6.5 Privileged wills

Section 11 of the Wills Act 1837 provides that the provisions of s 9 of the Wills Act 1837 relating to the formalities necessary for a will to be valid – due execution, for example – do not apply to 'any soldier being in actual military service, or any mariner or seaman being at sea'. Those people may dispose of their estate without any formalities at all. Before the Statute of Frauds 1677 there had been no requirements as to formalities for dispositions of personalty by will, but that Statute introduced requirements for all but small personal estates which were, however, not required in the case of privileged testators. Originally, s 11 of the 1837 Act was worded so as to cover only personalty, but the privilege was widened by the Wills (Soldiers and Sailors) Act 1918 to cover realty as well.

6.5.1 No formalities required

A privileged will may be written or it may be oral; there is no requirement as to formalities, not even that a privileged will should be in writing. It may be made by a person under the age of majority and requires no attesting witnesses, so if someone does witness the will then provided it is intended to be an informal will, they may still take a gift under the will. This appears analogous with the provision of the Wills Act 1968 relating to supernumerary witnesses, but predates it. The Wills Act 1968, however, only amended s 15 of the Wills Act 1837; the formalities of the 1837 Act have never applied to privileged testators.

The privileged testator in *Re Limond; Limond v Cunliffe* (1915) was a lieutenant whose regiment remained on the Indian frontier at the conclusion of the Waziristan operations in 1895, escorting a frontier delimiting party in the Tochi Valley. He was mortally wounded by a sniper and dictated a will to his brother-in-law, under which the brother-in-law was the residuary legatee, before dying the following day. The will, which concerned personalty only, was signed by the testator and attested by the brother-in-law and another witness. The court held that the testator was on actual military service when he made the will, so the will was privileged and the brother-in-law would not fall foul of s 15 of the Wills Act 1837 and could take under it.

6.5.2 Requirements for capacity and intention

On the other hand, the privileged testator still needs to have testamentary capacity and testamentary intention, so if either of these is lacking there can be no privileged will.

6.5.3 Soldier or sailor

The interpretation of who is a soldier or sailor may be considered to be surprisingly wide. It has included nurses and typists as well as what one might think of as soldiers in the ordinary way of serving members of the armed forces ready to fight the enemy. The interpretation of whether someone is a privileged testator does not involve a construction of the words in the will so much as a construction of reality; the courts will usually lean to finding that a purported privileged will is valid, especially, it is sometimes felt, when they approve of the dispositions made.

6.5.4 Typist may be sailor

Sarah Hale was a typist on the *Lusitania*. She wrote to her mother, including some testamentary dispositions in her letter, from Southampton before she left on her last voyage. The letter was held to be admissible as a sailor's will under s 11 of the Wills Act 1837 (*Re Hale* (1915)).

6.5.5 Nurse may be soldier

The privileged testatrix in *In the Estate of Ada Stanley* (1916) was a nurse in the Territorial Force Nursing Service. She was mobilised for service and sent abroad in the First World War. During a period back in England in 1915, after receiving orders to re-embark for duty, she wrote to her niece, Ada Louise Stanley. The document was in the form of a letter, dated and signed but not witnessed. It began 'I give you full liberty to deal with my affairs' and set out how she wished her property to be disposed of in the event of her death. The testatrix died of dysentery in hospital in England in December 1915 after another tour of duty, leaving an estate of about £550. Ada Louise Stanley applied to the court for the document to be admitted to proof.

The court, considering the authority of *Re Hale* (above), held that Ada Stanley had been a soldier, and it granted probate of the will as a soldier's will.

6.5.6 Others who may be soldiers

The Air Force is included by dint of the Wills (Soldiers and Sailors) Act 1918.

According to Lord Denning in *In re Wingham deceased; Andrews v Wingham* (1949) (below), 'soldier' includes 'not only the fighting men but also those who serve in the Forces, doctors, nurses, chaplains, WRNS, ATS, and so forth'.

A member of the WAAF also fell within the Act. The testatrix in *In the Estate of Rowson* (1944) was a squadron officer serving in England when she sent her solicitors written instructions for a formal will; on her death those instructions were treated as a privileged will.

6.5.7 Actual military service

Actual military service begins when a soldier receives orders and is mobilised. Merely being a soldier during peacetime is not enough, in theory, although in *Re Colman* (1958) a soldier was found to have been on actual military service in Germany in 1954.

6.5.8 Is actual military service the same as active military service?

The court in *In re Wingham (deceased)* (1949) was considering a purported privileged will made by the deceased whilst an officer training as a pilot at a camp training school in Saskatchewan in Canada during the Second World War. The deceased's father applied to the court on the basis that the deceased was not in a position to make a privileged will because, when he signed the document, he was not on 'actual military service'. He succeeded at first instance, but failed on appeal. The Court of Appeal addressed specifically the question of the meaning of 'actual military service', and whether this meant the same as 'active' military service. (It also discussed the equivalent phrase in Roman law, 'in expeditione', and concluded that it was relevant to a soldier on Hadrian's Wall or in the camp at Chester, but not to an airman in Saskatchewan who was only a day's flying from the enemy.)

The conclusion it came to was that the words 'actual' and 'active' were not interchangeable, and that a person was entitled to make a privileged will 'if at the time he is actually serving with the Armed Forces in connexion with military operations which are or have been taking place, or are believed to be imminent'. The will was therefore admitted to proof.

6.5.9 What is a war and is it necessary?

War need not have been declared as such, which is particularly relevant in any cases of soldiers who were serving in Northern Ireland. In *Re Jones (deceased)* (1981), the deceased, David Jones, had died in Northern Ireland in 1978 'at a time of armed and clandestine insurrection against the government'. He was a member of armed forces deployed at the request of the civil authorities. He was shot and mortally wounded, and on the way to hospital said to two officers of his battalion: 'if I don't make it, make sure Anne gets all my stuff.' Anne was his fiancée. David Jones had made a previous valid will leaving everything to his mother. The mother contested the case claiming David was not entitled to make a privileged will. The Registrar referred the matter to the High Court on the question of 'actual military service' and the meaning of 'war'.

6.5.10 Insurrection and disturbances may be war

The court held that, although hostilities between two sovereign governments would constitute a war, previous cases, especially the 1874 case of *Re Tweedale*, showed that the definition was wider. In that case, it was held that the suppression of insurrection or disturbances within the ambit of the area of government, but contrary to the ordinances of that government, was a matter of actual military service where the military were called out to suppress the disturbances. It was held that, where a question arose as to whether the deceased was on 'actual military service', the answer depended on the nature of the activities of the deceased and the unit or force to which he was attached, not on the character of the opposing operations. It was irrelevant that there was no formal state of war or that the enemy was not a uniformed force. It was also not relevant whether there was a foreign expedition or invasion or a local insurrection. The court therefore held that David Jones' oral declaration should be admitted to proof; therefore Anne's application succeeded. (Anne had by this time married someone else.)

6.5.11 Mercenaries and others?

The cases leave open the question of whether all persons involved in hostilities and insurrections may make privileged wills under English law. Certainly, in *Re Donaldson* (1840), the testator served not the Crown but the East India Dock Company and was nevertheless held to be entitled to make a privileged will. A court sitting in 1840 may, however, have proceeded on an assumption that the East India Dock Company was an extension of the Crown by other means, or at any rate that it was not incompatible with the British government. It is questionable whether, for example, a person on the opposing side to David Jones would have been allowed to make a privileged will, as a matter of public policy.

6.5.12 Being at sea

The interpretation of the phrase 'being at sea' is at least as wide as that of 'soldier'. To see why a person who is not on board ship has been considered to be at sea, one should consider the reasons for making some testators privileged in the first place. They are persons who are both more likely than most to die – on the battlefield or the open seas – and less able than most to obtain the advice of a solicitor and to make their will in a formal fashion. This was perhaps a little strained in the case of *Re M'Murdo* (1868); the deceased was held privileged because he was a mariner on the HMS *Excellent,* which was permanently stationed in Portsmouth Harbour. The court found that he was a mariner in Her Majesty's Service and 'still he is subject to the restraints of the service, and might have no opportunity of making a will with the usual formalities if he was taken on board when no lawyer was at hand'.

6.5.13 At sea in Surrey

Ian Newland, the testator in *In the Goods of Newland (deceased)* (1952), was 19 years old in 1944, when the age of majority was still 21. He was apprenticed in the Merchant Navy and joined a ship which appeared on 4 July of that year to have docked at Liverpool (the details of the case were somewhat vague because the records had been left deliberately obscure for security reasons). He spent his leave in Surrey, a landlocked county, where he executed a will before leaving again to rejoin his ship. He remained in the service until October that year. In 1951 he died in India. His will was referred to the court on the question of whether he was 'a seaman at sea' when he executed the will in Surrey, because only if that were the case would the will, as one made by a minor, be admissible. The court held that Ian Newland was indeed 'at sea' because the will had been drawn up in contemplation of the forthcoming voyage, at a time when he was already under orders to rejoin his ship before a certain date.

6.5.14 Reasons for the privilege confirmed

In *Re Rapley's Estate; Rapley v Rapley* (1983), the deceased seaman, Clive Rapley, had purported to make a will in 1960, when he was still a minor. The document was not attested in accordance with s 9 of the Wills Act 1837. When he purported to make the will, he was apprenticed to a shipping company and was on leave in England awaiting orders to join a new ship with the same company. Twenty years later, he died in a typhoon in the Pacific. The plaintiff in the action was Clive Rapley's mother, Nettie. She had been granted letters of administration based on Clive's intestacy but then brought an action against Clive's father, seeking to propound the 1960 will and have the existing grant revoked, on the basis that the 1960 will was valid as the will of a 'seaman or mariner being at sea'. The court held that s 11 of the Wills Act 1837 (as clarified by s 1 of the Wills (Soldiers and Sailors) Act 1918) exempted mariners and seamen at sea from the provisions of the Act because they were unlikely to have legal assistance available to them and because they were under a greater risk of death than most people. It said that the words 'at sea' included, on consideration of past cases, mariners or seamen who were on shore under orders to join a ship, but they did not include Clive Rapley at the date he purported to make the will, because the facts showed that he had not then received instructions to join his new ship.

6.5.15 How long does the privilege last?

The privilege may continue after the end of hostilities if the soldier is part of an army of occupation. This is supported by the decision in *Re Jones* (1981) (above) that no current war as such is required to establish privilege.

6.5.16 How long does a privileged will last?

The limits of Roman law, which held that a soldier's privileged will ceased to operate a year after he was demobilised, do not apply.

The testator in *In Re Booth* (1926) was a Colonel Booth, who in 1882 was stationed in Gibraltar as a paymaster in the 46th Regiment. The regiment had received orders to start for Egypt when the Colonel made a document purporting to be a will but which was not executed in accordance with the formalities. Later, he gave the document to his wife, who kept it in a wooden plate chest in a locked closet in their home at Hawstead House. In 1916, Hawstead House burnt down. Colonel Booth died in 1924, aged 81, without having made any other will. The Colonel's widow sought to propound the will as a privileged will, and was opposed by the heir at law and the statutory next of kin. They would have had entitlements to the Colonel's realty and personalty on his intestacy under the pre-1926 rules. Their case was that the Colonel was not on 'actual military service' at the time of making the will, so the lack of formalities rendered it invalid. They also brought evidence that he knew of the (probable) burning of the will and regarded the will as having thus been revoked, and that he had referred to the need to make another. They further sought to introduce, from Roman law, the principle that a privileged soldier's will ceases to have effect one year from the date the soldier was discharged from the army.

The court held that the Colonel's actual military service began on receipt of the orders to proceed abroad for service in a campaign, so the will was a privileged will and therefore valid. It also held that the rule of Roman law that a soldier's will became invalid one year after his discharge was not part of English law, and that acquiescence in destruction of the will by fire did not amount to revocation. The will (which had not of course been physically in existence for the past 10 years) was therefore admitted to probate, with the widow bringing evidence about its contents.

6.5.17 Testamentary intent

The testator must intend deliberately to give expression to his wishes as to what should happen if he were to die. The cases in this area show that there may be a difficulty in distinguishing the fine borderline between a statement which constitutes a privileged will and one which is merely a statement of what the purported testator believes to be the case.

The testator in *In the Estate of Donner* (1917) said, 'I want my mother to have everything', but it was held that this did not show testamentary intention but, on the facts, an approbation of what the deceased had believed would happen to his estate on his intestacy. Similarly, the privileged testator in *In the Estate of Knibbs* (1962) said, 'if anything ever happens to me, Iris will get anything I have got'. It was held that this did not demonstrate the intention that the testator's words should take effect as his will and accordingly there was no will.

In Re Stable (deceased) (1919) demonstrates that although it is necessary for the privileged testator to have testamentary intention, that is not the same as believing that he is making a will. In this case, a young man said to his fiancee, in the presence of a witness (who was useful to the court in being able to give evidence of what was said, but not required for compliance with any formality), 'If I stop a bullet everything of mine will be yours'. These words were admitted to probate as a privileged will, the court accepting explicitly that the testator does not need to think he is making a will (see, also, *Re Berger* (1989) above, at 3.5.2).

In *In the Estate of Beech, Beech v Public Trustee* (1923), it was held that the a testator cannot make an approval of the words put into his mouth conditional upon their legal effect being what he desired. If the testator executes a will knowing and approving of the words in it, the court cannot exclude from probate the words on which the testator was mistaken as to their legal effect, even if his intention was such that, in those circumstances, he did not intend them to be valid. What must be intended is that the words of the will should have effect at death.

6.5.18 Revocation

Marriage revokes a privileged will as it does any other (see 7.2). This was held by Shearman J in *In the Estate of Wardrop* (1917) on the basis of the wording of s 18 of the Wills Act 1837, which provides that 'every will ... shall be revoked by ... marriage'.

A privileged will which is not nuncupative (oral) may be revoked by destruction in the same way as a formal will; that is to say, if the testator destroys it with the intention of revoking it, that will be effective.

In *In the Estate of Gossage* (1921), a formal will was declared to have been revoked by informal writing declaring an intention to revoke. (For details of the facts of this case, see 7.7.) The decision is phrased in terms of the making of a further testamentary instrument. It refers to there being no requirement 'for the revocation of a soldier's will that there should be the formalities necessary to revoke the will of a civilian', although when the case concerned the revocation of a formal will. The court held explicitly, however, that the informal or privileged writing would have revoked the will under the law pertaining before the Wills Act 1837 and, when s 11 of that Act stated that privileged testators were exempt from the formalities of the Act, it meant that what had to be examined was whether the acts done would have had effect under the common law, which allowed a soldier to make or revoke his will without any formality.

The court said: '... no formalities are required for the execution of a soldier's will, but soldiers are allowed to dispose of their personal estate as they might have done before the Act – that is, as they might have done before the Statute of Frauds ... In the case of a civilian's will certain formalities are required; in that of a soldier's will no formalities at all are necessary, and therefore upon the interpretation of the Act no formalities are required to revoke a soldier's will.' It held that, '... the power of revocation is merely another aspect of the power of disposition'. Thus, if a testator is privileged, he may use that privilege to revoke previous wills as well as to make new ones without being subject to the requirements of the Wills Act 1837 as to the formalities.

6.6 Foreign wills

If a will is made in accordance with the law of a foreign country, it will nevertheless be valid under English law if it is executed in accordance with the requirements in the country where the testator was domiciled or habitually resident, or of which he was a national when he made the will or when he died. If the testator had immovable property, his will is also valid if it conforms to the requirements of the jurisdiction in which the immovable property is situated. The position is governed by the Wills Act 1963 which applies where the testator died from 1964 onwards, regardless of the date of execution of the will.

Section 2 of the 1963 Act allows for liberal interpretation of whether or not a formality needs to be strictly complied with. If a requirement is one of form, it need be adhered to less strongly than if it is one of essence as to the validity of the will, such as testamentary capacity.

The rules of private international law provide that the law of inheritance in respect of movable property is governed by the law of the deceased's domicile at the date of his death, and that of his immovable property by the *lex situs* (the law of the country in which the immovable property is situated). This may come into play particularly where there is an intestacy or where the country concerned has restrictions on testamentary freedom. For example, an English person who buys a house in France will, to the extent of his immovable property in France, be subject to the rules of French law as to how far he may leave his property by will. A Consultation Paper on the integration of the system was published in 1990 by the Hague Convention on Succession.

6.7   International wills

Sections 27 and 28 of the Administration of Justice Act 1982 include the form of will which will be acceptable in all countries which ratify the International Convention on International Wills of 1973. That will be in addition to the provisions of English internal law.

The Convention combines the formalities of signature and attestation required under English law with that of notarisation, as found elsewhere. It requires, essentially, that the will be made in numbered and signed pages and attested by two witnesses and either a solicitor or a notary public, who under this legislation is an authorised person who will issue a certificate as to the compliance with the formalities. Such a certificate is conclusive save where there is evidence that the formalities were not complied with.

As yet, those sections of the Administration of Justice Act which deal with international wills are not in force.

6.8   Joint wills

Where two or more persons execute the same document as the will of both of them, it will be a joint will. Joint wills are lawful but not usually appropriate. A joint will operates as the separate will of each testator, and either (or any) of the testators may revoke or vary the joint will so far as it applies to him. It does not matter whether the other person is still alive or whether he consents.

If the joint will remains valid for another person after it is admitted to probate as the will of a joint testator who has died, it is retained in the Registry of Wills of Living Persons. This can be inconvenient, but does not mean that the will cannot be revoked or amended by codicil by any surviving joint testator.

Joint wills are rare in practice and useful only insofar as they can effectively exercise a power given to two persons jointly to appoint by will. A joint will may also be a useful way of making a mutual will (see below), although there is no necessary connection at all between the two.

6.9 Mutual wills

The doctrine of mutual wills is an equitable doctrine and the creation of the Court of Chancery. Mutual wills are those which are made on the basis that the mutual testators – for example, as is often the case, husband and wife – each leave their property, usually, to the other, on the condition that the second to die will necessarily then leave all their estate – including that of the first to die – to an agreed third party, for example, their child.

6.9.1 An irrevocable will?

A mutual will is perhaps the nearest thing that exists to an irrevocable will. No will is irrevocable in law, but in the case of a mutual will not only will the breach of the agreement be remediable in an action for breach of contract but also the property involved will be fixed by equity with a constructive trust in favour of the agreed beneficiaries who, if they can prove the existence of the mutual will, can obtain the same practical results in terms of property as if the will had not been revoked, even if they cannot prevent revocation of the will itself.

The contractual element in mutual wills has not been much pursued, presumably because the loser, in event of a breach of the original agreement, would in any event be a third party to the contract and therefore unable to obtain a remedy for its breach. This was confirmed in *Beswick v Beswick* (1968), where an uncle transferred his business to his nephew in return for the nephew's promise to pay £5 per week to the uncle's widow after his death. The uncle died but the nephew did not pay. The widow brought an action against him. The court held that she could not sue in her own personal capacity, as she was not a party to the contract. However, as administratrix of the uncle's estate she did have standing to sue, as the estate had suffered a loss by virtue of the nephew's breach. The loss to the estate being purely nominal, the estate could obtain only nominal damages. As this would be an inadequate remedy, the court granted specific performance of the contract, with the estate bound to pass the £5 per week to the widow in her personal capacity. However, in the case of mutual wills, the route of seeking enforcement by the estate rather than the beneficiary is of no particular assistance, since the estate will never have suffered an appreciable loss for which to obtain damages, and the remedy of specific performance is equitable and would be liable to be granted only in situations in which the relevant property would, in any event, be fixed with a constructive trust. It appears that the contractual route is not useful, but this may change.

The Law Commission, in its Report No 242 *Privity of Contract: Contracts for the Benefit of Third Parties* (1993), has recommended that contracts made for the benefit of third parties should be enforceable by them, and that the parties to the contract should be unable to revoke the contract without a court order if the third party has already relied on it. The draft Bill in the Report, though aimed primarily at commercial situations, such as those relating to builders' contracts, appears potentially to encompass mutual will situations, as it is predicated on a wide definition of reliance. It remains to be seen first, whether the Bill ever becomes law in that form and secondly, if it does, whether and how it is applied to mutual wills. At the very least, it should produce a more detailed examination by the courts of their contractual element.

6.9.2 When revocation may take place and be of practical effect

The leading case is that of *Dufour v Pereira* (1769). Lord Camden in that case defined a mutual will thus: 'A mutual will is a revocable act. It may be revoked by joint consent clearly. By one only, if he gives notice, I can admit. But to affirm that the survivor (who has deluded his partner into this will upon the faith and persuasion that he would perform his part) may legally recall his contract, either secretly during the joint lives, or after at his pleasure, I cannot allow.'

6.9.3 Requirements for mutual wills

Three things must be established for a court to find mutual wills:

(a) agreement between the two or more persons executing the wills who also make provision for each other;

(b) agreement that the survivor will be bound;

(c) occurrence of the binding event.

6.9.4 Separate or joint wills

The will documents can be separate or there can be a joint will, and the terms of mutual wills may vary widely. In *Re Green* (1951), the parties were a married couple, and the agreement was that they would each leave all their property to the other, and the survivor would then leave half his own estate to charity. The surviving husband took the wife's estate and then remarried, making a new will leaving most of his property to his new wife. The court held that he could deal only with the half of his property that was not fixed with the trusts arising under the mutual will.

6.9.5 Proof of mutual wills

The agreement to be bound normally means that the survivor has promised not to revoke his own mutual will. Although it is usual for mutual wills to be in similar terms, the fact that close parties such as a husband and wife have made wills in the same terms does not amount to proof that the wills are mutual wills. There must be evidence of the agreement that the second to die will not revoke the mutual will. In *Re Oldham* (1925), a husband died after making a will in favour of his wife in the same terms as hers in favour of him. She subsequently remarried and made a new will in favour of her new husband. The court looked at the correspondence between the parties and their solicitor but found no evidence that there had been an agreement not to revoke.

In *Re Goodchild (deceased)* (1996), parents had made wills in similar terms benefiting their son, Gary, but the father had remarried after the mother's death, and had made a new will which was much less beneficial to Gary. Gary sought to show that the wills were mutual wills and brought considerable evidence from family and friends to suggest that his parents had considered themselves bound by irrevocable mutual wills. However, the court preferred the evidence of the solicitor who had advised the parents. The court found that any obligations the parents had were moral only, and did not have the necessary force of contract. It held that the wills were ordinary, separate wills and, along with a failed appeal on the mutual wills point, Gary proceeded with a family provision claim instead (see 15.21.5).

6.9.6   When does the final beneficiary's interest vest?

In *Re Hagger* (1930), a joint mutual will was made by a married couple by which they left property to each other for life and thereafter upon trust for various persons. The question arose as to when the interests of the beneficiaries of the trust vested and whether that was on the death of the first to die or the death of the second. It was a relevant question in this case because one of the beneficiaries had died after the wife but before the husband. If she had taken a vested interest on the death of the wife, her interest under the trust would be an interest in remainder postponed to the life interest of the husband, and the property would fall into her estate on his death. If she were not to take a vested interest until the death of the husband, her interest would lapse because she predeceased him.

It was also relevant to consider whether the interest which vested at the date of death of the first to die was the beneficiary's interest in the estate of the first to die or whether, at that point, the beneficiary also obtained a vested interest in the estate of the second to die.

6.9.7   Does the trust arise on death of the first to die or when the second to die takes a benefit?

The court held that the beneficiary's share vested on the death of the wife in *Re Hagger* (above) and that it vested in all the property covered by the mutual wills, that is, including all the property of the second to die that was involved in the agreement between the mutual testators. Clauson J held that the arrangement became binding in equity on the survivor when the first of them died.

There remained, however, a question mark over what the binding event was and thus when it occurred. It was not clear whether the trust came into operation when the first testator died leaving his mutual will unrevoked and believing the agreement as to the mutual wills still stood, or whether it did not arise until, that first death having already occurred, the survivor accepted a benefit under the will. The latter appeared to be implied by the reasoning for the imposition of a trust in *Dufour v Pereira* (above). However, Clauson J in *Re Hagger* (above) had held that the arrangement bit in equity on the death of the first to die 'even though the survivor did not signify his election to give effect to the will by taking benefits under it', but this remark was *obiter*, though the same had been said in *Gray v Perpetual Trustee Co* (1928) some two years before.

6.9.8 Survivor does not need to take any benefit for the doctrine of mutual wills to come into operation

The question appears to have been settled recently by *Re Dale* (1993). In that case, the terms of the mutual wills made by a married couple were that their property was left to their son and daughter in equal shares. After the death of the husband, the widow revoked her will and made a new one leaving very little to the daughter. On a preliminary hearing, the court found that the doctrine of mutual wills could apply even where the second to die had not received any benefit under the will of the first to die. In that case, the first of the two possible interpretations mentioned above necessarily applied so that the mutual wills would come into operation in equity on the death of the first to die.

The view that the event upon which the enforceability of mutual wills arises is the death of the first mutual testator was confirmed and refined in the recent case of *In re Hobley (deceased)* (1997). In that case, Mr and Mrs Hobley had made mutual wills in 1975 benefiting each other with substitutional gifts to various others which would come into operation when the second spouse died. The fact that the wills were mutual wills when they were made was not apparently in issue. One of the gifts was a house in Leamington Spa which was to go eventually to a Mr Blythe. Mr Hobley then revoked that gift by codicil, leaving the house in Leamington Spa to fall into residue. When he died in 1980, all his property, including that house, passed to Mrs Hobley. In 1992, she executed a new will, entirely different from the 1975 will, under which Mr Blythe did not get the house in Leamington Spa; she died the following year. If the mutual wills were still valid, then the property would be fixed with a constructive trust for those nominated in Mrs Hobley's 1975 will. The court held, however, that the effect of Mr Hobley's codicil had been to make an amendment which, whilst minor, was sufficiently significant to make it impossible for the court to embark upon an assessment of whether or not it was unconscionable for Mrs Hobley to have left her property elsewhere than as agreed. In the circumstances, she had been discharged from her obligations, which were no longer enforceable in equity, and her 1992 will was effective.

6.9.9 Practical difficulties with the doctrine of mutual wills – dissipation of assets by the second to die

A considerable problem with the doctrine of mutual wills is that it does not necessarily impose any duty on the second to die to account for property received from the estate of the first to die. Thus, the interests of the intended beneficiaries may possibly be defeated by the survivor of mutual testators dissipating all the assets.

6.9.10 Later acquisition of assets by the second to die

The converse of this is that the trust arising on the death of the first to die may include the after-acquired property of the second to die. For example, if the agreement is that each party will leave all their property to the other and thereafter to a specified third person, as is commonly the basis of the arrangement, the second party to die will never be able successfully to leave any of his property anywhere else, even if he outlives the first to die by many decades and amasses an unforeseeably large fortune.

6.9.11 A solution to the problem?

In *Re Cleaver* (1981), dealing with the problem of dissipation of assets in particular, the court implied into the agreement between the parties certain provisions which were arguably not really there and for which the authority seemed doubtful. The mutual wills were made by a married couple, and after the death of the husband the wife, taking the husband's whole estate, revoked her mutual will and made a new one by which, instead of the estate going equally to the husband's three children on her death, went to only one of them. The court held that a constructive trust had arisen over all her property at the death of her husband, including that which she obtained from his estate, the terms of which were that it would be shared amongst the husband's three children on her death. It went on to say, however, that she could not make large voluntary dispositions from the property, although she could otherwise use the property as she wished for her own benefit. This solution has the advantage of being practical and perhaps embodying the intentions of the parties, but it is not entirely certain whether it accords with the authorities or where the borderline between acceptable and unacceptable lifetime dispositions lies.

6.9.12 A better practical solution?

A much better idea might be for all the terms of mutual wills to be made clear on the face of them, since the court will not be able to imply terms where there are express provisions. This would also concentrate the minds of the mutual testators on the possible consequences of their actions.

The field of mutual wills appears to be mined with potential for negligence actions against solicitors. There has been something of an explosion recently, with several cases being reported during the last few years, possibly reflecting the amount of capital now often owned at death by those who do not take advice from specialists on estate planning. This area merits particular professional caution in advising on the effects of mutual wills, and careful contemporaneous recording as to whether or not wills made in similar terms are indeed mutual wills.

6.9.13 Enforcement of mutual wills

If the three requirements for mutual wills are met, and there have been no invalidating alterations to either will during the parties' joint lifetime, the practical effects of the arrangement can be enforced against the survivor in equity. The survivor cannot be prevented from revoking his mutual will, but he will be frustrated in equity and the property subject to the constructive trust may itself be bound by the terms of the mutual will.

SPECIAL WILLS

There are various special kinds of will which have different formalities or modes of operation from ordinary wills.

A statutory will is one made by the court under the Mental Health Act 1983 for a person who is not mentally capable of making a will for himself. The court in question is the Court of Protection, which is part of the Chancery Division of the High Court. The court orders a will to be made in the terms it believes the patient would have done had he been capable, and where he has never been capable then it assesses what it thinks a normally decent person would have done in the circumstances of the patient. The Mental Health Act sets out the formalities for execution of the statutory will, which are that it is expressed to be signed by the patient acting by the person authorised by the Court of Protection to execute the will for him, and it is actually signed by the authorised person with the patient's name and with his own, in the presence of two or more witnesses present at the same time who attest and subscribe in the presence of the authorised person; the will must then be sealed by the Court of Protection.

A person who may lose capacity can, since the Enduring Powers of Attorney Act 1985, make an Enduring Power of Attorney to allow another person to deal with his property during his lifetime once he becomes incapable, though he must still make any will dealing with property after his physical death himself. There is no equivalent statutory provision for allowing control by another of medical consents after a loss of capacity – so-called living wills – but developments now allow for enforceable directives as to medical treatment to be given in advance of loss of capacity, and there are proposals for Parliament to amend the law to allow for the appointment of health care proxies who can give or refuse consent on behalf of a patient who has become incapable. Enduring Powers and 'living wills' are not wills as such and the Wills Act 1837 does not apply to them.

Privileged wills are those made under s 11 of the Wills Act 1837, which provides that soldiers on actual military service or mariners or seamen being at sea are excused from the requirements for formalities laid down by the Wills Act itself. This includes being excused from the requirement to have reached the age of majority. The interpretation of who is a soldier on actual military service or a sailor is quite wide and may include a typist or nurse during a war or a member of the armed forces during an armed disturbance. The meaning of being at sea is similarly wide and has included sailors under orders to embark even if they are still on dry land. A privileged will may be made without the need for witnesses or even for writing, so it may be made orally or be in the form of a letter, and if there are any witnesses who are also beneficiaries they may still take under the will if it is privileged. The lack of requirement for formalities does not mean however that proof of testamentary intention is not required; sometimes there can be difficulty in establishing this, particularly with an oral will.

A will made under foreign law will be valid in England if it conforms to the requirements of the testator's country of habitual residence, domicile or nationality at death. Succession to movable property is governed by the law of the testator's domicile at death, but where immovable property is concerned it will be governed by the law of the country in which the immovable property is situated.

The Administration of Justice Act 1982 sets out a form of will which is to be acceptable in all countries which ratify the International Convention on International Wills. However, as yet, these provisions are not in force.

Two or more persons may execute the same document as a will; this will be valid as a joint will. However, it operates as the separate will of each person and can be revoked by them as they wish.

Mutual wills are made on the basis that each mutual testator makes his will in the terms that he does in reliance on the other making his will in particular agreed terms. If this occurs, then when one mutual testator dies, it is too late for the other to change his mind about the agreement. Although he may still change his will at law, equity will fix the property concerned with a trust so that it is redirected in accordance with the original agreement and is not disposed of in the terms of the new will. Just making wills in similar terms does not constitute making mutual wills. Whether wills are mutual is a matter of fact to be proved, though if they are identical that may be weighty evidence. Mutual wills can have unforeseen consequences if a surviving mutual testator either dissipates all the assets gained from the first person's estate or becomes much richer or remarries after the death of the other; the courts have sought to mitigate the effects of this.

CHAPTER 7

REVOCATION OF WILLS

7.1 A will is ambulatory

A will is ambulatory; it is of no effect until the testator's death. It can be revoked by the testator, provided he has the capacity, at any time. That is part of the essential nature of a will. However, it is not as easy to revoke a will as some people think, and many attempts to do so have failed. Equally, wills have been revoked without the testator having intended that they should be.

7.1.1 Ways of revoking a will

There are, in essence, four ways of revoking a will. All are governed by the Wills Act 1837, by s 18 in respect of marriage and by s 20 in respect of the other methods.

A will may be revoked by:

(a) marriage;

(b) destruction with intention to revoke;

(c) later will or codicil;

(d) duly executed writing declaring an intention to revoke.

Note that divorce does not revoke a will, though it may have an effect on some of the appointments and dispositions made (see 10.9).

7.1.2 Proof of revocation

If it is alleged, when a will that is otherwise valid comes to be proved, that it has been revoked, the legal burden of proving the revocation falls on the person alleging the revocation. There is no way in which a will may be revoked simply by becoming obsolete, so the making of a will cannot be regarded as a final act by anyone who countenances a change in their circumstances, whether in regard to the persons they intend to benefit under their will or in respect of what they have to leave them. If a person of 25 makes a will leaving everything (at that point, his bicycle and his savings of £25) to his best friend, and does not change the will before he dies at 50 having made millions, the best friend, with whom he has no doubt fallen out, will inherit the millions.

The testator will have the capacity to revoke a will provided he is over 18 and mentally capable; the mental capacity required to revoke a will is the same as is required to make one, with the proviso that this means the capacity to make a simple will rather than to make a complex one (see *Re Park* (1953) at 4.3.1).

7.2 Marriage

Section 18 of the Wills Act 1837 provides that, subject to certain exceptions, 'a will shall be revoked by the testator's marriage'.

Note that it is not the case that the ending of the marriage, whether through death, divorce or annulment, restores the previous position as regards the parties' wills, though a marriage which was void *ab initio* (and thus may have been the subject of nullity proceedings) will have had no effect in the first place.

7.2.1 Automatic revocation of will

It is immaterial whether someone intends by their marriage to revoke their will; it happens automatically by operation of s 18 of the 1837 Act. The Law Reform Committee's 22nd Report *The Making and Revocation of Wills*, published in 1980, considered the justifications for the continuance of the old rule and the points against it. As justifications for the rule, they concluded that marriage remained as fundamental a change in a person's life as ever, and that most testators would wish their spouse and children to inherit on their death and so should not inadvertently leave their property elsewhere through a failure to make a new will after marrying. They also felt that most people are aware of the rule that marriage revokes wills, so they were unlikely to fall foul of that rule itself. Against the retention of the rule, they mentioned particularly the change in the situation of married women, so that their property no longer passed automatically to their husband on marriage; this had made them less in need of protection than before, as they would now have their own property. If they did not, they could claim under the wider family provision rules, as could children, though their claims under those rules were more limited. The rule that marriage revokes a will was, on balance, retained.

7.2.2 Other ways of protecting the new spouse?

Note that the situation in this jurisdiction differs from that in the US, for example. The Uniform Probate Code implies a provision that, where a testator who had made a will before marriage fails to provide for his spouse by will after the marriage, the omitted spouse receives whatever she would have obtained on intestacy unless it appears from the will that the omission was deliberate or the testator provided for her otherwise and in lieu of a gift by will. The Family Law Act of Ontario in Canada gives an entitlement under s 5, and s 6 of the Act provides that the spouse may take that entitlement instead of a gift under the deceased's will or her entitlement on his intestacy, as she prefers.

The Law Reform Committee in its 22nd Report concluded that consideration should be given to repealing the rule that marriage revoked all wills partly because such revocation took with it the testator's gifts to charity as well. It suggested that Parliament was leaning towards equalising the legal position of married and cohabiting couples, and that this was a good reason for either abolishing the rule or extending it to cover the point at which cohabitation was established; the latter was, however, difficult to pinpoint. Since that report was published in 1980, the political and social climate has changed, and it seems unlikely that Parliament would now have any wish to equate cohabitation with marriage in any event.

7.2.3   Void marriage does not revoke a will

A void marriage, that is, one which the law does not recognise at all, does not revoke a will. The current grounds on which a marriage is void are set out in s 11 of the Matrimonial Causes Act 1973. The widowed testator in *Mette v Mette* (1859) married, or purported to marry, his late wife's half-sister; this relationship was then within the prohibited degrees of affinity and the marriage was thus void. The court held that it had not revoked the testator's will. In *Re Gray* (1963), a void marriage was held to make no difference to the parties' testamentary position, whereas a valid one did. In that case, the wife, not realising the marriage was void for the husband's bigamy, made a new will after the purported wedding. On the later death of the first wife of her 'husband', she contracted a valid marriage with him. She was held to have died intestate, because although it was clear she made her will in the belief that she was already married, the subsequent true marriage still revoked it. In *Warter v Warter* (1890), the testator had been the co-respondent in divorce proceedings; he went through a form of marriage with the respondent on 3 February 1880, after the decree absolute had been pronounced on 27 November 1879. That marriage was void because it took place within six months of the decree absolute, which at the time was not permissible. The testator executed a will on 6 February leaving all his property to his 'reputed wife'. On 2 April 1880 the couple went through another form of marriage. It was held that the will had been revoked by the second marriage, which was valid.

7.2.4   Voidable marriage does revoke a will

A voidable marriage, however, is one which is valid when contracted but subject to later annulment in court proceedings for the reasons set out in the Nullity Act 1971 (now in s 12 of the Matrimonial Causes Act 1973). A voidable marriage, being recognised in law when it takes place even if it is later annulled, does revoke a will even where the marriage is later annulled. The 1971 Act shifted the boundaries of void and voidable marriages, so that some situations which had fallen into one category under the system of canon law which previously obtained subsequently fell into the other. This included the situation where one party to a marriage did not consent to it, which had previously rendered the marriage void but which now merely renders it voidable. Thus such a marriage will now revoke a will, even if it is later the subject of a successful petition for nullity.

The case of *Re Roberts* (1978) turned on this point; the person who would have benefited under the pre-marriage will alleged that the testator's marriage had been void because he did not have the mental capacity to contract it. The Court of Appeal held, however, that such lack of capacity only made the marriage voidable, so that it would revoke a will. Once the will has been revoked by a valid marriage, the ending of that marriage, whether by annulment or divorce, does not alter the position that the voidable marriage was valid when contracted and revoked the will at that time.

The question of lack of consent to a marriage arises most frequently in respect of those who are unable to consent due to lack of capacity; after their marriage much or all of their property will necessarily pass to their new spouse in accordance with the rules of intestacy (see Chapter 9), as they may be incapable of making another will. Such a situation may be a cause of considerable concern and the occasion of an application to the court for a statutory will to be made under the Mental Health Act 1983 (see 6.1).

7.2.5 Exceptions to rule that marriage revokes a will

In certain limited circumstances, a will may not be revoked by the testator's marriage.

7.2.6 Will expressed to be made in contemplation of a marriage

It is not uncommon for a person who is to be married to want to arrange matters such as their will before the wedding, rather than having to think about it when they are embarking on, for example, their honeymoon safari. The Law of Property Act 1925 dealt with this situation by amending s 18 of the Wills Act 1837 to allow that a will expressed to be made in contemplation of marriage should not be revoked by the solemnisation of the marriage contemplated. That provision is in s 177 of the 1925 Act and applies to wills made after 1925 and before 1983 only. For wills made after 1982, there was a further amendment to s 18 of the Wills Act 1837 made by s 18 of the Administration of Justice Act 1982, so the current provisions of the 1837 Act as amended apply to wills made after 1982.

7.2.7 Wills made after 1925 but before 1983

For s 177 of the Law of Property Act 1925 to operate, the will must be expressed to be made in contemplation of the particular marriage which later takes place. Thus, the express statement in the will should refer to particulars of the marriage in order to fulfil the requirements of the section. The testator in *Pilot v Gainfort* (1931) gave by will 'to Diana Featherstone Pilot my wife all my worldly goods'. At the time of making the will, he was living with Diana, but their marriage came later. The court held that the will was not, however, revoked by the marriage because it 'practically' expressed contemplation of the marriage.

This case can be usefully compared with that of *Sallis v Jones* (1936), where the testator's will ended with the words 'this will is made in contemplation of marriage' but the court held that it was, nevertheless, revoked by the marriage contracted by the testator a few months after making the will. The problem was that the testator, despite apparently using the statutory wording, had not made it clear that he was contemplating a particular marriage, but appeared to be contemplating marriage in general. In the former case of *Pilot v Gainfort*, however, the marriage in question, to Diana Featherstone, was clear.

7.2.8 Whole will must be involved

It appears from the cases that the whole will or all its dispositions must be expressed to be made in contemplation of the particular marriage in order to satisfy s 177 of the Law of Property Act 1925. The testator in *In the Estate of Langston* (1953) executed a new will after the death of his wife leaving all his property to 'my fiancée Maida Edith Beck'. It was held that this was sufficient to satisfy the requirements of s 177 of the 1925 Act. However, in *Re Coleman* (1975) the testator by his will made gifts to 'my fiancée'. Two months later, he married her, and a year after that he died. The court held that the will had been revoked by the marriage, because it construed s 177 as requiring the will as a whole to be expressed to be in contemplation of marriage. The problem was that the testator could not be said to have made the will itself, as opposed to the particular dispositions to his fiancée, in contemplation of his forthcoming marriage.

7.2.9 The Law Reform Committee and the Administration of Justice Act 1982

The Law Reform Committee mentioned the case of *Re Coleman* (1975) in particular in its 22nd Report, finding the requirement for reference to the whole will too strict. They accordingly recommended that the law be changed so that '... if a will or any part of a will is shown by its language to be intended to survive a particular marriage, the presumption should be that the whole will survives ... capable of being rebutted to the extent that the will shows affirmatively that any particular provisions were not intended to survive the contemplated marriage'.

These recommendations were implemented by the Administration of Justice Act 1982.

7.2.10 Wills made after 1982

For wills made after 1982, the position appears therefore more relaxed. A will is not revoked by a marriage if it appears from it firstly that at the time it was made the testator was expecting to be married to a particular person and secondly that he intended that the wills or any disposition in it should not be revoked by the marriage. It is not clear whether the wording of the re-amended s 18 of the Wills Act 1837 after 1982 includes every situation covered by the section as amended only by s 177 of the Law of Property Act 1925 – is every will made in contemplation of marriage also necessarily made in expectation of marriage? Megarry J in *Re Coleman* (1975) (above) thought so – probably. There are no cases on the point, but it is suggested that if one arose, the courts would construe the later provisions as widening rather than merely altering the earlier ones.

7.2.11 Marriage and wills in other circumstances

The above provisions relating to the revocation of wills by marriage do not affect other provisions; for example, a will may be conditional on a marriage taking place, and provided it is also made in expectation of that particular marriage, then it will come into effect, but only if and when the marriage is contracted. The ending of a marriage does not revoke a will, although since 1982 it may affect the appointments or dispositions in the will. Note also that a covenant or contract not to revoke a will is valid insofar as the covenant itself goes, but does not affect the testator's ability to revoke the will. If he does so, the covenantee may sue for damages, but he cannot enforce or have revived the old will by his action. In *Re Marsland* (1939), the testator had covenanted not to revoke his will but did so by marrying. The beneficiaries under the old will sued, but were unsuccessful because the court held the will had been revoked not by the testator himself but by operation of law (s 18 of the Wills Act 1837); construing the covenant as one not to remarry would have been against public policy, which protects marriage. On the other hand, a suggestion that a contract should be found invalid in itself because its breach by marriage would offend public policy was rejected in *Robinson v Ommanney* (1833).

7.2.12 Appointments by will

Section 18 of the original Wills Act 1837 provided that an appointment made by will is not revoked by the testator's subsequent marriage if 'the real or personal estate thereby appointed would not in default of such appointment pass to his or her heir, customary heir, executor, or administrator, or the person entitled as his or her next of kin under the statute of distributions'.

This involved the awkward and complex question of who those people might be, applying the rules which were in effect before the legislation of 1925 came into force in 1926. If the exception does apply, it saves the appointment, but not the rest of the will, from revocation.

The Law Reform Committee considered this in its 22nd Report. It discussed the case of *Re Gilligan* (1950), where the court considered the principal purpose of the section. The Law Reform Committee concurred with the view of Pilcher J that the intention of the section was that the fund under appointment should devolve as on an intestacy if the testator's will were revoked. This would mean the widow would take her statutory share of the estate. They thought this rule should remain as it was by the Administration of Justice Act 1982 but that the language of the section should be modernised.

Thus, if the appointment is made in a will made after 1982 then the amended section provides that 'a disposition in exercise of a power of appointment shall take effect notwithstanding the testator's subsequent marriage unless the property so appointed would in default of appointment pass to his personal representatives'. Essentially this re-enacts the earlier provision but with reference not to the persons who would have been entitled under the pre-1926 rules but to the persons entitled to the testator's own estate on intestacy.

7.3 Destruction

Section 20 of the Wills Act 1837 provides that the whole or any part of a will or codicil is revoked 'by the burning, tearing, or otherwise destroying the same by the testator, or by some person in his presence and by his direction, with the intention of revoking the same'. Both those distinct elements – of physical destruction and of intention – must be fulfilled.

7.3.1 Destruction must be physical, not symbolic

The act of destruction of the will must be physical; cutting may be included in 'otherwise destroying', as was said in *Hobbs v Knight* (1838). The complete scratching out of the signatures of the testatrix and witnesses was also regarded as physical destruction within the meaning of the section in *Re Morton* (1887), but not in *In the goods of Godfrey* (1893) where the signature was struck through but remained legible.

Destruction which is not physical but symbolic will not do. In *Cheese v Lovejoy* (1877), the testator tried to revoke his will by crossing through part of it, writing 'revoked' on the back and throwing it away. When, after his death, the will was produced by his maid, who had retrieved it from a heap of old papers, the court had to decide whether his revocation had been successful. There was no problem with the testator's intention. The difficulty was whether the acts of destruction performed by the testator were sufficient under the Act. The court held that they were not, and admitted the will to probate, saying 'all the destroying in the world without intention will not revoke a will, nor all the intention in the world without destroying; there must be the two'.

7.3.2 Destruction of a will does not revoke a codicil to that will

Note that the revocation of a will by destruction does not revoke a codicil to that will. In *In the Goods of Turner* (1872), the testator gave by codicil a legacy to be held under conditions stated in the will. The will itself was later revoked by destruction. It was held, however, that this did not revoke the gift by codicil.

7.3.3 Sufficient destruction

To revoke the will, the destruction need not be of the whole will, but it must be of enough of it so as to impair the entirety of the will. It is therefore enough to burn, tear off or cut out or completely obliterate the signatures of the witnesses or the testator, as in *Hobbs v Knight* (1838) (above).

What amounts to sufficient destruction is somewhat reminiscent of what amounts to a sufficient signature (see 5.5 above); in *Perkes v Perkes* (1820), the destruction of the will by the testator's tearing it into four pieces with a definite intention to revoke it was held not be sufficient to revoke the will, because the testator was then stopped, partly by the devisee, whose behaviour had caused him to try to revoke the will, apologising. The testator then fitted the pieces back together, saying 'it is a good job it is no worse'. The court held the tearing insufficient to revoke the will because it was not all the destruction that the testator had intended to carry out. Thus, the sufficiency of destruction, like the sufficiency of a signature, may be determined by measuring what the testator did against what he intended to do.

7.3.4 Destruction of part of the will

Where part of the will is destroyed, it may be shown that there was revocation of that part only. In *In the Goods of Woodward* (1871), the testator had made his will on seven sheets of paper, each one signed by him and his witnesses at the end. The first eight lines of the will had been torn off and there was no information as to what they had contained. There was no proof of an intention to revoke the whole will and it was admitted to probate in its incomplete state. In *Re Everest* (1975), the lower half of the front page of the will was cut away. There was, again, insufficient evidence to establish that the testator had intended to revoke the whole will. It was admitted to probate without the missing first part.

7.3.5 Destruction by another person than the testator

If another person is to carry out the act of destruction, it must be in the testator's presence and at his direction. Both these elements need to be observed. The testator in *In the Estate of de Kremer* (1965) telephoned his solicitor to say that he wished to make a new will, asking him to destroy the old one. The solicitor, in the absence of the testator, did so. The court held that the destruction of the will had not revoked it. It also said that the solicitor concerned had committed a 'considerable professional error'. The will could not be revoked in the testator's absence; he could revoke it himself by destruction, but the extension allowing the revocation of a person's will by destruction by someone other than the testator himself should be considered to be a provision, like that for the signing of a will by a person other than the testator, to be used only as a last resort where there is some good reason, such as physical incapacity, why the testator cannot perform the act himself. Even then, the requirement for the testator's presence must be taken very seriously.

In *Re Dadds* (1857), the testatrix had called for assistance in revoking her will as she was too ill to manage by herself. Unfortunately, her assistants took the will out to the kitchen in order to burn it; it was held that this was not done in her presence and therefore was not effective to revoke the will. In the light of the improbability that the intestacy rules will satisfy the particular desires of any person, it is far better for practical purposes always to revoke a will at the same time as making further provisions for the disposal of property on death and by the same document.

7.3.6 Intention to revoke

Accidental destruction will not revoke the will; nor will destroying it intentionally but without the intention of revoking it. The first of these concepts is easy to see, but the second can cause some practical difficulty. It arises not infrequently, however, where a person mistakenly believes that a will has been revoked already or is invalid for some other reason, and therefore destroys it without the intention of revoking it – so far as they know, it does not need revoking. This was what occurred in *Giles v Warren* (1872), where a testator destroyed a will under a mistaken belief that it was invalid; the will was not revoked by that destruction. Likewise, in *Scott v Scott* (1859), the will was destroyed in the mistaken belief that a later will had already revoked it. The destroyed will was therefore not revoked by the destruction.

The testator's errors in these circumstances result in the earlier will being valid, albeit physically destroyed, and the later will in *Scott* being worthless. In *Re Jones* (1976), the court addressed directly the question of the testatrix's state of mind when destroying a will she believed to be invalid in any event. It held that a testator who tore up a will under the mistaken impression that it was of no effect 'may have merely torn it up, thinking that it was no longer worth the paper it was written upon ... the right inference to draw was that he did not intend to revoke it at all; he was merely disposing of what he thought was rubbish'.

A testator may have some intention of destroying his valid will but not the intention to revoke it. This occurred in *In the Goods of Brassington* (1902), where the testator had made a will leaving everything to his wife and appointing her sole executrix. He was always liable to become drunk and incapable and as time wore on he got worse until one day whilst particularly incapable he tore up his will. He subsequently tried to stick it back together and also told his doctor that he had torn up his will while he did not know what he was doing. It was held that the destruction had not revoked the will and it was admitted to probate.

The same applies where a will is destroyed accidentally, as occurred in the case of *Gill v Gill* (1909). The testator had got drunk and so annoyed his wife that she tore up his will in anger. The court subsequently held that there was no revocation because the destruction had not been at his direction, and acquiescence to the destruction did not equate with the necessary intention to revoke.

Acquiescing in destruction was also insufficient in *Re Booth* (1926) (see 7.7). The will was propounded by the deceased's widow, the court refusing to allow that the deceased's apparent acquiescence in its destruction amounted to that sufficient to revoke the will. If a will has been accidentally destroyed, just as where it has been lost, it is no longer available for revocation by destruction, as the destruction must take place in the limited circumstances allowed under the Act in order to revoke the will.

7.3.7 Destruction of parts and inferences of intention

If the testator destroys his signature on the will, this will raise an inference that he intended to revoke the whole will (as in *Hobbs v Knight*, above), but destruction of a part of the will that is not vital to the validity of the rest of the will does not affect it. In *In the Estate of Nunn* (1936), the testator had cut a strip out of the middle of his will and stitched the rest back together again. The court held that only the strip removed had been revoked and the rest of the will remained valid. Where, however, a will makes no sense without the destroyed parts, it will probably be considered to have been revoked in its entirety. The testator in *Leonard v Leonard* (1902) had destroyed the first two sheets of a will which consisted of five sheets of paper. Without the first two sheets, the remaining three were practically unintelligible and made no sense as a will. The court held that the testator had intended the revocation of the whole will. It should not be thought that actions of this kind will never be met in the course of the practice of an ordinary solicitor. Practitioners are well aware that, if there is some bizarre action that can be committed, there is an unexpectedly strong likelihood that sooner or later one of their clients will commit it.

7.3.8 Presumptions

There are two rebuttable presumptions in respect of the destruction of wills. These are that a will in the testator's possession which is missing at his death is presumed to have been revoked by destruction, and that a will found mutilated is presumed to have been mutilated with the intention of revocation.

7.3.9 Will missing at death

If the will was last known to be in the testator's possession but cannot be found at his death, it is presumed that the testator destroyed it with the intention of revoking it. How strong that presumption is, and thus how difficult to rebut, will depend on how safely the testator was known to keep the will. As with all presumptions, this one may be rebutted. Evidence may be adduced as to a wide range of facts that will tend to show the testator did not intend to revoke his will. For instance, it may be shown that his possessions were stolen in a burglary or destroyed by enemy action in wartime. In the Canadian case of *Lefebvre v Major* (1930), the presumption of destruction *animo revocandi* (with the intention to revoke) was rebutted by evidence that the testator had remained on good terms with his sister, whom his will benefited, that his things (possibly including his will) had been burned after his death and, according to the court, by evidence of 'the simple character of the man himself'.

7.3.10 Proving a missing will

It should be remembered that the difficulty of proving a will that cannot be found does not have any direct bearing on whether or not it is valid and has to be proved. Where a will cannot be found but it is shown that it has not been revoked, it can be proved by evidence of its contents. It is often the case that the only person who can give useful evidence about what was in the will is the beneficiary as in *Re Phibbs* (1917) (see 5.15.3), which might at first seem to render their evidence insufficiently weighty. However, as with most matters connected with wills, and indeed most family matters, the only persons likely to have any relevant knowledge about a matter usually are the close family members who are directly affected.

Evidence as to the contents of a lost will was given by the wife of Colonel Booth, whose privileged will reading: 'I leave everything to my wife absolutely. I hope she will have regard to my sister Mary' was believed to have been burned some eight years before his death. Mrs Booth was able to give evidence to the court of the contents of that will sufficient for it to be admitted to proof and thus to disinherit the heir and next of kin who would have taken on his intestacy (*Re Booth* (1926)).

In the case of *Sugden v Lord St Leonards* (1876), the handwritten will was not found, though many long codicils were. The will was proved in almost all its complexity on the evidence of the testator's daughter Charlotte. The testator had been Lord Chancellor, and the court accordingly found that 'Miss Sugden's position is exceptional; of her integrity there can be no doubt', although Hannen J was not entirely happy about the lack of evidence from a lawyer. He felt that would have been 'more satisfactory than the evidence of a non-professional person, above all the evidence of a lady'.

7.3.11 Will found mutilated

If at the testator's death the will which was in his possession is found mutilated, the presumption, again rebuttable, is that the testator mutilated it with the intention of revoking it, in whole or in part.

7.3.12 Capacity and the presumption of revocation by destruction

Tearing or mutilation during a period of insanity will not revoke the will, because the testator must always have the capacity to revoke the will in order to carry it out successfully. Showing that the testator was insane when he had possession of the will which it is alleged was revoked by him will reverse the burden of proof which would otherwise have operated, because it will mean that the presumption that the testator revoked the will by destruction will not operate. If the testator was insane during any part of the period when he had possession of the will, it will be necessary for anyone alleging he had revoked the will by destruction during that period to prove that he was mentally capable when he carried out the destruction.

7.4 By later will or codicil

Section 20 of the Wills Act 1837 provides that the whole or any part of a will may be revoked by another duly executed will or codicil.

7.4.1 Express revocation

Most wills, including will forms from a newsagent's shop, contain a revocation clause revoking all previous wills; this is normally the first clause of the will and comes immediately after the preamble stating who the testator is and what he is doing. Many codicils revoke a specific clause or paragraph of a specific will. Once they are duly executed, they are effective to revoke the will or clause or paragraph to which they refer. No particular form of words is necessary, but the phrase 'this is my last will' does not revoke earlier wills. It was said in *Lowthorpe-Lutwidge v Lowthorpe-Lutwidge* (1935) that a great deal of evidence is required to show that a general revocation clause is ineffective for want of intention since it is presumed that the testator knew and approved of the contents of his will. On the other hand, it was said in *Marsh v Marsh* (1860) that a general revocation clause worded as to revocation of 'all former wills' leads to the inference that the deceased intended to leave a subsisting will. If it can be found that the intention to make the revocation effected by a clause was based on a condition which has not been satisfied, the revocation will be ineffective (see below).

There has to be some clear statement of revocation. In *Re Hawkesley, Black v Tidy* (1934), the testatrix made a will in 1927 which she described as her last will. However, it did not expressly revoke earlier testamentary dispositions, and she had also made a will in 1922, to which she had added a codicil in 1925. The earlier will and the codicil thus remained valid, and the combined effects of the documents had to be considered.

7.4.2 Effect of words of revocation included by mistake

Where the testator includes in his will words of revocation which he does not in fact intend to operate, whether they do so or not will depend on how far he was aware of the words being in the document, not on how far he was aware of their legal effect. Thus, in *Collins v Elstone* (1893), where the testatrix was unaware (having been wrongly advised) of the true legal effect of the revocation clause in her will, but was clearly aware that it was there, it was held to be valid and thus to revoke her previous dispositions. In *Re Phelan* (1972), however, the testator was held to have been insufficiently aware of the revocation clauses in his last testamentary documents, so they were excluded from probate, thus achieving the result he intended as to his dispositions. The basis of the decision, however, appears to have everything to do with the testator's knowledge and approval of the contents of his will and nothing to do with his intention, or otherwise, of revoking his will.

7.4.3 Revocation clauses and wills for other jurisdictions

It may be questionable how far a revocation clause operates if there are wills made by the same testator which refer to other jurisdictions. The testator may, however, make provision. In *Re Wayland* (1951), the testator made a will dealing with his Belgian property under the provisions of Belgian law. Later, he made an English will which contained a general revocation clause but also declared 'this will is intended to deal only with my estate in England'. The court construed the revocation clause as dealing also only with his English wills and admitted the Belgian will to probate as well.

7.4.4 Inoperative revocation clauses

A revocation clause in a will does not operate if it is contained in a conditional will which is inoperative owing to the specified condition not being satisfied, or if it is itself subject to a condition which is not satisfied.

7.4.5 Implied revocation

If a later will contains provisions which are inconsistent with or merely repeat provisions in an earlier will, without that will or the provisions in it being expressly revoked, the earlier will is impliedly revoked insofar as that applies. The inconsistency does not revoke the earlier will as a whole. Taking a later provision rather than an earlier one when there is inconsistency between the two is a general rule of construction which was confirmed in *Birks v Birks* (1865). A court will read all the testamentary provisions together, since that is how they constitute the testator's 'will', and later provisions prevail over earlier ones with which they are inconsistent. If the inconsistency or repetition is partial, it will be a question of construction as to which provisions the testator intended to take effect at his death. In *Dempsey v Lawson* (1877), the testatrix had made a will in 1858 disposing of all her property and leaving the residue to Roman Catholic convents. In 1860 she made another, without revocation or residuary clauses. The court held that she had intended to replace the earlier will and the residuary beneficiaries under the earlier will received nothing.

7.4.6 Implied revocation by codicil

A common reason for making a codicil is to revoke gifts made in a will. If the codicil is clear, as well as properly made, then the revocation will be effective. If, however, it is not effective, the gift will still stand. In the situation where there is doubt about whether the codicil is sufficiently clear, there is an old case suggesting that the courts will incline to retain the provisions of the will intact. In *Hearle v Hicks* (1832), the testator left his copyhold house to his wife for her life. Later, he executed another will, leaving his freehold and copyhold land to his daughter for her life. The court held that the clear gift to the wife should stand and was not revoked by the more general gift in the subsequent codicil.

In *Re Wray* (1951), the testator appointed an executor and left him a legacy. The residue was left on the basis that, if the named beneficiary predeceased, the property should devolve as part of his estate. Later, the testator directed by codicil that his will should be read as though the name of the executor were admitted and that person were dead. It was held, however, that this did not mean that person was excluded from the life interest in the residue which he took as part of a gift under the will of the testator's residuary beneficiary.

7.4.7   Proof of revocation

If a will or codicil is revoked by a later will or codicil, that revocation takes effect immediately and continues whether or not the later will or codicil can be produced at the testator's death. However, it will be necessary to establish that the later document was duly executed and that its contents were such as expressly or impliedly to revoke the earlier document. Evidence such as a copy, or oral evidence, may be adduced to support this contention.

The situation can arise where a will or codicil is inadmissible to probate and yet it may still revoke an earlier will. In *Re Howard* (1944), the testator left his estate to his son by will. He later executed two wills on the same day. One was in favour of his wife and the other in favour of his son. Unfortunately, each of those two contained a revocation clause revoking all previous wills, and the court held that the two wills effectively revoked the earlier will, though neither could be admitted to probate as they were inconsistent and there was nothing to show which was executed first.

The decision in *Re Howard* may be compared with that in *Re Phelan* (1972). There, the testator had executed even more wills on the same day, and the court got round the problem by omitting the revocation clauses for want of knowledge and approval. In that case, however, the wills were not inconsistent with each other, whereas in *Re Howard* they were. In effect, in *Re Howard,* the court viewed the revocation clause as effective where the rest of the will was not, and in *Re Phelan* it viewed the wills as effective whereas the revocation clause was not. Note that the reasoning in *Re Phelan* was that the testator, on the facts, did not know and approve of the revocation clauses, so they were omitted; in *Re Howard*, admitting either will would have involved the court making some more positive finding about the testator's intentions.

7.5   Duly executed writing declaring an intention to revoke

Section 20 of the Wills Act 1837 provides that 'some writing declaring an intention to revoke' a will and executed in the same manner as a will revokes the will. The testator in *In the Goods of Durance* (1872) had written a letter to his brother which was attested by two witnesses. It directed his brother to obtain his will and burn it without reading it. The letter was held to constitute duly executed writing declaring an intention to revoke. The codicil of the testator in *In the Goods of Gosling* (1886) was obliterated, and at the foot of it was written 'We are witnesses to the erasure of the above'. It was signed by the testator and attested by two witnesses. This was held to be writing declaring an intention to revoke and effective, within the meaning of the section, to revoke the codicil. The testatrix in *Re Spracklan's Estate* (1938) had written a letter containing the words 'will you please destroy the will already made out'. The letter was duly attested and was addressed to the manager of the bank where her will was held. The court, on the question of whether this letter was effective to revoke the will, held that it had been revoked immediately on the execution of the letter.

7.6   Conditional revocation

The intention to revoke may be absolute or it may be conditional. If the intention to revoke is absolute, then it takes effect immediately once the formalities for revocation – destruction (with intention), later will or codicil or duly executed writing declaring an intention – are satisfied. If a will is revoked as a result of a misunderstanding of fact, it will be a question of construction whether the revocation was conditional on the fact being true (*In the Estate of Southerden* (1925) (below) – here the misunderstanding was of the nature of the intestacy rules).

7.6.1   Conditional intention

If there is conditional intention, revocation will not take place until the condition is fulfilled. Thus, if a testator has said, in a manner that complies with the formalities, that his will should be revoked only if he returns from a certain voyage, then whether or not his will has been revoked will turn on the question of fact of whether or not he did return. Questions of law and of fact should be distinguished very clearly in this area; the law is clear that a will may be made subject to conditional revocation. Assuming it is clear what event constitutes the condition, then the question is always whether that event has in fact occurred.

7.6.2   Revocation conditional on validity of another will

Sometimes the condition makes revocation dependent upon the validity of another will or codicil. This sort of conditional revocation is referred to as dependent relative revocation, or conditional revocation. A will destroyed after it was believed a second will had replaced its provisions was held still to be valid in *Re Middleton* (1864) when the second will failed for want of due attestation. Where a first will was revoked with a general view to making a new one, however, in *Re Jones* (1976), the Court of Appeal held that the necessary conditional intention was lacking, as the first will had been destroyed with the intention of revoking it, the replacement will being a separate matter.

In this area, establishing whether or not the revocation was conditional often involves considering evidence about the circumstances in which the testator made the new will, because it would be unusual for the testator to make it clear that his old will (which he clearly considers to be in need of updating) is only revoked if his new one is valid. However, this involves stretching the principles of the law somewhat. Testators rarely give a thought to what would happen if their new will were invalid, since they tend not to countenance the possibility. They cannot therefore be said really to have an intention about the validity of their old will; though the courts will uphold an old will as not revoked because of the failure of the new will, finding that the testator's intention to revoke was conditional can involve inferring a great deal into the state of mind of the testator – effectively, predicting what the answer would have been to a certain question (would you have wanted to revoke your old will if the new one were not valid?) when no such question was asked of or occurred to the testator.

7.6.3 Revocation partial and conditional

In *Re Finnemore* (1992), the testator had made three successive wills leaving most of his estate to the same person each time but varying the beneficiaries of the remaining quarter of residue. The last two wills, both containing express general revocation clauses, were witnessed by the main beneficiary's husband, so she stood to lose her gifts under s 15 of the Wills Act 1837. The court found two good reasons to save the gift. Firstly, it found that the revocation clause, construed distributively, applied to some provisions absolutely and conditionally to others. Secondly, as an alternative, it found that the doctrine of conditional revocation would apply so that the revocation of the first will was conditional upon the validity of the main gift in the last will. This might appear to be a court fitting its findings around facts which are apparent but with which the law does not easily deal well.

7.6.4 Conditional revocation by destruction

Where the (purported) revocation of the old will was by destruction, it will be a question of fact whether the intention was conditional. In *In the Estate of Green* (1962), however, the testator made a new will and then destroyed his old one. The new will failed for want of due execution. The court looked at the testator's intention when he destroyed his old will, and held that his intention to revoke it was absolute and the old will was revoked immediately on its destruction.

The Law Reform Committee expressed some concern in its 22nd Report that the doctrine of conditional revocation was being used against testators' intentions. However, in *Re Jones* (1976) (above), the court showed that it was alive to this possibility. The testatrix had formed the intention of making a new will benefiting a different set of relatives, and she destroyed her old one; evidence of a testatrix's intention to make a new will is not conclusive, however, as to her intention to make the revocation of the old will conditional. The court held that the testatrix's intention was to disinherit the person who would have taken under the original will and that it was irrelevant that its revocation resulted in an intestacy.

In respect of these decisions, note that the fact that the old will had been destroyed, whilst it might have made it difficult to prove the old will, did not affect that will's validity. A will may be valid even though it has been destroyed, if it was not destroyed with the necessary intention. If the revocation was really to have been effected by a revocation clause in a new will, it might well be that there was no intention to revoke by destruction, but that the testator was, as was said in *Re Jones* (1976) (above), disposing of so much rubbish. In that case, if the new will containing the revocation clause were invalid, the old will would not be revoked and so would have to be proved, even if that were inconvenient or difficult given that it had been destroyed.

7.6.5 Conditional intention where there is mistaken belief of revival of an old will

If a will has been revoked by a later will, the subsequent revocation of that later will does not revive the first one. If, therefore, the destruction of the later will is intended to revoke it conditionally on the revival of the first will, the revocation of the second will will be ineffective.

In *Powell v Powell* (1866), the testator executed a will in 1864 revoking all his former wills. He destroyed it in 1865 with the express intention of substituting it for a will of 1862 which he held. The court found the revocation by destruction to be conditional on the validity of the 1862 will, which had been revoked by that of 1864 and which was not valid. Therefore, it was held that there had been no revocation by destruction of the will of 1865. Sir JP Wilde said: '[T]he principle [is] that all acts by which a testator may physically destroy or mutilate a testamentary instrument are by their nature equivocal. ... It is ... necessary in each case to study the act done by the light of the circumstances under which it occurred, and the declarations of the testator with which it may have been accompanied. For unless it be done with *animo revocandi*, it is no revocation.'

The testator in *Cossey v Cossey* (1900) had executed a series of wills. In 1887, he left a legacy of £2,000 to his niece and then all the remainder to his wife. In 1897, he executed another will leaving his property to his wife for her life, with the remainder to his sister-in-law. In April 1899, he made a third will, revoking the second will of 1897, and benefiting his wife more than by the second will but less than by the first. In May 1899, he said to his wife, on their anniversary, that he wished to revoke the 1899 will and go by that of 1887. His servant tore up the 1889 will in his presence and at his direction. The purported revocation took place in the belief that the 1887 will would thereby be revived. This was wrong, and it was held that the revocation of the 1899 will was conditional on its being true. The purported revocation was therefore ineffective and the will of 1899 remained valid.

The same happened in the Canadian case of *Re Janotta* (1976). The testator was wrongly informed by his niece that the revocation of his second will, of which the terms were almost identical with his first, would revive the first will. The court held that the second will was revoked only in order to revive the first, *and* conditionally on that occurring. It therefore admitted the second will to probate because its revocation had been ineffective.

7.6.6 Intention conditional on certain devolution of property

Similarly, if a will is destroyed conditionally upon a particular devolution on intestacy which is not satisfied, or a substantial misunderstanding about the nature of the testator's estate, it will not be revoked. The testator in *In the Estate of Southerden* (1925) (above) had made a will giving all his property to his wife. Later he burnt it, on the understanding that his wife would be entitled to all his property under his intestacy. The court held that this was a revocation conditional on that particular devolution on intestacy, and since that did not occur the condition was not fulfilled and the revocation was ineffective. The testator in *Re Carey* (1977) revoked his will because he had nothing to leave and considered the will superfluous. However, he came into an inheritance. The court managed to hold that the revocation had been conditional on the testator having nothing to leave, and that therefore, in the light of his inheritance, it was ineffective.

7.6.7 Conditional express revocation

A revocation clause in a will or codicil may be subject to an express condition which, if the condition is not satisfied, will mean that the clause does not operate. This may be a far simpler situation, as where the testator manages to state clearly his position about the revocation being dependent on a certain, ascertainable event. However, a revocation clause may also be construed as being conditional because of something expressed in it even if the condition as such is not express.

7.6.8 Implying the circumstances for revocation

In *Campbell v French* (1797), the testator gave legacies to his sister's two grandchildren, who were living in America. Later, by a codicil, he revoked the legacies to the grandchildren, 'they being all dead'. In fact, they were not dead. The revocation was held to be conditional on their being dead and,

153

therefore, ineffective. The testator in *In the Goods of Hope Brown* (1942) had a will prepared by solicitors by which he carefully disposed of all his property. Some years later he made a will for himself, properly executed but not well drafted. This later will contained a full revocation clause revoking all previous testamentary dispositions, and gave a life interest to the testator's wife, directing for the payment of pecuniary bequests free of duty (but making no such bequests) and directing his trustees to divide his property, after his wife's death, to after-mentioned beneficiaries who were not, in fact, mentioned. The court managed to find that the revocation clause was conditional on the testator concluding his later will, and the later will was admitted to probate without the revocation clause.

7.6.9 Conditional implied revocation

Implied revocation is what occurs when the testator makes a later gift of the same property of which he has disposed in an earlier will, without expressly revoking the earlier will or gift in it. It is a question of construction whether a gift is impliedly revoked by a gift of the same thing in a later will if that later gift subsequently fails. The question to be asked is, as with the revocation of a will, whether the revocation of the earlier gift was conditional on the later gift being effective.

The testatrix in *Re Robinson* (1930) gave her estate by will upon trust to pay an annuity to her son and after his death to divide her estate equally between her grandchildren who attained 21. By a later will, she gave her whole estate to her son absolutely, but the disposition was void because her son's wife was an attesting witness. The court found no intention to revoke the earlier will in any event, since the only indication of such an intention in the later will was the different, failed, disposition. The revocation of the earlier provision was therefore ineffective.

7.7 Revocation and privileged wills

Privileged wills – those made in circumstances where the testator is excused the need to comply with the formalities – are revocable in the same way as other wills, save that an oral (nuncupative) will cannot, of course, be revoked by destruction. They will be revoked if the testator makes a further will revoking them, whether that is a privileged will or not. Whether or not the testator can make a further privileged will depends on his situation at the time of making it. If he is not entitled to make a privileged will, he is not entitled to revoke a will without the formalities either.

The Court of Appeal considered the revocation of privileged wills in *In the Estate of Gossage; Wood v Gossage* (1921). (Note that the headnote to this short case is somewhat misleading.) The testator made a formally executed will in 1915, appointing his fiancée executrix and leaving her the residue of his estate after certain legacies. He then left with his regiment for South Africa, where he changed his mind and wrote to his fiancée asking her to give the will to his sister, which she did. In 1918, he wrote to his sister giving her instructions about the disposal of his property and saying, 'As regards the will, if you haven't already done so, I want you to burn it for I have already cancelled it'. The sister accordingly burnt the will, but after the death of the testator later that year, a copy of it was found amongst his possessions. The fiancée sought a declaration that the will should be admitted to probate. The deceased's next of kin claimed that the letter to the sister was writing declaring an intention to revoke. The court of first instance agreed with the next of kin and the fiancée appealed to the Court of Appeal.

The Court of Appeal held that s 11 of the Wills Act 1837 meant that privileged wills were outside the formalities of that Act completely, and therefore they continued to be governed by the law which applied before the 1837 Act. Lord Sterndale MR commented:

> There can be no question as to the intention of the testator to revoke his bequest to the plaintiff ... Obviously it would be a great injustice if the plaintiff were to take the property, but I hope that that fact does not influence me to strain the Act of Parliament against her. It is said ... that there is no valid revocation here because by s 20 a soldier's will cannot be revoked, though it can be made without the formalities required ... This appears to me to be an absurd result, but, however absurd it is, effect must be given to it if that result arises from the Act. I do not think, however, that it requires any straining of the language of the Act of Parliament to arrive at an opposite conclusion. It is quite clear that, apart from the Wills Act, a soldier could at common law make or revoke his will without any formality ... If one reads ss 9 and 11 together, no formalities are required for the execution of a soldier's will, but soldiers are allowed to dispose of their personal estate as they might have done before the Act – that is, as they might have done before the Statute of Frauds.

Younger LJ said: '... it is not required for the revocation of a soldier's will that there should be the formalities necessary to revoke the will of a civilian. Nothing more is required by s 11.'

The question of the revocation of privileged wills was also addressed in *Re Booth* (1926), where the testator had made a privileged will when starting out for Egypt with his regiment in 1882. It was made in writing but would have been inadequately executed had the testator not been in a position to make a privileged will. After that war, he gave the document to his wife, who kept it in a wooden plate chest in a locked closet in their home at Hawstead House. In 1916, that house burnt down. Colonel Booth died in 1924, aged 81, without having made any other will. The widow sought to propound the will; the defendants made various objections. They brought evidence that he knew of the (probable) burning of the will and regarded the will as having thus been revoked. They showed that the Colonel had referred to the need to make another will. The court held, however, that acquiescence in destruction of the will by fire did not amount to revocation. The defendants also suggested that there should be imported into English law the principle of Roman law that a privileged will was automatically revoked by operation of law one year from the end of the testator's privilege – for example, a year after a sailor returns home or a soldier ceases to be on actual military service. The court declined to accept these objections and held that the will was valid.

REVOCATION OF WILLS

A testator may, provided he has the necessary mental capacity, revoke a will at any time. The capacity required is the same as to make a simple will. The burden of proving that a will is valid is with the person alleging the validity; the burden of proving that a valid will has been revoked is with the person alleging revocation.

A will may be revoked in four ways:

(a) marriage;

(b) destruction with intention to revoke;

(c) by later will or codicil;

(c) by duly executed writing declaring an intention to revoke.

Marriage revokes a will, including a privileged will, by operation of s 18 of the Wills Act 1837 whether or not the testator wishes it. A void marriage does not revoke a will, but a voidable one does. The position under the Wills Act 1837 was changed by s 177 of the Law of Property Act to provide that a will expressed to be made in contemplation of a particular marriage would not be revoked by that marriage. The Administration of Justice Act 1982 then provided that the will would not be revoked by the marriage if it appeared from the will that the testator was expecting the marriage and that he did not intend the revocation.

If destruction is to revoke a will in accordance with s 20 of the Wills Act 1837, then it must be physical destruction of all, or the vital parts, of the will, and it must be accompanied by the intention to revoke. The testator must either carry out the destruction himself or may have another person do it in his presence and at his direction. If the will is destroyed accidentally or without the necessary intention then there will be no revocation. A will known to have been in the testator's possession at death but which cannot be found will be presumed to have been destroyed by him with the intention of revocation, and a similar presumption applies where the will is found mutilated. However, presumptions as always are subject to rebuttal by evidence. Destruction during a period of insanity will not be sufficient as the testator will have lacked the necessary capacity even if he had the intention. The contents of a will which has been lost or destroyed but remains valid must be proved by whatever evidence is available.

Section 20 of the Wills Act 1837 also provides that the whole or any part of a will may be revoked by another duly executed will or codicil. Most wills expressly revoke all previous testamentary dispositions. Even if they do not, any valid dispositions which come later will impliedly revoke any earlier dispositions with which they are inconsistent.

Section 20 also allows for the revocation of a will by duly executed writing declaring an intention to revoke. This amounts, in essence, to a document which complies with the usual formalities for wills but does not contain dispositive provisions.

Revocation may be conditional on certain facts or, sometimes, on the validity of another will. This may be expressed by the testator or may be found by implication from the facts.

CHAPTER 8

ALTERATION, REPUBLICATION AND REVIVAL

8.1 Alteration

The basic rule is that alterations are not valid if they are made after execution – the words of the will are fixed at execution, and anything added afterwards will not have been executed and therefore cannot be admitted to probate. This is stated in s 21 of the Wills Act 1837, which provides that '... no obliteration, interlineation, or other alteration made in any will after the execution thereof shall be valid or have any effect, except so far as the words or effect of the will before such alteration shall not be apparent, unless such alteration shall be executed in like manner as hereinbefore is required for the execution of the will'.

It is also clear, however, that this basic rule gives no guidance as to what should be done if a will is found, duly executed, but containing alterations – provisions crossed out with new provisions inserted. The new provisions will be valid if they were made before the will was executed; how is anyone to tell whether they were or not?

It may be noted, but as an exception only, that r 14(2) of the 1987 Non-Contentious Probate Rules allows a registrar to grant probate of will including any unattested alterations without evidence that the alterations were made before execution, if the alteration appears to him to be 'of no practical importance'.

8.1.1 Alterations before execution

A finding as to whether an alteration was made before or after execution may begin with the application of presumptions. These presumptions are, as always, rebuttable; they will give a basis for a preliminary assumption, but if there is evidence to the contrary, that may overcome the presumption.

8.1.2 Time of alteration

The rebuttable presumption is that an unattested alteration (one which has not itself been executed) was made after the execution of the will or codicil it is contained in. In practice, small alterations are often made before execution – the testator, having approved his will, will only notice a mis-spelling of a beneficiary's name when he arrives at his solicitor's office to execute the will – but where substantial amendments have to be made, a professional adviser will have the will prepared afresh. If alterations are made before execution, it is the practice for the testator and witnesses to initial each alteration. It is then clear from the face of the will that the alteration existed before the will was executed. Extrinsic evidence, such as the statements of the witnesses, as to the circumstances of the execution, as well as the internal evidence of the contents of the will itself, may also be admitted in disputed cases.

8.1.3 Presumption of alteration after execution rebutted by internal evidence

There may also be other types of internal evidence which will rebut the presumption of alteration after execution. Where the will does not make sense without the alteration, it may therefore be found that the alteration was made before execution. In *Birch v Birch* (1848), the alterations consisted of filling in blanks which the draughtsman of the will had left for the amounts of legacies. It was held that the blanks had been filled in before execution. The alterations in *In the Goods of Cadge* (1868) consisted of interlineations in the same ink as the rest of the will. Without them, the will was unintelligible. It was held that they were made before execution and were therefore valid.

8.1.4 Due execution of alterations

If an alteration made after the will was executed is itself executed in accordance with the usual formalities for a will (as contained in s 9 of the Wills Act 1837), it will be valid. The alteration may be attested by the testator and witnesses signing by the alterations, usually in the margin, or by their adding a memorandum, itself attested, referring to the alterations.

8.1.5 What constitutes due execution of an alteration?

The cases on what constitutes due execution of an alteration show that the formalities must be adhered to strictly. In *Re Dewell* (1853), the testator inserted a small amendment after execution and acknowledged the document as his will, and the witnesses initialled the amendment. The execution of the amendment was accepted and the alteration admitted to probate. In *Re Shearn* (1880), however, the testatrix similarly discovered a small omission immediately after execution and inserted it by interlineation, acknowledging the document as her will to the two witnesses who then initialled in the margin near the interlineation. In that case, the court held that the alteration had not been duly executed because the testatrix had not signed it nor, before the witnesses signed, acknowledged her signature of the whole will as such to them.

8.1.6   'Not apparent' – revocation of part by obliteration

Alterations which make a part of the will 'not apparent' revoke that part of the will, provided that it can be shown that the testator intended by obliterating that part of the will to render it ineffective. As with revocation of a whole will by destruction, for revocation of part of a will by obliteration – since that is what this form of alteration amounts to – to be effective, there must be both the mental element of sufficient intention and the physical element of sufficient obliteration.

8.1.7   Examining the altered part – has it been made 'not apparent'?

Section 21 of the Wills Act 1837 foresees that some alterations may make part of the will not apparent, and provides that in those circumstances such a part will be revoked even if the alteration was not duly executed. This means not apparent on the face of the will itself.

Two related questions then arise – how far does the testator have to go to make the previous provision 'not apparent', and how far do the personal representatives and the court go in trying to establish whether the old provision is apparent or not?

Following the death of the testatrix in *In re Adams (deceased)* (1990), her will was found scribbled on with the signatures of the witnesses and the testatrix heavily scored with a ball-point pen. It was shown that she had intended to revoke the will. The court held that making the signatures not apparent in this way was sufficient to revoke the will.

8.1.8   Investigating and deciding

The question must then arise of what methods may or should be used in trying to work out what was written before the alteration took place. The cases have established what methods may be used to try to decipher the altered part. Any 'natural means' of discovering what the words are will be admissible, which appears to include anything which does not involve interfering physically with the will or making another document. If the original wording can be deciphered by natural means, it will be valid.

The testator in *Ffinch v Coombe* (1894) had attempted to obliterate some of the words in the will, after execution, by pasting slips of paper over them. It was held proper to try to read them by holding the paper up against the light framed with brown paper around the pasted-on slips. A decision on the same facts – indeed, the same will – in *In the Goods of Horsford* (1874) held that physically interfering with the will by removing the slips of paper was unacceptable.

8.1.9 Borderline between natural means and other means

It is difficult to define where the borderline lies between natural means, which may be used to see whether words are 'not apparent', and other means, which may not. It might at first sight appear to be the doing of any acts that require any equipment. However, in *Ffinch v Coombe* (1894) (above), the light from a window was used, but increased in effect by framing the will with brown paper, which itself might be considered an interference involving the use of equipment. The use of magnifying glasses was held to be permissible in *In the Goods of Brasier* (1899). An infra-red photograph showing the wording beneath a pasted-on strip of paper was, however, held inadmissible in *Re Itter* (1950) (below).

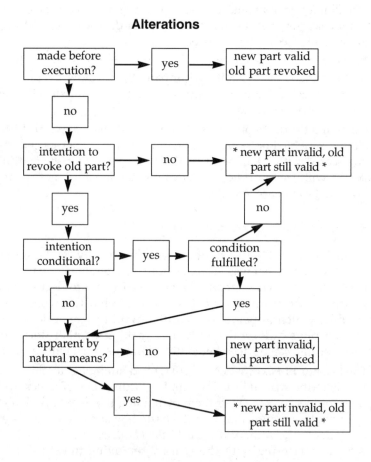

Alterations

* extrinsic evidence admissible as to
what the old part says *

There is no case to say whether the functions of an infra-red machine might be considered in the same light, as it were, as those of a magnifying glass, if the court were invited to look at the image directly rather than on a second document.

Altering – as opposed to clarifying – what means could be used to establish whether or not words have been made 'not apparent' could, however, alter the burden on testators when making obliterations. If any method could be used to decipher obliterated words, rather than just 'natural means', then the likelihood of the testator being able to tell whether or not he had sufficiently obliterated words would diminish greatly. Perhaps the answer lies in an unspoken inference that testators have magnifying glasses, but not infra-red machines.

8.1.10 Alteration without intention

As with the revocation of the whole of a will by destruction, it is necessary for both elements, the physical element of obliteration and the mental element of intention, to be present. Accidents do not suffice. If the obliteration was not deliberate, it will be necessary to establish what the provisions were so as to have them admitted to probate. This will also apply where the testator, though he had an intention that the obliteration should revoke the relevant part of the will, had only a conditional intention, and the condition was not satisfied.

8.1.11 Alteration with conditional intention

In the circumstances of both revocation of a will by destruction and revocation of part of a will by obliteration, the necessary physical acts may be accompanied only by a conditional intention. If there is no true intention to revoke, the revocation will not be valid. Thus, if conditional intention applies, and the condition on which the intention is based is not fulfilled, the word obliterated must be ascertained so that it can be admitted to probate.

8.1.12 Evidence

In these circumstances, a wide range of methods may be used to determine what the obliterated part said. The court is seeking not to decide whether the words on the will before the alteration are apparent or not – it may well be very clear that they are not apparent, just as it is very clear in the case of a will which has been burnt without being revoked that one cannot read what was in it – but to discover what the words were.

The question of whether the intention to revoke was conditional is one of fact. The admissible evidence of that also includes direct extrinsic evidence – direct evidence of the testator's intention which comes from outside the will – as to the testator's declarations of intention.

The testator in *In the Goods of McCabe* (1873) made a gift by will to his niece, believing the niece's mother to be dying. However, the mother recovered, and the testator substituted her as the beneficiary of the gift. The court admitted evidence of what the testator had declared to be his intention and it was held that the obliteration of the niece's name was conditional and her name was admitted to probate. This contrasts with *Townley v Watson* (1844) where an attempt to call the draughtsman of a will to give evidence as to what the words which had been obliterated were, failed. Sir H Jenner Fust said the construction which the courts had put on 'apparent' was 'apparent on inspection of the instrument itself'.

The testator in *In the Goods of Itter* (1950) attempted to substitute a different legacy for the one he had first made, though he did not attempt to change the legatee. The previous provisions could not be discovered except by the making of another document, in this case an infra-red photograph. That was unacceptable in the context of deciding whether the previous words were 'not apparent' and, since the infra-red photograph was not admitted, the words could not be deciphered and were indeed not apparent. The court held, however, that the intention to revoke the first legacy was conditional on the validity of the substituted legacy; the doctrine of conditional revocation applied. Extrinsic evidence such as the infra-red photograph was then admissible to discover what the previous words had been; the infra-red photograph was then admitted so the court could tell what words should be admitted to probate.

8.1.13 Deliberative and final alterations

Alterations before execution will not be valid if they are deliberative rather than final. There is a rebuttable presumption that pencil alterations are deliberative and ink ones final. In *Hawkes v Hawkes* (1828), it was said that each presumption is all the stronger if there are both pencil and ink alterations.

8.1.14 Alterations to privileged wills

There is a presumption that, if an alteration has been made to a privileged will, it was made while the testator was still able to make a privileged will. Such an alteration will therefore not be liable to fail for want of compliance with the formalities for execution laid down in s 9 of the Wills Act 1837.

8.2 Republication

'Publication' of a will originally meant a declaration by the testator, in the presence of witnesses, that the instrument produced to them was his will. The requirement that a will be published in this way in order to be valid was abolished by s 13 of the Wills Act 1837. It is still reflected, however, in the name of the doctrine of republication. When republication is talked about in practice, it may be called 'confirmation', reflecting the fact that the testator is making a later affirmation of the validity and contents of his will. Republication, or confirmation, occurs when a will is re-executed with the proper formalities. It may also be effected by codicil, and this is a fairly common occurrence.

Republication differs from revival (see below) in that revival, if successful, brings back a revoked will or codicil, whereas republication confirms an unrevoked will or codicil.

There are two methods of republication:

(a) re-execution with the proper formalities;

(b) by a duly executed codicil containing some reference to the will or codicil to be republished.

8.2.1 Intention to republish

The testator must have intended to republish his will, but a very low standard of proof is required, so that it may appear more accurate to say that all that is required is a reference to the will and a court will infer the intention. It has been found that merely referring to the codicil as being a codicil to a will identified by its date shows sufficient intention to republish the will. In *Re JC Taylor* (1888), a codicil which described itself as 'codicil to my will' was held to be sufficient to republish the will. A will is, however, commonly republished more emphatically by the testator making a codicil to a specified will, the new provisions being followed by some words such as 'in all other respects I confirm my said will'. In that situation, there is no room for doubt about the testator's intention.

It may be possible to show, by a codicil, that a testator was treating his will as unaltered. The testatrix in *Re Hay* (1904) struck out three legacies in a will, but the alteration by which she did this was unattested. Later, she made a codicil revoking only one of them. It was held that the other two legacies stood, as the testatrix's codicil was held to confirm her will without the alterations.

8.2.2 Effects of republication

Republication alters the date at which the will takes effect, so that it is no longer the original date of execution, but the date of republication. Before 1837, a will could not dispose of realty acquired after its own date, so a gift, for example, of 'all my real estate' would refer only to the real estate the testator had at the date of making the will. It was therefore necessary for a testator to update even the most generally worded of wills whenever he acquired any real property. If there had been no other developments of significance which justified making a new will, the desired effect could be achieved by simply republishing the will. The situation now is that, subject to contrary intention, the will speaks as to property from the date of death. Where a will is republished, that will validate a final alteration made after the previous execution but before the later one.

8.2.3 Time of alterations

Republication of an altered will by codicil will not, however, assist in validating the alterations in the will unless it can be shown that the alterations were made before the execution of the codicil. The presumption will still be that the alterations were made after execution. However, that presumption may of course be rebutted. The testator's will in *In the Goods of Heath* (1892) showed interlineations, but the court looked at the wording of the codicil and held that the interlineations in the will had been made before the codicil.

8.2.4 Date from which a republished will speaks

The general rule is that a will speaks from the date of the testator's death as to property and from its own date as to persons, save where there is contrary intention in the will (see 11.19–11.21). If a contrary intention is found so that a gift is held to be a specific gift of property which the testator had at the time of making the will, but which he no longer has at the date of death, the gift will fail by ademption (see 10.7).

Section 34 of the Wills Act 1837 deals with wills that are re-executed or revived as well as republished. It says that such a will is deemed for the purposes of the Wills Act to have been made at the time of its re-execution, revival or republication. A republished will operates, generally, as if it had been executed at the time of its republication.

This is, however, only a general rule, and will not be applied so as to defeat the testator's intentions. In *Re Moore* (1907), Barton J said: 'The authorities ... lead me to the conclusion that the courts have always treated the principle that republication makes the will speak as if it had been re-executed at the date of the codicil not as a rigid formula or technical rule, but as a useful and flexible instrument for effectuating a testator's intentions, by ascertaining them down to the latest date at which they have been expressed.'

8.2.5 No republication where change of date would defeat the testator's intention

As has been shown above, the intention to republish the will is readily inferred. In *Re Heath* (1949), however, a testator had executed a will containing a clause of a kind which it later became impossible validly to include, making a gift to his daughter with restrictions which could not be created after 1936. The relevant date was that of execution of the will. The court was asked to make a finding as to whether the testator had republished his will by his later codicil, because if he had then the clause would have been invalid. The court held that a finding that the original will had been republished would defeat the testator's intention and accordingly held that it had not.

8.2.6 Date of republication and objects of gifts

Generally, however, the effect of republishing the will is to make it speak from the date of republication. Persons referred to in it will be ascertained by reference to the date of republication, as, for example, in the case of *Re Hardyman* (1925), where the testatrix made a gift to her cousin's wife. The will was republished after the death of the wife who was alive at the time of the execution of the will, so at that time there was no specific person for it to refer to. Subsequently, the cousin remarried, and on the death of the testatrix it was held that the words used referred to the second wife, on the basis that, given there was no particular individual fulfilling that description at the date of republication, the reference must be taken to be any wife of the cousin.

Note, however, that by virtue of the provisions of s 1(7) of the Family Law Reform Act 1969, republication after 1969 does not mean that references to 'children' made before that date will change their effect as regards illegitimate children. Although the effect of s 15 of the 1969 Act was to include within the definition of 'children' all children, whether legitimate or illegitimate, unless a contrary intention appeared, s 1(7) specifically excludes from this any will or codicil executed before that Act came into force on 1 January 1970, even though the will or codicil was republished by codicil after that date.

8.2.7 Date of republication and subject matter of gifts

It is not clear whether republication can operate to save a specific gift which would otherwise fail by ademption. In *Re Galway* (1950), the testator had previously devised land, republishing the will after the Coal Act 1938 came into force bringing with it a right to compensation for the assets nationalised under it. The nationalisation removed some of the testator's interests in his land from his estate, but the republication of the will was held not to pass the compensation for the gift itself which had failed through ademption. In *Re Harvey* (1947), republication of the will after the asset had changed its legal nature saved the gift. The testator had made a will in 1912, which included an undivided share in land. By 1926, this had become personalty under s 35 of the Law of Property Act 1925. A codicil of 1927 which merely confirmed the cancellation of an earlier will was held sufficient to republish the will and preclude ademption. This might be considered the converse of the decision in *Re Hardyman* (above).

8.2.8 Republication of will with general revocation clause – effect on codicils

If a will is republished which contains a general revocation clause, this does not operate to revoke any earlier codicil to that will, even though logically it might appear to do so because the will, now speaking from a date later than that of the codicil, revokes all previous testamentary dispositions. In *In the Goods of Rawlins* (1879), however, the court held that *'prima facie* the re-execution of the will is a confirmation and not a revocation of the codicil, which became part of the instrument'.

8.2.9 Republication and s 15 of the Wills Act 1837

If a will contains a gift which is invalid because the will was witnessed by the donee or his spouse, the republication of that will by a codicil with other witnesses will validate the gift.

8.2.10 Republication – a trap for the solicitor?

It is clear from this that the implications of republishing a will are very great. Wills are frequently republished, however, by their confirmation in a codicil, and this is often done without careful examination – or even any examination – of whether the effect of their clauses will be altered by the change in date. There are no cases reported of actions for compensation by disappointed beneficiaries who have lost out unexpectedly through the operation of the rules relating to republication where the courts have not applied their ingenuity to saving gifts. This does not, however, mean, that there is no such case waiting to happen.

8.3 Revival

Section 22 of the Wills Act 1837 provides two ways for a will or codicil to be revived. Any part of a will or codicil which has been revoked may be revived by the testator, provided that it still exists and has not been destroyed. The methods available are:

(a) re-execution with the proper formalities;

(b) by a duly executed codicil showing an intention to revive the earlier document.

8.3.1 Revocation of a revoking document does not revive

If the first will is revoked by a second will, revocation of the second will does not revive the first one. This was demonstrated in *In the Goods of Hodgkinson* (1893), where the testator had made a first will giving all his property to his dear friend Jane. He later made a second will giving his realty to his sister Emma. This impliedly revoked the first will so far as the gift in the first will consisted of realty. The testator then revoked the second will by destruction. The Court of Appeal was asked to decide whether the revocation of the second will to Emma had effectively revived the gift of realty to Jane in the first will. It held that the testator's realty would pass on intestacy because the revocation of the second will did not revive the part of the first will that had been impliedly revoked.

8.3.2 Intention

There is a greater burden of proof of intention to be satisfied for revival than for republication; there must be much more than a mere reference to the will. The court will inquire into the testator's intention and will not infer it. The court in *In the Goods of Steele* (1868) was dealing with a codicil; it was asked how much intention to revive must be shown in the codicil for the revival to be effective. It held that the intention must '... appear on the face of the codicil, either by express words referring to a will as revoked and importing an intention to revive the same, or by a disposition of the testator's property inconsistent with any other intention, or by some other expressions conveying to the mind of the court, with reasonable certainty, the existence of the intention in question'. The court in *Marsh v Marsh* (1860) held that an intention to revive must, since the Wills Act 1837, appear from the codicil itself, and could not be established from any act dehors (outside) the codicil such as merely tying the codicil to the revoked will, as in that case.

8.3.3 Admissibility of evidence

Extrinsic evidence may be admissible in construing a codicil. The testator in *In the Goods of Davis* (1952) made a will giving all his property to one Ethel Phoebe Horsley, a lady who was not his wife. A year later he married her, thus revoking the will. Subsequently, he wrote 'The herein named Ethel Phoebe Horsley is now my lawful wedded wife' on the envelope containing the will, signed what he had written and had it attested. Ethel's sister gave evidence that she had pointed out to him that the marriage had revoked the will just before he made the writing. The court held that writing on the envelope amounted to a codicil showing the testator's intention to revive the will, and declared itself baffled as to what other intention the deceased could possibly have had except to revive the will.

8.3.4 Effects of revival

Section 34 of the Wills Act 1837 provides that a revived will is deemed for the purposes of the Act to have been made at the time of its revival. If there is a partial revocation of a will followed by a revocation of the whole will, a subsequent revival does not extend to the part first revoked unless an intention to the contrary can be shown. Note that revival may validate an unattested alteration made before the revival, or may incorporate a document which came into existence after the first execution of the will or codicil but before the revival.

ALTERATION, REPUBLICATION AND REVIVAL

Alterations made after execution are not valid. The will should be proved as it was at the time of execution.

If however intentional alterations made after execution have made the old words of the will not apparent by natural means, they will effectively have revoked those words.

Alterations made after execution which are not intentional will not be effective, and the same applies to alterations made with a conditional intention where the condition is not satisfied. Where such an alteration is made, then the old words remain valid and extrinsic evidence may be admitted to discover what they are.

It is presumed – subject to rebuttal – that alterations to privileged wills were made while the testator was still privileged.

A will which has been republished or revived is deemed by s 34 of the Wills Act 1837 to have been made at the time of its republication or revival.

A will which is valid may be re published by re-execution in accordance with the formalities or by being confirmed by a duly executed codicil referring to it. The result will be that the effective date of the original will becomes the date of re-publication, save in certain cases where that would defeat the testator's original intention. Alterations which can be shown to have been made before republication will therefore be validated even if they were made after the date of the original execution.

A will which has been revoked may be revived if s 22 of the Wills Act is complied with. It will not be revived by revocation of the document which revoked it, though the expectation that it will may make the second revocation conditional on a condition which is not satisfied. Revival will validate alterations made after the original execution in the same way as republication.

CHAPTER 9

INTESTATE SUCCESSION

9.1 Meaning of intestacy

A person who dies without leaving a valid will is said to be intestate; a person who does leave a valid will which fails to deal with all his property is said to be partially intestate. There are rules of law governing what happens to a person's property in either situation. Many people have particular ideas about what will happen if they die intestate, and sometimes fail to make a will for that reason. For example, they often have the impression that their spouse, if they are married, will inherit everything they have when they die. This will not necessarily be the situation if they have a substantial estate – in some cases, that may just mean a family house – and other relatives such as parents or children.

9.1.1 General structure of the intestacy rules

The rules are supposed to give the intestate's family something akin to what the legislators believe he would have left them had he made a will.

There used to be different provisions for realty, which devolved onto heirs ascertainable by a complex system, subject to curtesy or dower for the widow or widower, and personalty, which was governed until 1890 by the Statute of Distributions 1670 allowing provision for a widow or widower, issue and next of kin according to degree.

The history of the rules of intestacy demonstrates the historic differences between the ownership of property resulting from the different legal and social roles of husbands and wives, but those differences have now been abolished at least so far as the letter of the law is concerned. The original provision of the Law of Property Act 1922 was that the spouse would be entitled to the first thousand pounds of the intestate's estate; this was designed to give her the whole estate in the majority – 98% – of cases. The basic current provisions are still those laid down in the Administration of Estates Act 1925, although they have been amended and the spouse's entitlement increased by subsequent legislation. The previous distinctions between the devolution of personalty and realty have also been abolished and new categories of entitled persons have been set up.

The system of distribution set up in 1925 was described by Lord Cairns as 'a will made by the legislature for the intestate' and based on the presumed intentions of the deceased. It has been suggested that the stirpital construction of gifts – that where grandchildren take in the place of their parents who have predeceased, they take a proportionate part of their parent's share, not so much per grandchild – is inconsistent with this presumption, as most people would divide their property according to the number of recipients.

9.1.2 The Morton Committee Report 1951 and the Intestates' Estates Act 1952

This area of law was substantially reviewed in 1951, after the Morton Committee reported on the state of the law of intestate succession. It made four basic recommendations:

(a) an increase in the fixed entitlement for the spouse on intestacy;

(b) a right for the spouse to retain the matrimonial home;

(c) the avoidance of life interests in small estates;

(d) the extension of the family provision legislation to totally intestate estates.

As a result, the Intestates' Estates Act 1952 was passed. The spouse's statutory legacy was increased, but s 49(1)(aa) of the Administration of Estates Act 1925 was introduced to compensate for this. It requires the spouse to bring into account benefits she receives under the will on a partial intestacy (see below).

9.1.3 Law Commission Report No 187 (1989)

In 1989, the Law Commission made several suggestions for improving the system in its Report No 187 *Family Law: Distribution on Intestacy*. It recommended:

(a) that a surviving spouse should receive the whole estate;

(b) that the hotchpot rules (see below under 9.5 and 9.8) should be abolished;

(c) that a person should have to survive the deceased by 14 days in order to inherit from his estate on his intestacy.

It did not recommend, however, that cohabitants should inherit automatically on intestacy, but did suggest changes to the family provision rules (albeit this was outside their brief) to make it easier for them to bring a claim. The recommendations in this report have been acted upon, to an extent.

9.1.4 Disadvantages of relying on the intestacy rules

A person who appreciates the effects of the law of intestacy is very likely to want to make a will in order to avoid them. Apart from the dictation of who would receive the property in the estate, in many cases the lack of appointment of an executor and the restriction to the statutory powers on administration would involve inconvenience for the deceased's personal representatives and beneficiaries. The statutory trusts in particular cause difficulties where there are minor children entitled under the intestacy. As no-one can be sure when they will die or how much property they will have when it happens, not making a will leaves them with a lack of control over their property which may have unpredictable consequences. For example, if the intestate left more property than is covered by the spouse's entitlement, or the spouse dies before him, his property may be tied up on awkward and expensive trusts which he would have wanted to avoid. Intestate estates also attract liability to Inheritance Tax just as any other estate does, but by failing to make a will the deceased has lost the chance to organise his affairs so as to minimise the liability to tax.

9.1.5 Administering the estate

Where there is a valid will appointing executors, they take their authority from the will and so there are people to deal with the estate from the moment of the testator's death, but where the deceased died intestate there has to be some provision of law because no-one has authority to deal with the estate until they are granted authority to administer it by the court. The personal representatives in the case of an intestate estate are called administrators and they are required to deal with the estate in accordance with the rules of intestacy. They do not have a discretion to do what they think the deceased wanted; if he did not want the intestacy rules to operate, he should have made a will. The rules cannot be varied: a Canadian testator attempted to exclude the rules by making a will stating that he did not wish his separated wife to benefit from his estate, but as he failed to make any alternative provisions in his will, she took under the intestacy rules anyway (*Re Snider* (1974)).

On the death of an intestate, his property used to vest, by operation of law, in the President of the Family Division of the High Court pending a grant of letters of administration. The property remained legally vested in that person until the grant, and did not pass with his office. The Law Commission, in its Report No 184 *Property Law: Title on Death* (1989), recommended a change to this rule, and this was implemented by s 14 of the Law of Property (Miscellaneous Provisions) Act 1994, so that s 9 of the Administration of Estates Act 1925 now provides that the property of an intestate is vested in the Public Trustee until the grant of administration.

9.1.6 Statutory trust – s 33 of the Administration of Estates Act 1925

Where a person dies intestate as to any property, that property will pass to his personal representatives under s 33 of the Administration of Estates Act 1925 on trust, with a power to sell.

Note that there are particular rules in the Intestates' Estates Act 1952 relating to the house in which the intestate's spouse was living when the intestate died (not quite the same thing as a matrimonial home for the purposes of divorce matters). Schedule 2, para 4(1) says that whatever interest the intestate had in that house must not be sold without the resident spouse's consent until 12 months have elapsed from the first grant of representation to the estate, unless there is no other way of finding the money to pay for the administration of the estate.

9.1.7 Administrators

The personal representatives hold the proceeds of the sale to be distributed in accordance with the provisions of s 46 of the Administration of Estates Act 1925, after payment of funeral, testamentary and administration expenses, debts and other liabilities of the estate. Where there is a partial intestacy, they also hold the fund subject to the legacies in the will. Therefore, in the usual wa, no-one, including the deceased's spouse, can receive anything from the estate by operation of the intestacy rules unless all the payments under these categories have first been satisfied in full.

9.2 Entitlements on intestacy

Though the details of the entitlements can be quite complex, it is first of all useful to consider their basic shape. If there is a surviving spouse, she will obtain the personal chattels and a lump sum fixed by law; if there is still something remaining in the estate after she has had this sum, how much of it she gets will depend on whether the deceased also left issue or, if not, whether he left any other relatives within a fairly narrow category. If there is no spouse, the deceased's issue takes the whole estate. There is a wider category of people who may inherit where the deceased leaves neither spouse nor issue; only if all this fails will the property go to the government. Where there is anything substantial in an estate, a relative will usually appear to claim it.

The Law Commission recommended in 1989 that the surviving spouse should be entitled to the whole estate, and simplicity was one of its reasons. However, this recommendation was not accepted by the government even in principle and there is no likelihood of such a change in the foreseeable future.

In the Australian case of *Re Morrison* (1945), the intestate's widow was also his cousin. It was held that she took her entitlements on intestacy in both capacities. This could not arise under English law, however, since where there is a surviving spouse, all those who may inherit with her are within the prohibited degrees of affinity for marriage.

However, it is theoretically possible for a person to obtain two entitlements under the English intestacy rules. The widower whose deceased wife was also his adopted sister may take in both capacities.

9.2.1 Surviving spouse – definition

The definition is the 'lawfully married spouse alive at the death'. Thus, this will not include a divorced spouse, nor one whose marriage is null and void. Nor will it include a judicially separated spouse, because although judicially separated spouses are still technically married, their marriage not having been dissolved, they are excluded from entitlement by s 18(2) of the Matrimonial Causes Act 1973. Provisions of this kind about judicially separated spouses date from 1970. Note that when a spouse ceases to be entitled under the intestacy rules differs from when she ceases to be entitled to gifts or to take up an appointment as executor in a will, in that the latter applies only where the marriage has been dissolved or annulled (s 18A of the Wills Act 1837 as amended by Administration of Justice Act 1982).

It is for the surviving spouse to prove a valid marriage, but if she can show that a lawful ceremony was apparently concluded, then it will be for anyone disputing that to disprove the validity of the marriage. They may be able to do so by showing the marriage was void for bigamy, for example, as occurred in *Re Peete* (1952), where the purported widow's evidence of the death of her first husband was disputed and rejected. Where, however, the dispute relates to a defect in the formalities of the marriage proceedings, it is not clear whether the standard of proof is 'beyond reasonable doubt' (*Mahadervan v Mahadervan* (1962)) or merely 'firm and clear' (*Re Taylor* (1961)).

There are no statutory provisions or court decisions on whether a spouse of a polygamous marriage is entitled on intestacy. However, the Matrimonial Proceedings (Polygamous Marriages) Act 1972 allowed the parties to polygamous marriages to seek relief in the English courts, and in *Re Sehota, Kaur v Kaur* (1978) the spouse of a polygamous marriage was held to be entitled to apply under s 1(1)(a) of the Inheritance (Provision for Family and Dependants) Act 1975 as a spouse of the deceased. It is thus likely that a court would follow that decision by analogy.

9.2.2 Unmarried cohabitants

Unmarried cohabitants have no rights under the intestacy rules at all. They may of course have property rights just as spouses may. For example, they may be joint tenants in equity of a property they owned together with the deceased, in which case they will be entitled by virtue of the right of survivorship to the deceased's share of the property. They may also set up, as may a spouse, a claim in equity based on their contributions to a property in the sole name of the deceased. The Law Commission in its Report No 187 of 1989 did not suggest broadening the category of those entitled under the intestacy rules to include unmarried cohabitants, although they did suggest they should be able to establish a claim under the Inheritance (Provision for Family and Dependants) Act 1975 more easily than they could under that statute as it then stood (see Chapter 15).

In some other jurisdictions, the intestacy rules do provide for unmarried cohabitants to take under the intestacy of their partners. In British Columbia, there is a discretionary allowance for 'common law spouses'. In Queensland, the spouse takes all the estate on intestacy (the recommendation made by the Law Commission here which has been rejected by the government), and 'spouse' includes a cohabitant of two years' standing or a person living with the deceased intestate at death who is a parent of the intestate's child; where there is both an established cohabitant within these rules and a lawfully married spouse, they share the estate as to half each.

9.2.3 Survival

It used not to matter how long the spouse survived the deceased; even if it were only for a few minutes, the property of the first to die would pass on his death. Thus, if intestate spouses were involved in a road accident, one being killed instantly and the other being found alive but dying on the way to hospital, the spouse entitlement would pass from the estate of the one killed immediately and then, within minutes, into the estate of the second to die. Thus, much of a person's estate might pass to someone else's family, for example, to his parents-in-law, instead of perhaps to his own parents as he would have wished. Taken in conjunction with the *commorientes* principles, this had potential for injustice as well as distress.

9.2.4 *Commorientes*

Sometimes it is not possible to tell who died first. Such a situation is clearly likely to occur in particular where spouses are involved, since what is required for this difficulty to arise is people who are beneficiaries of each other's estates and who die together; this is likely to happen to people who travel together in cars or aeroplanes, or take extended holidays in far-flung places, as people do when they retire.

Wherever it cannot be told who died first, the *commorientes* rule (dying together) is applied. The rule under s 184 of the Law of Property Act 1925 is that where two persons die in circumstances in which it cannot be told who died first, there will be a presumption that the elder did. There is, however, an exception to this rule which applies where the people in question are spouses and the elder of them dies intestate. In those circumstances, s 46(3) of the Administration of Estates Act 1925 provides instead that it shall be deemed that the younger spouse did not survive the older intestate. This prevents the scenario envisaged above from occurring where the couple are properly *commorientes*, but if there is evidence, as in that example, that one did survive the other even by a short period, neither the *commorientes* rule nor its exception applies. Adducing such evidence is potentially very painful, however.

9.2.5 Survivorship

Where a person is making a will, they will usually make any gift conditional on the beneficiary surviving them by a specified period, usually about 28 days or a calendar month (see 10.6.9). This makes it more likely that the beneficiary will take the property and be able to enjoy it rather than, as would be the case should the two die in quick succession, perhaps as a result of the same accident, the property passing from one to the other and then directly to the other's family.

On intestacy, however, there was, until recently, no such provision, and there was a particular risk that the law would operate unfairly. For example, a couple might die as a result of a road accident, the wife being killed outright and her husband dying later in hospital. If the wife were intestate a large amount, or all, of her property would pass to her husband; it might then pass under his will to his family, with nothing going to her family at all even though her husband was unable to enjoy the property himself as the intestacy provisions would intend. The Law Commission investigated, and recommended a statutory survivorship period of 14 days, in relation to spouses only, feeling that any longer period could cause too great a delay in the administration of an estate. However, the situation was rectified by the insertion of a survivorship period of 28 days, in relation to spouses only, as s 46(1)(2A) of the Administration of Estates Act 1925 by s 1 of the Law Reform (Succession) Act 1995. This relates to deaths on or after 1 January 1996.

9.3 Spouse entitlement

A spouse is not automatically entitled to the estate of the deceased. The entitlement to the whole estate will arise only if the estate is small enough to fall within all the provisions below, or if the deceased had no issue, siblings or their issue, or parents alive when he died. The spouse is entitled first of all to the personal chattels, as defined by s 55(1)(x) of the Administration of Estates Act 1925.

9.3.1 Personal chattels – s 55(1)(x) of the Administration of Estates Act (AEA) 1925

These are 'articles of household or personal use or ornament'. The wording of the section begins with 'carriages' and has been criticised as being inappropriate as well as unclear, so that it is difficult for a personal representative to be sure whether a particular item falls within it. Note that the statutory definition excludes chattels used for business purposes, money, or securities for money.

Defining whether an article falls within the section may be difficult. Reference may be made to past cases which are not intestacy cases but which nevertheless involve the definition of personal chattels. In *Re Collins* (1971), a reference in a will to 'personal effects' was regarded as analogous to one to 'personal chattels'; the court went on to hold that the definition included collections of coins and stamps and a motor car.

In *Re Crispin* (1975), where the court had to decide what was included in a gift in a will of personal chattels it was held that the relevant question was whether the article came within the ordinary meaning of the word used in the section. Here the word 'furniture' was held to include clocks which the deceased had maintained as a collection. The Court of Appeal said that since clocks fell within the relevant definition, it did not matter what use they were put to.

Motor cars were held in *Re White* (1916) not to come within the definition of 'carriages' in the list provided by the section, but to be acceptable within the more general definition of articles of personal use. It is not clear whether items subject to hire purchase agreements are included. New Zealand legislation expressly does so, but this throws no light on the subject, since it may mean either that decisions in this country would follow that principle by analogy or, conversely, that it is necessary for there to be an express provision for them to be included.

A relevant consideration will, however, be the user of the item. If it is used for business purposes, even in part, it will not be a personal chattel within the meaning of the section. In *Re Ogilby* (1942), the deceased intestate's herd of cattle did not fall within the definition of personal chattels because they were used for farming purposes, even though they were a total failure as a business venture because they were farmed at a loss. The category of 'horses' was, however, held in *Re Hutchinson* (1955) to include racehorses, given that their use by the deceased was recreational rather than for business purposes.

The definition of personal chattels provided by the section has been criticised by the courts. In *Re Reynolds Will Trusts* (1966), the court called it a 'curious collection of terms', and the court in *Re Chaplin* (1950) employed some spoof Latin to express its opinion that the wording was 'an omnium gatherum ... The enumeration of specific articles in the definition is neither happy nor clear'.

9.3.2 Fixed net sum

As well as the personal chattels, the spouse is entitled to a fixed sum absolutely, the figures differing according to whether issue or other relatives survive or not. If the deceased is survived by issue, the spouse gets £125,000. If the deceased died without issue but leaving a parent or sibling of the whole blood as well as the spouse, the sum the spouse receives is £200,000. (If there is a spouse but no issue, parents or siblings, the spouse takes the whole estate.)

The figures are updated by order of the Lord Chancellor from time to time; the last update was December 1993. The sums carry interest (SI 1977/1490) as from specified dates, the rate of which is also varied from time to time. The sum can be used to 'buy' the matrimonial home (see below). The sudden uprating of the statutory legacy figures (for example, the increase in December 1993 was from £75,000/£125,000 to £125,000/£200,000) was felt by the Law Commission to lead to unacceptable discrepancies in the intestacy provisions relating to deaths either side of the relevant date, and to be a further good reason for providing that the surviving spouse should take the whole estate.

In *Re Collens (deceased)* (1986), the court had to consider the question of how the spouse's rights under English law interact with her rights under foreign law. In that case, the deceased died intestate in 1966, domiciled in Trinidad and Tobago, leaving a widow and several children from a previous marriage. His estate consisted of property in Trinidad and Tobago and Barbados as well as property in the UK, some of which was immovable. The widow accepted $1,000,000 in satisfaction of her rights in the Trinidad and Tobago estate. She also obtained one third of the rest of the estate under the law of the deceased's domicile, which governed succession to movable property. She then also claimed the statutory legacy of (then) £5,000 under s 46 of the AEA 1925 in respect of the English estate. The court held that even if under s 46 of the AEA 1925 the residuary estate of the intestate meant all his worldwide property, it could only regulate succession to the deceased's immovable property in England and could not charge assets where succession to them was regulated by foreign law. Therefore s 46 could not regulate succession to the deceased's movable property because it was regulated by the law of the deceased's domicile. Thus, the charge on the English immovable assets could not be said to have been satisfied out of the overseas assets of the deceased. The widow's benefits in Trinidad and Tobago were obtained by virtue of the intestacy laws of Trinidad and Tobago or the deed of compromise in the proceedings, and did not satisfy the charge on the English immovable property. Therefore, the widow was entitled to the statutory legacy under English law.

9.3.3 Remainder of the estate

The surviving spouse will always have an entitlement to more from the estate than the personal chattels and her fixed net sum – provided there is more! – but the amount and mode of her inheritance depends on whether other relatives of the deceased survived him.

9.3.4 Surviving spouse and issue

If there are surviving issue of the deceased, the spouse also gets a life interest in half the residue. The residue is calculated as being what is left from the estate (net of liabilities) after deduction of the personal chattels and fixed sum which she has already received. Remember that issue means not only children of the deceased but also remoter descendants such as grandchildren or great-grandchildren, and it includes issue *en ventre sa mere* (in gestation) at the date of the death. Remember too that 'children' in this context does not refer to people who are under age, but to a person's offspring, in the sense in which, whatever our age, we are all children. The Law Commission thought that the administration of estates would be 'easier, cheaper and shorter' without the inconvenience of life interests, even if in some situations they answered a need for provision very well.

9.3.5 Capitalisation of life interest

The spouse may capitalise her entitlement if she wishes, provided it is in possession, rather than have it as income for the rest of her life. (If she is under 18, she will not receive the capital until she reaches that age.) The relevant provision was inserted into the Administration of Estates Act 1925 by the Intestates Estates Act 1952, so that it is now s 47A of the AEA 1925. She must elect for this procedure within 12 months from the first grant, unless the court extends that period. The procedure for doing this is laid down in the Act, and requires her to give notice in writing, which she may retract only with the consent of the personal representatives. If the spouse is herself the sole personal representative, the notice should be given to the Principal Registrar of the Family Division. There are regulations in a statutory instrument, the Intestate Succession (Interest and Capitalisation) Order 1977, which set out how the figure for the capital sum is to be calculated. This is in essence the same system that an insurance company would use, based on interest rates and a calculation of how long the spouse is expected to live according to actuarial tables which take into account, for example, her age and other considerations. The costs involved in this come out of the estate.

9.3.6 Surviving spouse, no issue, specified other relatives

If there are no issue but there are specified other relatives, the interest the spouse takes in half the residue will be absolute. She therefore obtains a *life* interest only where there are issue. The relatives specified for these purposes are parents and siblings of the whole blood, that is, brother and sisters with the same mother and the same father as the deceased.

9.3.7 Surviving spouse, no issue, no specified other relatives

If there are no issue and no specified other relatives, the spouse is entitled to the whole residue absolutely.

Note that there the category of 'other' relatives who may be entitled to inherit property is wider when there is no surviving spouse.

9.3.8 Matrimonial home

The intestacy rules give the spouse no automatic entitlement to the matrimonial home as such. Believing that such an entitlement exists is another common error; a man who thinks he need not make a will because he has no valuable property apart from his interest in the matrimonial home in which his family lives may not realise that, on his death intestate, the house may have to be sold to satisfy the entitlements of his various relatives under the intestacy rules.

The spouse may be entitled to the house, or a share in it, by virtue of her interests under normal property law, however, and so her entitlement on intestacy will be in addition to what she already has.

9.3.9 Jointly owned property

Often, the property will be in the joint names of the deceased and his spouse. They must be joint tenants at law; the question of the passing of the deceased's beneficial interest will depend on whether they were joint tenants or tenants in common in equity. If the spouses were joint tenants in equity, then the deceased's interest passes to his spouse by operation of the right of survivorship or *jus accrescendi* and it never falls into his estate. The spouse therefore receives his interest in the house, as well as her full entitlement under the intestacy rules, if she and the deceased were joint tenants. Only if a house jointly owned at law by the spouses is held by them as tenants in common in equity will there be any question at all about whether the surviving spouse can effectively keep the matrimonial home. If a wife was a tenant in common, she may have to make such financial sacrifices in terms of losing her statutory legacy or even taking on extra debt to buy her husband's share of the house that she really cannot then afford to keep the house and family going. Many widowed spouses are in no position to raise cash by way of mortgage because they have insufficient earning capacity and years of working life remaining to obtain a mortgage, or perhaps because they have the care of children and cannot take paid work.

9.3.10 Resulting or implied trusts

Even where the property is in the deceased's sole name, it may be possible to show that the surviving spouse has obtained an entitlement to a share in the property by virtue of her own contributions. The types of contributions the courts are willing to countenance as giving rise to an interest in property in such circumstances varies, but a close consideration of the principles of the so-called 'new model' constructive trust will not be made here.

9.3.11 Proprietary estoppel

A person – whether spouse, cohabitant or anyone else – may also be able to establish a property right to a share in land by virtue of proprietary estoppel. This is what happened in *Re Basham (deceased)* (1987), where the plaintiff was the deceased's stepdaughter. The deceased had married the plaintiff's mother when the plaintiff was 15; she gave up hairdressing to help her stepfather in various business ventures. Both she and her husband carried out work on a house belonging to the deceased which it had always been understood would be left to the her as payment for all her work, and they were dissuaded from moving away from the area by the deceased on the promise of that gift of the house. The rest of the family also believed the plaintiff would be left the house. Unfortunately, the deceased failed to make a will to that effect. The plaintiff, as a stepdaughter, had no entitlement under the intestacy rules, under which everything would go to two nieces of the deceased. She brought a claim based on proprietary estoppel and, on the basis of the evidence, succeeded.

The area of proprietary estoppel seems to be broadening at present, perhaps because the courts are narrowing the definition of constructive trusts. It may widen still further as a result of the disappearance after the Law of Property (Miscellaneous Provisions) Act 1989 of the doctrine of part performance, so that where a contract does not fulfil the requirements of s 2 of that Act, proprietary estoppel may be the best, or only, way to establish an entitlement to the property.

9.3.12 Appropriation of the matrimonial home

The surviving spouse can require the personal representatives to appropriate the matrimonial home to her in satisfaction of any absolute interest in the intestacy. This means that she can force them to let her have the house in lieu of an interest of equivalent value, for example, the fixed net sum (statutory legacy). Absolute interests do not include the life interest which a spouse obtains in half the residue where there are issue, but that may be capitalised if the spouse so elects.

The deceased's share in the matrimonial home may be worth more than the fixed net sum or other interests available to the surviving spouse from the deceased's estate. In that case, the spouse may have to pay 'equality money' making up the difference in value. In *Re Phelps (deceased)* (1979), the court held that a spouse may require the personal representatives to appropriate the matrimonial home partly in satisfaction of that spouse's absolute interest and partly in return for the payment of equality money. In a case where a surviving spouse is trying to raise a sum to give by way of equality money in order to keep the matrimonial home, it can be particularly useful to establish that she has a property entitlement under trust rules, because that will reduce the sum of money she has to find by the amount to which she is held to be entitled.

There is a rule that any beneficiary of an estate may avoid (have declared invalid) the purchase of an asset from an estate by a personal representative. This would obviously be a risk in the not uncommon situation where an intestate leaves a surviving spouse who wishes to keep the matrimonial home but needs to pay equality money to do so, and where the estate exceeded the spouse's entitlement so that others are also entitled. The spouse would also be entitled to the grant of representation (see 12.17). There is therefore a limited exception to the rule, to deal with this situation, in the Second Schedule to the Intestates' Estates Act.

Problems have arisen with the appropriation of the matrimonial home to the spouse because the fixed net sum is valued at the date of the intestate's death, whereas the value of the house is taken at the date of appropriation. When house values were rising very quickly during the 1970s and the mid 1980s in particular, this meant that the surviving spouse could find that, although at the date of the deceased's death she could have 'bought' his share of the matrimonial home with her fixed net sum, by the time the paperwork came to be dealt with, there was a huge shortfall. In *Robinson v Collins* (1975), the matrimonial home was valued at £4,200 at the date of death, but by the date of appropriation the value was £8,000. The sum the spouse had to provide was the latter. In a period when property prices are relatively stable, there is less practical difficulty with this provision, and, of course, when prices were falling a spouse might have obtained an unexpected advantage. Its potential for causing unwarranted mischief for the surviving spouse remains, however, and its existence was one of the reasons the Law Commission gave in its Report No 187 (made in 1989, after the property market explosion of the 1980s) for recommending that the surviving spouse of an intestate be entitled simply to the whole estate.

9.4   Issue

Issue means children or remoter direct descendants, for example, grandchildren or great-grandchildren. It does not include step-children or children of the family in the sense in which they are included in matrimonial proceedings; the Law Commission considered this question in its Report No 187 but felt that it would lead to uncertainty as to who was included in the definition and therefore to litigation and expense beyond any advantage it might bring.

The definition of issue does, however, include those who are adopted or legitimated (see, also, 11.17).

Until the Family Law Reform Act 1969, illegitimate children had no claim on the intestacy of their parents. However, in respect of deaths from 1970 onwards, s 14 of the 1969 Act provided that the child and his parents would stand in relation to each other in the same way as if the child were legitimate.

This Act did not, however, affect relationships other than those between parents and children, so it gave an illegitimate child no claim for example on the intestacy of grandparents or siblings, and if an illegitimate child died intestate without parents, his estate would pass as *bona vacantia* to the Crown, even if he was close to his siblings or grandparents.

The Family Law Reform Act 1987 applies to the estates of those who die intestate after April 1988. Section 19 of the Act provides that in the tracing of a child's relationships, it no longer matters whether the child's parents were married to each other or not.

9.4.1 Statutory trusts

Where there are issue entitled on intestacy, they take 'on the statutory trusts'. This means that their entitlement is held in the way prescribed by statute until they attain an absolutely vested interest when they reach the age of majority. This was set at 21 until the Family Law Reform Act 1969 took effect in 1970, lowering the age to 18.

The statutory trusts are set out in s 47 of the AEA 1925.

9.4.2 Stirpital entitlement

Under the statutory trusts, the issue take *per stirpes* (s 47(1)(i)). This means that the intestate's estate is divided in proportion to the number of children he had, and where remoter issue are entitled, they take the share of the estate which falls to their branch. Remoter issue are entitled only where the person or persons through whom they claim have predeceased the intestate: a grandchild may claim from his grandparent's estate only if the relevant parent died before the grandparent. Therefore, if a widowed intestate died leaving three children, each with two children of her own, and one of the intestate's children had died before her, the two surviving children would take one-third of the estate and the two grandchildren whose relevant parent had died would take one-sixth each.

Entitlement *per stirpes* on intestacy

Imelda (dies intestate)

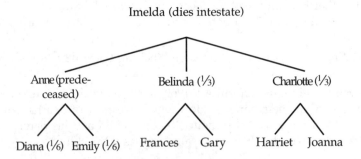

Anne (predeceased)   Belinda (⅓)   Charlotte (⅓)

Diana (⅙) Emily (⅙)   Frances   Gary   Harriet   Joanna

Note that if any child entitled on intestacy does not reach the age of 18, their entitlement fails. Thus, if Diana died at 17, her share would be divided amongst the others entitled at Imelda's death per stirpes, so that Emily, Belinda and Charlotte would each take ⅓ of Diana's share.

9.4.3   Maintenance and advancement

The provisions of ss 31 and 32 of the Trustee Act 1925 as to maintenance and advancement apply to the entitlement of issue on intestacy (s 47(1)(ii) of the AEA 1925). This means that the amount of income and capital that can be applied before the relevant person becomes entitled is somewhat limited. Section 31 provides, in brief, that the trustees may apply the income from the fund for the maintenance, education or benefit of the child and otherwise will accumulate it, and s 32 provides that up to one half of a person's presumptive share of capital may be applied for the advancement or benefit of that person before they become entitled.

The limitations of these powers were discussed by the Law Commission and also by the Law Reform Committee. The Law Commission thought them too strict, since it is often when a child is young that money is most needed for him.

The Law Reform Committee, on the other hand, considered the matter in its 23rd Report *The Powers and Duties of Trustees* (1982), and concluded that as the recipients of the money were persons only contingently entitled, the provisions were sufficient.

Obviously, had the Law Commission's recommendations as to the surviving spouse taking the whole estate been accepted and implemented, then where there was such a spouse, the statutory trusts would not arise. However, where the spouse had predeceased or the marriage had ended in divorce, or the relevant parties had never been married, the statutory trusts could still apply.

9.5   'Hotchpot' (death before 1996)

Children of the intestate – but not remoter descendants – entitled on an intestacy arising before 1996 have to set against their share of the intestate's estate the value (as at the date of the intestate's death) of certain benefits conferred on them by the intestate during his lifetime. The setting off of such benefits against an entitlement under the intestacy rules is what is meant by hotchpot.

9.5.1   Advancements

Giving an advancement is akin to setting someone up in business or assisting them in making their way in the world; marriage gifts probably seemed more easily to fit into the same category in 1925 than perhaps they do today. As well as applying to intestacies arising before 1996, the rules on what constitutes an advancement may be relevant in situations other than hotchpot.

In *Taylor v Taylor* (1875), it was held that the payment of the admission fee to an Inn of Court for an intending barrister and the purchase of a mining plant for a son's business were advancements, but the payment of a fee to a special pleader for an intending barrister to read in chambers, payments made to a curate to assist him in his living expenses and payment of an army officer's debts did not constitute advancements. In *Re Hayward* (1957), nominations amounting to £507 in favour of a son aged 43 were held not to be *prima facie* an advancement for the purposes of hotchpot on intestacy, though it was thought that had the son been 20 years younger the answer might have been different.

9.5.2   Hotchpot and contrary intention

Section 47(1)(iii) of the AEA 1925 also said that the hotchpot rule was excluded by 'any contrary intention ... expressed or appearing from circumstances of the case'. Therefore, an intestate's child who received a substantial sum from his parent during his life might well seek to establish that that parent still wanted him to have the same share of the estate as his other siblings. The onus of proving a contrary intention is on the person who asserts it, so if an intestate's child is saying that he should not have to bring an advancement into hotchpot, he has to show that the parent intended that that should not happen. In *Hardy v Shaw* (1976), Goff J said that the test of contrary intention was not objective; it was not what the intestate's intention would have been likely to be had she thought of everything. The court should look at all the circumstances of the case and decide whether, subjectively, they required an inference that her intention was that the gift should not be brought into hotchpot.

9.5.3   Accounting for advancements

The mathematical side of accounting for advancements is fairly simple, once it has been established what has to be brought into hotchpot in relation to an estate arising before 1996. The value of the advancements should be added to the distributable residue, so that if the five branches of issue were to share between them £47,000, but one of them had to account for an advancement worth £8,000, the sum to work with would be £55,000. That sum should then be divided by five, for each of the branches of issue, giving an entitlement of £11,000 per branch. The £8,000 is then deducted from the share of the child who has to account, so that he receives £3,000 and each of the four other branches receives £11,000, making a total of £47,000. Note however that where the advancement received exceeded the child's entitlement, he would not have to make any repayment into the estate, and the distributable residue should simply be divided amongst the others.

9.6 Other relatives

Where no spouse or issue survives the intestate, the order of entitlement set out in s 46 of the Administration of Estates Act 1925, based on a widening circle of relationships, is as follows:

(a) parents absolutely (if both then in equal shares);

(b) brothers and sisters of the whole blood on the statutory trusts;

(c) brothers and sisters of the half blood on the statutory trusts;

(d) grandparents absolutely (if more than one in equal shares);

(e) uncles and aunts of the whole blood on the statutory trusts;

(f) uncles and aunts of the half blood on the statutory trusts;

(g) *bona vacantia*.

Each category should be exhausted before the next applies, and persons in the same category are equally entitled. Thus, if there are no parents or brothers or sisters of the whole blood, but there are brother and sisters of the half blood and also grandparents, the grandparents will get nothing and the brothers and sisters of the half blood will split the money equally amongst themselves. Hotchpot never applied to these other relatives, and the relationships must be blood ones. Thus, the wife of a parent's brother is not an aunt for these purposes.

Note that the term *bona vacantia* refers only to goods – that is, personalty. Where there is no owner of land, by virtue of the doctrine of escheat, the property belongs to the Crown.

9.7 Failure of intestate benefits

An entitlement to an interest on intestacy may fail. Usually this will be because the beneficiary disclaims the benefit.

9.7.1 Disclaimer

A beneficiary entitled under the intestacy rules may disclaim his interest, just as anyone entitled under a will may do (see, also, the subject of disclaimer at 10.5). In *Re Scott* (1975), the deceased's brother and sister disclaimed their entitlements under both her will and the intestacy rules. The question then arose as to what would happen to their shares, namely whether they would go to the Crown as *bona vacantia* or would go to the persons entitled had the brother and sister predeceased rather than disclaiming. The court held that if a beneficiary disclaims his interest under both the deceased's will and the deceased's intestacy, the disclaimer will operate as though the brother and sister had predeceased the intestate, so the further next of kin would take the undisposed-of interest on the testatrix's partial intestacy.

If there is a life interest with a contingent gift in remainder, the remainder will be accelerated, save while the remainder remains contingent. Therefore, where a spouse disclaims her life interest, the issue do not still have to wait until she dies to obtain their shares, but they do have to wait until they attain the age of 18 and their entitlements are still contingent on their attaining that age.

9.8   Partial intestacy

Where the estate is partially intestate – that is, there is a valid will which fails to deal with the whole estate – the position is governed by s 49 of the AEA 1925. Section 55(1)(vi) of the AEA 1925 provides that 'intestate' includes a person who leaves a will but dies intestate as to some beneficial interest in his real or personal estate. The general principle is that the same rules as those on a total intestacy apply, subject to the provisions of the will. This means such provisions as are operative, and not those relating to a gift which has failed and of which the subject matter is now undisposed; in that situation the provisions the testator has made directing how the gift is to be treated will be redundant and will not operate (*Re Thornber* (1937)). The operation of the rules in this section causes considerable problems, and many people would agree with the judge who called it 'as bad a piece of draughtsmanship as one could conceive, in many respects' (Dankwerts J in *Re Morton* (1956), referring, however, to s 49(1)(a)).

It is important to distinguish between residue and undisposed of property. There may be a gift of residue which fails in part, for example, where a testator leaves a residuary gift to four people, one of whom predeceases him. Unless the wording of the will provides that his lapsed share should then be divided amongst the other three, or there is some other provision as to what should happen to it, it will be property undisposed of by the will, and s 49 will come into operation.

9.8.1   Hotchpot on a partial intestacy (death before 1996)

On a partial intestacy, the deceased's spouse and issue used to have to account for benefits under the will as against their entitlements under the intestacy rules. The provisions under which the spouse and issue of the deceased must account were contained in s 49(1)(aa) (spouses) and (a) (issue, specifically excluding other persons). This was repealed for deaths after 1995 by the Law Reform (Succession) Act 1995, but still applies where the partial intestacy arises before 1996, like the provision on total intestacy that children – but not remoter issue – had to bring into account benefits received by them from the deceased during his lifetime, under the rule in s 47(1)(iii) (see 9.5).

The spouse caught by the pre-1996 rules must account for testamentary benefits against the entitlement to the statutory legacy; this does not affect her entitlement to the personal chattels, so if there are personal chattels undisposed of by the will, the spouse will get them. The testamentary benefit should first be identified and valued. If it is a life interest, actuarial tables will have to be used to give a figure for the capital value of the future entitlement to income. The value of the testamentary benefit should then be subtracted from the value of the statutory legacy. This general principle arises from the case of *Re Bowen-Buscarlet's Will Trusts* (1971), which interpreted s 33(1) of the AEA 1925. That case contradicted, on the point of the time for payment of the statutory legacy, an earlier case, *Re McKee* (1931).

9.8.2   Payment of spouse's statutory legacy

Section 33(1) of the AEA 1925 provides that on the death of a person intestate as to any real or personal estate, such estate shall be held by his personal representatives on trust with the power to sell. This can create a particular problem in the situation of a partial intestacy where there may also be an express trust under the provisions of the will.

In *Re McKee* (1931), the deceased had made a will leaving his residuary estate on trust for sale for his wife for life and then for those of his brothers and sisters who survived her. None of his brothers or sisters survived her, so there was a partial intestacy. The court held that s 33(1) of the AEA 1925 did not apply to an asset of the deceased's estate if the deceased had effectively disposed of some beneficial interest, for example, a life interest, in the whole of that asset by his will. Nor could s 33(1) apply to an asset held upon an express trust for sale imposed by the deceased's will, because the express trust for sale excluded the statutory trust for sale imposed by s 33(1); there cannot be two subsisting trusts for sale at the same time. The effect was that the intestacy should be treated as arising on the death of the wife, and that her estate should receive the statutory legacy and interest on it.

The effect of this decision was to establish that a partial intestacy may arise some time after the death of the testator, on the death of a life tenant, and that the intestacy rules relating to the payment of the spouse's statutory legacy will be applied at that time. It also established that s 33(1) will apply to an asset if the deceased dies wholly intestate as to that asset, or as to a share in that asset, if the will imposes no trust for sale on that asset. Where, however, there is an express trust for sale, that will effectively displace the statutory trust for sale; they cannot exist together. Section 49(1) operates as if the legislature had inserted at the end of every deceased's will an ultimate gift of any undisposed-of property or interest in property in favour of the persons beneficially entitled on intestacy, and it applies irrespective of whether s 33(1) imposes a statutory trust for sale.

Re McKee may come into its own again. It predates the provision in s 49(i)(aa) of the Administration of Estates Act 1925 relating to hotchpot on a partial intestacy (see 9.8.1). That provision was inserted by the Intestates' Estates Act 1952 and removed again by the Law Reform (Succession) Act 1995.

The deceased in *Re Bowen-Buscarlet's Will Trusts* (1971) left a widow and a married daughter. His will directed his trustees to hold his residuary estate for his widow for her life, but unfortunately failed to say what should happen thereafter. A partial intestacy therefore arose, bringing into operation the statutory rules. Had there been no daughter, the widow would have been entitled to the whole estate, subject to her own life interest; she could have merged the two interests and claim the whole estate immediately. However, where there is issue in such a situation, what the widow can claim under the intestacy rules is the fixed net sum or statutory legacy and a life interest in half the residue. Here, that claim had to be fitted in with the widow's claims under the will. The question was how the residuary estate should be held, since the life interest under the intestacy rules failed because the widow could not enjoy it after her own death when her life interest under the will would end.

The Court of Appeal held that, under the will, the estate was held on trust for the widow during her life and thereafter under the intestacy rules. Under the intestacy rules, subject to the payment to the widow of the statutory legacy and interest thereon, the estate was held on trust for the daughter absolutely, because of her absolute entitlement under the statutory trusts for the deceased's issue. The widow was entitled to immediate payment of the statutory legacy with interest, because her interests under the two sets of terms merged (rejecting the Court of Appeal on that point in *Re McKee*).

It has been generally felt that the decision in *Re Bowen-Buscarlet* is the preferable one. *Re Bowen-Buscarlet* was followed in an Australian case, *Re Wade* (1980), but in that case the court went further. Reasoning that the intestacy was supposed to occur on the termination of the widow's life interest, it said that she did not have to account for the value of that life interest.

9.8.3 Issue – s 49(1)(a) of the AEA 1925 (hotchpot – death before 1996)

In relation to estates arising before 1996, s 49(1)(a) of the AEA 1925 says that the provisions of s 47 as to bringing property into account shall apply to beneficial interests acquired by issue under the will. It specifically excludes beneficial interests so acquired by other persons. Section 47(1)(iii) refers to *inter vivos* advancements being brought into account by an intestate's child. Clearly a contrast, if not confusion, arises, because of the different references to 'issue' and 'children'. In particular, there is the practical question of exactly what benefit has to be brought into account, in the situation, for example, where the testator gives a life interest to his daughter, with remainder to her issue.

The deceased in *Re Young* (1951) left his residuary estate to his wife for life and directed that thereafter it was to be divided into seven parts. A one-seventh part was to go to each of five of his six children, and another seventh on trust to apply the income or capital at the discretion of the trustees for the maintenance of his sixth child and his children during his life, and after his death on trust for those children absolutely. The deceased made no provision as to what would happen to the remaining seventh share after his widow's death, so the intestacy rules came into play. The first five children had to bring their one-seventh shares into account against their entitlement on intestacy; the question was how much the sixth child, whose interest in his one-seventh share was only a life interest, had to account for. The court held that the relevant value was the whole capital value, rejecting the argument that only the very limited interest of that child in that one-seventh share was liable to be brought into hotchpot. Harman J construed s 49(1)(a) as if it referred to accounting for benefits being done not by individual beneficiaries but by branches of the family; as though accounting, as well as entitlement, were based on a *per stirpes* rules. He said that 'issue' in s 49(1)(a) must mean children or remoter issue and 'any member of the family belonging to a certain branch must bring in everything that has been taken or acquired under the will by that branch'.

That decision, as well as the awkward wording of the section itself, has been heavily criticised. Dankwerts J in *Re Morton* (1956) commented that 'to value the interest as being equivalent to a gift of capital in a case where a person takes no more than a life interest seems to me contrary to fairness, common sense and everything else'. The decision in *Re Young* was followed in *Re Grover* (1970), where a child had to account for his testamentary life interest at its capital value, but the judgment of Harman J was criticised. Pennycuick J thought the section contained 'great difficulties of language' and that Harman J's statement was 'in extremely wide terms'. He suggested an alternative construction, under which the testator's descendants accounted for beneficial interests they themselves received under the will as against their own entitlements on intestacy, but not for interests received by other members of their branch of the family.

Note that, for deaths after 1995, this provision has been repealed by the Law Reform (Succession) Act 1995.

INTESTATE SUCCESSION

If a person dies without leaving a valid will they are said to be intestate. If someone leaves a valid will which does not deal with all their property, they are said to be partially intestate. In both cases, the law provides rules as to the administration and disposition of their estate, which are set out in the Administration of Estates Act 1925. The entitlements (s 46) are based on family relationships. A spouse must survive the intestate by 28 days in order to inherit. Directions by a testator in a valid will that the intestacy rules should not operate are ineffective. The only way to exclude them is to make valid alternative provisions.

The property is fixed with a statutory trust by s 33 of the Administration of Estates Act 1925, but there are directions to the personal representatives as to what property they should sell or keep after settling debts.

If the testator left a spouse, she will first have his personal chattels and the statutory legacy, which is now £125,000 where the deceased left issue and £200,000 where he did not. If there is no issue, she will also have half any remainder of the estate, but if there is issue that interest will be a life interest only, unless she chooses to capitalise it (when it will be worth considerably less than half). Only if there are no specified other relatives will she be entitled to the whole of the remainder of the estate. She is not entitled to the matrimonial home as such, but if she can afford to buy it from the estate then she may compel the estate to sell it to her (s 47A of the AEA 1925).

Issue means children or remoter direct descendants, who become entitled to their inheritance at eighteen. They will have the intestate's estate subject to the entitlement of any surviving spouse. If an intestate's own child dies before attaining his inheritance, that child's descendants share out his inheritance amongst themselves. If the children are minors, how their entitlements are managed until they attain their majority at 18 is governed by the usual statutory rules set out principally in the Trustee Act 1925.

Unmarried cohabitants are not included in the definition of spouse and step-children are not included in the definition of issue. However, 'issue' does include adopted and illegitimate children.

Those entitled when there is no spouse or issue are first of all parents and then siblings, followed by half-siblings. After this, grandparents are entitled and then uncles and aunts, followed by half-uncles and half-aunts. If there are none of these, the deceased's property will go to the State.

The complex 'hotchpot' provisions no longer apply, save where an estate arising before 1996 is concerned.

CHAPTER 10

THE CLASSIFICATION AND FAILURE OF GIFTS

10.1 Classification of gifts

Gifts may be specific, general, demonstrative or residuary. It is the classification of legacies which gives rise to the most frequent difficulties and the most important consequences. How a legacy is treated in various circumstances depends on what category it falls into, so it is necessary to be able to distinguish them.

10.1.1 Specific legacies

A specific legacy is the gift of a particular piece of the testator's personal property. The will is construed to ascertain whether the testator intended the piece of property to pass to the beneficiary *in specie*, that is, whether he intended the particular item itself to pass. If a court has to construe whether or not a particular gift is a specific gift, it will usually lean against finding that it is and will prefer to find that it is general, because specific legacies are liable to fail by ademption, although they hold a more privileged position than general legacies where the estate is insufficient to meet all the gifts in the will (see ademption and abatement, below).

A specific legacy may be indicated by the use of the word 'my' when the gift is being described, though if the testator describes the gift as a general gift, it will not be found to be specific (*Re Compton* (1914)). In *Bothamley v Sherson* (1875), the testator made a gift of 'all my shares or stock in the Midland Railway Company'. This was held to be a specific legacy, the court defining a specific legacy as 'what has been sometimes called a severed or distinguished part' of the testator's estate. Two gifts of shares in a private family company were held to be specific bequests without the use of the possessive pronoun in *Re Rose* (1949).

In the early case of *Innes v Johnson* (1799), the testator left his sister the interest on a £300 bond for her life and thereafter left her daughter the interest due on the bond and the capital. The testator left various bonds, but it was held that this was a specific gift of the one of that value. In *Re Wedmore* (1907), the testator in his will forgave his children all their unsecured debts to him. Two of his sons owed him such debts. It was held that the forgiveness of them was a specific legacy.

10.1.2 General legacies

A general legacy does not refer to any particular piece of the testator's estate. Gifts of stocks and shares are usually general gifts, although they may be made specific if the testator describes them as 'my' shares in the particular company. In *Re Willcocks* (1921), the testatrix made a gift of £948 3s 11d Queensland 32% stock. She died owning exactly that sum of that kind of stock, but the court held that the gift was nevertheless a general legacy (compare *Re Rose* (above)).

A gift of a piece of property which the testator does not own, if it is a general gift, will be fulfilled by the personal representatives purchasing the property for the beneficiary from the funds in the estate. For example, if Nick's aunt had been a keen sailor but died without owning any yacht at the date of her death, the effect of a gift to him of 'my yacht' would be completely different from that of a gift of 'a yacht'. In the former case, the gift would be a specific gift, and where it is no longer in the testatrix's estate it would fail by ademption, because she left Nick a particular item which is not available. However, in the latter case, she will have left him a yacht – no particular yacht – and the personal representatives will buy him one, provided his aunt left enough money to cover the purchase.

10.1.3 Demonstrative legacies

Demonstrative legacies are legacies which the testator directs to be satisfied out of a specified fund or pool of property. The classic example of the demonstrative legacy is a sum of money to be paid out of a particular bank account.

Demonstrative legacies operate as specific legacies unless they fail because the specific property is not available. Insofar as the specific property to answer the gift is lacking, they operate like general legacies. In *Re O'Connor* (1970), the testator had directed that a gift be satisfied only out of specified property. The court held that this could not be a demonstrative legacy, because it was an essential characteristic of a demonstrative legacy that it operated as a general legacy if the fund was insufficient. In *Re Webster* (1937), the testator gave a legacy of a sum to be paid out of his share in the family business. This was held to be a demonstrative legacy. Therefore when it was found that the deceased's share in the business was worth less than the gift, there was no failure for that reason. The beneficiary was entitled to have the sum paid out of the testator's general estate instead.

In *Walford v Walford* (1912), the testator gave to his sister 'the sum of £1,000 to be paid out of the estate and effects inherited by me from my mother'. This included a gift in remainder subject to the life interest of his father, who died seven years later. The House of Lords held that the legacy was demonstrative and it was irrelevant that it was to be paid from a sum to be received later.

10.1.4 Pecuniary legacies

The phrase 'pecuniary legacy' can cause difficulties, because it refers to different things depending on the context in which it is used. It is primarily a gift of money, which may be specific, general or demonstrative. A pecuniary gift of the money in the testator's piggy bank may be construed as a specific gift, and will then fail if there is nothing there. A general pecuniary gift is a sum of money; a demonstrative one is directed to be paid from a particular fund. It was said in *Re O'Connor* (1948) that the term 'pecuniary legacy' is insufficient; it must be ascertained whether the particular gift is specific, demonstrative or general.

However, where the mechanics of the administration of the estate are concerned, the expression is defined at s 55(1)(ix) of the AEA 1925 to include a general legacy, an annuity, any tax payable on a gift which the testator has directed to be paid free of tax and any part of a demonstrative legacy that cannot be discharged out of specified property.

10.1.5 Annuities

An annuity is a form of pecuniary legacy; it was described by the court in *Re Earl of Berkeley* (1968) as 'a series of legacies payable at intervals'. It may be specific (in which case it is liable to fail by ademption), general or demonstrative, depending on the construction of the will. An annuity is payable from the date of the testator's death unless he states otherwise. The personal representatives will usually appropriate (see 13.10) certain assets to make reasonably certain of the payment of the annuity, or may purchase an annuity from the estate. If the testator has directed for the purchase of an annuity, the annuitant may take the purchase price instead.

10.1.6 Devises

A devise is the gift by will of real property. Devises are usually specific – 'my freehold house at 24 Acacia Avenue', for example. It used to be the case that only a specific devise would function, because wills were not ambulatory as to real property and could not operate to pass realty acquired by the testator after the date of the will. Now, however, devises may be general, as with a gift of 'all my freehold property', for instance, and may also be residuary – 'my house at 24 Acacia Avenue to Anne and all the rest of my land to Belinda'.

10.1.7 Residuary gifts

Every properly-drafted will should have a provision for the application of residue, preferably one which foresees all reasonably possible events of failure such as divorce or predecease. The residuary gift includes whatever remains after all the debts and liabilities have been cleared and the legacies and devises paid out. Residuary gifts may be divided, for example, as to realty and personalty, or shared out between beneficiaries. If there is no residuary gift, or such residuary gift as there is fails, there will be property undisposed of by the will and the rules of partial intestacy will apply.

Sometimes, it may be unclear whether a gift is residuary or specific. This may need to be ascertained so that the personal representatives know what the proper distribution of the estate will be. The testator in *Re Green* (1880) left a leasehold pub with directions for it to be sold. He gave a legacy to a beneficiary of the rents and profits until sale and of the proceeds of sale, and left the residue and other residuary real and personal estate to his two daughters. The court held that all the gifts to the daughters were residuary. In *Re Wilson* (1966), the testatrix gave pecuniary legacies and then left 'all my real estate and the residue of my personal estate' to her daughter. The personal estate was insufficient to pay the pecuniary legacies, so the question was whether the gift of 'all my real estate' was residuary or specific. (If the latter, it would take precedence over the pecuniary legacies.) The court held that the gift was residuary.

10.2 Different effects

It may be necessary to be able to distinguish what class of legacy is being dealt with because, as shown in *Re Wilson* above, different rules apply to the different categories.

10.2.1 Ademption

If the property mentioned in a specific legacy or a specific devise is not part of the testator's estate at his death, the gift is adeemed. This means that the legatee or devisee will receive neither the property itself nor anything representing it, for example, the proceeds of sale of a house left to him in the testator's will but in fact sold before the testator's death. General and demonstrative legacies do not fail by ademption.

For further details, see below on failure of gifts.

10.2.2 Abatement

This relates to the payment of the liabilities of the estate. Part II of the First Schedule to the Administration of Estates Act 1925 regulates where the burden of the liabilities will fall. Specific gifts rank behind general gifts in the statutory order of application of property to the discharge of liabilities and gifts in the same class abate at the same rate. A testator may vary the statutory order by his will.

For further details, see below on failure of gifts and 13.13–13.15 on the incidence of debts and legacies.

10.2.3 Income and interest

Specific legacies and devises carry with them their own income or profits accruing from the testator's death, whereas general or demonstrative legacies carry interest at a fixed rate and only from the date at which they become payable (generally from the end of the 'executor's year', as was the case with the interest on the demonstrative legacy in *Walford v Walford* (1912) (above)). The details of the rules as to payment of interest and the exceptions to the rules are numerous and complex.

10.2.4 Expenses

There are also different rules about where the expenses of the different parts of the estate fall. Expenses incurred by the personal representatives in preserving specific gifts must be reimbursed by the relevant beneficiary. The court in *Re Rooke* (1933) said it could not see on what principle a beneficiary should get the income and profits from a specific gift if he were not liable for the expenses. Expenses incurred in preserving the subject matter of general or demonstrative legacies are payable out of the estate as part of the costs of administration.

10.3 Failure of gifts

Even if a will is valid, individual gifts made in it may fail.

There are several reasons why a gift made in a will may fail:

- the beneficiary disclaims;
- the beneficiary predeceases the testator (lapse);
- a specific gift is adeemed;
- the beneficiary or his spouse witnesses the will (s 15 of the Wills Act 1837);
- a gift to the testator's spouse fails following divorce or annulment of the marriage (s 18A of the Wills Act 1837);
- by reason of public policy or because it promotes an illegal purpose;
- the gift is contrary to the principle of inalienability;
- abatement or insolvency;
- uncertainty;
- the gift is contingent on a condition which is not satisfied;
- the gift was made as a result of fraud on the testator.

Some of these reasons for failure may also apply on intestacy, for example, disclaimer, forfeiture or lapse.

10.4 Effect of failure

The subject matter of a gift which fails in any well-drawn will either falls into residue and forms part of the gift to the testator's residuary beneficiary or passes to the person the testator has specified as the substitutional beneficiary. If there is no residuary beneficiary and no substitutional gift or other arrangement (see below), the property will pass on intestacy. The property will also pass on intestacy if there is a residuary beneficiary but the testator has shown an intention that the subject matter of the gift should be excluded from his residuary bequest in any event. If the gift which fails was a life interest, then the interest in remainder will be accelerated.

10.5 Disclaimer

Generally speaking, any beneficiary may disclaim a gift by will or an entitlement on intestacy. This includes a beneficiary who is a company or an unincorporated association. Abbot CJ in *Townson v Tickell* (1819) said, 'The law certainly is not so absurd as to force a man to take an estate against his will'. The position with gifts under a will has been clear for a very long time. The beneficiaries under the deceased's intestacy may also disclaim. In *Re Scott* (1975), the two siblings of the deceased took under the intestacy rules on the deceased's partial intestacy. They both disclaimed, the court being asked to decide whether, as a result, the property disclaimed would pass to the Crown as *bona vacantia* or to the persons who would have been next of kin but for the two siblings; it held that it would pass to the next of kin.

10.5.1 The act of disclaiming

Disclaimers are often made by deed, especially where the beneficiary is disclaiming as part of a deed of arrangement, but that need not be the case. Disclaimer can be effected by simple writing or even by conduct. It may be done at any time provided the beneficiary has not accepted the gift or derived any benefit from it; the disclaimer may then be retracted if no-one has placed any reliance on it, whether other beneficiaries or the personal representatives. Once the disclaimer has been made it will be read back to the date of death.

10.5.2 Reasons for disclaiming

There are various reasons for disclaiming:

(a) gift brings with it obligations the beneficiary does not want to fulfil;

(b) personal unwillingness to accept testator's gift;

(c) tax.

Of these, the last, at least, is certainly not uncommon. However, disclaimer and variation of benefits by will may be motivated by generosity or a feeling that the testator has been unfair.

In *Crowden v Aldridge* (1993), it was held that a document signed by the 16 beneficiaries of an estate confirming their agreement to the variation of the estate was enforceable even where the form of agreement had not been executed as a deed and some of the beneficiaries changed their minds after signing. The deceased had left his housekeeper £100, and it was agreed amongst the family that this was insufficient and that she should have £5,000 and the bungalow in which she lived. The last four beneficiaries to sign the memorandum of agreement then suggested that the housekeeper should take only a life interest in the bungalow and declined to proceed on the original basis. The court held, however, that the original signed agreement was enforceable.

10.5.3 Tax savings

A beneficiary may disclaim because the result of his disclaimer is a minimising of liability to tax, usually Inheritance Tax but sometimes also Capital Gains Tax. This is usually seen in the form of all the beneficiaries effectively rearranging the provisions of the testator's will or intestacy between them; this can be done whenever the relevant beneficiaries are all of full age and all consent to the rearrangement. The Inland Revenue will accept a deed of variation made within two years of death as effective for tax purposes, provided notice is given to it within six months of the deed (though if there is a prior disclaimer, rather than a variation, notice is not required). It will read the provisions back to the date of death by virtue of s 142 of the Inheritance Tax Act 1984 and the Taxation of Chargeable Gains Act 1992. Deeds of variation may also be used in the same way on intestacy, so as to vary the statutory provisions to result in a tax saving. This is the process sometimes known as 'post-death tax planning' (see 14.20).

10.5.4 Personal feelings

The beneficiary may disclaim for any reason. Thus, if he would feel embarrassed to take any sort of gift from the testator for personal reasons, he may disclaim. He need not give reasons.

10.5.5 Gift carries obligations which the beneficiary does not wish to fulfil

Some gifts come bearing obligations, either because of their nature – the freehold of a house subject to a long lease containing onerous landlord's covenants, perhaps – or because the testator has stated in his will that the gift can be taken only if the beneficiary fulfils certain conditions.

10.5.6 Partial disclaimer not possible

The person who finds the obligations which come with a gift cannot avoid them and still take the benefit by attributing the obligations to one part of the gift and taking the rest.

10.5.7 Disclaimer of one of two or more separable gifts

A beneficiary may disclaim one gift and accept another provided the two are truly separable; otherwise, the doctrine of election may apply (see 11.13). In *Guthrie v Walrond* (1882), a gift of 'all my estate and effects in the Island of Mauritius' was held to be an indivisible gift, so that it could be disclaimed as a whole or not at all.

Re Scott (1975) (above) showed how a disclaimer may lead to a partial intestacy even where the will appears to provide for all eventualities, if there is no specific provision for a gift over of property otherwise undisposed-of. The testatrix left a gift of income to her brother and sister, to pass on the death of the second of them to those of her brother's children who attained 21 or, being female, married under that age. Thereafter, the fund went to two charities absolutely. The brother and sister disclaimed. The question was whether the income was accelerated, so that pending the birth of a child of the brother it went to the charities, or whether it should be accumulated for 21 years, or until the deaths of the brother and sister, and added to capital, or whether it should devolve on partial intestacy, or what should happen to it. The court held that it should devolve on partial intestacy, the gift to charity being contingent and therefore not liable to be accelerated, and the testatrix having evinced an intention against accumulation by disposing of life interests.

10.6 Lapse

The doctrine of lapse holds that a gift fails if the beneficiary predeceases the testator. This is because the will is of no effect until the testator dies. The same applies to gifts to a limited company or other corporate body which has been dissolved and also to gifts made by way of nomination rather than by will (see 2.3.1). The doctrine of lapse cannot be excluded by a provision in the will (*Re*

Ladd (1932)), although a testator may make a substitutional gift to the beneficiary's personal representatives or to his children which is to take effect should the beneficiary predecease. There are also certain exceptions to the doctrine.

10.6.1 Joint tenants and tenants in common

The doctrine of lapse does not apply where there is a gift to joint tenants (*not* to tenants in common) or a class gift, since the subject matter of the gift will go to the other joint tenant(s) or the remaining members of the class. This is the reason for the phrase often seen in wills which leaves a certain gift 'to such of my children as survive me and if more than one in equal shares'. The phrase 'to such of my children as survive me' ensures that the effect of a child predeceasing will still be to pass his share into the pool to be divide amongst the others, but the use of the words 'in equal shares' ensures that the beneficiaries receive the gifts, as amongst themselves, as tenants in common.

10.6.2 Gifts to issue

The doctrine of lapse is altered by s 33 of the Wills Act 1837 as amended by s 19 of the Administration of Justice Act 1982. It was also held in *Re Meredith* (1924) that the statutory provisions do not operate if there is a contrary intention appearing in the will.

10.6.3 Section 33 of the Wills Act 1837

Section 33 of the 1837 Act states that a gift made by a testator's will to any of his issue, provided that the testator was survived by some issue and that the gift was one not determinable at or before the named beneficiary's death, would be effective as though the beneficiary had died immediately after the testator. This provision now includes deceased issue who are members of a class, so that where the gift is to the testator's children, the issue of a child who has predeceased may take his share.

10.6.4 Benefit *per stirpes*

The shares under s 33 are taken stirpitally, so that the benefit is divided not according to the absolute number of persons who will take a benefit, but according to the number of branches of the family. Thus, where there are two surviving children, and two have predeceased, one leaving two grandchildren of the testator and one leaving no grandchild but three great-grandchildren, there will be four branches of the family, one for each child of the original testator. Each of his two children will take a quarter share. The two grandchildren will share their deceased parent's quarter share, taking one-eighth each, and the three great-grandchildren will take one-twelfth each, making up the last quarter-share.

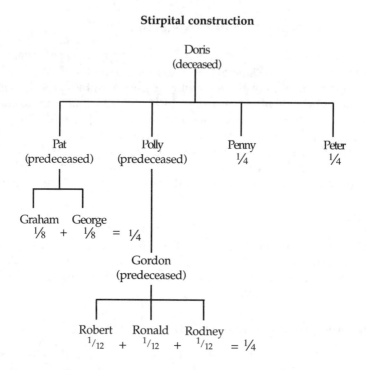

Stirpital construction

Doris
(deceased)

| Pat | Polly | Penny | Peter |
| (predeceased) | (predeceased) | ¼ | ¼ |

Graham   George
⅛   +   ⅛   =   ¼

Gordon
(predeceased)

Robert   Ronald   Rodney
$^1/_{12}$ + $^1/_{12}$ + $^1/_{12}$ =   ¼

10.6.5 *Commorientes*

The presumption, introduced by s 184 of the Law of Property Act 1925, is that where two persons have died in circumstances in which it cannot be told which died first, the older died before the younger. Note that the persons do not have to die together – one may be lost at sea on a completely unspecifiable date whilst the other dies in hospital on land. Like all presumptions, it may be rebutted by evidence. Thus, if someone could be found who had seen the deceased sailor still alive at a time when his younger land-based colleague was known to be already dead, then the presumption would not operate. In that situation, survivorship may be found on evidence on the balance of probabilities (*Lamb v Lord Advocate* (1976)).

The question of when the presumption was applicable was discussed in detail in *Hickman v Peacey* (1945) by the House of Lords. In that case, five bodies were discovered in the remains of a house bombed during the Second

World War. The deceased had left various gifts to each other; there was some suggestion that they had not all died together as their bodies were found in different places. However, the court cited Lord Cranworth LC in *Underwood v Wing* (1855), 'It cannot be assumed to be proved, or probable, or possible, that two human beings should cease to breathe at the same moment of time ...' and Lord Macmillan said that the question to be answered was a practical one – 'Can you say for certain which of these two deceased persons died first?'. If not, the presumption applied.

10.6.6 Purpose of *commorientes* rule

The presumption in s 184 is designed to avoid the frustration of the testator's intentions by passing his property to someone who cannot enjoy it. However, the presumption itself may frustrate those intentions, in that it may operate in some cases to pass all the property of the elder to the younger, if that person is the sole beneficiary under the elder's will, though where they have died together, the younger will not have time to enjoy the property, which will immediately pass to her own beneficiaries under her will or intestacy.

10.6.7 Exception to the *commorientes* rule for spouses where the elder is intestate

The presumption in s 184 of the Law of Property Act (LPA) 1925 is excluded by s 46(3) of the Administration of Estates Act 1925 if the two persons being considered are spouses and the older of them dies intestate. The reason for a different provision for intestate spouses was that they are likely to die together and, before the application of a survivorship period of 28 days in cases of spouses' intestacy under the Law Reform (Succession) Act 1995, the result would be merely to pass all the property of both spouses to the family of only one of them.

The exception for spouses does not apply in cases where the older spouse is not intestate, even where the will contains no survivorship clause. In *Re Rowland* (1962), a married couple were lost at sea. The husband left a will without a survivorship clause, in favour of his wife. The existence of the will excluded the exception under s 46(3) of the AEA 1925 to the usual *commorientes* rule under s 184 of the LPA 1925. Therefore, that rule operated and, as he was older than his wife, he was presumed to have predeceased her, and his property passed to her and then, she being dead too, to those entitled to her estate.

Lapse on intestacy and *commorientes*

Was the beneficiary
the intestate's spouse?

Yes   No

Did the beneficiary
survive the intestate
by 28 days?

Did the beneficiary survive
the intestate (on the balance
of probabilities)

No   Yes   Yes   Can't tell   No

Beneficiary's
entitlement to
intestate's
estate goes to
beneficiary's
estate

Was the beneficiary
younger than the
intestate?

Yes

No

Beneficiary's entitlement
to intestate's estate has
failed by lapse

10.6.8 *Commorientes* rule operates without court discretion

Although the statutory presumption, and its exception for spouses, is designed to make the operation of the rules easier to deal with, its own existence and method of application does not bring with it any discretion for the court to decide when or whether to apply it. It was held in *Re Lindop* (1942) that although the statutory presumption under s 184 of the LPA 1925 may be rebutted by evidence, there is no discretion given to the court to disregard it on the ground that it would be unfair or unjust to act upon it.

10.6.9 Survivorship clauses

It is usual to see a 'survivorship clause' in a will, which passes the property only if the beneficiary survives the testator by a certain period, usually about one month. Since 1995, there has been a statutory survivorship period of 28 days in cases of intestacy with respect of spouses. This provides a way of dealing with the practical question of how to avoid passing an estate to someone who dies in such rapid succession that they have no chance of enjoying the property, and passing it to them means, effectively, passing it to whoever benefits under their will or intestacy. It also avoids the problem that arises where there is evidence that one person was still alive at the scene of a disaster, even if they died of their injuries shortly thereafter. Section 184 is not brought into operation where it is certain who died first.

A period of up to six months will allow for the tax advantages of avoiding two incidences of Inheritance Tax, which potentially comes into operation whenever a gift is made, but such a long period would risk delaying the administration of an estate. Whilst the appropriate length of a survivorship period ought to be considered in each case, in practice, a period of 28 days or one month is standard.

10.7 Ademption

Specific gifts may fail by ademption, though general and demonstrative legacies do not. In the early case of *Ashburner v Macguire* (1786), the testator's gift of 'my £1,000 East India Stock' was held to be a specific gift and therefore to have been adeemed because the testator had sold that stock during his lifetime. In *Gordon v Duff* (1861) the testator left 'the sum of £2,000 Long Annuities standing in my name in the books of the Bank of England'. At his death, he had only £300 worth. The testator's gift was held to be specific and, despite his leaving a great deal of other property, most of it was adeemed.

As courts lean towards finding gifts valid, they also lean in cases of doubt towards construing a gift as general rather than specific. In *Re Gage* (1934), the testator gave to his niece by will 'the sum of £1,150 War Loan 1929–47 stock and to MG the sum of £500 New South Wales Five per cent stock now standing in my name.' The court construed the gifts separately and held that the niece could take cash in the place of the gift of the War Loan.

If there is something in the wording of the will which shows the testator had a particular asset of his in mind at the time of making the will, and that wording cannot be construed as referring generally to articles of that type, the gift will, however, be a specific gift and liable to fail by ademption. The testator in *Oliver v Oliver* (1871) recited his entitlement to receive £5,602 Consols from his sister's estate and left part of that gift to his son. However, he received the Consols during his lifetime and sold them. The gift to the son was held to have failed by ademption.

A specific gift which speaks from the death of the testator (s 24 of the Wills Act 1837 provides that a will speaks from the date of death in respect of the estate comprised in it; see 11.20) will fail only if the gift does not form part of the testator's property at the date of his death.

Note that, for the purposes of ascertaining whether a specific gift has failed by ademption, there is something rather like a commorientes rules for the testator and his property. Where the two perish in the same disaster, the rule stated in *Durrant v Friend* (1852) holds that, in the absence of any evidence to the contrary, the property is assumed to have been destroyed before the testator died. This means that a gift of a car written off in a fatal road accident will be adeemed, rather than the beneficiary obtaining the proceeds of any insurance policy on it, as would have happened had it been destroyed after the testator's death.

10.7.1 Does the subject matter of the specific gift still exist?

It was held in *Re Slater* (1907), where the court was considering a gift of shares in a water company which had been taken over by a local water authority, that a specific gift will fail if the testator, at the time of his death, had no assets of the description given in his will. The court asked itself: '... where is the thing which is given? ... it is no use trying to trace it unless ... you find something which has been changed in name or form only, but which is substantially the same thing.' A specific gift will be adeemed where there has been a change in its subject matter, that is, the thing itself, but where there has merely been a change in name or form, there will be no ademption.

Re Slater was applied in *Re Kuypers* (1925), where 15% shares had been reduced to 8% shares and new shares issued in compensation. The tenant for life was held to have no right to the income from the new shares. The court said that the name of the old shares had been changed and they had lost some of their attractiveness, but they remained the same shares. Consequently, the tenant for life took them as they were.

Re Slater was also applied in the recent case of *Re Dorman* (1994). Edward Dorman died in 1985 leaving his widow the income from a trust, which she used for living expenses, paying the rest into a deposit account. The widow made a will giving the balance of her deposit account back to the trust. She also gave an Enduring Power of Attorney (see 6.3); her attorney, unaware of the terms of the will, transferred the money to a higher-paying account with the same bank. The court held that the gift was not adeemed, because the reference was essentially to the fund of money, the details of the account being for identification only. The change was not one of substance, as in *Re Kuypers*. The court also distinguished the Scottish case of *Re Ballantyne* (1941), where, on similar facts, the gift was adeemed, because in that case there had been a change of bank.

10.7.2 Changes in name or form do not lead to ademption

The change in name or form of the subject matter of the gift will not cause it to be adeemed, however, provided that it remains substantially the same property.

The testator in *Re Clifford* (1912) gave a specific gift of twenty-three of his shares in a certain company. After the will was made – but before the testator's death – the company changed its name and sub-divided each share into four new shares of one-quarter the value each. The court held that the gift would not be adeemed, because the new shares were 'identical in all but name and form' to the old shares; the legatee therefore took 92 of the new shares in place of the original 23 old ones. The difference between this situation and that in *Re Kuypers* (above) is that, in the later case, the shares had been changed and not simply subdivided.

In *Re Leeming* (1912), the testator's gift was a specific legacy of 'my ten shares' in a named limited company. Between the making of the will and the death of the testator, the company was voluntarily liquidated. After reforms, a new company was created under the same name as the old one. The court looked at what the practical effects of these changes were, rather than at the dissolution of the company in which the testator had had his shares, and held that the specific legacy had not been adeemed. The beneficiary took the shares in the new company.

10.7.3 Ademption by operation of law

A gift will still be adeemed even if the subject matter has vanished from the testator's estate by operation of law, as happened under nationalisation. The question may then arise as to whether the original gift is replaced by whatever compensation the law offers for the property, or whether the gift is simply adeemed.

In *Re Galway* (1950), the testator made a gift of land. After the making of the will but before his death, the Coal Act 1938 was passed, nationalising the property rights in the coal so that they could not pass under the will, but providing for the payment of compensation. The question before the court was whether the beneficiary could take the compensation in place of the coal, or whether the compensation was separate personalty which would, in this case, fall into residue. It was held that in these circumstances, if there was no contrary intention in the will sufficient to pass the compensation on nationalisation instead of the property which had been nationalised, the specific gift of the nationalised property would fail by ademption. The compensation therefore went to the residuary legatee.

10.7.4 Ademption, the doctrine of conversion and the Trusts of Land and Appointment of Trustees Act 1996

Similar questions may be posed in respect of equitable interests in land. It is not unknown for testators to leave their realty to one person and their personalty to another. Before 1926, there was no difficulty because a half share in a parcel of land was realty in law, no doubt echoing what the lay testator would expect from applying his own common sense. However, the changes made by the sweeping property legislation of 1925 had what may have been unexpected consequences in succession terms. In accordance with the blurring of the boundaries between real and personal property and, especially, the overall aim to make land more readily commerciable, s 35 of the Law of Property Act 1925 provided that a trust for sale would arise automatically, by operation of law, in all cases of joint ownership of land. To this principle was applied the equitable doctrine of conversion, holding, on the basis that equity regards as done that which ought to be done, that land subject to a trust for sale was considered in equity to have been already converted into money. The beneficial interests were therefore not in the land, but in the proceeds (or potential proceeds) of sale. They were, therefore, not beneficial interests in realty.

The courts were therefore often asked to say how a pre-1926 will which was worded in terms of realty should be applied to the estate when the testator died after 1925 and the share of realty had been converted by operation of s 35 of the Law of Property Act 1925. Such gifts failed unless saved by, for example, republication (*Re Harvey* (1947)).

The courts were, however, generally uncomfortable with the operation of the doctrine of conversion in family, as opposed to commercial, situations. The idea that a married couple who jointly owned their matrimonial home should have an interest not in the house itself but only in the proceeds of its sale was described by Lord Wilberforce in *Williams and Glyn's Bank v Boland* (1980) as 'just a little unreal'. After some years of being ignored by a variety of courts, presumably on the basis of common sense, the operation of the doctrine was laid to rest by s 3 of the Trusts of Land and Appointment of Trustees Act 1996 in relation to trusts for sale. Again, as they were before 1926, equitable interests in land are formally recognised as realty as from the beginning of 1997.

10.7.5 Specific gifts subject to a binding contract of sale

The position with property which is the subject of a specific gift and which the testator has contracted to sell (but of which he has not completed the sale) is rather complex. If the will is made first and then the contract entered into, the beneficiary may enjoy the property until the contract is completed, whereupon it is adeemed.

However, if the contract predates the will, the doctrine of conversion operates on the gift in the will itself, so that the beneficiary will receive the proceeds of sale.

In neither case can the beneficiary retain the property itself.

10.7.6 Options

The position with property over which the testator has granted an option to purchase to a third party is governed by the anomalous rule in *Lawes v Bennett* (1795). This deems the conversion to occur at the date of the option. Nevertheless, on the exercise of the option, the gift is adeemed.

In *Re Sweeting* (1975), the testator died leaving properties subject to contracts of sale, which were held to be enforceable despite being conditional, since the widow had consented to the sales. The conditional contracts were treated as options under the rule in *Lawes v Bennett*, and therefore the gifts of the properties were adeemed on completion of the contracts.

10.7.7 Practical ways of dealing with the risk of ademption

There is nothing to be done to reverse the effects of nationalisation on the will of any individual testator, and any testator who has not altered his will in respect of property which has been nationalised since the date of the will needs to make a new will to deal with the altered state of his property. Problems with the doctrine of conversion operating on real property should not arise when a will has been properly drawn. A testator may ensure that his intention to make a gift will not be totally frustrated by the ademption of a specific gift, however, by making a substitutional gift, a course approved in *Mullins v Smith* (1860). Thus, the testator may, for example, leave his Steinway grand or such other piano as he has at the date of his death or if he has no piano then some other, general gift.

10.8 Witnessing of the will by beneficiary or beneficiary's spouse

By s 15 of the Wills Act 1837, any gift to an attesting witness or his spouse is 'utterly null and void'. (See in this respect also 5.17.) Where, however, the attesting witness and the beneficiary marry after the date of attestation, the beneficiary will not lose the benefit by reason of the later marriage (*Thorpe v Beswick* (1881)).

10.8.1 Signature as other than attesting witness

Section 15 of the 1837 Act does not apply when that person signs the will otherwise than as an attesting witness. This occurred in *Kitcat v King* (1930), where a supernumerary witness signed to indicate approval of the contents of the will. Nor, since the Wills Act 1968, will it apply if there are still sufficient attesting witnesses if that person's signature is discounted (see, further, 5.17 and the case of *Re Bravda* (1968)).

10.8.2 How a gift to an attesting witness may be saved

Gifts to the attesting witness on trust for someone else do not fail, nor do gifts to someone else on secret trust for the attesting witness. A gift made or confirmed by another will or codicil, if that is properly witnessed, may thus be validated.

This area of the law is still not as clear as it might be. The courts have found some latitude for interpretation in the wording of the statute.

10.8.3 Charging clauses

It is fairly common for a person to instruct his solicitor to prepare a will in which that solicitor or his firm is appointed executor (see, also, 12.12.2 below). Most lay executors would in any case pass their paperwork to a solicitor to deal with it; appointing the solicitor as executor enables the testator to choose who deals with his estate. The fees of a solicitor appointed by the executors, or by any other administrators of the estate, are administration expenses of the estate, but where the solicitor is appointed by the will as executor, he may not make what are effectively those same charges unless there is a direct provision in the will for him to do so.

An executor or trustee may not be paid for his services in dealing with the estate unless there is a specific provision to that effect in the will. This rule was confirmed in *Re Orwell* (1982), the case which concerned the estate of the writer George Orwell. In that case, however, the court declined to construe the charging clause for the trustees so as to exclude payment to the firm of literary agents of one of the executors.

It is therefore standard practice to include a 'charging clause' authorising such payment whenever solicitors are appointed as executors or trustees. It allows them to charge the estate for their professional services in executing the will and administering the estate. (For an example of such a clause, see 3.7.) The Law Commission has suggested that there should be an implied statutory charging clause, subject to contrary intention, for anyone who does not obtain any benefit or remuneration under the will (Consultation Paper No 146 *Trustees' Powers and Duties* (1997)).

10.8.4 Attesting solicitors and charging clauses

The benefit of a charging clause is, however, a benefit under the will, so if the solicitor named as executor also witnesses the will, he will be prevented from charging under the charging clause. In *Re Pooley* (1888), the will was attested by a solicitor who was appointed executor under it. The will contained a charging clause. The court held that the payment the solicitor might obtain under the provisions of the charging clause was a benefit under the will, and because he had witnessed the will he could not therefore claim for his services.

Where an attesting witness derives a benefit under a later appointment, that may also be treated as analogous more with the situation of the solicitor who is appointed by the administrators of the estate than with that of the solicitor appointed in the will by name as executor. He may then be able to keep the benefit of a relevant charging clause. In *Re Royce* (1957), one of the attesting witnesses to the will was a solicitor. After the testator's death, he was appointed trustee of the will. The court held that he could rely on the charging clause in the will even though he had been an attesting witness.

10.8.5 Benefits to attesting witness confirmed by codicil attested by others

The case of *Re Trotter* (1899) also concerned a solicitor who witnessed a will appointing him executor and containing a charging clause. He later also attested a second codicil to the will. Nevertheless, the court held that he could take the benefit of the charging clause in the will under the first codicil which confirmed the will and which he had not attested himself.

10.8.6 Gift to beneficiary as trustee

Re Ray (1936) is authority for the assertion that a beneficiary who takes as trustee, as opposed to being beneficially entitled to the gift, will not be deprived of the gift because he was also an attesting witness. In applying the decision in this case more widely, however, care must be taken with the precise facts. The testatrix was a nun and left her property by will to whomever should be the abbess of her convent at the date of her death, upon trust for the convent. The will was witnessed by two other nuns. When the testatrix died, one of the attesting nuns was the abbess of the convent. The court's decision rested not only the grounds that the attesting nun was not beneficially entitled to the gift but also on the grounds that a gift made to a person described by a formula referring to their station at the date of the testatrix death should not fail because that station was then filled by someone who had witnessed the will, if the testatrix could not have known at the time of making the will who would fill that station at the date of her death.

It is submitted that the second limb of this decision would not be sufficient alone where the witness was beneficially entitled and the sole point on which the case turned was the use of the formula to identify the beneficiary.

10.9 Dissolution or annulment of marriage

In historical terms, widespread divorce is a recent phenomenon. It has been suggested by sociologists that the duration of marriages has not in fact altered much over time; what has happened is that people's life expectancy used to be so much less that the number and pattern of divorces now mirrors the number and pattern of marriages which previously ended early through the death of one party. Laws are not, on the whole, created to deal with something which is not perceived to present a difficulty. The historical pattern of succession law addressed what happened when one spouse died; that was the likely outcome. It did not address what would happen on divorce.

10.9.1 Section 18A of the Wills Act 1837, introduced by the Administration of Justice Act 1982

Section 18 of the Wills Act 1837 deals with the revocation of wills by marriage. Section 18A was added to the Wills Act 1837 by s 18(2) of the Administration of Justice Act 1982, originally amending the original section so as to provide that any gift by will to a spouse would lapse if the marriage were later dissolved or annulled by a court, unless a contrary intention appeared in the will.

10.9.2 *Re Sinclair* (1985)

The deficiencies in this formulation rapidly became apparent in the case of *Re Sinclair* (1985). In that case, the testator made a will leaving his whole estate to his wife. There was a gift over to the Imperial Cancer Research Fund if she predeceased him or failed to survive him for one month. The marriage was dissolved and the testator died, but the former wife lived on. The Court of Appeal held that the gift to the Imperial Cancer Research Fund was effective in accordance with the terms of the will, namely only if the testator's former wife had indeed predeceased him or died within a month of his death. As neither of these things had happened, the estate passed under the rules relating to intestacy.

10.9.3 Section 18A amended by Law Reform (Succession) Act 1995

The Law Commission's Report No 217 of 1993 considered the effects of *Re Sinclair* (1985) (above). It recommended an amendment to s 18A so that a divorced spouse was treated as having predeceased. This was implemented in respect of estates arising after 1995 (that is, deaths on or after 1 January 1996, regardless of the date of the will, or of the divorce or annulment) by s 3 of the Law Reform (Succession) Act 1995. This applies where a will appoints a spouse as executor or trustee, or gives her a power of appointment, or if a gift is made to her by the will. If the marriage is later dissolved or annulled, the spouse is treated as having died on the date of the divorce or annulment unless a contrary intention is expressed in the will. This would have produced the correct result in *Re Sinclair*, had the testator died after 1995. Note, however, that the divorced spouse is not treated as having predeceased for all purposes, so, for example, a gift to a third party dependent on the spouse not predeceasing would still take effect. Care should also be taken if the substitutionary gift should be effective in other circumstances of failure of the original gift, such as disclaimer or death within the survivorship period; the current practice of specifying that the substitutionary gift should operate if the original gift fails for any reason may still be advisable, although in respect of gifts to third parties of which the operation really is dependent on the predecease of a spouse, extra care should be taken that the effect of the two spouses' wills is not to give an unintentional double gift to the third party because of the effect, for example, of a survivorship provision.

10.9.4 Judicial separation

Note that judicial separation has no effect on gifts by will, though it does affect entitlement on intestacy.

10.10 Public policy and illegality

A gift may be held void as being in contravention of public policy, for instance if it is held that it tends to promote the ending of an existing marriage. A gift will likewise fail if it promotes an illegal purpose. The rules relating to this area are the same as those for *inter vivos* trusts. Thus, a gift to a wife provided she divorces her husband will be invalid. A gift which, though the same in practical effect, is phrased so as to provide for her in the event of her no longer being married (and thus no longer dependent on her husband) may well be valid.

10.10.1 A person may not profit from his own crime

A common reason for a gift by will or entitlement on intestacy being held void for reason of public policy is, however, the rule that a person may not profit from his own crime. In the context of succession, this is seen as the rule that a beneficiary who is guilty of the murder or manslaughter of the deceased may not take a benefit from the estate of the deceased. This applies whether the benefit comes through the will or the intestacy of the deceased, or under a nomination or *donatio mortis causa* or some form of trust including a joint tenancy (note that homicide by one joint tenant of another joint tenant severs the joint tenancy).

10.10.2 The forfeiture rule

The forfeiture rule is the name given to that rule of public policy which states that a sane person who commits murder or manslaughter should not be allowed to benefit from the estate of his victim. It is a rule of public policy and not one arising under statute; the Forfeiture Act 1982 (see below) did not create the forfeiture rule, but modified it.

There is an interesting provision in Scotland, under the Parricide Act 1594. This provides that where a person is convicted of the murder of his parent or grandparent, he and all his descendants are precluded from taking from the murderee's estate. The idea of 'corruption of the blood' is thought to have arisen by analogy with the rules pertaining to treason (since abolished). The Act is so complex that it has never been successfully applied. In a near-miss case, *Oliphant v Oliphant* (1674), a man killed his mother but escaped from custody and so was never convicted of murder; therefore the Act did not apply.

10.10.3 Homicide by the insane does not lead to forfeiture

If a person is not convicted of murder or manslaughter, the forfeiture rule does not come into operation. Thus, if they are found insane and not convicted for that reason, they may keep any benefits under the will or intestacy of the deceased.

10.10.4 Conviction leads to forfeiture

The rule does not operate on the basis of moral culpability. In *Re Giles* (1971), a woman who had killed her husband was found not guilty of murder but guilty of manslaughter by reason of diminished responsibility, and was sent to Broadmoor. She sought her benefit from her husband's estate on the basis that she was not morally, only criminally, guilty of the killing, but the court held that the benefit was still forfeited.

10.10.5 Operation of the rule

The rule was exemplified in the case of *Re Crippen* (1911), the murderer who tried to escape to America but was caught by the use of the transatlantic telegraph. He had murdered his intestate wife; before her estate was administered, he was executed for his crime. It was held that the forfeiture rule prevented her estate from passing to him. Therefore, the beneficiary of Crippen's will could not claim the estate of the murdered wife, because it had not passed to Crippen during his life and did not form part of his estate.

10.10.6 Where the subject matter of a gift goes if the gift fails under the forfeiture rule

Where a gift fails under the forfeiture rule, it falls into residue like any other failed gift. Because so many homicides are committed within the family, this can often create difficult practical questions. In *Re Callaway* (1956), the testatrix, who was a widow, was murdered by her daughter. She had left her whole estate by will to that daughter, who was disentitled to her benefit under the will by operation of the forfeiture rule. All the deceased's property therefore should have passed under the intestacy rules, but the operation of those rules meant the convicted daughter would share the estate with the deceased's son. Her murder of the deceased also disentitled her to her share under the intestacy rules. The question arose as to where that share would go. The Crown claimed the daughter's half share as *bona vacantia*. However, the court rejected this suggestion and awarded the whole estate to the son, as though the daughter had predeceased.

10.10.7 Forfeiture Act 1982

Note that statute is not what gives rise to the forfeiture rule itself; that is a creation of public policy. The forfeiture rule existed long before the 1982 Act, but before that Act there was no possibility of seeking relief from the effects of the rule. This Act is not what deprives the homicidal beneficiary of his gifts but is what may allow him to avoid the effects of the forfeiture rule and keep the gifts. (It would have been helpful if the Act had been called the Relief From Forfeiture Act.)

10.10.8 Provisions of the 1982 Act

Section 2 of the 1982 Act allows for the modification of the effects of the forfeiture rule in cases of manslaughter, though not murder. Anyone convicted of murder will still lose all benefit from the deceased's estate and the court has no power to grant them relief from the effects of the forfeiture rule.

Proceedings under the 1982 Act for modification of the forfeiture rule must be brought within three months of the conviction for manslaughter. If the court is satisfied that the justice of the case so requires, it can grant complete or partial relief from the effect of the forfeiture rule. The decision is in the court's discretion and it will have regard to the conduct of both the offender and the deceased and to any other material circumstances.

In *Re K* (1985) a wife was convicted of the manslaughter of her husband on the grounds of diminished responsibility. He had been persistently and seriously violent towards her over a long period. She was sentenced to two years' probation for his manslaughter. On her application for modification of the forfeiture rule, the court allowed her to take his interest in their family home, which was jointly owned, and her benefits under his will. Compare this with *Re Giles* (1971) (above), before the 1982 Act.

In an Australian case on similar facts, *Public Trustee v Evans* (1985), in the New South Wales Supreme Court, Young J said that the exclusion from benefit rule was essentially judge-made and the courts should recognise that there may be good reasons for departing from it.

In the more recent case of *Jones v Roberts* (1995), the court considered a man's application for relief from the forfeiture of his interest in the estate of his father. He had been convicted of the manslaughter of both his parents on the basis of diminished responsibility because, although his actions were deliberate, he was found to be suffering from paranoid schizophrenia and to be deluded that his parents were persecuting him, though not to the extent that he was considered criminally insane (which would have meant acquittal). The court considered the pre-Forfeiture Act case of *Gray v Barr* (1971) in which it had been said that the forfeiture rule should apply, as a matter of public policy, in cases of deliberate, unlawful and intentional violence or threats of violence. Distinguishing *Re K* (1985), which has a different factual background, the court said that public policy in this respect had not moved on and that therefore relief from forfeiture should not encompass cases such as this, where there were 'deliberate and intentional acts of violence' resulting in death. The application for relief therefore failed.

10.11 Inalienability; perpetuities and accumulations

If a gift offends against the perpetuity rule, it will be void for that reason. In *Ward v Van der Loeff* (1924), a codicil was held partly inoperative for perpetuity; Lord Haldane found this a good reason for awarding costs out of the estate since 'the difficulty has been entirely caused by the testator himself'.

The courts may, however, construe the terms of a will so that the rule against perpetuities is not offended. In *Re Vaux* (1939), the residuary fund was appointed by clauses 11 and 12 of the will. Clause 11 offended against perpetuity and was therefore void. Clause 12, however, was debatable; it gave full discretion to the trustees of the fund (so that the rule against double portions did not apply – see Chapter 11) and was expressly limited to whatever period fell within the law against perpetuities. The court held that the rule could be cited without reference to lives in being and that where a gift was limited in this way, it would be saved.

In *Re Drummond* (1988), the settlor had settled property for himself for life and thereafter to such of his three daughters as were living at his death and attained 21 or married, and for the issue of any daughters who predeceased, on the same contingencies. One daughter who survived the settlor died later without issue. The gift was held not to offend the rule against perpetuities because it could be construed as referring to lives in being; each of the daughters had *ab initio* (from the outset) identifiable contingent interests in their sisters' shares. It was held that the share of the deceased daughter went as to one-third to each remaining sister and one-third on resulting trust to the settlor's estate (and not as is suggested in the headnote to the case).

10.12 Insolvency and abatement

A gift may fail because there is insufficient property in the estate to satisfy it. This may be because the estate is insolvent, so that there is simply no property available from which the gift may be satisfied, or because the estate is insufficient to pay all the gifts in full, so that they abate, in which case a beneficiary may receive part of the gift. For the order of payment of debts in an insolvent estate, see 13.7.

10.12.1 Insolvency

The estate is insolvent if it cannot meet its debts and liabilities. Those payments are met first, and none of the beneficiaries has any claim on any property in the estate until they have been made in full.

10.12.2 Abatement

Where the estate can meet all its debts and liabilities in full, the personal representatives will then deal with any remaining property in it in accordance with the deceased's will or intestacy. On intestacy, the rules are clear; the surviving spouse, if any, has a first claim on the estate, and thereafter the division of any residue is prescribed amongst the deceased's family. Where the deceased left a will, however, there may be various provisions of different kinds which the personal representatives cannot implement in full because there is insufficient in the estate to do so. The rules of abatement provide how the gifts should be dealt with when they cannot all be made in full.

10.12.3 Different rules depending on type of gift

Residue abates first, then general legacies and lastly specific and demonstrative legacies. Each class abates completely before the next class begins to abate, and gifts in the same class abate at the same rate, on the principle that 'equality is equity'.

In practical terms, this means that, after payment of debts and liabilities, all the specific and demonstrative legacies are paid out first in full if possible, and then if there is anything remaining it is used to pay general legacies. Only if those are all paid in full will there be any residue.

10.12.4 Interest

Interest may be payable on legacies; if it is, it is payable in full and does not abate with the legacy, as it is not treated as a legacy.

10.12.5 Inheritance Tax

Where a testator has specified that a specific gift which would otherwise bear its own tax should be paid free of tax, the tax that is payable on it is treated as a pecuniary legacy. Thus, a beneficiary may receive his specific gift in full but have to pay part of the tax on it because the deemed pecuniary legacy represented by the provision that the gift be free of tax has abated in the next class of gifts because of a lack of funds in the estate.

10.12.6 Subject to contrary intention in the will

The rules of abatement are subject to any contrary intention shown in the will. The testator may have indicated by the terms of his will that he wanted the gifts to be paid out in a particular order of priority. In *Sayer v Sayer* (1714), the testator directed that the pecuniary legacies given by his will should be taken out of the whole personalty. As there was insufficient in the estate to pay both the pecuniary legacies and the specific legacies in full, the question arose as to whether the direction meant that the pecuniary legacies would take precedence over the specific legacies. The court held that it did mean that, and the specific legacies abated.

How expression of a contrary intention works in practice is discussed further in 13.15. What is discussed here are the rules implied by law, which operate where there is no such contrary intention.

10.13 Uncertainty

A gift will be void if it is uncertain either as to its subject matter or as to its object (beneficiary). The court will lean to construing a gift as being certain, however, and may admit evidence to establish the identity of either. For the details of this, see 11.4–11.10. Note, however, that so far as uncertainty of object is concerned, no charitable gift will ever fail for want of an object. If the gift is clearly charitable, the court can direct which particular charities will receive it. In *Re White* (1893), the testator left a gift on trust for 'the following religious societies' without naming any. The court treated it as *prima facie* confined to charities and so it was held valid as a charitable gift even though the objects were not named and therefore, had it not been charitable, it would have failed for uncertainty of objects.

Uncertainty may render a gift void even where it appears certain on the face of it. The testator in *Re Gray* (1887) made a gift of company shares, which was a general legacy. However, the company had been wound up before the testator's death. The gift failed for uncertainty because the personal representatives could neither purchase the shares nor ascertain their value so as to satisfy the gift in money.

The courts have evolved rules to deal with common sorts of uncertainty. In *Re Poulton; Smail v Litchfield* (1987), the testatrix left property to a life tenant with the direction that she should on her death divide it 'among her own relatives according to her own discretion'. The life tenant left a share to her cousin for life and then to the cousin's children, who were not that original life tenant's statutory next of kin. The plaintiff claimed that this was not permissible given the rule of construction that 'relations' were the same as 'next of kin'. However, the court held that this rule existed purely to save gifts which would otherwise be void for uncertainty.

10.14 Non-compliance with condition

A gift by will may be subject to a condition. The condition may be a condition precedent or a condition subsequent, and it may be valid or void.

10.14.1 Condition precedent

A condition precedent is one which has to be satisfied before the event contingent upon it can take place. Thus, a gift might be conditional on the beneficiary attaining a certain age or giving a certain piece of his property to a third party (in which case it is unclear what sort of interest – whether in the property itself, or as a charge on it, or personally only against the beneficiary – the third party obtains in the property if the beneficiary obtains it without fulfilling the condition). Only when this had happened could the gift pass. If the testator prescribes a period during which the condition must be satisfied, that will probably need to be adhered to precisely if the gift is not to fail, although there is some Commonwealth authority for the proposition that a court may extend the time limit laid down by a testator where the condition is largely fulfilled (*Re Bragg* (1977) CA). If a condition precedent is void, the gift itself will fail.

10.14.2 Condition subsequent

In the case of a condition subsequent operating as a condition of defeasance, the beneficiary loses the gift if the condition is not satisfied. If a condition subsequent is void, the gift becomes unconditional. In the case where the condition of defeasance is ambiguous, evidence may be adduced.

In *Re Tepper* (1987), the testator made gifts conditional on the beneficiaries remaining in, and not marrying outside, the Jewish faith. The court held that, though the gift appeared to be void for uncertainty, the condition was one of defeasance rather than a condition precedent and accordingly evidence should be filed as to the meaning of the phrase 'the Jewish faith'.

10.15 Fraud

If a beneficiary has committed a relevant fraud on the testator, that will disqualify him from taking a benefit under the will. The testator in *Wilkinson v Joughlin* (1866) believed himself to be married to the woman whom he named as 'my wife' when leaving her a benefit under his will. The court held, however, that she had deliberately misled him about her marital status – she was already married, and the marriage to the testator was void because of her bigamy – and that this amounted to fraud. She, therefore, did not take the benefit under the will of her 'husband'. In *Re Posner* (1953), the testator similarly left a gift to the person he called 'my wife' but to whom he was not legally married. However, in that case, there was no element of fraud and indeed neither party had realised that the marriage had not been valid. The 'wife' therefore took her benefit under the will of the testator.

THE CLASSIFICATION AND FAILURE OF GIFTS

Gifts are classified in different ways. Legacies may be specific, demonstrative, general or residuary. How a legacy is classified may have important practical effects on whether or not a beneficiary receives the gift or whether it is used to pay the debts of the estate. A 'legacy' is a gift of personal property, whereas 'devise' refers to a gift of land.

(a) Specific gifts are gifts of a particular, severable part of the testator's property.

(b) General gifts do not refer to any particular part of the estate and if a testator makes a general gift of something that is in the estate, the personal representatives will have to buy that gift for the beneficiary.

(c) A demonstrative legacy is a gift out of a particular fund. Insofar as the fund exists, the gift is specific, but if the fund is insufficient to meet the gift, the rest of the gift operates as a general legacy.

(d) Residuary gifts are gifts of all the remainder of a particular kind of property or all the remainder of the estate after the specific, general and demonstrative gifts have been taken out.

(e) Pecuniary legacies are gifts of money, which may fall into various categories. Annuities are regarded as a series of pecuniary legacies, but are governed by particular rules as to their administration.

The fact that a testator leaves someone a gift by will does not necessarily mean that person will receive the specified property. Gifts may fail in various ways.

A beneficiary may disclaim a gift made to him. This may have an effect on what other beneficiaries receive, in that they will receive more or receive it sooner.

If the beneficiary predeceases (dies before) the testator, his gift will lapse, subject to the provisions of s 33 of the Wills Act 1837 which relate to gifts to predeceased children being saved by the existence of a remoter issue in the same line. The doctrine of lapse does not apply where there is a joint tenancy or a class gift.

Specific gifts fail by ademption (or 'are adeemed') where the specified property does not form part of the testator's estate at his death.

Where a beneficiary or his spouse has been an attesting witness to the will, the gift will fail under s 15 of the Wills Act 1837. This does not apply if the beneficiary is a spouse who married the witness after the execution of the will, or if the witness can be excluded because there are sufficient other witnesses without him.

If a marriage is dissolved or annulled, then any gift to the former spouse or appointment of that person as executor will be treated as though that person had predeceased under s 18A of the Wills Act 1837, as amended by the Administration of Justice Act 1982.

A gift will fail if it is contrary to public policy, especially if it falls foul of the forfeiture rule which says that a person who has been convicted of killing another may not benefit from the deceased's will or intestacy. However, in the case of manslaughter (but not murder) the beneficiary may apply to the court for relief from forfeiture under the Forfeiture Act 1982.

Where the estate is insolvent – there is insufficient in it to meet its debts and liabilities – then no beneficiary will receive any gift. The creditors will be paid in an order laid down by statute. Where the estate is solvent but there is insufficient to meet all the gifts, they will also be paid out in an order laid down by statute, according to their classification, unless the testator has specified otherwise in the will. Gifts within a class are paid out proportionately; they abate rateably within the class.

Gifts which contravene the rules against inalienability or perpetuities and accumulations will fail for that reason. Gifts also fail if they are insufficiently certain, do not comply with a valid condition or if they have been obtained by the fraud of the beneficiary.

CHAPTER 11

CONSTRUCTION OF WILLS

11.1 General principles

The construction of a will is the way its wording will be interpreted. Questions of knowledge and approval may dictate what parts of a will may have to be omitted from probate as invalid; questions of construction arise when considering what the import of the valid parts of the will may be. Construction deals with how the meaning of particular words and phrases will be established, and what will be done to resolve cases of ambiguity. No two persons use language the same way, and there is always the risk that what was perfectly clear to the testator may be rather less clear to his personal representatives or indeed to a court. Moreover, even if the personal representatives knew the testator well and are satisfied that, though he appeared to say one thing, he definitely meant another, it would not be a satisfactory state of affairs to allow them to interpret the testator's will in accordance with their own beliefs or their own agenda in a way that gave scope for their rewriting it. That would mean that the testator's family and friends, rather than the testator himself, wrote the will.

There have to be rules which state how certain words are to be interpreted or what is to be done with particular kinds of ambiguity. In the early case of *Jones v Westcomb* (1711), for example, the court had to decide how to deal with a will by which the testator devised a term of years to his wife for life and then the child *en ventre sa mère*, with one-third of the gift to the wife if the child died before the age of 21, when the wife was not in fact pregnant – it held that the devise was good, though the contingency had never occurred. There may be cases in which the implementation of those rules does an injustice which is manifest to onlookers, but there are others where the rules will bring a resolution and allow the administration of an estate to proceed when otherwise the arguing could have continued indefinitely. Moreover, once the meaning that the law will attribute to words is clearly established, future testators and their advisers may be confident in the knowledge that, as far as the legal interpretation of their wills goes, they have said what they mean.

Again, the problem in this area as in others is that by the time the question arises it is too late for the testator to be asked to clarify his position. It is often the general function of the law to provide rules to resolve difficulties and ambiguities.

11.1.1 Function of the rules of construction

The object of the rules of construction is to ascertain the testator's expressed intention. This should be clearly distinguished from simply attempting to ascertain the testator's actual intention. If that were the object, then the will document itself would be just one piece of evidence about something which is probably undiscoverable and certainly cannot be checked. The rules of construction are rules on how to construe the will itself, as the expression of the testator's intention. The testator must be taken to have meant what he said when he said it; however, many rules have to be followed in order to establish what, legally, he did mean. To go behind the words to the extent of passing over them as the fundamental expression of his testamentary wishes would be to deprive him of the ability to do exactly as he wished. In *Higgins v Dawson* (1902), Lord Shand said of a particular proposal to lead evidence that it was 'to supply a basis for inferring the intention of the testator and to take one away from the true construction of the will as showing that the testator intended something different from what he has said'; that is not the function of a court of construction and the evidence was not admitted.

It would also contradict or at best render irrelevant the statutory requirement in s 9 of the Wills Act 1837 that the will be 'in writing'; the importance of what is written must be preserved, and the courts must not overstep the bounds of interpreting wills so as to allow themselves to go so far as writing them. Lord Simon LC said in *Perrin v Morgan* (1943) that: 'The fundamental rule in construing the language of a will is to put on the words used the meaning which, having regard to the terms of the will, the testator intended. The question is not, of course, what the testator meant to do when he made his will, but what the written words he uses mean in the particular case – what are the "expressed intentions" of the testator.' Thus, if what the testator says is clear, then however unlikely it may seem, it must stand, and must not be interpreted to the extent that the court is not interpreting, but writing, the will.

11.1.2 Construction or re-construction?

There may sometimes be a temptation to stretch the rules of construction, no doubt so that the testator's real and true intention (as often discernible by his family and friends) may be honoured rather than what he appears to have said, without meaning it. There may often be a genuinely disappointed relative who truly believes that their great-uncle meant to benefit them by leaving them the Mercedes he had when he died, but if his will leaves the Mini he had when he made the will and which he no longer has, without any substitutional provision relating to the Mercedes or such other cars as great-uncle might have at his death, who is to say that the omission was not deliberate? Perhaps there had been a row which the great-nephew has not mentioned. It is too late to ask the testator personally.

The court of construction's function is not to improve upon what the testator has said, only to give effect to what is in the will itself, described by Jenkins LJ in *Re Bailey* (1951) as 'the dispositions actually made as appearing expressly or by necessary implication from the language of the will applied to the surrounding circumstances of the case'. Thus, in some situations a court will look at the circumstances around the case and take evidence as to what was said or done – but this is with a view to the proper interpretation of the will itself, not in order to see whether it could be improved upon. Rules as to when a court will look at evidence from outside the will – extrinsic evidence – have also evolved and are adhered to strictly. They do usually have a discernible logic.

11.1.3 How much latitude does the court have?

The court cannot interfere with what the will actually says, even if it appears likely that it would achieve a better result. The only way a court can alter the provisions of a will is under the Inheritance (Provision for Family and Dependants) Act 1975, and what it does then is not so much alter the provisions as amend their effects – the will itself remains, but the implementation of its provisions is partly undone by the implementation of the subsequent court order. Nevertheless, a court may often have some latitude in its decision, being able to justify more than one construction of the will or, for example, being able to decide which of two meanings with nothing to choose between them constitutes the more probable representation of the testator's intention; in this area, as in others, there may often be a lingering doubt as to whether a court's view is based on the law or on the facts of the case.

In *Underwood v Wing* (1854), the testator's will gave his personalty on trust to William Wing for the testator's wife absolutely, but if she died in his lifetime on certain trusts (which failed), and subject to this to William Wing. The testator and his wife were lost at sea together and there was no evidence as to who died first. It was held that the gift to William Wing was dependent on the testator surviving his wife and the mere failure of the practical operation of the gift did not mean William Wing was entitled. But in a similarly difficult situation in *Re Whitrick* (1957), the court construed the testatrix's true intention to the opposite effect. She had left her estate to her husband or, if he died 'at the same time' as her, to three named beneficiaries. He predeceased her. The court construed 'at the same time' effectively to include 'or before' to save the gifts, as this appeared to be the testatrix's clear intention. (For the *commorientes* rule, see 9.2 and 10.6.)

11.1.4 Practicalities of construction – where do you take the problem?

The construction of a will may well be a contentious point, and it is possible to take the matter to a court for its decision. If a case does need to go to court, it is not a matter of sending off a postal application to the local Probate Registry, as suffices with a solicitor's usual application for a grant of probate. Where a matter becomes contentious, although it would normally go to the Family Division of the High Court for the question of the validity of the will to be dealt with, questions of construction usually go to the Chancery Division of the High Court.

The Chancery Division has historically been concerned with wills and those who practise in it, on both sides of the bench, have long experience of construing deeds of trust and settlements. The Chancery Division in particular is felt to be very lawyer-like in its approach, and some people (particularly those who find a decision has gone against them, perhaps) feel that it is too pedantic and too much biased towards the interpretation a lawyer would put on words rather than the meaning which to them appears obvious and which they feel should be recognised by the court.

11.1.5 Why different courts for different functions?

The system under which the courts deal with different questions about wills may appear to be one of those systems which, if you did not have them already, you might not invent. The court to which one usually refers when talking about probate matters is the Family Division of the High Court, usually in its incarnation as a local District Probate Registry where it generally exercises its judicial function in a way that is essentially not judicial at all, but administrative. The Family Division is the renamed Probate, Divorce and Admiralty Division of the High Court, which took its new title under the Administration of Justice Act 1970. By then it had already exercised its probate functions for a century under the organisation of the courts which took place under the Judicature Acts in the 1870s. That organisation assigned construction functions, however, to the Chancery Division.

11.1.6 The division of functions between courts

The present structure is at least clearer than what went before, although it reflects it. That was involved with the different jurisdictions of the ecclesiastical courts, the common law courts and the Court of Chancery. The ecclesiastical courts imported a great deal from Roman law. They retained jurisdiction over the *validity* of wills of personalty for a very long time. The Court of Chancery, also importing many principles of Roman law, gradually managed to obtain jurisdiction over the *interpretation* of wills of personalty.

The courts of common law, which also brought in Roman law principles, tended to hold simply that realty devolved to the devisee named in the will or else to the heir upon intestacy; both they and the Court of Chancery would adjudicate on the *interpretation* of wills of realty.

The division of functions between courts is largely historical; that is certainly its origin. It is possible to observe a sense in the structure of the system. The Family Division is concerned with disputes about people and what they do, and so perhaps it is the right place for decisions about the validity of a will and, if the question comes up, exactly what form of the will is the right one to be accepted as valid. The Chancery Division has always been concerned with property and with the meaning of settlements and other disposals of property which are set out in disputable language, and so if a question of construction of any substance arises, it considers itself a more appropriate venue than the Family Division. However, in *In the Estate of Fawcett* (1941), the probate court held that where it was considering a question of validity, it had a limited jurisdiction to construe a will and a duty to exercise that jurisdiction to save costs.

11.1.7 Where do you find the rules?

There are various presumptions and rules which have evolved over the course of the centuries of case law, and there are statutory provisions. Some of these relate directly to the construction of wills, for example those which set out what certain expressions will mean as a matter of law or which deal with the evidence a court may look at in a construction matter, and some of them are of more general application, for instance rules about the age of majority.

11.1.8 What will the court do?

The court will construe the will as a whole. Lord Halsbury in *Higgins v Dawson* (1902) (above) said: 'Where you are construing either a will or any other instrument ... you must look at the whole instrument to see the meaning of the whole instrument, and you cannot rely upon one particular passage in it to the exclusion of what is relevant to the explanation of the particular clause that you are expounding.'

In *Re Macandrew* (1963), the testator's will of 1900 directed his trustees to hold his son W's share of the residue during his life on discretionary trusts for one or more of a class including W and his wife and issue if any. After W's death, the trustees were to pay the income to W's widow and then in trust for his children. The testator had then provided that 'if my said son W shall not leave a child or widow' then the fund should be held of trust for certain children of another son. Where the testator left a widow but no children, the court construed the will as a whole and held that 'or widow' was superfluous as well as incongruous, so that the widow took her life interest and then the fund passed in trust for the children of the other named son.

The court will apply all the rules which have evolved from past cases as well as statutory rules of construction (see below). It will also try to read the will so as to make it cover all the testator's property, rather than allowing its construction of the will to lead to an intestacy. Esher MR in *Re Harrison* (1885) justified this by suggesting that a testator who 'has executed a will in solemn form ... did not intend to make it a solemn farce ... to die intestate ...'. However, this can be done only where there are genuine alternative readings of the will. The court cannot step completely outside the boundaries of the law just to save a will from failing. Extrinsic evidence (evidence not found on the face of the will itself) may be admissible, and if that is the case then the court will use it. (For the circumstances in which extrinsic evidence is admissible, see below.) In respect of the wills of testators who died after 1982, s 20 of the Administration of Justice Act 1982 allows for rectification where it can be established that there was a clerical error or a failure on the part of the testator's solicitor to understand his instructions; this involves (apparently) changing the wording of the will rather than simply construing it. It may, however, resolve similar difficulties.

11.1.9 What will the court not do?

The court will not readily read words into a will. In *Scale v Rawlins* (1892), the testator made a gift of three houses for his niece for her life. He provided that if she died leaving no children, the houses should go instead to his nephews. The House of Lords would not imply a provision that if, as occurred, the niece should die leaving children, they should take the gift. The testator's provisions were clear and, even if it also seemed clear they were not what he intended, they had to stand as they were. In some cases, however (see *Re Whitrick*, above), it may be possible for the court to overcome such difficulties by construing the offending parts of the will in the light of the rest of the provisions and holding that, in the light of those other provisions, effectively something must be implied into the will for it to make sense as a whole.

There are procedures for resolving ambiguity by looking outside the will; there are none which allow an ambiguity which does not appear from the will to be created by the introduction of evidence from outside the will. If this were done, it would be tantamount to the court writing, rather than interpreting the will, and would contradict the fundamental requirement that a will be in writing.

11.1.10 Rectification

If the testator dies after 1982, the court is empowered by s 20 of the Administration of Justice Act 1982 to rectify the will, including by inserting words into the will, in the cases of clerical error or a failure to understand instructions. If neither of those conditions is satisfied, s 20 does not apply. The provision does not assist where the testator has misunderstood the legal effects of his words, or where there is a lacuna in the will.

It is thus not a method of construction proper, since that deals with the correct interpretation of the wording of the will, but it is a matter related to establishing the contents of the will, albeit on the facts of a case the borderline may not always be discernible and the two functions may operate together. For a discussion of how the two functions operate differently, see the judgment of Latey J in *Re Morris* (1970), predating the 1982 Act (see below at 11.6).

11.2 Basic presumption – words have their ordinary meaning

There is a presumption, set out in *Re Crawford* (1854), that ordinary words will be given their ordinary meaning; the same goes for ordinary phrases. This presumption can, however, be unhelpful where the ordinary word has more than one meaning and is thus ambiguous, or where the testator has used words which appear ordinary and unambiguous but which he is known to have used in a particular way that was out of the ordinary.

11.2.1 The 'dictionary principle'

A testator may supply his own dictionary – that is, give instructions as to the interpretation and meaning of the words he uses. Thus, a testator who clearly says that he gives his house to his beloved may also state that, when he says his beloved, he means Susan Jones of 24 Acacia Avenue, and the instructions will be effective. A 'dictionary' may be implied. The testator in *Re Davidson* (1949) was held to have supplied his own definitions sufficiently by naming his stepson but referring to him as 'my son' and to one of the stepson's children as 'my granddaughter'. Therefore the stepson's children took a share of the residuary gift which the testator left to 'my grandchildren'.

It may not always be completely obvious where the borderline is between the courts holding that the testator was using words in a particular way – supplying his own dictionary – and their finding that a word may be ignored. In *Pratt v Matthew* (1856), for example, the testator referred to 'my wife Caroline' where the purported marriage had not been valid and so Caroline was not the testator's wife, but the court discounted the word 'wife'. In the case of *Re Smalley* (1929) (below), however, the use of the word 'wife' in similar circumstances was found to be a particularly wide use of the word and valid for that reason.

11.2.2 Obvious and secondary meanings

In the absence of a dictionary supplied by the testator, where the obvious meaning of a word makes no sense, it may be shown that a secondary meaning of the word makes sense in context. However, this rule cannot always be used to cure poor writing on the part of the testator. The obvious meaning of words has to be shown to give a result which is essentially nonsensical before a court would agree to looking elsewhere than their obvious import for a meaning.

In *Gilmoor v MacPhillamy* (1930), the Privy Council said: 'In order to justify a departure from the natural and ordinary meaning of any word or phrase there must be found in the instrument containing it a context which necessitates or justifies such a departure. It is not enough that the natural and ordinary meaning may produce results which to some minds appear capricious or fail to accord with a logical scheme of disposition.'

The testator in *Re Smalley* (1929) left a gift to 'my wife Eliza Ann Smalley'; his wife was called Mary Ann. Although Eliza Ann with whom he lived was not his lawful wife, the court held that the testator was using the word 'wife' in a secondary meaning of 'reputed wife'.

11.2.3 Technical words

If the testator has used technical words, even if they might reasonably be felt to mean something different to the layman and therefore arguably to have a different 'obvious' meaning, they must be interpreted in their technical meaning. This is a great pitfall for the writer of a home-made will, especially one who feels that the document will be all the better if it contains legal-sounding language and expressions even if he is not certain of their precise meaning. The word 'heir', for example, has persisted in the popular vocabulary although it has no current application since the 1925 legislation; if it were to be used in a will, undoubtedly it would be found to refer to whoever would have fulfilled the category of 'heir' under the pre-1926 rules, something which few, if any, students or solicitors would know. The presumption that technical words will be given their technical meaning may, however, be rebutted in the same way as the presumption that ordinary words will be given their ordinary meaning.

11.3 Particular points

There are many particular rules of construction which have evolved to resolve particular kinds of ambiguity; some are encountered more often than others.

11.3.1 Construction *ejusdem generis*

Ejusdem generis is a Latin phrase which means 'of the same kind'. It is the name given to the rule which says that, when there is a list of words, they will be construed so that they all have the same scope of reference. Where some of the words have, on the face of them, a wider scope and some have a narrower scope, the wider ones will be limited by the narrower. It is not a rule which will be applied if there is any indication of a contrary intention. For example, the word 'effects' is a very wide word, capable of meaning personalty in general, and that is how it was construed in *Re Fitzpatrick* (1934), the gift being of 'my house and all my furniture and effects'. In *Re Miller* (1889), however, the word was used at the end of a list and, in that context, the court held that the words did not include share certificates and banknotes, because it held that this did not accord with the other items on a construction *ejusdem generis*.

11.3.2 Erroneous use of legal words – the do-it-yourself lawyer

The testatrix in *Re Cook* (1948) made a home-made will which made gifts of 'all my personal estate whatsoever' to certain named relatives. Her estate consisted mainly of real property. The court accepted that it was unlikely that she had meant her realty to devolve on intestacy, but that she had chosen to use a term of art and had been so clear in stating in legal terms that she was dealing only with her personalty that there was no room for construing the phrase otherwise than in its usual legal sense. 'Testators can make black mean white if they make the dictionary sufficiently clear,' said Harman J, 'but the testatrix has not done so.' In *Re Bailey* (1945), however, another testatrix who made a home-made will and made a similar, but less clear, error was luckier. She made gifts of realty and personalty to named persons, concluding with a gift to 'my residuary legatee'. The word 'legatee' is, of course, appropriate only to a person receiving personalty; a person receiving realty is a devisee and the general term covering both is 'beneficiary'. However, the court found that, in the context of the will, the word 'legatee' was used to mean 'beneficiary' and the gift to the 'residuary legatee' included real property.

11.3.3 Inconsistency

Where there is inconsistency between two provisions of the will, the later of two provisions will prevail if no other solution can be found. Usually, however, this 'rule of despair', as it was described in *Re Potter* (1944), can be avoided. If it is clear from the will itself both that there has been an error in the wording and what the correct version is, the correct provisions may be carried out. The courts may ignore part of a description of something if it turns out to be untrue in the light of the facts, or they may interpret the words which produce the difficulty not as an essential part of a description but as restricting the scope of the words which do apply on the facts. Sometimes, the legal basis for the decision as to what is 'correct' is less than clear or convincing, even if the result seems to be sensible; this might be felt to show the gap between what the law should do and what it does do, or perhaps the difficulty of formulating laws and principles of law which can be applied to produce sensible results in the right cases without leaving scope for each individual court to make up, on the hoof, what law and principles it will apply.

11.3.4 Problems with allowing courts latitude to arrive at 'sensible' decisions

There are two basic problems with allowing courts to do as they wish in any particular case. One is that it is often felt to be wrong in principle to allow judges to make the law – that is the job of Parliament. The other is that, if there is no set basis for decisions, they become very unpredictable. What is a sensible decision to one person (usually the person who benefits from it) may be the contrary to another (who loses out). Therefore, cases are less likely to be settled, or abandoned before they begin, by the parties' lawyers advising them that an offer is good or a case hopeless; this leads to a proliferation of litigation, which is always considered to be a bad thing (save by some lawyers, for example litigation lawyers).

11.4 Ambiguity

If the words of the will are ambiguous, the court may look at evidence from outside the will to assist with construing its meaning. Ambiguity may arise either on the face of the will – where a person looking at the will can see that there is an ambiguity – or in the light of the circumstances surrounding the testator and the provisions of the will. Different systems of law provided different rules for the admissibility of evidence depending on what the problem was which needed solving. In *Guardhouse v Blackburn* (1866), Sir JP Wilde said: 'I venture to think that the Ecclesiastical Courts created a difficulty (perpetually recurring) for themselves, when they attempted to adopt the well-known rules as to parol evidence and patent and latent ambiguities, existing in the courts of law and equity, to cases of probate to which such rules were not properly applicable.'

Amendments to the common law position on the admissibility of extrinsic evidence were made by s 21 of the Administration of Justice Act 1982 (see below at 11.11).

11.4.1 How does the court decide in cases of ambiguity?

It may appear that it would be helpful to look at either or both of the will and other evidence, for example, statements of the testator's intention – evidence of these can be given by the persons who heard them where admissible.

11.4.2 The will itself

The grant is conclusive as to the words of the will, and a court of construction cannot admit evidence of what the deceased's original will contained in order to deal with any alleged errors. Nor can it do so in order to fill in blank spaces. The original will is, however, admissible to prove how its contents are set out – for example whether there are commas or indentations (*Re Steel* (1979)).

11.5   Extrinsic evidence

Extrinsic evidence is evidence which comes from outside the will. It may be direct or circumstantial. Direct evidence will refer to the provisions the testator intended to make by his will. Circumstantial evidence will not refer directly to testamentary provisions but will assist in ascertaining what they mean.

For example, where the testator has made a gift to 'my beloved daughter', that will be a latent ambiguity, since it becomes clear that it is ambiguous only once one discovers he had three daughters. The testator may have said to other persons that he intended to benefit his daughter Linda; that is direct extrinsic evidence, which can be given to the court by those other persons. If the same testator always referred to his daughter Linda as his beloved, and never referred to any other daughter that way, evidence of that may be circumstantial evidence of the meaning of the words in his will.

11.5.1   Extrinsic evidence – existence of subject matter

Evidence from outside the will is always called extrinsic evidence. A court will always hear evidence as to whether the property in the will or the beneficiary who is to receive it exists. It would clearly be impossible for a court to make any helpful statement about the practical effects of a will if this were not the case.

11.5.2   Extrinsic evidence – patent and latent ambiguity

What kind of extrinsic evidence the court will admit as to the testator's intention depends on whether the ambiguity arises on the face of the will (patent ambiguity) or whether it is apparent only in the light of surrounding circumstances (latent ambiguity). Thus, if a person looking at the will, but knowing nothing about the testator, his property or his nearest and dearest would be able to see that the will was ambiguous, the ambiguity was held to be patent and the rules for dealing with ambiguity on the face of the will would apply. However, if the ambiguity was latent, and could be discovered only when there was an attempt to apply the provisions of the will to reality, then a different set of rules applied.

11.6   Patent ambiguity – pre-1983 rules

In respect of patent ambiguity where the testator died before 1983, direct extrinsic evidence would be admissible only where there was equivocation.

This was discussed by Latey J in *Re Morris* (1970), who was dealing with a will which required rectification but to which the reforms of 1982 obviously did not apply. The testatrix had stated in her codicil that she revoked clauses 3 and 7 of her will, when it was clear from the instructions she had given her solicitor that she had intended to revoke not clause 7 in its entirety but clause 7(iv). Latey J, explaining that his options were either to pronounce against the whole instrument or to exclude part and admit the rest, went on to say: 'Of course, the ambiguity being a patent one, the court of construction will not be able to admit the external evidence which makes the testatrix's intentions as clear as crystal, or to have regard to the findings of fact in that regard in this action. One can only say that that is a situation which WS Gilbert would have found ripe, but is otherwise unattractive.'

11.7   Latent ambiguity – pre-1983 rules

Where the language of any part of the will was shown to be ambiguous in the light of evidence other than that of the testator's intention, both direct and circumstantial evidence could be admitted to assist with the construction of the will.

11.8   Ambiguity after 1982

Since the Administration of Justice Act 1982 came into force, referring to testators dying after 1982, the situation has been governed by s 21 of that Act (see further below), and both direct and circumstantial evidence is admissible whether the ambiguity is apparent on the face of the will or appears only when the provisions of the will are applied to reality.

11.8.1   What if the extrinsic evidence does not answer the questions?

In *Re Williams* (1985), however, the court was unassisted by evidence about what the testatrix had meant by her lists of those to whom she had intended to give gifts. It rejected the extrinsic evidence of a letter to her solicitor. The court held that where the construction of the language used was concerned, 'language' includes numerals as much as words or letters, but it was not decided whether it would include the division of legatees into three groups. Declining, however, to hold that the ambiguity was one of language in any event, it proceeded to construe the will without the aid of any helpful extrinsic evidence as giving equal gifts to each of the named beneficiaries.

11.9 Direct extrinsic evidence

Direct extrinsic evidence is admissible under the common law where there is equivocation or to rebut particular presumptions of equity.

11.9.1 Equivocation

Where there is equivocation – a description which applies to more than one person or thing – then direct extrinsic evidence of the testator's meaning is admissible. There is no equivocation where the testator's meaning can be ascertained by using the 'armchair principle' (see below).

11.9.2 Equitable presumptions

Direct extrinsic evidence of the testator's declaration of intention is also admissible to rebut certain equitable presumptions. Note that these equitable presumptions are not themselves rules of construction. They are presumptions that a legacy in a will satisfies certain other obligations.

The presumptions are:

(a) that a legacy satisfies a debt;

(b) that a legacy satisfies another legacy;

(c) that a legacy satisfies a portion-debt.

11.9.3 Satisfaction of a debt

If the testator owed a debt and he leaves a legacy which appears to refer to the debt, without saying that the creditor should have the legacy as well as being able to claim the debt from the estate, then equity may presume, if all the requirements are satisfied, that the testator intended the legacy to satisfy the debt. The testator must owe the debt before the date of the will (since he can hardly be presumed to have intended to satisfy a debt he did not have), and he must leave the creditor by will a legacy equal to or greater than the debt. The legacy must be of the same general nature as the debt and must also be as beneficial to the creditor as the debt.

11.9.4 Satisfaction of another legacy

The rule is that the legatee will take only one of two similar legacies in the same instrument. If, however, they are not similar – for example they are of different amounts or the subject matter is different, or the testator gives different reasons for giving them – then the legatee will take both. If the legacies are contained in different instruments, for example in a will and then in a codicil, then the legatee will take both. However, an exception to this latter rule was stated in *Hurst v Beach* (1821) so that when the testator has stated his reason for giving the gift and it is the same in both cases, only one legacy is payable. This presumption is, as always, subject to the contrary intention of the testator.

11.9.5 Satisfaction of a portion or portion-debt

A portion is a gift from the testator to a child of his, or someone whom he treats as a child, to establish him permanently in life. Note that the provision of a portion *inter vivos* will lead to the ademption of a subsequent legacy of a portion, which is the corollary of the rule that a portion-debt will be satisfied by a legacy; essentially, the child cannot take the gift of a portion twice. The reason that the gift of one-third of a fund to a child of the testatrix in *Re Ashton, Ingram v Papillon* (1897) did not have to be brought into account against her subsequent share of the rest of the fund was that the donor, being the child's mother and not her father, was not considered to be *in loco parentis*. It is not clear, there being no cases on the point, whether the rules, which were formulated and generally applied in different social conditions from those prevailing today, would treat a substantial gift of the right kind from a mother to her child as a portion in the same way as such a gift from a father today.

Where a testator had created for himself during his lifetime the obligation to give a portion, then a portion-debt arises. If, however, the testator was under an obligation to fulfil a portion-debt and he makes a legacy of substantially the same nature, without expressing a contrary intention that the donee should be able to claim both the portion and the legacy, then equity will presume that the legacy was made in satisfaction of the portion-debt.

11.10 Circumstantial extrinsic evidence – the armchair principle

The 'armchair principle' of construction allows for the admission of circumstantial extrinsic evidence where there is uncertainty or ambiguity in the will. In order to arrive at the correct intention of the testator, the construer places himself 'so to speak, in the testator's armchair' (*Boyes v Cook* (1880)) and considers the circumstances by which he was surrounded when he made his will.

11.10.1 The armchair principle and the object of the gift

It is usually used to ascertain the identity of the object of the gift, that is, person to whom it is given. In *Charter v Charter* (1874), the testator had appointed 'my son, Forster Charter' as executor and left him his residuary estate. The testator had had a son of that name, but he had died some years before the will was made, something of which he was obviously aware.

Therefore, he could not have intended, in saying 'my son, Forster Charter', to mean that son. At the date of the will, he had two sons, William Forster Charter and Charles Charter. William obtained common form probate, and Charles successfully applied for the grant to be revoked, showing that, in the circumstances, the will really referred to himself. In *Thorn v Dickens* (1906), the court admitted evidence to show that the testator, whose will read simply 'All for mother', always called his wife 'mother'.

11.10.2 The armchair principle and the subject matter of the gift

The armchair principle may, however, also be used to ascertain the identity of the subject matter of the gift. In *Kell v Charmer* (1856) the testator left 'to my son William the sum of i.x.x. To my son Robert Charles the sum of o.x.x'. Evidence as to the system of symbols used by the testator in his jeweller's business was admitted to show that these symbols meant £100 and £200 respectively.

11.10.3 Limits of the armchair principle

The armchair principle does have it limits. Circumstantial evidence may clarify the meaning of ambiguous or uncertain words, but it may not give them a meaning which they are incapable of bearing. In *Higgins v Dawson* (1902) (above), Lord Davey said: 'The testator may have been imperfectly acquainted with the use of legal language ... he may have used language the legal interpretation of which does not carry out the intentions that he had in his mind ... that fact should not induce the court to put a meaning on his words different from that which the court judicially determines to be the meaning which they bear.'

More recently, Nicholls J said in *Re Williams* (1985) (above at 11.8.1): 'if, however liberal may be the approach of the court, the meaning is one which the word or phrase cannot bear, I do not see how in carrying out a process of ... interpretation ... the court can declare that meaning to be the meaning of the word or phrase. Such a conclusion, varying or contradicting the language used, would amount to rewriting part of the will ...'

11.10.4 Ambiguity must be present to be interpreted

Moreover there must be an ambiguity; the armchair principle cannot be used to create one, as that would, again, amount to ignoring the clear instructions in the written will. In *Higgins v Dawson* (1902), again, Lord Shand said: 'In the class of cases in which you cannot tell exactly what is given or to whom it is given because of obscure or doubtful expressions ... you must have recourse to extrinsic evidence in order to ascertain his meaning. But here ... the will is in its expression and language ... unambiguous, and that being so, no proof in reference to the amount of the testator's estate at the date of the will can affect its construction ... Even if it could be shown that the intention of the testator was something different from the language of the will that intention would not prevail ...'

In *NSPCC v Scottish NSPCC* (1915), the testator gave legacies to various Scottish charities, and also one to 'the National Society for the Prevention of Cruelty to Children'. This was the exact name of an English charity, but there was evidence that the Scottish National Society had been brought to the testator's attention shortly before his death. There was no evidence as to his having paid any attention to the English charity at all. The House of Lords held, however, that there was no ambiguity which it needed to cure and the English society therefore took the gift. (Note, however, that such an error could now possibly be established as falling within the terms of s 20 of the Administration of Justice Act 1982 as a clerical error, so that the court could consider rectifying the will by adding in the word 'Scottish'.)

11.11 Section 21 of the Administration of Justice Act 1982

This section widened the areas in which extrinsic evidence is admissible. In respect of testators who die after 1982, direct and circumstantial extrinsic evidence of their intention is admissible to assist with the interpretation of the will in three situations:

(a) Where any part of a will is meaningless, as, for example, were the gifts in *Kell v Charmer*, above. Note that the meaninglessness of a blank is not assisted with, however, as that cannot be 'interpreted'. Nor can this provision assist with a gift which is quite clear on its face, even if someone feels – or is – quite justified in claiming that it was meant to signify something completely different. This provision deals only with the situation where there is something in the will which is meaningless in itself.

(b) Where the language of any part of will is ambiguous on the face of it. Circumstantial extrinsic evidence only would be admissible before 1983; after 1982, direct extrinsic evidence is also admissible.

(c) Where evidence other than evidence of the testator's intention shows that the language used in any part of a will is ambiguous in the light of surrounding circumstances. This provision may assist where the will appears to make sense on its face, but does not do so when it is applied to reality.

11.12 Decisions the courts have reached

It may be helpful to consider some of the decisions the courts have reached, applying the rules of construction.

In *Bristow v Bristow* (1842), the testatrix left a bequest of £800 to the four eldest children of her cousin George Bristow and £200 to the three remaining children of her uncle of the same name. Her cousin had seven children; her uncle had one child, but had had four grandchildren, of whom three remained. The court eventually decided that the £200 went to the three youngest children of the cousin. In *Re Rickit* (1853), the testator left a gift to his 'niece, the daughter' of his late sister Sarah. This was taken by his nephew, the son and only child of the testator's late sister Sarah Ann.

In *Ellis v Bartrum* (1857), the testator left gifts of 10 guineas to the surgeon and resident apothecary of the Southern Dispensary. There were two surgeons and no apothecary, though there was a dispenser. The court held that the gift to the 'resident apothecary' went to the resident dispenser, although the two words are not interchangeable, and the effect of the will was that the three persons took 19 guineas each.

A comparatively recent example of a court looking at all the circumstances and interpreting the will in a way that might appear to go against the words in it is *Re Fleming* (1974). In that case, the testator held a leasehold of a house in Hampstead and had left that leasehold, specifically referring to it as such, to the Hampstead Old People's Housing Trust. However, after the will was made, the testator had also acquired the freehold of the house, and he had not merged the two. It appeared, therefore, that the freehold fell into residue and it was accordingly claimed by the residuary beneficiaries. Whilst this interpretation might accord with the law on a very strict interpretation, the court nevertheless held that the freehold passed with the leasehold.

It based this interpretation on a line of decisions in cases with similar facts, where the courts had held that such expressions as 'my leasehold house' referred to the whole of the testator's interest in the property, because the implications of saying 'leasehold' were not apparent at the time the will was made. At that time the word was merely a description of the testator's whole interest, not a limitation of any kind. In *Struthers v Struthers* (1857), the court had said that the gift of a lease of four houses passed the freehold which the testator subsequently acquired because 'the words were used to express the whole extent of property he might leave at his death, not anticipating that he should then be entitled to any greater interest'; in *Saxton v Saxton* (1879), a gift of 'all my term and interest in the leasehold ... premises ...' also passed the later-acquired freehold because the court held there was 'nothing more clear than that this testator intended to give the house as a provision for his wife, and he intended by the words he used to give any interest he might have in that house'.

11.13 The doctrine of election

There is a general principle that, in order to take a benefit under a will, a person must comply with all the provisions of the will as a whole. The doctrine of election was set out in full by Lord Cairns in *Codrington v Codrington* (1875). It applies where a testator has given someone a gift by will and, at the same time, purported to give some property which belongs to that person to a third party. It may not be the case that the donee under the will can both keep his own property and take the gift made under the testator's will. The doctrine of election asks him to choose, or elect, whether to keep the gift under the will and pass on the property the testator purported to give, or to keep his own property and forgo the gift under the will. If he wishes to have both, the doctrine of election says that he may do so only if he compensates the third party for the loss of the gift the testator purported to make to him by will.

The doctrine of election applies wherever the above situation arises and the testator has not expressed a contrary intention; there is no requirement for an actual intention that the doctrine should operate to be established. The basis of the doctrine is questionable, but the Court of Appeal has said that the view that it is a creature of equity is the correct one. This view says that equity imposes the election on the conscience of the donee, so that it will not allow him to take the gift to him without his complying with the condition, which equity imposes, of making the gift to the third party.

The view that the doctrine of election is a doctrine of equity was first clearly stated in *Re Mengel* (1962). The testator's gifts of property had to be construed in the light of the Danish law of community of property within marriage, which meant that some of the things he had purported to leave by will were not entirely his to give away. He had left all his personal and household goods to his wife, and the remainder on trust for his wife during her life. He had also left two specific gifts, subject to the gifts to his wife, of his books to his niece and his collection of etchings and mountain photographs to his nephew. It was held that the doctrine of election depended not on the testator's intention but on his having purported to dispose of property of which he could not validly dispose. His widow therefore had to elect for the books, etchings and photographs under the gift to her of personal and household goods, because the testator was purporting to give what was not his, but not under the gift of the remainder of his property.

11.14 Absolute or lifetime gifts?

By virtue of s 28 of the Wills Act 1837, unless a contrary intention appears in the will, a devise of real property without any words of limitation passes the fee simple or other existing whole interest which the testator has the power to dispose of. Note, however, how far the apparent expression of a contrary intention may be ignored; see the cases applied in *Re Fleming* (1974) (above). The same principle also applies to personal property.

11.15 The rule in *Lassence v Tierney*

The rule in *Lassence v Tierney* (1849), also called the rule in *Hancock v Watson*, states that if there is an absolute gift to a legatee, with trusts then imposed on that gift which fail, then the absolute gift will still stand. The question of whether there is an initial absolute gift is one of construction; the gift may be directly to the beneficiary or to trustees on trust for him.

In *Hancock v Watson* (1902), the testator left a residuary gift of personalty to his trustees, on trust for his wife for life and thereafter to be divided into portions. Two of these portions were left to one Susan Drake, but the testator then said 'it is my will and mind that the two fifth portions allotted to her shall remain in trust, and that she be entitled to take only the interest ... of the shares so bequeathed to her during her natural life'. There were other trusts which were to come into operation after Susan Drake's death. Those other trusts failed, and the court, looking at the words 'I give' and 'allotted' which were used in the will in respect of the gift to Susan Drake, held that she should take the two portions absolutely.

11.16 Exercise of power of appointment by will

Section 27 of the Wills Act 1837 states that a general devise of the real estate of the testator includes any real estate which he has power to appoint in any manner he may think proper, unless a contrary intention appears in his will. This means, if the testator has any such power of appointment, that there is no need for the testator to state in his will that he is exercising the power. Although the operation of s 27 is excluded by any contrary intention in the testator's will, describing the property as 'my' property is not sufficient to establish a contrary intention. Section 27 applies only to general powers of appointment, not to special powers, nor to a hybrid power to appoint in favour of anyone save certain named persons (see, also, delegation of testamentary powers at 3.6).

11.17 Children

A testator may identify his beneficiaries by reference to their relationship to himself or others, especially as 'children'.

11.17.1 Adopted children

In respect of any testator who dies after 1975, an adopted child is treated by virtue of s 39 of the Adoption Act 1976 as the lawful child of his adopter(s) and not the child of his natural parents, subject to contrary indication. The adopted child also stands in the relationship of sibling to its adoptive parents' other children. The date of the adoption order is irrelevant, even if it comes after the testator's death.

If the gift in a will depends on the date of birth of the child, then, subject to contrary indication, an adopted child will be treated as having been born on the date of his adoption. Two children adopted on the same day will be treated as having been born on that day in the order of their age. References in the will to the age of the child are not affected, however, by these provisions (s 42(2)).

The development of the law traces a pattern of increasing acceptance of adoption. If the testator died before 1976, the adoption order must have been made before his death, which is no longer required. Where, however, the date of execution of the relevant will or codicil was also before April 1959, the adoption order has to have been made before that date (note the possible effects of republication however) but after 1949 in order for the child to take.

11.17.2 Legitimation

The position before the Family Law Reform Act 1987 (see below) could depend on the operation of the Legitimacy Act 1976. The Legitimacy Act 1976 states that, in respect of a testator dying after 1975, a legitimated person may take as though he had been born legitimate, subject to contrary indication. In respect of the children of void marriages, it mattered whether the child was born before or after the ceremony. In *Re Spence* (1989), it was held that a child born before the celebration of a void marriage would not be legitimated by that marriage.

After 1 April 1988, the position is governed by s 28 of the Family Law Reform Act 1987. Since that Act came into force, the situation has changed and the result in the *Re Spence* situation would now be different, because whether a child was illegitimate or not would be irrelevant.

11.17.3 Illegitimate children

At common law, references to 'children' were presumed to mean legitimate children only. By s 15 of the Family Law Reform Act 1969, however, in wills or codicils made after 1969 references to children were presumed (that is, the testator could exclude the presumption by making a gift explicitly to his legitimate children only) to include illegitimate children, and relationships traced through an illegitimate line were also included. However, this applied only where the illegitimate children, or those claiming through them, were to benefit. It did not allow, for example, a child's unmarried father to claim from that child's estate. Nor did it apply where reference was made, for instance, to a gift to someone 'if he dies without leaving children', which was still presumed to mean legitimate children only, subject to contrary indication.

Until the Family Law Reform Act 1969, illegitimate children had no claim on the intestacy of their parents save in very limited circumstances. However, in respect of deaths from 1970 onwards, s 14 of the 1969 Act provided that the child and his parents would stand in relation to each other in the same way as if the child were legitimate. This Act did not, however, affect relationships other than those between parents and children, so it gave an illegitimate child no claim, for example, on the intestacy of grandparents or siblings, and if an illegitimate child died intestate without parents, his estate would pass as *bona vacantia* to the Crown, even if he was close to his siblings or grandparents.

The Family Law Reform Act 1987 applies to the estates of those who die intestate after April 1988. Section 19 of the Act means that in the tracing of a child's relationships, it no longer matters whether the child's parents were married to each other or not.

The Family Law Reform Act 1987, s 19, also applies to wills or codicils made after 3 April 1988 and provides that references, whether express or implied, to any relationship between two persons are to be construed without regard to whether the father and mother of either of them, or of any person through whom the relationship is deduced, were married to each other at any time or not, subject to contrary intention.

11.17.4 AID and in vitro fertilisation

Children born after April 1988 as a result of artificial insemination by donor were regarded by virtue of s 27(1) of the Family Law Reform Act 1987 as the children of their mother and, subject to contrary proof, of the mother's husband if she is married. From August 1991 the position has been governed by s 28 of the Human Fertilisation and Embryology Act 1990, which includes children born as a result of in vitro fertilisation or egg donation. They are regarded as the children of the mother's husband, or the man with whom she obtained the treatment, unless it is shown he did not consent, to the exclusion of the donor.

11.18 Age of majority

The age of majority is the age at which a person ceases to be a 'minor' or 'infant' and becomes entitled to property as an adult of 'full age'. The age of majority is now 18, following s 1 of the Family Law Reform Act 1969, which came into force on 1 January 1970. Previously, it was 21. The date for ascertaining which age of majority is relevant is the date of execution of the will. A will executed before 1970 but republished after 1969 will not be treated as having been made after 1969 for these purposes.

11.19 Dates from which a will speaks

There are different rules for property – the subject matter of the gift – and for beneficiaries – the objects of the gift.

11.20 Property and s 24 of the Wills Act 1837

Section 24 of the Wills Act 1837 states that a will speaks from the date of death as to property, subject to contrary intention. This includes the subject matter of specific gifts, unless that is described so as to show that the testator intended a particular object which was in existence at the date of the will. In that case, one not unusual with specific gifts, a contrary intention will be found which excludes s 24. If it is held that the testator intended a particular object which existed at the date of the will but does not exist at the s 24 date – immediately before the testator's death – then the gift will be a specific gift and will fail by ademption. It is therefore very important to know exactly when a gift will be found to be specific rather than general in this context. In *Re Sikes* (1927), for example, the testatrix made a gift of 'my piano'. She had a piano at the time, but before her death she sold that piano and bought another. The court held that the phrase 'my piano' made the gift a specific gift of the piano she had at the time of making the will, and that it therefore failed by ademption.

11.20.1 'Now' and contrary intention

The use by the testator of the words 'now' or 'at present' will be found ambiguous as to whether this means the date of the will or the date of death. As a matter of common sense, one might assume that the testator, at the time of making the will, meant, by 'now', that time of writing. As a matter of law, however (an entirely different matter), it may seem that s 24 implies the date of his death. The question then arises as to whether the use of the words 'now' or 'at present' by the testator constitute an intention contrary to that imported by s 24. The cases do not appear to give any clear guidance as to how 'now' or 'at present' will be construed. Some courts, for instance the court in *Willis v Willis* (1911), have chosen to regard the words as no more than additional description, which can be ignored if the situation changed between the making of the will and the date of death. Others, however, have construed 'now' as showing a contrary intention, for example, that in *Re Edwards* (1890), where the court was asked to decide how much of a property a beneficiary could claim where the gift was of 'my house and premises where I now reside'. At the time of making the will, the testator owned and resided in the whole property; by his death, he had let part of it. However, the court held that the beneficiary took the whole property; note, however, that this concerned realty in respect of which wills were not ambulatory before 1926 (see 3.1.1). It is submitted that there is no clear rule at all in this area, and that either course can be justified with reference to the cases. The matter being therefore entirely in the lap of the individual judge, it may even be a question of which outcome he prefers.

11.20.2 Effect of republication

If the will is republished, it speaks from the date of republication. In *Re Reeves* (1928), the testator gave his daughter 'all my interest in my present lease'. The lease expired three years after the making of the will. The testator later took a further lease on the same property and then confirmed his will by codicil. The court (assuming that 'present' amounted to a contrary intention) held that the daughter was entitled to the new lease because the effect of the republication was to make the will speak as if it had been executed at the date of the codicil, and as the original lease was not specified in the will, as it would have been had it been described, for example, by reference to its dates, then the republication was effective to pass the subsequent lease.

11.21 Beneficiaries

A will speaks from its own date as to the object of a gift, subject to contrary intention in the will. (This is not altered by s 24 of the Wills Act 1837, which refers to real and personal *property*, ie, the subject matter of the will, only.) It still may not be immediately clear whether a person is entitled to take under the will, because even where the person in the will is described by his situation in life and that situation is filled by someone at the testator's death, in the absence of a clear provision for the substitution of the situation by another person the description will be taken to refer to the particular individual who filled it at the date of the will. Thus, if that person has predeceased the testator, the gift will lapse. In *Re Whorwood* (1887), the testator gave to 'Lord Sherborne and his heirs my Oliver Cromwell cup'. The person who was Lord Sherborne at the date of the will predeceased the testator. The court held that the gift lapsed, even though the gift had been made explicitly 'for an heirloom', because that did not amount to a substitutional gift to Lord Sherborne's heir.

11.21.1 Contrary intention

The testator may show a contrary intention in his will, giving an alternative time for the ascertaining of the beneficiaries. In *Re Daniels* (1918), it was held that the testator's gift to 'the Lord Mayor of London for the time being' had sufficiently expressed a contrary intention by the words 'for the time being' so as to pass the gift to the person who was Lord Mayor at the time of death.

A contrary intention will be implied if the provision of the will would make no sense if the time for ascertaining the beneficiary were the date of the will; in *Radford v Willis* (1871) a gift to the 'husband' of an unmarried woman was construed as one to the man she subsequently married. Something similar occurred in *Re Hickman* (1948), but in that case the gift was to the wife of the testator's unmarried grandson. The wife he had at the date of the testator's death was his second; the first was still alive, the marriage having ended in divorce. It was held that once the first wife had fulfilled the description, she did not lose her gift by the divorce. In our present society, which is much more used to and tolerant of divorce, it might be, however, that the courts would seek to distinguish this case, were similar facts to arise.

11.21.2 Effect of republication

The testatrix in *Re Hardyman* (1925) gave a legacy 'in trust for my cousin his children and his wife'. At that time, the cousin was married, but that wife died not only before the testator but also before he republished his will by codicil. It was shown that the testator, at the date of republication, was aware of the death of the wife. The court held on that basis that the effect of the republication was to make the will refer to any woman the cousin might marry, so the legacy did not lapse. Instead, the cousin's second wife took the interest originally intended for the first wife.

11.22 Class gifts

A class gift in the strict sense is one by which something is to be shared out, so that the size of the gift to each person depends on how many persons there are in the class (*Pearks v Moseley* (1880)). If it is established that a gift is a class gift, the class closing rules will apply to govern the category of persons who fall within the class. If they did not, the class could remain open for a very long time, preventing the estate from being distributed subject always to the provisions of the Perpetuities and Accumulations Act 1964.

11.22.1 Class gift proper and individual gifts to members of a class

If there is an individual gift to each member of a class, the class will close at the testator's death, just as it would in any other case of ascertaining the object of a gift. The difference between individual gifts to each member of a class and a class gift is the difference between '£100 to each of A's children' (of whom he has five) and '£500 to A's children' (as a class). Although the effect in each case is the same if A has five children, only the latter is a class gift in the strict sense. If one of the children predeceased, in the case of individual gifts then each of the remaining four children would still take their £100, but the £100 which would have gone to the other child will go elsewhere. In the case of the latter class gift, however, the £500 would be divided amongst the remaining four children, giving them £125 each.

11.22.2 Naming individuals

The mentioning of particular individuals by name is not fatal to a finding that a gift is a class gift. This was stated in *Kingsbury v Walter* (1901), where it was held that, on the proper construction of the will, the testator had intended the gift to take effect as a class gift. As well as importing the class closing rules, such a finding can exclude the doctrine of lapse; therefore a reference to a person who had predeceased the testator will not entail the doctrine of lapse.

11.23 Class closing rules

These apply where there is a class gift in the true sense. The personal representatives need to know that a class has closed in order to be sure that they can distribute the whole of the property to be shared out amongst the members of the class. They do not want to run the risk of a further class member appearing in the future wanting his share. Of course, closing the class early may exclude some persons whom the testator, had he been specifically asked, would have liked to include. On the other hand, it would not be in the general interest for the distribution to be delayed for a protracted period or even indefinitely.

11.23.1 Closing of a class entitled to an immediate gift

The basic rule, of when a class entitled to an immediate gift closes, is as set out in *Viner v Francis* (1789). In the case of an immediate class gift where each member takes a share at birth, the class closes at the testator's death if any member of the class is then in existence. Where, however, there is no member of the class in existence at the testator's death, then no class closing rule applies and the class remains open indefinitely (*Shepherd v Ingram* (1764)).

11.23.2 Closing of a class entitled to a postponed gift

A gift may be immediate or postponed, for example, to vest after a prior life interest. In *Re Chartres* (1827), it was said that if there is a postponed class gift, the class will close when the postponement ends. If, however, there is no member of the class when the postponement ends, then, as with the situation where there is an entitlement to an immediate gift but no member of the class in existence at the testator's death, no class-closing rule will apply and the class will remain open indefinitely.

11.23.3 Closing of a class where there is a contingency imposed on the class members

Where there is a contingency imposed on each member of the class (for example, to the children of A who attain the age of 18) the relevant class-closing rule is the rule in *Andrews v Partington* (1871). This says that if the gift is an immediate one, the class will close as soon after the testator's gift as there is anyone who satisfies the contingency.

It was held in *Re Wernher, Lloyds Bank Ltd v Earl Mountbatten* (1961) that the rule in *Andrews v Partington* applies whenever a testator's words invite it. The use of words inviting the application of the rule will give rise to a presumption that the testator intended the will to be construed in accordance with it. In *Re Wernher*, there was a bequest of an aggregate fund to children as a class payable on their attainment of a given age or on marriage. The period of distribution was held to be the time when the first child was entitled to receive and children coming into being after that time were thus excluded.

If the gift is postponed, for example, by a preceding life interest, the class will close after the end of the postponement if any member of the class who was in existence after the testator's death has satisfied the contingency. If this does not happen immediately, the class will close when a class member does satisfy the contingency.

11.23.4 Difficult cases – gifts postponed to something which does not happen as expected

A particular problem arises if, as is not an unlikely combination, a gift is made to a person for their life and subsequently to others, and the life tenant disclaims. This is particularly likely to happen where the life tenant is the parent of the remaindermen and feels he or she does not need the life interest. The question arises as to when the class closes – at the date of disclaimer or the date of death?

If the former, then those children born after that date will be excluded by operation of the rules. It does not appear that this will necessarily accord with what the testator intended. If, however, the latter applies, then either the distribution of the property is held up, with complications arising as to how it is dealt with in the meantime, or the property is distributed, so that some may have to be returned to satisfy the claims of class members who appear later or those claims may go unfulfilled because the property has been dissipated and cannot be recovered.

11.23.5 Class closing at date of disclaimer (interpretation 1)

In *Re Davies* (1957), there was a gift for life with remainder to that beneficiary's issue; she had three children. The beneficiary disclaimed her life interest and the question before the court was whether the gift in remainder was accelerated and the class closed at that date, or whether it would close, as the testator would have expected, at the date of her death. Vaisey J held that the vested class gift in remainder was accelerated on disclaimer of a life interest and that it was not liable to be affected by the coming into existence of any future issue of the original beneficiary.

11.23.6 Class closing at date of death (interpretation 2)

On the other hand, in *Re Kebty-Fletcher* (1967), a gift on trust for X for life and after his death to his children was interpreted differently. In that case, the testator had left gifts to his nephews and nieces for their life and thereafter for the children of those beneficiaries at 21. One nephew had assigned and released his life interest by deed to the Public Trustee, on the basis that the original trusts remained. The question was whether the class closed in accordance with the rule in *Andrews v Partington*, as soon one of the nephew's children reached 21, or on his death.

Stamp J doubted the sense of *Re Davies* (above), and said he was content to treat it as applicable only to cases of acceleration. He did not accept that it could be applied to alter the composition of the class. He said: 'The release of a life interest in favour of children is one of the commonest features in the field of trusts and, so far as I am aware, it has never hitherto been suggested that such a release may have the dramatic effect now claimed of altering the membership of the class of children to take.' He held that the disposition of the life interest did not accelerate the interests of the nephew's children or alter the composition of the class. Discussing the rule in *Andrews v Partington*, he said: 'In my view ... that rule ought only to be applied where the testator ... must, or may, be taken to have intended a distribution at a moment of time which may be applied to the benefit of all the members of the class.'

In *Re Harker's Will Trusts* (1969) too, Goff J held that the rule in *Andrews v Partington* did not apply. He held that the class of beneficiaries whose interest had been accelerated and brought into possession by the disclaimer of the preceding life interest remained open until the death of the person who disclaimed. Therefore, although those members of the class took an accelerated benefit, it remained liable to be diminished by further class members in the future.

Re Harker's Will Trusts (1969) provides a practical solution to the question of whether and how to distribute property where a life tenant has disclaimed but the class has not closed. In saying that the beneficiaries may receive an accelerated interest, rather than that the property must be preserved pending final ascertainment of exactly what that interest should be, it preserves the class of beneficiaries the testator intended to benefit but avoids the problem of what to do with the property in the trust pending the closing of the class. This leaves the way open, however, for difficulty or unfairness to later beneficiaries if the property should be dissipated before they become entitled.

11.23.7 Excluding the class closing rules

It is possible to exclude the class-closing rules, but this must be done with care. It was held in *Re Tom's Settlement* (1987) that a settlor may supply his own 'closing date'. In that case, the court discussed the purpose of the class-closing rules. It said they were intended to resolve conflict between the testator's intentions to give a share of his estate to the members of a class whenever they were born and to give a share to a person as soon as they became entitled. However, where a testator had clearly specifically included a class-closing date, that could exclude the class-closing rules. References in the will to a specified date as 'the class-closing date' showed an intention that the class would remain open until that date, even if the application of the usual class-closing rules would have closed it earlier.

In *Re Edmondson's Will Trusts* (1972), it was held that the use of the phrase 'whenever born' was sufficiently emphatic to exclude the class-closing rules and equivalent to the phrase 'at whatever time they may be born'. In *Re Chapman's Settlement Trusts* (1978), it was held, confirming *Re Edmondson*, that the use in respect of children of a phrase such as 'now born or who shall be born hereafter' will not exclude the class-closing rules, because a phrase of that kind could simply refer to children born before the closing of the class.

CONSTRUCTION OF WILLS

Construing a will means interpreting the meaning of the words used in it. Construction should not be stretched to re-writing the will. The dividing line is sometimes difficult to draw.

Words are presumed to have their ordinary, everyday meaning. However, the testator may supply his own dictionary, providing an alternative meaning for any particular words he uses. Technical words are given their technical meanings.

Where the words used are ambiguous, this may be on the face of the will and apparent to anyone reading it, or may only become clear when the words are applied to reality. The former ambiguity is said to be patent and the latter latent.

The court will always admit extrinsic evidence – evidence other than just the will itself – about the property mentioned in the will.

Direct extrinsic evidence refers to what provisions the testator intended to make by his will. Circumstantial extrinsic evidence assists in interpreting the words used.

Where the question is what the testator intended the words of the will to mean, the court may be allowed to admit extrinsic evidence. The rules governing this were widened by the Administration of Justice Act 1982.

Before 1983, direct extrinsic evidence was admissible in the case of a patent ambiguity only where there was equivocation. In the case of a latent ambiguity, both direct and circumstantial evidence were admissible.

After 1982, direct and circumstantial evidence are both admissible in cases of ambiguity whether it is patent or latent.

Direct extrinsic evidence may be adduced to rebut the equitable presumptions of satisfaction of debts, portion-debts or legacies.

Admitting circumstantial extrinsic evidence means using the 'armchair principle' in order to see the meaning of the testator's words as he saw them himself. However, this may only be done where the words are ambiguous before the evidence is adduced, not in order to create the ambiguity itself, and it may not be stretched so far that the words come to carry a meaning which they cannot bear.

By s 21 of the Administration of Justice Act 1982, direct and circumstantial extrinsic evidence is admissible where any part of a will is meaningless, consists of patently ambiguous language or is shown to be ambiguous in the light of surrounding circumstances other than evidence of the testator's intention.

If a beneficiary is left a gift by a testator who also purports to leave part of that beneficiary's property to another person, the doctrine of election says that the beneficiary may not keep both items.

Gifts are assumed to be as absolute as the testator's interest in them unless he provides otherwise in the will. The rule in *Lassence v Tierney* holds that a gift to a person as trustee becomes absolute if the trusts fail.

The meaning of certain relationships, especially those of children and parents, has changed considerably this century. A general gift to children will now include adopted, legitimated and illegitimate children, and many children born by artificial insemination by donor or by in vitro fertilisation, as well as legitimate children and children *en ventre sa mère*. The age of majority was changed by s 1 of the Family Law Reform Act 1969 to 18, so references to infants, minors or adults will be construed accordingly.

A will speaks from the date of death as to property, subject to contrary intention, in accordance with s 24 of the Wills Act 1837. However, it speaks from its own date as to beneficiaries, again subject to contrary intention.

A class gift is a gift to be shared out amongst a particular set of individuals, so that how much each receives depends on the number in the class. In order that the property in a class gift should not remain in trust indefinitely, there are rules for ascertaining when the class will close so that the trustees can be sure that no further members will materialise. This allows them to distribute the fund without fear of creating problems later although, where a life tenant disclaims, accelerated benefits may create such difficulties. The class-closing rules may be excluded by careful drafting.

CHAPTER 12

PERSONAL REPRESENTATIVES

12.1 What is a personal representative?

Personal representatives are the people who administer the estate left by the deceased. They are sometimes described as stepping into the deceased person's shoes; they stand in relation to the property in his estate very much as he did when he was still alive. Personal representatives may be either executors or administrators, depending on whether or not they are appointed by the testator's will, but all personal representatives have essentially the same duties. Those duties are aimed at dealing with everything in the testator's estate so as to wind it up with everyone concerned getting exactly what they should and nothing being left over. The duties involved in administering and winding up the estate are, in essence, to collect in the assets, pay the liabilities and, probably, then to distribute what remains. If there is property which then has to be retained on a continuing trust, the personal representatives should pass it to the trustees.

12.1.1 Duties of the personal representatives

More specifically, the personal representatives must first ascertain what the assets and liabilities of the estate are, calculate the Inheritance Tax payable and accordingly pay it and obtain any grant of probate or letters of administration. They must then collect in the assets and pay the debts and liabilities in the estate, and fulfil any gifts made by will. The tax position must be confirmed and the expenses of the administration paid, and then estate accounts prepared confirming all assets received and payments made and showing the balance due as residue. The residue will then be transferred to beneficiaries direct or to their trustees.

12.1.2 Executors or administrators?

In any properly drafted will, executors will be appointed to carry out the testator's wishes. The testator may thus choose whomever he likes to be the executors, and he may also make provision for the substitution of someone else of his choosing if his first choice is unavailable. A trust corporation, for example a bank, may be appointed executor. The executor will, almost always, deal with the estate as the result of the testator appointing him expressly and personally to do so, although in a few situations, considered below, an executor may be appointed by other means.

If there is no-one named as executor in the will who takes up the post (and none of the other, less usual, provisions applies) then the law provides who may deal with the estate. Such people, whose entitlement comes from general legal provisions rather than from those of a will, are called administrators. Executor and administrator are masculine terms: the feminines are executrix and administratrix (plurals: executrices and administratrices). Executors and administrators have the same essential duties, but there are some differences as to how they are carried out.

12.1.3 Specific differences – obtaining the power to deal with the estate

Executors obtain their power under the will. This means that, provided they are not disqualified as executors by reason of infancy, for example, or mental incapacity, the estate vests in them and they are entitled to deal with it as soon as the testator dies.

No-one is forced to act as an executor or administrator, but because the office of executor is thrust upon the relevant person automatically on the death of the testator, any executor who does not wish to take on that office must take the positive step of renouncing probate. Administrators, however, have no authority until a grant is made to them – in the meantime, the property vests in the Public Trustee. An executor may begin litigation relating to the estate at any time after death, but at the point where he needs to prove his title, he will have to produce a grant, since that is the means for doing so. An administrator, however, may not commence any action in his capacity as administrator until he has his grant of letters of administration. The administrator in *Mills v Anderson* (1984) settled a claim within court proceedings on behalf of the deceased's estate before obtaining his grant of letters of administration. The court held that the settlement was not binding because the administrator had no authority to make it.

12.2 Doctrine of relation back

By the doctrine of relation back, however, the letters of administration, once obtained, may in limited circumstances relate back to the death of the deceased. This doctrine enables an administrator to recover a loss to the deceased's estate from a wrongdoer who injured the estate in the time between the death and the grant of letters of administration. If there were no such provision, the administrator would be unable to bring the wrongdoer to account, since in general he can deal only with the estate after the date of the grant of representation to him. This doctrine does not enable an administrator to do anything before the grant, only to deal after the grant with certain matters which occurred before it.

12.3 What is a grant of representation?

A grant may be of probate, to an executor, or of letters of administration, to an administrator. (There are also variations on both themes, which are considered below.) The grant is confirmation of the executor's authority and title, and confers authority on the administrator. It is an officially sealed document obtained from a local Probate Registry, which is part of the Family Division of the High Court, in most cases without any need for anyone to attend the Registry or any court at all, since the paperwork is passed to a solicitor who will deal with the Registry in the post. A lay person has to attend in person, however. Where there is more than one lay executor, only one need attend.

Because a grant is needed to prove title in various circumstances, and it would be inconvenient and difficult to produce the original grant on every occasion when it is needed, the Probate Registry will for a small fee (25 p per copy) provide as many 'office copy' grants as are requested along with the original grant itself; these are sealed with the official seal and are used to prove title where necessary.

12.3.1 What if no-one takes out a grant?

The grant is issued to the personal representatives personally. If no-one takes out a grant, and any executor there may be renounces probate, any dealings with the estate must be dealt with through the Family Division. Proceedings can be issued against the estate by issuing a writ or originating summons against the estate and applying to the court under s 2 of the Proceedings Against Estates Act 1970 for an order appointing someone to represent the estate in the proceedings, possibly the Official Solicitor.

This situation must be distinguished from that where the deceased is only believed, not proven, to be dead; in that situation, it will be extremely difficult to have any dealings with the estate at all, at any rate until his death can be legally presumed from the passage of time or evidence of the circumstances of his disappearance. This could occur, for example, where a person on a walking holiday is believed to have been caught in an avalanche but his body has not been recovered. He is not considered legally dead, so there are no personal representatives to deal with his property. If there is really good reason to believe that he is dead, however, despite lack of the usual proof, an application for leave to swear death can be made under Non-Contentious Probate Rules (NCPR) 1987 r 53, supported by an affidavit including particulars of any life insurance policies (NCPR 1987 r 53) and any exhibits relevant to the cause of death.

During the period before a grant is taken out in relation to the deceased's estate, anyone interested in the estate may, however, apply to the Chancery Division of the High Court for the appointment of a receiver to protect the assets of the estate. The executor in *Re Sutcliffe* (1942) carried on the deceased's solicitor's practice for three years after his death; a creditor successfully applied to the court for the appointment of a receiver. Alternatively, the aggrieved person may be able to take out a grant (see 12.16).

12.3.2 Resealing

A so-called 'colonial grant' may be resealed, normally without leave, on the application of the person to whom the grant was made or on his written authorisation. The 'colonies' referred to include territories in, for example, Canada. The detailed rules are contained in the Colonial Probates Act 1892 as extended by the Colonial Probates (Protected State and Mandated Territories) Act 1927, and the territories to which these provisions apply are specified in the Colonial Probate Act Application Order 1965 (as amended).

12.4 Executors

Executors are those chosen by the testator to administer his will, though this general statement is subject to the qualifications set out below. They will usually be either family members, who perform the task for love and in the interests of seeing the estate properly administered, or professionals, such as a bank or other trust corporation, or a firm of solicitors, who will be paid for their work. Professional will-writers who are not practising solicitors are not currently authorised to administer estates, though they may (for a fee) advise lay executors as to the process for obtaining a grant and carrying out the administration without instructing (and paying) solicitors to deal with the work. It is, however, entirely proper for executors and administrators to instruct solicitors in this way and to pay them out of the estate. The only financial advantage to come to an executor personally from his office as such will be, exceptionally, if the rule in *Strong v Bird* (1874) can perfect a gift to him from the deceased (see 2.7.1), although the Law Commission has suggested a change to this in respect of implied charging clauses (see 5.17.1). There is no prohibition on executors taking gifts from the will and, indeed, beneficiaries may often be the most appropriate executors. This is reflected in NCPR r 20, where the next choice for personal representative after the executor appointed in the will is the residuary beneficiary.

Executors are usually appointed expressly, but may be appointed in other ways.

12.4.1 Failure of appointment of executors

If the will itself is valid, the failure of any appointment of executors in it – or the failure to make any such appointment – does not invalidate it. What it does is activate the provisions for authorising persons to act as administrators with the will annexed (see below); the will is annexed to the grant of letters of administration, and they must administer the estate in accordance with the terms of the will.

A failure to appoint executors who take a grant of probate does not render the estate intestate; that term refers to a failure to deal with property by will. An estate in which only some of the property is dealt with by will is said to be partially intestate, and the entitlement to the property in the estate will be the same whether the administration is carried out by executors or by administrators with the will annexed.

12.5 Express appointment

Express appointment occurs when the will contains a clause naming a particular person and stating that he is to be the executor. The reason for putting in the address and occupation of an executor is so they can be identified and found when the time comes; it is not a requirement of law but, as a practical act, is very sensible.

Express appointment enables the testator to appoint different executors for different parts of an estate or to deal with the estate only during a certain period. Obviously such provisions are very unusual where there is a small and ordinary estate. It may, however, be entirely appropriate to make such an appointment, especially where, for instance, an author wishes to appoint special people to deal with his literary works but a family member to deal with his ordinary family matters, or a parent wishes to leave all his property to his child, appointing executors to deal with the estate until the child attains his majority.

12.5.1 Number of executors

Although it may be usual to appoint two persons as executors and trustees, as a matter of law any number of executors may be appointed. Even where a trust arises, one executor alone may be appointed. Where there is a sole beneficiary of full age, for example, where the testator leaves all his property to his wife, it is most appropriate for that person to be the sole executor. Where many executors are appointed, however, probate will be granted to no more than four executors, in accordance with s 114(1) of the Supreme Court Act 1981. The executors will be chosen simply by reference to the first four named; probate will be granted to them with power reserved to the others, so that, for example, if the executors with the grant die, the others may more easily step in.

12.5.2 Conditional or substitutional appointment

The appointment of the executor may be conditional, but as always with anything in a will the condition should be clearly drafted. A condition may relate, for example, to the age of the executor; the appointment may be conditional on the executor having attained a certain age at the date of the testator's death.

A substitutional appointment may also be made, for example, where a particular person is appointed to the office of executor with a provision that another should take that office if the first one dies before the testator. Again, the drafting should be clear so that there is no doubt about the circumstances in which the substitution will operate. In this example, the substitutional executor would be appointed by the will only where the first died before the testator, so if the first one survived the testator by one day only, the appointment of the second would not be valid.

12.6 Implied appointment

Executors may also be appointed by implication of the wording of the will.

12.6.1 Meaning of 'executor according to the tenor'

An executor whose appointment is not express but implied is called an executor according to the tenor. The tenor means the general tone of the will or the way it reads. If the wording of the will implies clearly that its terms should be carried out by a particular person in accordance with the usual duties of a personal representative, but does not expressly appoint them as 'executor', they may be held to be an executor according to the tenor. In a professionally drafted will, an executor will always be expressly and unambiguously appointed; an appointment which is less clear can lead to queries from the Probate Registry, if not litigation, and thus obviously to delay and expense.

It is not the case that if a testator leaves all his property to one person, that person is impliedly the executor. It was confirmed in *Re Pryse* (1904) that a person who is the sole beneficiary, or the residuary beneficiary, will not be the implied executor for that reason. There must be something in the will which implies that the testator wanted the implied executor to carry out the terms of the will in an administrative capacity. Thus, it is possible for there to be an executor according to the tenor who has to deal with the estate and pass all the benefit under the testator's will to another person, without retaining anything for himself.

12.6.2 Examples of executors according to the tenor

The will must show the expectation that the person impliedly appointed will fulfil the essential duties of an executor. It was held in *In the Goods of Adamson* (1875) that the essential duties of an executor are to collect the assets of the deceased, to pay his funeral expenses and debts, to discharge the legacies and other gifts made by the will and to account for the residuary estate.

A particular example of what constitutes appointing a person to carry out these duties without quite expressly appointing them executor is the testatrix statement in *In the Goods of Cook* (1902) that she desired John Goodrick to pay all her just debts. Where the testator in *In the Estate of Fawcett* (1941) said: 'All else to be sold and proceeds after debts, etc, Barclays Bank will do this, to Emily Thompson', this was held impliedly to mean the bank was executor according to the tenor (though the action was essentially compromised and the bank renounced on the basis that Emily Thompson would take the grant instead).

Although it may be usual for a testator making express appointments to appoint the same persons as executors and trustees, this is not compulsory, and a person appointed as trustee by the will is not the executor solely for that reason. Where the testator in *In the Goods of Punchard* (1872) said: 'I wish PA Collins to act as trustee to this estate', it was held that Mr Collins was not the executor according to the tenor. This was because he was not required by the wording of the will to perform the essential functions of an executor, namely to pay debts or take on the general administration of the estate.

12.7   Settled land executors

Particular provisions apply to land settled under the Settled Land Act (SLA) 1925 which remains settled after the death of a tenant for life. Note that, following the implementation of the Trusts of Land and Appointment of Trustees Act 1996, although no new strict settlements can be created after 1996, all strict settlements already created before that date (including settlements created by will where the testator died before the end of 1996) remain valid by virtue of s 2 of the 1996 Act until they come to an end.

12.7.1   Appointment of settled land trustees – s 22 of the AEA 1925

It is unusual to see land settled under the Settled Land Act 1925 in practice, and therefore unusual to see settled land executors. However, where they are found, they are governed by special provisions under s 22 of the Administration of Estates Act (EAE) 1925. This states that a testator may appoint the Settled Land Act trustees as his special executors in regard to the settled land. If he does not appoint them expressly, then the section deems them to be appointed. This is the only statutory provision dealing with the deeming of an appointment as executor. Probate may be granted to such trustees specially limited to the settled land and the grant to the executors of the rest of the estate will specifically except the settled land.

What this means is that if the testator is entitled to settled land during his lifetime, and on his death the settlement continues, the law will appoint the trustees of the settlement to deal with the passing of that entitlement to the next person entitled under the trust, if he does not appoint them himself. This does not affect the appointment of executors for the rest of the testator's estate.

12.7.2 Where there are no settled land trustees – s 30 of the SLA 1925

If, however, the land is settled by will without the testator appointing settled land trustees, then s 30 of the Settled Land Act 1925 comes into operation. It is unusual to see a settlement under the Settled Land Act made deliberately. However, under the system of land trusts operating before the implementation of the Trusts of Land and Appointment of Trustees Act 1996, there were two separate ways, each with a different machinery, to create successive interests in land, which must subsist in equity, behind a trust, because they cannot exist at law (see s 1 of the Law of Property Act (LPA) 1925). There would be a strict settlement wherever no trust for sale could be found; trusts for sale were implied by statute in cases of co-ownership but otherwise had to be express. Thus, where a testator left a life interest without expressly creating a trust for sale, a strict settlement would arise. This might be seen in, for example, a home-made will by which the testator left his property to his wife for her lifetime and thereafter to their children. The interaction of the accidental creation of strict settlements and their possibly somewhat unexpected consequences, especially the provision that a Tenant For Life under a strict settlement has the power to sell the property regardless of a settlor's attempts to fetter such a power, was one of the reasons for the passing of the 1996 Act.

Where a pre-1997 strict settlement is found to have been created by will, s 30(3) of the Settled Land Act provides that the personal representatives of the deceased settlor are deemed to be trustees of the settlement until other trustees are appointed. This would mean that if the settlement arose under the terms of the testator's will, his personal representatives would become the settled land trustees and would continue to be those trustees even after the completion of the administration of the estate. On the subsequent death of the tenant for life, they would be his settled land executors.

12.7.3 Additional or special settled land executors

The trustees of a settlement under the Settled Land Act or any beneficiary of it may apply to the court for the appointment of an additional or special settled land executor.

12.8 Executors appointed under a power in the will

It is unusual for executors to be appointed under a power in the will. The situation arises where the testator nominates, by his will, another person to make the appointment to the office of executor. The testator may specify the group of persons from whom the appointees are to be chosen or may specify persons who may not be appointed under the power, or he may leave the choice completely open to the nominated person. In the absence of any contrary provision by the testator, the nominated person may appoint himself.

The testator may thus delegate the power to appoint executors. What the testator may not do is delegate the power to make the will itself. (If he tries to do this, the document he makes and by which he purports to give that power will not itself be a will: see the subject of delegation of testamentary powers at 3.6.)

12.9 Executors appointed by the court

The court has power to appoint executors in certain circumstances. This is very unusual, save perhaps in the case of a minority or life interest where there is only one personal representative to deal with the trust which then arises. The court's powers may arise in three alternative situations:

(a) where there is a minority or life interest;

(b) where a personal representative or beneficiary applies to the court for the appointment of a substituted personal representative; or

(c) where the trustees or a beneficiary of settled land apply to the court for the appointment of additional or special settled land executors.

12.9.1 Minority or life interest

Where a minority or life interest arises, and there is only one personal representative to deal with the trust, the court may appoint one or more further personal representatives to act with that person. This does not apply, however, if the lone personal representative is a trust corporation, for example, a bank. The application to the court can be made by any person interested (in the technical sense of having an interest such as a life interest in the estate) or their guardian or receiver.

12.9.2 Substituted personal representative

Anyone who is a personal representative or a beneficiary may apply to the court for an order appointing a substituted personal representative. The court's powers under s 50 of the Administration of Justice Act 1985 are wide. The substituted personal representative may be appointed to act with the existing representatives or instead of any or all of them. He will be an executor if acting with any other executor. Otherwise, if acting alone or with administrators, he will be an administrator.

12.10 Executor by representation – s 7 of the AEA 1925

An executor may obtain his power by virtue of the operation of the important provisions of s 7 of the Administration of Estates Act 1925. These provisions are usually called the 'chain of representation'. If there is more than one executor, then in the event of any of them dying, the other(s) will carry on. However, when the last one dies having already taken probate, then any executor of his will also be the executor of the first testator, provided he obtains probate of the second testator's will. That second executor cannot take on the office of the first executor's executor without also taking on the office of the original testator's personal representative, so if he does not want to deal with either, he must renounce both.

12.10.1 Chain of representation

This is how the 'chain of representation' works:

(a) T is the testator;

(b) X takes probate of T's will;

(c) X is T's last or sole executor;

(d) X dies without fully administering T's estate;

(e) Y obtains probate of X's will;

(f) Y is T's executor by representation.

All the conditions mentioned above must be fulfilled for the chain to function. If T or X fails to appoint an executor (for instance if either is intestate and for that reason has an administrator instead) or X or Y fails to take out probate, the chain will not operate. If the chain operates, Y becomes the executor by representation of T.

12.10.2 Recommendation for change

The Law Reform Committee in its 23rd Report *The Powers and Duties of Trustees* (1982) found the results of the operation of the chain of representation 'often unsatisfactory'. In particular, it was unhappy that a person could find himself unable to get rid of the obligation to administer an estate with which he had no real connection without renouncing the estate for which he was really appointed as well. They recommended that the retirement of personal representatives should generally be allowed more easily than at present, and that the case of an executorship acquired through these rules was a good example of a situation where, provided there had been no intermeddling, such retirement should be allowed.

12.11 Executors *de son tort*

'Executors *de son tort*' are not, in general, executors or personal representatives as such. They are persons who have intermeddled with the estate – dealt with it without authority – and who have thus incurred the liability to be treated as though they were personal representatives and to be held responsible to creditors in particular, especially the Inland Revenue, in respect of whatever they have intermeddled with.

12.11.1 Acts which do not make a person an executor *de son tort*

A person does not become an executor *de son tort* by carrying out acts of common humanity which are not connected with the essential functions of a personal representative. The distinction between acts which make a person an executor *de son tort* and those which do not is one of the nature of the acts, not their objective financial significance. Arranging for a funeral, for example, will not make a person executor *de son tort*, as was established in *Harrison v Rowley* (1798). Collecting assets and paying debts, as in *Re Stevens* (1898), will, however, render a person an executor *de son tort*, because those are the essential functions of an executor.

12.11.2 The personal representative as executor *de son tort*

Occasionally, a personal representative who acts wrongly is referred to as an executor *de son tort*. If a person entitled to a grant acts prior to the grant, he can be cited to take a grant; this applies equally to an executor appointed by will, who takes his power from the will, though he can only prove his title to the property in the estate by means of a grant of probate. If the executor acts as such without taking out the grant, he may also be called an executor *de son tort*. Although the word tort has to do with wrongdoing, the executor *de son tort* need not necessarily have committed any acts wrong in themselves, and if subsequently he takes out the grant of probate, an executor who has intermeddled as an executor *de son tort* will become an executor in the same way as if he had never been an executor *de son tort*. The same applies to an administrator who acts without authority before the grant but subsequently takes out a grant of letters of administration.

12.11.3 Executor *de son tort* who is entitled to a grant

The significance of a person intermeddling with an estate and becoming an executor *de son tort* depends on whether they are a person entitled to a grant to the estate or not. If they are, they can be cited to take a grant because the acts which made them an executor *de son tort* will constitute acceptance of the office of executor or administrator. This was the case with Mr Glew, the husband of the married couple appointed executors in the case of *In the Estate of Biggs* (1966). They were elderly persons in poor health. They both absolutely refused to take out a grant even though the husband had not only intermeddled with the estate but had also been specifically ordered by the court to take probate. The court could have imprisoned him for his disobedience of its order, but it was unwilling to do so – it appeared he would prefer going to prison to taking probate. (The court found another solution, considered below at 12.12.1.)

12.11.4 Executor *de son tort* who is not entitled to a grant

If the intermeddler is not entitled to a grant, then, as was confirmed in *Re Davis* (1860), he cannot be compelled to take one out. The true personal representatives will be bound by his acts only if they involve his having paid over money or assets to a person who reasonably believes he had authority to act as personal representative, or if what he has done is something the personal representatives were bound to do anyway.

12.11.5 Liability of an executor *de son tort* – Inheritance Tax

The liability of the executor *de son tort* to account to beneficiaries and creditors of the estate as though he were an executor or administrator includes a liability as to the payment of Inheritance Tax, pursuant to ss 199 and 200 of the Inheritance Tax Act 1984, on anything with which he has intermeddled. Cases involving the Inland Revenue provide a fruitful source of examples of executors *de son tort*, because companies can become executors *de son tort* by dealing with the deceased's shareholdings. They can then be fixed with the obligation to pay the tax on the deceased's estate and comparatively easily located in order to oblige payment. It is stated in s 55(1)(ix) of the Administration of Estates Act 1925 that so far as liability to pay Estate Duty (now Inheritance Tax) is concerned, the term 'personal representatives' includes executors *de son tort*. They are helpfully defined in that subsection as persons who take possession of or intermeddle with the deceased's property without the authority of the personal representatives or of the court. It is the liability for tax which is often the cause of greatest concern to a person who finds himself executor *de son tort*.

In *New York Breweries Co Ltd v Attorney General* (1899), the English company which registered the transfer of shares from the name of the deceased to his American executors was held to have made itself executor *de son tort* by doing so, and was therefore liable to pay the Estate Duty on the English estate of the deceased, who had died domiciled in America.

12.11.6 Extent of other liabilities of an executor *de son tort*

The executor *de son tort* does not have the personal representative's duty to get in and collect, and account for, all the assets of the estate. He is liable to account only for those items with which he deals. If they are used to discharge liabilities in the same way that a personal representative should have done, the executor *de son tort* will be given credit for such payments by virtue of s 28 of the Administration of Estates Act 1925. Therefore, if he discharges only debts which would have been discharged anyway, or otherwise gives the property where it should properly have been given, he will not incur any further liability. If he himself was a creditor of the estate, he may keep anything properly obtained by him in satisfaction of a contractual debt to him. This must be proper, however; if he has paid himself out of turn and deprived a person with a prior claim of their rightful entitlement, he will be liable. He may also keep any expenses a personal representative could lawfully keep, such as the deceased's funeral expenses if he has paid them.

12.12 Who may be an executor

A testator may appoint anyone he wishes as executor. Any person or trust corporation may be appointed. Whether and when they can act as such will, however, depend on the circumstances. A minor or a mentally incapacitated person may not act as an executor; if a minor is appointed, he can take probate at 18 but not before.

12.12.1 Who may be granted probate or letters of administration

Probate may be granted to a sole executor, or to any number as appointed, up to a maximum of four for any part of the estate. Two is the usual number for which a will drafter strives, save where there is a sole adult beneficiary who is also the executor. A court may pass over an executor 'by reason of any special circumstances', by virtue of its power under s 116 of the Supreme Court Act 1981. The executrix whose appointment was considered in *In the Estate of S* (1968) was serving a sentence of life imprisonment for the manslaughter of the testator, which the court felt made it quite impossible for her to act as executrix. Both of the two executors appointed by the testator in *In the Estate of Biggs* (1966) (above) refused to take probate, even though the husband had been cited to take out a grant. The court declined to use its powers to imprison an elderly man in poor health, who appeared more willing to go to prison than to comply with the court's order. There was also the thought that even had either or both of the couple taken probate, they would have done so under protest and probably carried on causing difficulties. The court used its powers under s 116 and appointed an administratrix with the will annexed instead.

12.12.2 Appointing a firm of solicitors – the Horgan clause

It is fairly common for a firm of solicitors to be appointed to the office of executor, usually by a clause appointing the partners in the specified firm, or its successor, at the date of the testator's death, as its executors. The testator may express the desire that a specific person act if he is available, or that only two partners act in the proving of the will, but such provisions will be precatory only (expressing an unenforceable wish). It was confirmed in *Re Horgan* (1971) that the appointment of a firm of solicitors in this way will be valid and a clause which appoints a firm of solicitors is usually called a 'Horgan clause'. The usual formulation is to appoint the firm and to request that a particular person acts.

12.12.3 Appointing solicitors rather than lay persons

Most lay executors pass the administration of the estate to solicitors for them to deal with; such expenses of the administration as payment of the solicitors' fees come out of the estate, not the executors' own pockets. If the executor is a lay person, they will not be able to obtain a grant through the post but will have to attend the probate registry personally; many people do not have the time or inclination to do this and prefer to have solicitors deal with the estate anyway. Appointing solicitors as executors in the will effectively enables the testator to choose which firm is appointed. However, the solicitors will not be entitled to charge for their services unless a clause allowing them to do so is included in the will, because of the general rule that executors and trustees may not be paid for fulfilling the functions of their office unless specifically authorised (see, also, 5.17.1 and 10.8.3 above). Note that even if they are authorised to charge for their professional services, that will not cover charging for services which are not professional (*Re Chapple, Newton v Chapman* (1884)), unless the charging clause will also cover non-professional services. If the charging clause is left out, it is rather likely the solicitors will renounce probate. If a trust corporation such as a bank is appointed, again that appointment must be made on the terms and conditions of that trust corporation, or it will renounce.

12.13 Renouncing probate

Anyone appointed executor may accept or renounce probate before acting without giving any reason. This also applies to those deemed to have been appointed as special executors in relation to settled land. However, renunciation is a positive step and will not happen simply by the executor doing nothing. There are precedents to be found in the appropriate practice books for forms by which to renounce. The renunciation takes effect once the signed form is filed with the probate registry. Partial renunciation is not possible. Where an executor Y by taking out probate of the will of X becomes the executor by representation of T, under s 7 of the Administration of Estates Act 1925, he may not renounce the executorship of T's will without renouncing that of X as well. Having renounced probate, an executor may retract his renunciation only with the leave of the court, which will be given only if the court thinks it in the interests of the estate. Having been wrongly advised and therefore renounced will not entitle an executor to retract his renunciation (*In the Goods of Gill* (1873)).

12.14 Citation

If the executor neither accepts nor renounces probate, the court may issue a citation summoning the executor to make a formal decision one way or the other. Obviously, the court will not do, or be able to do, this automatically. There is no central authority overseeing the day-to-day administration of estates. Anyone who would, if the executor renounced, be entitled to letters of administration, may apply to the court for a citation to be issued.

12.14.1 If the executor intermeddles

Acceptance can be constituted not only by taking out probate but also by intermeddling, as in *In the Estate of Biggs* (1966) above. Any executor who has intermeddled but does not then take out a grant of probate may be cited by anyone interested in the estate, who may alternatively ask for that executor to be passed over so that the grant may be issued to someone else.

12.14.2 Failure to take out grant causing loss

If something is lost to the estate through the failure of an executor to take out probate, the decision in *Re Stevens* (1898) shows that the beneficiary cannot claim against him for that reason.

12.15 Administrators

The term 'administrator' applies to a personal representative appointed not by the testator but by virtue of the provisions in the Non-Contentious Probate Rules 1987, which are made under s 127 of the Supreme Court Act 1981. Administrators take a grant of letters of administration rather than of probate. Obviously, if there is no will, no executor will have been appointed, but administrators are also appointed where there is a will but it does not name anyone who can or will act as executor. Such a person must, nevertheless, administer the estate in accordance with the terms of the will, and they will be granted letters of administration with the will annexed – the grant will have the will attached to it. There is no obligation on anyone to be an administrator if they do not wish to do so.

12.16 Order of priority where there is a will – NCPR r 20

The order of those who may take a grant where there is a will is regulated by r 20 of the Non-Contentious Probate Rules; the first is the executor, but the rest of the rule applies equally even if no executor was ever appointed. This list follows a pattern based on the entitlement to property in the estate.

The provisions of r 20 as to the order of priority of entitlement to a grant where there is a will are as follows:

(a) the executor;

(b) any residuary legatee or devisee holding in trust for any other person;

(c) any other residuary legatee or devisee (including one for life) or where the residue is not wholly disposed of by the will, any person entitled to share in the undisposed of residue under the intestacy rules;

(d) the personal representative of any residuary legatee or devisee (but not one for life, or one holding in trust for any other person), or of any person entitled to share in any residue not disposed of by the will;

(e) any other legatee or devisee (including one for life or one holding in trust for any other person) or any creditor of the deceased;

(f) the personal representative of any other legatee or devisee (but not one for life or one holding in trust for any other person) or of any creditor of the deceased.

12.16.1 Operation of NCPR r 20

After the executor himself, the person most nearly carrying out his functions is a trustee of the residuary estate; such a person is accordingly the next in line to take out a grant where no executor is available. If there is no trust of residue, then the person who takes residue himself has the closest function to that of executor and is accordingly the most appropriate person to deal with the estate as a whole.

12.16.2 Resolving a dispute as to who will take a grant

If persons entitled in the same degree cannot decide who should take the grant, the court may decide. The general rule according to which it will make its decision is that the best person to deal with the claims of the beneficiaries and creditors will take the grant, although in practice this means proving that another potential applicant is not of the right character to take the grant.

If there is a dispute as to who of the persons entitled in the same class should take a grant, the court will in appropriate cases apply r 27(5) NCPR. This states that a grant should go to a living person in preference to the personal representative a deceased person, and to a person of full age in preference to guardian of a minor.

12.17 Order of priority where there is no will – NCPR r 22

There is a very different rule of entitlement where there is no will at all and the deceased died wholly intestate. The structure of the provisions of r 22 is based on family relationships. Entitlement to a grant under this rule also depends on a beneficial entitlement to property under the intestacy rules, which, again, are based on the same family relationships. The rules of entitlement to a grant of letters of administration on intestacy are as follows:

(a) Provided they have a beneficial interest under the intestacy rules:

- the surviving husband or wife;

- the children of the deceased and the issue of any deceased child who died before the deceased;

- the father and mother of the deceased;

- brothers and sisters of the whole blood and the issue of any deceased brother or sister of the whole blood who died before the deceased;

- brothers and sisters of the half blood and the issue of any deceased brother or sister of the half blood who died before the deceased;

- grandparents;

- uncles and aunts of the whole blood and the issue of any deceased uncle or aunt of the whole blood who died before the deceased;

- uncles and aunts of the half blood and the issue of any deceased uncle or aunt of the half blood who died before the deceased.

(b) In default of any person having a beneficial interest in the estate, the Treasury Solicitor (or solicitor for the Duchies of Lancaster or Cornwall, depending on the residence of the deceased) if he claims *bona vacantia* on behalf of the Crown.

(c) If all prior persons entitled to a grant have been cleared off, a creditor of the deceased, or the personal representative of such creditor, or any person who may have a beneficial interest in the event of an accretion to the estate.

Again, if persons entitled in the same degree cannot decide who shall take a grant, the court may decide.

12.18 Clearing off

Where a person wishes to apply for a grant but they do not come at the top of the list of those entitled to one, they must establish that those with a prior entitlement to the grant can be passed over. Clearing off is the process of getting rid of someone with prior entitlement. Thus, anyone applying for a grant of administration in relation to the estate of an intestate ('simple' administration) must establish that everyone entitled with priority has either renounced his right to administration or has been cited to accept or refuse a grant of administration.

12.19 Grants of representation

Grants are the form of court order issued to personal representatives giving them authority to deal with an estate. They are technically court orders, but acquiring a grant does not usually involve attending any court and nor does it usually involve anyone exercising any judicial function. If every grant had to be ordered by even a junior form of judge, there would need to be a huge number of courts of probate sitting many hours each week. In practice almost all applications for grants are dealt with not judicially but, in reality, administratively, by clerks. They will deal with all non-contentious or 'common form' business, as defined in s 128 of the Supreme Court Act 1981, which is dealt with by the Family Division of the High Court in the form usually of the local District Probate Registry of the executors' solicitors. Contentious, or 'solemn form' business is generally assigned to the Chancery Division, to be begun by writ, though actions over smaller estates may be brought in the county court.

12.19.1 Need for a grant – Administration of Estates (Small Payments) Act 1965

With respect to certain funds in an estate, it may not be necessary to obtain a grant before being able to use them. The Administration of Estates (Small Payments) Act 1965 provides a list of assets, including National Savings, building society accounts and arrears of salary or superannuation benefits due to state employees, which may be paid over without the need to produce a grant. The limit is £5,000. The fact that the authority concerned has power to make such payments does not, however, mean that it can be compelled to do so, and it may have its own particular regulations about when it will make payment. In some estates, the only substantive assets may be covered by these provisions.

12.19.2 What is admissible to probate

A will is admissible to probate if it appoints executors, even if they renounce, or if it contains a disposition of property within the jurisdiction. Thus a will which only appoints a guardian for a child or only revokes a previous will without making further dispositions is not admissible to proof unless the court exercises its discretion. It must be remembered, however, that in every case it is necessary for the will to satisfy all the criteria for validity, both as to the state of mind of the testator when he made the will and (save in the case of a privileged will) as to compliance with the formalities in the Wills Act 1837.

The court's powers of discretion are wide, and they will be exercised if the court sees fit. Although in theory the court has no jurisdiction at all over property outside England and Wales, it may issue a grant in respect of a will dealing exclusively with such property, though the application for the grant must include a recital of the reason for seeking a grant in such circumstances. In *Re Wayland* (1951), the court admitted to probate a will which dealt exclusively with property outside the jurisdiction, namely the deceased's Belgian will, in order to clarify the effect of a revocation clause in the deceased's English will (see 7.4.3 above).

12.20 Obtaining a grant

The application for a grant may be made to the Principal Registry of the Family Division, which is at Somerset House in the Strand in London, or to a local District Probate Registry. No grant may be issued within seven days of death where there is a will, or 14 days in the case of administration on intestacy (NCPR 1987 r 6).

12.20.1 Papers to be submitted

The registrar may require any papers he thinks necessary, but it will usually be clear to a solicitor dealing with an estate what papers are needed in any particular case. The usual papers are the oath form – an affidavit sworn, or affirmation made, by the proposed personal representatives confirming that they are entitled to a grant and will duly administer the estate –, any wills or codicils, which should be duly referred to in the affidavit, and affidavits or affirmations giving evidence as necessary on any extra points. Note that it is not necessary to send the death certificate; the evidence of the person applying to take the grant that the deceased is dead is sufficient. If any documents are difficult to settle (draft) then they may be submitted to the Probate Registry for settling at a fee of £5 per document; the settled draft should then be submitted with the papers on the application for a grant.

12.20.2 Contents of the oath form

The oath form deals with the details of the deceased and of his death, and the details of the person applying for a grant. It asks them to explain what their entitlement to the grant is – for example, that they are the executor appointed by the will or the surviving spouse of the intestate, and to swear (or affirm) that they will duly administer the estate according to law.

12.20.3 Personal representatives liable for Inheritance Tax (IHT)

The personal representatives are liable under s 200(1) of the Inheritance Tax Act (IHTA) 1984 for the IHT payable on:

(a) any property which was not immediately before the deceased's death comprised in a settlement; and

(b) any land in the UK which immediately before the deceased's death was comprised in a settlement and which devolves upon or vests in the personal representatives.

However, the personal representative is only liable for tax to the extent he receives (or should have received but for his own neglect or default) the property as personal representative (s 204(1)).

12.20.4 No grant until IHT paid

No grant of probate or administration will be issued unless the Probate Registry is satisfied that any Inheritance Tax due on the estate has been paid. There are obvious administrative advantages in not enabling anyone to get their hands on the estate until after the Inland Revenue has been satisfied; it could be considerably more awkward to enforce payment later. Thus, although the probate forms for a small estate may be very simple, for a substantial estate, even where the dispositions are simple, considerable paperwork may be required with respect to tax. The prescribed forms of oath contain a specific reference to tax and current commercially-available pre-printed oath forms also give the relevant figures in their marginal notes.

12.20.5 Thresholds for IHT paperwork

The tax paperwork will differ depending on the amount in the estate. If the personal representatives swear in the application for the grant that the estate is worth less than £180,000, the estate will be an 'excepted estate'. No tax will be payable and no account need be submitted to the Inland Revenue. If the estate is worth more than the present £180,000 limit for excepted estates, but less than the current IHT threshold (at present £223,000), a short account in Form 202 is usually the appropriate form to be submitted with the application for a grant. It requires not only that no IHT should be payable but also that the deceased should have been domiciled in the UK, all the estate should be situated in the UK and should not include any interest in settled property, that there should be no Potentially Exempt Transfers to be taken into account and that the gross estate before exemptions and reliefs should not be twice the current IHT threshold. On Form 202, the personal representatives set out what is in the estate and how it has been valued so it can be confirmed that no IHT is payable. If IHT is payable, a full Inland Revenue Account (IRA) in Form 200 must be submitted, the tax paid and the account duly receipted by the Inland Revenue, in order for the application for the grant of probate or administration to proceed.

12.20.6 Paying the IHT

The personal representatives must deliver any Inland Revenue account within 12 months from the end of the month of death, or, if later, three months from the date when they first acted. Interest is payable on tax unpaid after six months from the end of the month of death; thus, to avoid paying interest, the personal representative have to have submitted the account and paid the tax by then.

There is clear potential for a practical difficulty here. One of the purposes for which the property in the estate may be needed is for the payment of the IHT on the estate, but the tax has to be paid before the property can be obtained and used for any purpose. One solution to this paradoxical situation which is often adopted is for the personal representatives to pay the IHT by means of a loan to the estate from a beneficiary who stands to gain from the estate and has some cash available. The consequent speeding-up of the probate process is a considerable encouragement to such a beneficiary. Alternatively, a commercial loan may be sought from a bank, since an estate which has enough in it to require the payment of IHT will be sufficient to service and repay a commercial loan.

12.20.7 Common minor problems in seeking probate

The fact that there are problems with some particular aspect of the application for the grant will not necessarily lead to a court hearing. It is comparatively common for a will to be found in a poor state and for an 'affidavit of plight and condition' to be submitted with the application for probate to explain how this came about, avoiding any need to investigate questions of destruction, for example. Affidavits are also fairly frequently required where the testator has attached something to the will, for example, a note to his solicitor confirming that he has obeyed all instructions (including the one not to attach anything to the will). Otherwise the Probate Registry may raise queries about what the document was and why it was attached.

12.20.8 Obtaining letters of administration

The process of obtaining letters of administration is broadly similar to that of obtaining probate. Where there is a will to be annexed to the grant, whether or not it covers all the property in the estate, it will be referred to on the oath form; where the deceased died wholly intestate, that fact will be referred to. The applicant for the grant will have to recite their entitlement to the grant by reference to r 22, rather than r 20, of the NCPR in the case of total intestacy.

12.21 Caveats – NCPR r 44

The entering of a caveat will prevent the sealing of a grant until the caveator's objections have been dealt with. The caveat is a notice as specified by r 44 of the Non-Contentious Probate Rules 1987 sent to the Family Division of the High Court; the applicant for the grant will be told about it and may then issue a warning to the caveator, who should then state his contrary interest to that of the applicant, or else issue a summons for directions if he has no such contrary interest. Otherwise, the caveat expires after six months if it is not extended.

12.22 Omissions from probate

There may be some reason why even a will, or part of a will, which has been properly executed and is otherwise valid will not be admitted to probate. This will apply where there is fraud or forgery, or where the testator did not know and approve of the will or part omitted. The relevant parts will not be included in the probate because the testator did not fulfil the necessary conditions as to state of mind and *animus testandi* (intention to make a will) in relation to those parts of the will.

It is not permissible for documents which are valid to be omitted from probate even by the agreement of all the beneficiaries. If the beneficiaries agree to vary the provisions of the will, they should negotiate from the starting point of the gifts in the will; the agreed variation can then be effected, formally, once the will has been proved. A variation or disclaimer can then be read back into the will for tax purposes (see 10.5 above and 14.20 below). Even where a document's validity is doubtful and it is agreed by all parties that it is not valid, it should be propounded by the executor. This was held by the court in *Re Watts* (1837), where the testator was a proven lunatic; the court nevertheless refused to grant letters of administration on the basis of the agreement of almost all the persons involved that the will should be ignored.

12.23 Revocation of grants

The court has power not only to make but also to revoke grants, although the particular circumstances in which a grant may be revoked are not specified by statute. The power to revoke grants is contained in s 121 of the Supreme Court Act 1981. A grant may be revoked for various reasons, but it will usually be either because it was wrongly made in the first place or because of subsequent events.

12.23.1 Grant wrongly made

Where the grant is wrongly made, then this has usually been caused by the applicant for the grant having made a false statement. That may, however, have been inadvertent.

12.23.2 Wrong statements by applicants

The deceased may prove not to have been dead after all. The application for revocation of the grant in the case of *In the Goods of Napier* (1809) was made to the court by the 'deceased' who had not, after all, died on the field of battle. He had been left there for dead by his fellow-soldiers and the applicant for the original grant had been quite unaware that he was still alive.

The applicant may have made some false claim as to their relationship to the deceased, so that once the truth was known it was apparent that the grant should not have been made to that person. The applicant in *In the Goods of Moore* (1845) claimed to be the widow of the deceased, but it turned out that she had not actually been married to him. The grant to the deceased's relative in *Re Bergman's Goods* (1842) was revoked when it was discovered that he was illegitimate and therefore not entitled to the grant for that reason; the law today in respect of illegitimacy is different.

12.23.3 Contravention of procedure

Grants have been revoked where a caveator was not given notice before the making of the grant, as in *Trimlestown v Trimlestown* (1830), and where persons entitled in priority to the grantee were not cited and cleared-off before the grant was made, in *Ravenscroft v Ravenscroft* (1671).

12.23.4 Other matters discovered later

It may become clear after a grant has been made that it should not have been because the will of which probate was granted, for example, later turns out not to have been valid. A will may be found after a grant of letters of administration has been made, or a later will found after a grant of probate. A codicil may be found appointing different executors, or the grantee may turn out to be an infant. It may also transpire that the deceased had remarried after making the will which was proved, so that it was revoked, as occurred in *Priestman v Thomas* (1884).

12.23.5 Subsequent events

Where a grantee becomes incapable and there are other grantees, the original grant will be revoked and a fresh grant made to the other(s). If, however, there are no other grantees, the grant will not be revoked; rather a grant of letters of administration *de bonis non* (see below) for the use and benefit of the grantee will be made. This occurred, for example, in the case of *In the Goods of Galbraith* (1951), where, six years after the original grant to two executors, both were too physically and mentally infirm to act. The court made a grant *de bonis non* with the will annexed. A grantee who wishes to be relieved of his duties may ask the court to revoke the grant to him, but he will have to have some very good reason. Advanced age and ill health might, again, be such a reason – see the removal and retirement of personal representatives at 12.31 below.

The court may revoke a grant where it becomes apparent that the grantee will not carry out the administration properly. Where the grantee disappears before administration is completed, the court may decide to make a fresh grant on the grounds that the first one has turned out to be 'abortive or inefficient', as occurred in the case of *In the Goods of Loveday* (1900). In that case, the deceased's widow obtained a grant of letters of administration and later disappeared without carrying out the administration of the estate.

A grant may be revoked because the grantee has committed a breach of duty. Not every breach will be considered serious enough to warrant revocation, however, and the standard of breach required may appear quite high. In *In the Estate of Cope* (1954), the administrators of the estate submitted estate duty accounts which turned out to be inaccurate in that certain assets were omitted and a disputed debt (owed by the deceased to one of the administrators) was included. The court thought there might be a case for ordering the administrators to account to the court for their administration but did not think the breach warranted revocation of the grant.

In *Re Flynn* (1982), however, the estate had appeared insolvent until further property fell into it. The court refused to strike out an action to revoke the grant on the basis of delay, as the delay was not unreasonable in the light of the previous apparent futility of such an application. It appeared, however, that the court would be unwilling to strike out any such action before a hearing save if it were frivolous, vexatious or otherwise an abuse of the process of the court.

12.24 Powers of amendment

The court also has power to amend a grant under r 41 of the Non-Contentious Probate Rules. This applies only where the amendment is not of any great substance.

12.24.1 Will proved in solemn form

Most wills are proved in common form. There are no court proceedings in the sense that is usually meant, but an application on paper to the Probate Registry for a grant, supported by affidavits as necessary. Where, however, there is a major dispute (the entering of a caveat or the issuing of a citation does not of itself take the matter out of the realm of 'non-contentious' business) about the validity of a will, there may be court proceedings in which the court makes a final order as to the validity of the will. This then becomes *res judicata* (a matter about which the court has adjudicated) and that question cannot be reopened save in exceptional circumstances, for example, the finding of a later will or proof of fraud. In *Re Barraclough* (1965), for instance, there was a claim that the deceased had lacked testamentary capacity; the plaintiff, on losing her legal aid certificate, compromised the claim and was later prevented by the *res judicata* rule from re-opening the question in further court proceedings.

12.25 Effect of revocation

Clearly where someone's authority to deal with an estate is revoked, that could have serious and far-reaching consequences. There is a set of rules protecting persons who have dealt with a personal representative whose authority to deal with the property in the deceased's estate is later revoked.

12.25.1 Protection for persons who have dealt with former personal representatives

A person who has purchased property from the former personal representative is protected by various statutory provisions, in particular s 204(1) of the Law of Property Act 1925 and s 37 of the Administration of Estates Act 1925.

12.25.2 Revoked court orders – s 204(1) of the LPA 1925

A purchaser will be protected by the provisions of s 204(1) of the Law of Property Act 1925, which states that any person acting under a court order whilst that order is in force will be specifically protected if the order is subsequently revoked because of some irregularity. A grant is technically a court order. The section further states that its protection operates even for a person who was aware of the irregularity or impropriety. In *Re Bridgett & Hayes' Contract* (1928), land was settled on Emily Bridgett for life and after her death on trust for sale. She died in 1926, the estate being vested in her as tenant for life. John Jackson was the sole trustee of the settlement. Emily's executor, Thomas Bridgett, contracted to sell the land to a purchaser, who objected to his title on the ground that the legal estate was vested in Mr Jackson as Emily's special executor (see settled land executors above). The court held Thomas Bridgett could make a good title, because the settlement ended at Emily's death, and the legal title vested in Thomas Bridgett as from the grant of probate.

12.25.3 Conveyances and revoked grants – s 37 of the AEA 1925

Section 37 of the Administration of Estates Act 1925 states that a conveyance will be valid notwithstanding subsequent revocation of the grant. 'Conveyance' under this section includes most dispositions made by deed, including mortgages, leases and vesting instruments, provided the purchaser acquired the interest in good faith and for valuable consideration.

12.25.4 Payments to or by the former personal representative – s 27(2) of the AEA 1925

Provided that any transaction has been carried out in good faith by the person seeking to rely on the sub-section, s 27(2) of the AEA 1925 provides that the receipt of a former personal representative given whilst his grant was still in force is a good discharge. It also allows a personal representative to reimburse himself for payments properly made by him in the administration of the estate whilst his grant was still in force.

12.25.5 Indemnity of former personal representative – s 27(1) of the AEA 1925

A personal representative who has acted in good faith during the subsistence of his grant of representation will be protected by s 27(1) of the Administration of Estates Act 1925. This provides that every person who makes a disposition under a representation shall be indemnified and protected in so doing, regardless of any defect or circumstances affecting the validity of the representation.

12.26 Special and limited grants

The grant of representation will usually authorise the grantee to deal with all the deceased's property and wind up the estate. However, this is not always the case.

12.26.1 Special grants

There are certain situations in which the court will make a grant limited to the carrying out of a particular purpose which cannot wait for the appointment of personal representatives under a full grant. This will apply where there are assets in the estate which need to be collected in speedily or where legal proceedings need to be dealt with. The first is a grant *ad colligenda bona* (for the collection of goods), and the second may be a grant *pendente lite* or a grant *ad litem* (pending suit or during litigation). The former confers rights over the assets in the estate whereas the latter merely confers the right to represent the estate in proceedings, for example, as in the case of *Re Knight* (1939), where the Official Solicitor took out a grant *ad litem* so that a claimant could start proceedings against the estate for personal injuries under the Law Reform (Miscellaneous Provisions) Act 1934. It is also possible, and simpler, to deal with actions against the estate by invoking s 2 of the Proceedings Against Estates Act 1970, but this confers only the right to represent the estate as defendant in proceedings which would have lain against the testator himself and so is no use where the estate is to be the plaintiff in the proceedings or where the action is one such as a claim under the family provision legislation, which would not lie against a testator during his lifetime.

12.26.2 Limited grants

A grant of limited probate will be made where the executors are not to deal with all the testator's property or are not to carry on dealing with it indefinitely. Section 113 of the Supreme Court Act 1981 provides that the court may make limited grants as it sees fit. There are narrower provisions relating to insolvent estates.

Limitations as to property commonly apply where there is a grant limited to settled property where the settlement continues after the testator's death (if it does not, the property ceases to be settled property), where the testator has appointed particular executors to deal with a specified part of his estate, for example, literary executors, or where the administrator, having taken out a previous grant, fails to complete the administration of the estate, perhaps by dying without an executor taking on the first estate by a chain of representation. This last form of limited grant is called a grant *de bonis non administratis* (grant of the goods which were not administered); where the personal representative had become a trustee, his own personal representatives would have the power under s 36 of the Trustee Act 1925 to appoint a new trustee, and no grant would be needed. If a grant limited as to property is to be made, the grant relating to the rest of the estate will be made stated to be 'save and except' the property to which the limited grant relates; if the limited grant has already been made, the grant relating to the rest of the estate is called a grant *caeterorum* (of the other things).

Limitations as to time arise in various circumstances, although the only one commonly met in practice is where the will appoints a minor as executor. By s 118 of the Supreme Court Act 1981, a minor is prevented from taking a grant until he reaches his majority. There may be a grant of administration *durante minore aetate* (during minority). The grant will be specified to last until the minor attains his majority. It will be made to the person entitled to the residuary estate if the minor has no interest in the estate but is appointed sole executor (NCPR r 32(1)), or otherwise to the minor's parent(s) or guardian unless the district judge or registrar appoints another person to act alone or jointly under his overriding discretion (NCPR r 32(2)). It may then only be renounced on the minor's behalf by order of the registrar. The only limit to the grantee's rights and liabilities is the minor's minority.

Other grants limited as to time are grants of administration during mental incapacity, administration *pendente lite* and administration *durante absentia* (in absence). A grant of administration *pendente lite* may be made where there is a dispute about the validity of the will or the right to administer the estate. It will be made only if the court thinks it necessary and 'proper in all the circumstances', to someone unconnected with the action, for example an accountant, who can do nothing with the estate save with leave of the court. A grant *durante absentia* may be sought where the personal representative remains out of the jurisdiction; the court may issue the grant to any person interested in the estate, including a creditor. Where there is known to be a valid will in existence which cannot be found, it is also possible for the court to make a grant 'till the will be found', as was done in the case of *Re Wright* (1893).

12.27 Other grants

Other particular types of grants may be appropriate in certain circumstances.

12.27.1 Double probate, cessate grants, attorneys and settled land

Where one executor, having given notice to the others, obtains a grant to act alone, that grant will state that there is power reserved to the others should they wish to apply for a grant later. If they do so, the result will be 'double probate'; the first grant is not recalled.

A cessate grant is one which is issued following the expiry of a period of administration under a previous grant. In this it differs technically from a grant *de bonis non administratis*, since in theory it is a renewal of the whole grant rather than a new grant dealing only with the remaining property. However, the practical effect is the same.

A person's attorney may take a grant on his behalf, which will be revoked if the principal calls for his own grant or, alternatively, dies.

The particular rules relating to the appointment of settled land executors are discussed above at 12.7. Where there is settled land, they will take a separate grant in their separate capacity limited to the settled land, and the grant relating to the rest of the deceased's estate will be save and except the settled land.

12.28 Personal representatives or trustees?

The personal representatives' duties are not the same as those of the trustees, though both are in a fiduciary position so they must act in good faith, putting the interests of the estate before their own and taking no profit from their position (save where specifically authorised). Personal representatives must act for the benefit of the estate as a whole, but trustees owe their duty to the beneficiaries as individuals (*Re Hayes* (1971)).

Personal representatives and trustees have different powers and duties under the general law. Trustees will be needed if there is any property which will not be distributed immediately, for example where it is held pending the fulfilment of a condition such as the beneficiary attaining a certain age, or where any recipient will not get an absolute title to the property, for instance a life interest under a trust for sale.

12.28.1 Personal representatives who are also trustees

Although it is usual to appoint the same persons as trustees as are appointed executors, their functions are different and it is possible to appoint different persons. The reason they are often the same is that the elements which make a testator choose a person to be his executor – he trusts them to deal honestly and efficiently with his property – are the same elements that would make him choose them as his trustees.

The personal representatives will also become trustees where the nature of the estate calls for them – because a trust arises – but no trustees have been expressly appointed. This is certainly the case where there is a trust created under a will and the testator has failed to appoint trustees, but the situation may be more difficult where the trust arises on an intestacy.

12.29 Personal representatives and trustees: different rules and roles

The personal representative's function is to wind up the estate and distribute the assets appropriately. The personal representative retains his function for life, so that even where an estate has apparently been finally wound up, if something further accrues to the estate or proceedings are commenced against it, he is bound to deal with it, whereas the function of the trustee is to hold the title to the property pending the end of the trust.

12.29.1 Acting jointly

Personal representatives may act severally – each one by himself – including in the giving of receipts, whereas the authority of trustees is joint and they must act unanimously unless given authority by the will to do otherwise. The situation when personal representatives deal with land is somewhat different. The rule that one personal representative could bind all of his colleagues to convey land by entering into a contract to do so (see *Fountain Forestry Ltd v Edwards* (1975)) was altered by s 16 of the Law of Property (Miscellaneous Provisions) Act 1994, amending s 2(2) of the Administration of Estates Act 1925 as from 1 July 1995. All personal representatives must now concur in both the contract and (as before the 1994 Act) the conveyance for them to be valid. Practitioners should beware of the situation where, on the death of a legal joint tenant, the beneficial ownership is, or may be, held on a tenancy in common; the deceased's personal representatives will need to concur in any contract.

12.29.2 Overreaching

Where there is only one personal representative, he can overreach equitable interests on the sale of property from the estate. Where, however, the person selling the property from the estate is a trustee, he cannot overreach equitable interests if he is acting alone (save in the case of a trust corporation, under s 27(2) of the LPA 1925 and s 18(1) of the SLA 1925).

12.29.3 Appointment of new persons to act

Where the sole or last personal representative is still acting as such when he dies and the administration of the estate remains incomplete, someone else will have to take out a further grant of representation to the estate. Where, however, the person is a trustee, a new trustee of the existing trust can be appointed by the personal representatives of the last surviving trustee, under the powers in s 36 of the Trustee Act 1925. If a new trustee is required whilst there are trustees still in office, they can appoint one of themselves under powers in the same section.

12.29.4 Ceasing to act

Retirement is difficult for a personal representative once he has taken out a grant, and the appointment of additional representatives is equally difficult unless he is a sole personal representative and the estate is one which calls for two (where there is a minority interest, for example; see 12.9 above). Under s 36 of the Trustee Act 1925, however, a trustee has the power to appoint additional or substitutional trustees.

On the death of a sole personal representative without completing the administration of the estate, then either the chain of representation under s 7 of the Administration of Estates Act 1925 (see 12.10 above) will operate or an application will have to be made by the person entitled for a grant *de bonis non administratis*. The trust property of a trustee devolves on his personal representatives.

12.29.5 Limitation

There are different limitation periods relating to the time during which an action against personal representatives and trustees may be brought, save where there is fraud or the personal representative or trustee keeps the relevant property himself, when there is no limitation period. An action must be brought against a trustee within the usual period of six years of the cause of action accruing, whereas in the case of a personal representative the relevant period for actions in respect of personalty (save interest on legacies) is 12 years.

12.29.6 Personal representative who has become trustee

Where a personal representative has become a trustee, the rules relating to trustees apply to him. In *George Attenborough & Son v Solomon* (1913), one of the testator's two sons who were appointed personal representatives sold valuable items of silver plate 10 years after the testator's death. It was held that the preparation of the residuary account showed that all the debts and legacies had been paid before the purported sale and that the personal representatives had become trustees by the time of the sale. Therefore the one son could not act alone, and the transaction was invalid.

12.29.7 Law Reform Committee 23rd Report *The Powers and Duties of Trustees*

The Law Reform Committee in its 23rd Report *The Powers and Duties of Trustees* (1982) recommended that the rules for personal representatives should be aligned with those for trustees, so they could no longer act alone, though in practice they could have power delegated to them by co-personal representatives. The powers of personal representatives and trustees were brought closer by the Trusts of Land and Appointment of Trustees Act 1996, but are still far from fully aligned.

12.30 When does a personal representative become a trustee?

Personal representatives are supposed to wind up the deceased's estate; trustees hold property and administer it in accordance with the terms of the trust, until the trust comes to an end. Where the two roles are performed by the same persons, it may be difficult to tell when the transition occurs.

12.30.1 Under a will

It is not unusual to find the same persons appointed as executors (personal representatives) and trustees in a will. In *Re Grosvenor* (1916), it was held that once personal representatives have indicated by an assent that the subject matter of a specific gift is not required to meet debts and expenses, they hold that asset on trust for the beneficiary.

The situation is less clear so far as residue is concerned. In *Harvell v Foster* (1954) (below), the Court of Appeal held that personal representatives remain liable as such in respect of residuary property until it is vested in the entitled beneficiary, which may be delayed considerably where that beneficiary is a minor at the testator's death. The decision in *Re Yerburgh* (1928) (below), however, left open the possibility that personal representatives become trustees once their essential functions of collecting the assets and paying the debts, expenses and legacies are complete and the residue has been ascertained. Although *Re Yerburgh* was an intestacy case, it would seem logical for the rules to be the same in both situations.

12.30.2 Particular problems on intestacy

An administrator who has not paid the funeral and testamentary expenses, debts and legacies (if any), cannot be said have duly administered the estate according to law – this wording is part of the promise an administrator makes on oath when he applies to the court for a grant authorising him to deal with the estate in the first place. If, however, he has done all those things and then received the money to be held in a continuing trust, the question is whether he has automatically become a trustee or whether he is still an administrator.

12.30.3 Pre-1926 – administration completed, administratrix becomes trustee

The deceased intestate in *Re Ponder* (1921) left a widow and two infant sons. The widow obtained letters of administration, paid the expenses and debts, and invested her sons' shares of the personal property in her own name. Sargant J held that she had become a trustee and the Public Trustee could therefore be appointed to be a trustee jointly with her. Had she still been a personal representative, the court would have had no such power.

12.30.4 Post-1926 – the old rules apply, but is a vesting assent needed?

It is not clear whether it is necessary for a personal representative to make an assent to himself, vesting property in himself as trustee, in order to make the transition of status.

In *Re Yerburgh* (1928), the deceased died intestate in 1926, just after the major legislative changes of the previous year came into force. He left a widow and two infant children. His administrators wound up the estate save for the continuing trusts. They were unsure how to proceed thereafter and applied to the court for directions, because the new law did not make it clear. Romer J said that s 33 of the Administration of Estates Act 1925 had imposed certain duties on legal personal representatives, and when the estate had been fully administered in accordance with those duties, they became trustees on the basis that the old law applied and determined the time at which they ceased to be legal personal representatives and became trustees for sale. He held that at that point the personal representatives ought to make a vesting assent to themselves under s 36 of the Administration of Estates Act 1925.

Unfortunately, it was not clear from Romer J's judgment whether he meant the making of the assent was desirable (as evidence of the automatic change in status) or essential (to effect it), although obviously if he meant the latter, that could have greatly assisted in solving the problems about when and whether, in any particular case, the personal representatives become trustees. The old law, however, as can be seen from *Re Ponder* (above), did not require an assent.

12.30.5 Doubts cast on *Ponder* and *Yerburgh*? The position where the deceased dies testate

The decision in *Harvell v Foster* (1954), however, departed from those in *Re Ponder* and *Re Yerburgh*. The testator appointed his daughter sole executrix and gave her all his estate, but she was a minor at his death and a grant of administration was made to her husband. He entered into an administration bond (these have now been replaced by guarantees) with two solicitors as sureties. The solicitors acted for the husband in the administration of the estate paid over the balance to him. He decamped with most of the money and failed to pay to the daughter when she reached full age.

The Court of Appeal, reversing the decision in the court below, held that the two solicitors were liable to the daughter for the missing money. It based its decision partly on the wording of the administration bond, and partly on the limited nature of the husband's grant. Evershed LJ said that a personal representative's duties included retaining residue in trust where it could not be distributed immediately because the intended beneficiary was an infant. The court disagreed with the implication in *Re Ponder* that the offices of personal representative and trustee were mutually exclusive. Unfortunately, the court did not explain precisely when, in that case, it considered that a personal representative does become a trustee.

12.30.6 A robust approach

Dankwerts J in *Re Cockburn* (1957) had no doubt about the matter at all. He held that personal representatives, whether executors or administrators, became trustees automatically once they had completed the administration in due course. Thereafter they held the property for the beneficiaries under the terms of the will or on intestacy, and were bound to carry out the duties of trustees.

Unfortunately, again, his explanation of how his reasoning related to that of *Harvell v Foster* was not entirely satisfactory or helpful, because he dismissed the suggestion that there was any substantive contradiction between that case and the decision in *Re Ponder*.

12.30.7 The problem identified? – but not entirely solved?

Some of the problems have arisen because of the possibilities of alternative readings of the words of the statute. This problem was identified and discussed in *Re Kings Will Trusts; Assheton v Boyne* (1964). The testatrix in this case had appointed executors and trustees and made specific devises upon trust. After two executors had taken probate, one of them died, and the other appointed a further trustee of the will. The other original executor then died, and his executor became executor by representation of the will of the original testator. He appointed the plaintiff to be a trustee of the will and then he too died. No-one had ever made a written assent to the vesting of the legal estate of the land in accordance with s 36 of the Administration of Estates Act 1925.

The question was whether the plaintiff held the legal estate in the land, as trustee of the will, or whether it was held by the defendant, the executor by representation. Pennycuick J held that the legal estate in the land still vested in the executor by representation of the original testator, rejecting the argument that, prior to the appointment of the other further executor, the legal estate had become vested in the second of the original executors.

He discussed the construction of s 36(4) of the Administration of Estates Act 1925, which falls into two parts.

The first part of that subsection states that an assent to the vesting of a legal estate must be in writing, signed by the personal representative and naming the person in whose favour it is given. This will operate to vest the relevant legal estate in the named person. The judge held that this laid down a rule applicable to any assent to the vesting of a legal estate, including an assent by a personal representative in his own favour.

The second part of s 36(4) says that 'an assent not in writing or not in favour of a named person shall not be effectual to pass a legal estate'. The judge held that this set out the consequences if this rule were disregarded, and it did not create an exception to that rule. He held that the appointment of new trustees by deed did not lead to the implied vesting of the legal estate in them, because for that to happen, the person making the appointment by deed had himself to hold the property as trustee.

Academic writers have criticised the decision in this case, but the courts followed it in *Re Edwards* (1981).

Although the Law Commission considered the question, it reported in its Report No 184 in 1989 (*Property Law: Title on Death*) that solicitors reported little problem in practice in dealing with assents. The implications of the decision in *Re King's Will Trusts* being quite well known, the practice had become to make a written assent in any event, thus avoiding potential difficulties.

12.31 Removal and retirement of personal representatives

The court may, where there are special circumstances, pass over someone in appointing a personal representative under the powers conferred on it by s 116 of the Supreme Court Act 1981. Once the personal representative has been appointed, however, the powers to remove him are much more limited, even where he actively desires to retire. There was no power at all until the passing of the Administration of Justice Act 1985. Section 50 of this Act implemented the recommendation of the Law Reform Committee who, in their 23rd Report, said the court should be allowed the discretion to accede to the application by, or on behalf of, a personal representative or beneficiary for a personal representative to be removed or replaced.

PERSONAL REPRESENTATIVES

Personal representatives are the individuals who administer the deceased's estate in accordance with the law. They may be either executors, appointed expressly or impliedly in a valid will, or administrators, who can apply for a grant of representation if they fall within the rules laid down under the law.

There are different rules for settled land executors and for executors by chain of representation under s 7 of the Administration of Estates Act 1925.

Executors take their power from the will and so technically do not need a grant to deal with the property in the estate, but they do need the grant to prove their title to property. Administrators have no power to act before a grant is made to them.

The personal representative's duty is to the estate. A person who intermeddles with the estate (deals with the property in it when he has no authority to do so) is called an executor *de son tort* and is liable to the estate like a personal representative in respect of the property he has dealt with.

Anyone may be appointed executor but a person who is incapable by reason of mental incapacity may not act, and a person who is under eighteen cannot act until he reaches his majority. A grant of probate will be issued only up to a maximum of four individuals. A trust corporation such as a bank may also be appointed. An executor may renounce without reason if he does not wish to act.

The Non-Contentious Probate Rules lay down, in order, the persons who are entitled to be administrators and take out a grant of letters of administration. Rule 20 deals with the situation where there is a will. If the executor does not take a grant of probate, the person who takes the grant of letters of administration will have the will annexed to the grant and must administer the estate in accordance with its terms. Rule 20 is structured in accordance with entitlements to property. Rule 22 deals with the situation where there is no will and thus an intestacy. This rule, like the entitlement to property itself on intestacy, is structured around family relationships. Who takes out the grant does not affect the entitlements themselves.

The Administration of Estates (Small Payments) Act 1965 says that certain assets may be paid over without a grant.

In order to obtain the grant, the personal representatives first have to calculate the value of the estate and pay any Inheritance Tax on it. This may mean taking out a loan on behalf of the estate, because it is not always possible to get hold of a sufficient amount of the estate's property to pay the tax without being able to produce a grant.

If any person objects to a particular grant, they may enter a caveat by sending a notice to the court. No grant will be issued until the caveator has had a chance to present their objections to the court.

Grants of probate may be revoked if they were wrongly made or a grantee becomes incapable or does not carry out his functions. Grants may also be amended.

There is statutory protection for a person who purchases property from a personal representative whose grant is subsequently revoked. Section 204(1) of the Law of Property Act 1925 protects a person acting under a court order whilst it is in force and s 37 of the Administration of Estates Act 1925 states that a conveyance (widely defined) will be valid notwithstanding the subsequent revocation of the grant. Personal representatives making or receiving payments are protected by s 27(2) of the LPA 1925 and s 27(1) protects them where they make a disposition, in both cases provided that they are in good faith.

There are special grants and limited grants to deal with the situation where the usual grant cannot be waited for or the personal representatives are not dealing with all the property in the estate for the total duration of the administration.

Personal representatives administer and wind up the estate. Trustees administer a continuing trust. Not only do the two have different functions but also different rules apply to them. The Law Reform Committee thought that the two systems of powers should be aligned. Where the two are the same persons, there may be considerable difficulty in deciding when they cease to hold property as personal representatives and become trustees in relation to it. Because of the different rules which apply to the two offices, the difference may be important. The most difficult question is whether a vesting assent is needed to pass the property from a person as personal representative to himself as trustee, and this has not been answered satisfactorily by the courts.

CHAPTER 13

ADMINISTRATION OF ESTATES

The task of the personal representatives is to collect in the assets of the estate, pay the debts, liabilities and legacies and distribute the residue. The process of doing this is the administration of the estate.

13.1 What is in the estate?

At common law, only personalty devolved upon the personal representatives, and realty went directly to the devisee by will or the heir on intestacy. The position as to realty altered in the late 19th century and is now governed by s 1 of the Administration of Estates Act 1925. The estate now comprises all the deceased's personalty and all realty in which the deceased was entitled to an interest not ceasing on his death. Examples of interests ceasing on death are an interest under a joint tenancy, or a life interest.

The estate should be valued as at the date of death. However, valuation is, on occasion, as much an art as a science, and it is involved with questions of liability to pay tax. For more about this, see below at 14.17.

13.1.1 Assets available to meet debts and liabilities

The assets of the estate available for the payment of debts and liabilities are defined in s 32(1) of the Administration of Estates Act 1925 as any property the deceased owned, to the extent of his beneficial interest, property subject to a general power exercised by the deceased by will and entailed property disposed of by the deceased under s 176 of the Law of Property Act 1925.

13.1.2 Other assets available

Other assets may, however, fall into the estate of the deceased, and they are included in the assets available. The commonest of these will be income arising in the estate after the date of death. Property appointed by will may also be available, as may the subject matter of a *donatio mortis causa*, according to *Re Korvine* (1921), if there is nothing else to satisfy the debts of the estate.

13.1.3 Property not available

Property subject to a special power is not available, and neither is property the deceased held under a trust but in which he did not have the beneficial interest. This latter point is of great practical use; it was held in *Re Webb* (1941) that the proceeds of a life policy, on which the deceased had paid the premiums but which he had written in trust for his son, did not form part of his estate. Some property may be unavailable to the personal representatives as a matter of practicality, such as foreign property.

One of the amendments made to the law by the Administration of Justice Act 1982, in this case by s 19, was to the way gifts were saved by s 33 of the Wills Act 1837. Section 33 of the Wills Act 1837 provides that a gift to issue of the testator will be saved where that issue, though predeceased, leaves issue of his own; before 1983, such gifts were first of all available as assets of the estate of the predeceased issue to satisfy any unmet debts and liabilities before passing to the beneficiaries. After 1982, however, they passed straight to the beneficiaries, thus bypassing the estate of the predeceased and avoiding the liability to satisfy his debts.

13.2 What has to come out of the estate and when?

It is important to know the order in which funds are applied because there may be insufficient to meet all the liabilities. The personal representatives must pay the funeral expenses, the administration expenses, the debts of the estate at the date of the deceased's death and debts of the estate arising thereafter, in that order of priority. Thus, if the deceased died insolvent, owing large sums of money when all that is in the estate is enough to pay the funeral bill, the personal representatives must pay that before they look at settling the liabilities to creditors at all. However, the personal representatives may make only reasonable payments for funeral expenses; though 'reasonable' is interpreted broadly in the case where the deceased was wealthy, in the case of an insolvent estate only an amount to cover necessary expenses will be allowed.

The assets must be applied first to the obligations incurred by the deceased during his lifetime, before obligations incurred by the personal representatives after his death. It may seem unfortunate, in the light of this, that liability to Inheritance Tax (IHT) arises under s 4(1) of the Inheritance Tax Act 1984 on the deceased's deemed disposal of all his property immediately before death. However, the personal representatives will in any case have had to pay any IHT on the estate in order to obtain the grant.

13.2.1 Other action at the personal representatives' discretion

Personal representatives have a power to settle or abandon debts and claims, provided they do so in good faith. They may also seek a termination of any contract not automatically frustrated by death.

13.2.2 The executor's year

The personal representatives' duty is usually said to be to deal with the administration within a year, so that during the so called 'executor's year' they cannot be called upon to make payments and those not made will not usually incur interest. It is, however, technically to deal with the estate and make payments 'with due diligence', which may vary from case to case according to the circumstances (*Re Tankard* (1942)). Sometimes delay will be justifiable, and in that situation the personal representative will not be liable for loss caused by it.

13.3 Dealing with the assets and liabilities

The personal representatives must collect in the assets and meet all the debts and liabilities before distributing the estate to the beneficiaries.

Some amendments to how personal representatives deal with land were made by the Law of Property (Miscellaneous Provisions) Act 1994, which allows registration of land charges in unregistered conveyancing to be made against the name of the deceased rather than the personal representatives. It also allows service of notices, as it were, on the deceased where the server had no reason to believe he had died and, where the server did know of the death, allows service on the personal representatives of the deceased at his last known address.

13.3.1 Ascertaining the debts and liabilities before distribution

The basic rule is that the personal representatives are liable to pay all the debts which the assets of the estate will cover, save those which are statute-barred (though they have an exceptional discretion to pay these). This remains the same even where they have distributed the assets to the beneficiaries on the assumption that no more debts can be discovered, unless they have complied with the obligations set out by statute for personal representatives and trustees to obtain protection against such later claims.

13.3.2 Protection against later claims – s 27 of the Trustee Act 1925

The personal representatives can obtain protection against later claims by creditors by complying with the provisions of s 27 of the Trustee Act (TA) 1925. The personal representatives should place advertisements requiring any person interested in the estate to send them particulars of their claim on the estate within the time specified in the notice; this must be at least two months. The advertisements required are placed as a matter of course by practitioners in this area in every administration. The personal representatives must give notice of their intended distribution in the *London Gazette* and, where there is any land in the estate, in the newspaper in circulation in the area where the land is; for personal property, the *London Gazette* alone is enough. If there is some difficulty or query, the personal representative should apply to the court for directions as to what notices should be placed. Once the two months (or greater specified period) have expired, the personal representatives may distribute the estate on the basis of the claims of which they have actual or constructive notice.

In *Re Aldhous* (1955), the testator died partially intestate. The executors advertised in accordance with s 27 of the Trustee Act 1925, but no claims were received and they passed the estate to the Treasury Solicitor as *bona vacantia*. When the next-of-kin turned up later making demands, the executors were protected against them by having complied with the provisions of s 27.

13.3.3 Declaration of the court

In the case of *Re Gess* (1942), the deceased died intestate domiciled by choice in England, though he was originally from Poland. His administrators paid the debts of which they knew and were then declared by the court to be at liberty to distribute the remaining £1,092 held by the Custodian of Enemy Property.

13.4 Ascertaining the beneficiaries

Where there is a will, usually the beneficiaries will be named; usually, they will be family members and the personal representatives will know who they are and where to find them.

13.4.1 Benjamin orders and authority from the court to distribute

Sometimes, a personal representative will be aware of the existence of a beneficiary – for example, one who is named in a will – but will not know how to find him. In most cases, the executors of a will or members of the deceased's family can provide all the necessary information, but sometimes neither that nor the expedient of advertising in newspapers or even employing someone to trace the beneficiary is successful.

It may transpire that, to the best of anyone's knowledge, a named beneficiary is dead, though this cannot be proved. This occurred in the case of *Re Benjamin* (1902), where the deceased left a gift to his son, who had last been heard of some while previously on the return journey from France. The personal representatives made inquiries and advertised for the son, to no avail. Eventually, they applied to the court and obtained an order allowing them to distribute the estate as though that beneficiary had predeceased.

However, it was said in *Re Green's Will Trust* (1985) that 'the true view is that a *Re Benjamin* order does not vary or destroy a beneficial interest. It merely enables trust property to be distributed in accordance with the practical probabilities'. Thus, if the deceased's son had turned up after the court order, awkward readjustments would have been necessary.

Another situation that may arise is, for example, that in *Re Pettifor* (1966) where the personal representative sought authority from the court to distribute the estate on the basis that a woman of 70 would not have another child. Pennycuick J criticised such applications as of no practical use and a waste of time. The legal treatment of this question was reviewed extensively in the case of *Figg v Clarke (Inspector of Taxes)* (1997).

13.5 Dealing with an estate pending distribution

The personal representatives have wide powers to collect in the deceased's assets and to hold them pending distribution of the estate. Their powers in respect of the way in which they may deal with the property within the estate once they have it are however limited, unless the testator has widened them in his will.

13.5.1 Powers to collect in the estate

The personal representatives will probably obtain possession of most or all of the deceased's estate by virtue of their office. Where this is not the case, usually the person who does have possession will hand the property over on the personal representative's request and on his production of evidence of authority, usually the grant of representation. If, however, a request does not succeed, the personal representatives may sue under their general power to do so in order to recover assets. They may also commence court proceedings to recover liabilities to the deceased's estate or to pursue a tort claim on the estate's behalf, in order to maximise the assets.

13.5.2 Court actions as assets (or liabilities) of the estate

The common law rule is that the right to sue dies with the plaintiff. However, this was altered by the Law Reform (Miscellaneous Provisions) Act 1934 so that most causes of action survive an individual's death, whether or not the proceedings had actually commenced during the deceased's lifetime, though no awards of exemplary damages may be obtained.

In *Rickless v United Artists* (1987), the court held that the estate of the actor Peter Sellers included his right under s 2 of the Dramatic and Musical Performers' Protection Act 1958 to consent to the reproduction of his performances. Actions in defamation do not, however, survive death – hence the outpouring of journalists at the death of Robert Maxwell; neither he nor his estate was in any position to take any action about it.

13.5.3 Fatal Accidents Act actions

Actions under the Fatal Accidents Act 1976 are usually brought by the personal representatives for the benefit of the deceased's relatives, as opposed to the situation with other actions where they are brought for the benefit of the estate. Of course, the personal representatives, the beneficiaries and the deceased's relatives are often drawn from the same group of persons. Fatal Accidents Act claims are for the loss of dependency or for bereavement. Loss of dependency claims can be very large, representing years of a breadwinner's wages; bereavement claims are for a fixed sum, currently £7,500, per deceased person, claimable by a very limited range of relatives.

13.6   Is the estate solvent?

If there is sufficient in the estate to meet the funeral and administration expenses and pay all debts and liabilities in full, the estate is solvent. All these payments must be made before any gift in the testator's will or entitlement under his intestacy is considered. The creditors in a solvent estate will be paid in full before the legacies are paid and the assets distributed.

13.6.1 Dealing with the debts

Just because an estate is solvent does not mean that the beneficiaries will all be paid in full what they expect to receive. It may be that the testator has left legacies amounting to more than remains in the estate after payment of all the liabilities, or the beneficiary may be expecting to receive a house whereas that house was subject to a heavy mortgage liability – what occurs in these circumstances will be discussed in more detail later.

13.7   What if the estate is insolvent?

The personal representatives may still administer an insolvent estate, or, alternatively, an administration order can be obtained from the court or an order may be made for the administration of the estate in bankruptcy. The priority of debts in an insolvent estate is governed by s 34(1) of the Administration of Estates Act (AEA) 1925, which states that funeral, testamentary and administration expenses (including expenses of litigation ordered to be paid out of the estate) are to be paid first, and thereafter payments are to be made as they are in respect of the distribution of the property of a living person who has declared bankrupt. The testator cannot alter that order by the terms of his will. The only situation in which it does not apply is where the debt is secured; for example, a debt secured by way of mortgage on a house will be met in full from the value of the house, provided that value is sufficient to cover the debt. Any debt remaining thereafter ('negative equity') will be unsecured.

13.7.1 Payment of debts in an insolvent estate – s 34(1) of the AEA 1925

The order of priority in respect of unsecured debts is as follows:

(a) specially preferred debts

(money held by the deceased in certain official capacities in connection with friendly societies or military duties)

(b) preferred debts

(income tax for employees for the 12 months preceding death, VAT and road tax for six months before death and National Insurance Contributions and certain other taxes for 12 months, arrears of pension contributions and four months' wages owing to employees)

(c) ordinary debts

(almost anything which is not in any other category)

(d) interest on any debts in the previous categories

(e) deferred debts

(such as loans between spouses)

Each class must be exhausted before payments are made under the next. Failure to observe the proper order, or to distribute equally within the same class, will render a personal representative liable personally to pay any debts superior to those he has paid, provided he had notice of them, or to make good the unequal distribution, save where he had no reason to believe the estate was insolvent when he made a payment.

13.8 Managing the property in the estate

Many will trusts will now be effectively governed by the provisions of the Trusts of Land and Appointment of Trustees Act 1996. The 1996 Act defines a 'trust of land' as any trust of property which consists of, or includes, land. Trustees of land have all the powers of a beneficial owner, subject, of course, to the provisions of the individual trust and to the trustees' general fiduciary duties.

The amendments made to trustees' powers by the 1996 Act represent a radical change from the law applying before 1997. That gave trustees only very limited powers, though the Law Reform Committee had long since recommended, in its 23rd Report *The Powers and Duties of Trustees* (1982) that they should be widened, not least because they so restricted trustees as to make them unable to deal with property in accordance with the general scheme of the Trustee Act 1925, which emphasises the standards expected of an ordinary prudent man of business.

The old law still applies, however, to trusts which contain no land and consist only of personalty. Moreover, the partial abolition of the doctrine of conversion by s 3(1) of the Trusts of Land and Appointment of Trustees Act 1996 does not apply where the trust was created by the will of someone who died before 1997 (see 10.7.4).

It has been proposed by the Law Commission, in its Consultation Paper No 146 *Trustees' Powers and Duties* (1997), that all trustees, including those of personalty only, should have the power to purchase a legal estate in land in England and Wales, and to do so with the aid of a mortgage. Such a provision was apparently omitted from the Bill which became the 1996 Act for reasons of time and expediency. The Law Commission has further proposed that trustees of personalty only should also have power to insure trust property as if they were its beneficial owners, and should generally have a duty to do so as a reasonably prudent person would, with a discretion to apportion the payment of premiums as they think fit.

Personal representatives have by s 18 of the Trusts of Land and Appointment of Trustees Act 1996 the same powers as trustees of land, though with modifications as to consents, consultation and court applications in cases of dispute, where a post-1996 estate contains land. Personal representatives have powers under the Trustee Act 1925 and the Trustee Investments Act 1961 to use banking facilities and to invest in certain authorised securities; the investment powers though are fairly limited and it is usual practice to widen them in a will. They may pay calls on shares and take up (or renounce) rights issues, and they may also concur in schemes to reconstruct a company or modify the rights attached to its shares.

13.8.1 Powers to insure

The personal representatives' powers to insure personalty are very limited (s 19 of the TA 1925) and the widening of powers to insure in a will is particularly important. The statutory powers are to insure to three-quarters of the value of the insured property, save where the personal representative is bound to transfer property immediately to a beneficiary (s 19(1) of the TA 1925), when there is no power at all.

13.8.2 Powers to carry on the deceased's business

The personal representatives' powers to carry on the deceased's business are very limited, and if a person wishes his business to be dealt with by them then again he should put some specific provision in his will. Explicit powers are needed specifically because they are not implied, and they should be full and clear, because the cases show that the courts take a very restrictive view of the what is authorised in practice by a direction simply to carry on the testator's business. In *M'Neillie v Acton* (1853), the court held that such a direction did not authorise the personal representative to have recourse to any assets other than the capital already in the business to carry it on, so that a security given over property in the estate for that purpose was invalid against the beneficiaries. The personal representatives' powers are limited to carrying on the business with a view to selling it as a going concern.

13.8.3 Pros and cons of carrying on the business

A business is, of course, worth far more as a going concern, with all its goodwill, than it is if it has been allowed to collapse and lose all its trade. A personal representative is however personally liable to those he deals with if he carries on the deceased's business. This was described by the court in *Re Garland* (1804) as 'very hard', but the court pointed out that no-one is obliged to take on such liability. 'He becomes liable, as personally responsible, to the extent of all his own property ... But he places himself in that situation by his own choice.' He is, however, entitled to indemnify himself from the estate.

13.8.4 How long can a sale of the business be postponed?

The testator in *Re Crowther* (1895) left his estate on trust for sale and gave his trustees power to postpone such sale and conversion 'for such period as to them shall seem expedient'. At the time of his death, he had two businesses, one of which he ran alone as sole proprietor and the other which he ran in partnership with his son, who was one of the trustees of the will. Twenty two years later, the trustees were still running both businesses, not with a view to their sale but for the benefit of his widow, who was the life tenant under the deceased's will. The question before the court was whether the trustees had authority to carry on both the businesses in this way under their power to postpone sale. In this case, the court held that the power to postpone the sale of a business involved a power of continuing the business in the meantime.

13.8.5 Effect of carrying on the business without authority

In *Dowse v Gorton* (1891), it was held that personal representatives not only have authority to carry on a business with a view to selling it as a going concern, but may also claim indemnity from both beneficiaries and creditors, provided they are carrying on the business with a view to the proper realisation of the estate. However, if the business is carried on under an authority in a will but not with a view to proper realisation, indemnity may only be claimed against beneficiaries and not against creditors. This may, however, not be the case with a particular creditor if he has assented to the carrying on of the business.

13.8.6 Creditors' acquiescence in unauthorised carrying on of business

Where, however, a creditor has not assented to the carrying on of the business, and the business has been carried on but not with a view to proper realisation, as occurred in *Re Oxley* (1914), the creditor of the estate may treat the continuance of the business as improper. He is then entitled to be paid out of the value of the assets which existed at the death of the deceased, and the personal representative has no right to be indemnified in priority to him. Assenting to the carrying on of the business has to be more than just knowing about it and doing nothing to stop it. The court in *Re Oxley* held that, for a personal representative to succeed in asserting that a creditor has assented to the carrying on the business, it was necessary to show an active affirmative assent. The court held that mere standing by with knowledge and doing nothing was not sufficient. The application in this case was made by persons who had become creditors of the estate in the course of business carried on by the personal representatives. They were seeking a declaration that they had priority over those creditors who had allowed the personal representatives to carry on unauthorised business transactions; the court refused their application.

13.9 Assents

When the property in the estate vests in the person entitled, the assent of the personal representatives is required. At common law, an assent can be made expressly, even though not in writing, by a few informal words spoken by the executor (*Barnard v Pumfrett* (1841)).

However, under statute an assent by a personal representative to the vesting of a legal estate *in land* in another person, in whatever capacity – beneficially or as trustee or personal representative of another deceased person – is governed by s 36(4) of the AEA 1925, which says that: '... an assent to the vesting of a legal estate shall be in writing, signed by the personal representative, and shall name the person in whose favour it is given and shall operate to vest in that person the legal estate to which it relates; and an assent not in writing or not in favour of a named person shall not be effectual to pass a legal estate.' Note that a vesting assent is one of the forms of conveyance listed in s 52(2) of the Law of Property Act 1925 which are effective to pass a legal estate in land despite not being a deed.

It has long been unclear whether the provisions of s 36(4) of the AEA 1925 mean a personal representative needs to assent to the vesting of a legal estate in land in himself, in whatever capacity. In *Re King's Will Trusts* (1964), Pennycuick J held that the same rule applied to an assent by a personal representative to the vesting of a legal estate in land in himself (whether beneficially, as trustee, or as personal representative of another deceased) as to an assent by him in favour of another person. Whether or not that decision is questionable, on the basis that it rests on an interpretation of s 36(4), the signed written assent by the personal representative in his own favour is still be highly desirable, as documentary evidence of the title to the legal estate. Indeed the Law Commission, investigating the point, found that it was the usual practice to make such an assent, solicitors having generally absorbed the implications of *Re King's Will Trusts*.

However, in the later case of *Re Edwards Will Trusts* (1982), a woman who owned real property died intestate, leaving her husband solely entitled. Her husband obtained letters of administration and occupied the property for 20 years before dying without at any time making an assent in writing in his own favour. It was held that the husband had by his conduct assented to the vesting of the equitable interest in himself, so that it passed to his executors.

Section 36(6) of the Administration of Estates Act 1925 provides some protection for a purchaser (or mortgagee or lessee) of a legal estate in land in good faith for money or money's worth. A person purchasing from a personal representative should check the grant to see whether a previous assent or conveyance to trustees or beneficiaries has been made and a notice of this appended to the grant – the trustees or beneficiary can require this to be done. If, however, it has not been done, s 36(6) provides that a statement in writing by the personal representative that he has not given or made an assent or conveyance in respect of the legal estate shall be sufficient evidence of that in favour of the purchaser. In practice, the conveying personal representative will insert such a statement in a conveyance of unregistered land. Unfortunately, it was held in *Re Duce and Boots Cash Chemists (Southern) Ltd's Contract* (1937) that such a statement may be sufficient, but it is not conclusive.

13.10 Appropriation

Section 41 of the AEA 1925 gives personal representatives a power to appropriate assets in satisfaction of testamentary or intestate benefits. It applies whenever the deceased died, and whether he died testate or intestate, and to any part of the estate.

There are two principal consequences of a personal representative exercising the right:

(a) the beneficiary's interest transfers to the appropriated assets, so if they increase or decrease in value, he bears that (*Ballard v Marsden* (1880));

(b) the appropriation clears the other assets for distribution.

The personal representative may exercise the power as he thinks just and reasonable, according the rights of those interested in the estate.

The consent of the beneficiary is however required:

(a) from a beneficiary absolutely entitled;

(b) from the trustee (not being the personal representative) or the person entitled for the time being to the income of any settled legacy, share or interest.

Consent maybe given for an infant by his parents or guardian or by the court.

The personal representatives must have regard to the rights of anyone who is not consenting, though they will be bound by an appropriation duly made.

The assets are valued at the date of appropriation, not at the date of death. In times of fluctuating house prices in particular, this can have harsh results. The value of the house in *Re Collins* (1975), for example, was £4,200 at the death in 1972 and £8,000 when the court heard the case in 1974.

The power in s 41 is not prejudiced by any other powers of appropriation conferred by law or under the deceased's will. It is quite common to see a provision in a will allowing appropriation but without the consents required by s 41, as this can make the administration easier.

13.11 Does a beneficiary have a proprietary interest?

The position of the beneficiary is not entirely clear-cut; the legal title to property devolves on the personal representatives, but it is less easy to say what becomes of the beneficial interest. It cannot be said, for example, that the beneficial interest in the deceased's house has passed to you just because the deceased left it to you in his will; it may be mortgaged to the hilt, without any other provision for the satisfaction of the secured debt, or the estate may be insolvent, so that in reality the deceased had nothing to leave you. Unfortunately, in those circumstances, although you will know the deceased probably intended well towards you, you will not obtain any interest in anything of any practical value.

13.11.1 Beneficiary's interest in an unadministered estate

A beneficiary does, however, clearly have some interest in the estate. What needs to be established is when and how that arises, and what its nature is.

13.11.2 No interest in residue until it is ascertained

In *Dr Barnardo's v Commissioners of the Income Tax Acts* (1921), which concerned a gift of residuary estate, the court held that the legatee of a share of residue has no interest in any of the property of the testator until the residue has been ascertained. The same was held in *Lord Sudeley v Attorney General* (1897), which concerned a gift of a share of the residuary real and personal estate. The beneficiary claimed a share of mortgages in New Zealand, but the court held that the entitlement was to a share of the estate once ascertained, not to anything in it in particular.

In *Commissioner of Stamp Duties (Queensland) v Livingston* (1965), the question was important because the beneficiary, although she survived her husband (or her gift would have lapsed), died before his estate had been administered. The question was not whether her interest could be passed on to her estate; that clearly could happen, as she had survived the deceased and there was no provision preventing it, for example a condition that she survive the deceased by a certain length of time which she had failed to fulfil. The question was whether, at the time of her death, she already had a proprietary interest in her share of the property in the deceased's estate. If she did, taxes would have been payable. The Privy Council, hearing the matter on appeal from the High Court of Australia, said that, as a general rule, a beneficiary under a will or intestacy has no legal or equitable proprietary interest in the unadministered assets of the deceased's estate. The entire ownership of the unadministered assets is in the deceased's personal representatives. It was said that whatever property comes to a personal representative by virtue of his office comes to him 'in full ownership without distinction between legal and equitable interests. The whole property [is] his'.

The case of *Eastbourne Mutual Building Society v Hastings Corporation* (1965) concerned the interest of a widower solely entitled to his estate, being the next-of-kin on intestacy where the estate was quite small. The date at which he acquired his interest was relevant because the house was to be compulsorily purchased by the council, who would pay compensation at the full market value if it was occupied by the person who acquired it or a member of the family of that person who was also entitled to an interest in the house. The level of compensation otherwise would take no account of the buildings on the land, but pay the value of the site only. The widower carried on living in the house but never took out any grant of representation or had the title to the house transferred to himself. The question for the court was whether he nevertheless had an interest in it, and unfortunately for the mortgagee, who was the interested party, the court held that he did not.

13.11.3 Interest in specific bequest at death

However, in *Inland Revenue Commissioners v Hawley* (1928), it was said that a beneficiary entitled under a specific bequest or devise took an equitable interest in the subject matter of the gift at the death of the testator, and this was confirmed in *Re K (deceased)* (1985).

This did not assist the son living in the testator's bungalow in *Barclay v Barclay* (1970), however, because the testator had expressly directed that it be sold and the proceeds divided between his five sons and daughters-in-law.

The son refused to move out and the daughter-in-law who took the grant brought possession proceedings against him. The Court of Appeal held that she should succeed, but Lord Denning MR also said that an equitable interest in property itself could arise under the will if it were appropriately worded.

13.11.4 Ensuring of due administration is a chose in action of the beneficiary

It was held in *Re Leigh's Wills Trusts* (1970) that the ensuring of due administration is a chose in action of the beneficiary. This means he is entitled to bring an action about the administration of the estate and, insofar as that entitlement constitutes property, it is the property of the beneficiary. This entitlement was what led Colonel Wintle to acquire part of the testatrix's estate in *Wintle v Nye* (1959) (see 4.9.7); he wished to be in a position to take Mr Nye, the solicitor, to court.

In *Re Leigh's Will Trusts*, the testatrix had made a specific gift in her will to Frederick Durbridge of 'all shares which I hold and any other interest ... which I may have' in a sheet metal company. The deceased had never had any such shares or interest, but at her death she was the sole administratrix and sole beneficiary of the unadministered estate of her husband, who had died intestate owning some shares in, and a debt due from, the company. The court held that the specific gift to Mr Durbridge took effect by the testatrix having transmitted to her executors her chose in action of the right to ensure due administration. As sole beneficiary, the testatrix had a right to require the new administrator to administer the husband's estate in any manner she or her executors might require, consistent with the rights of anyone else against the estate. The specific gift in the will imposed a duty on the executors to exercise this right so as to ensure so far as possible that the shares and the debt became available to satisfy the specific gift.

13.12 Apportionments

There are rules designed to ensure that all beneficiaries are treated fairly, namely the rules of equitable and legal apportionment. These are extremely awkward to apply in practice, involving somewhat complex calculations. In professionally drafted wills where they might apply, they are expressly excluded.

The rules of equitable apportionment are briefly outlined here principally so that the need to exclude them may be fully appreciated.

13.12.1 Rule in *Howe v Dartmouth* (1802)

The rule in *Howe v Dartmouth* (1802) is the duty to maintain equality between beneficiaries entitled in succession to unspecified personalty under a will. The duty is to convert certain property (wasting assets, unauthorised investments and reversionary interests) into authorised investments.

13.12.2 Rule in *Earl of Chesterfield's Trusts* (1883)

The rule in *Earl of Chesterfield's Trusts* (1883) is the duty to divide the sum realised on the falling into possession of a reversionary interest between capital and income so that the tenant for life receives a sum representing what he would have received had the reversionary interest been sold within the executor's year, calculated on a figure which would have grown to the sum realised if invested at the testator's death at 4% compound interest.

13.12.3 Rule in *Allhusen v Whittell* (1867)

The rule in *Allhusen v Whittell* (1867) is the duty to ensure that when distributions are made and debts are paid, some of the cost is charged to income so that the life tenant does not take the income from those parts of the estate that should have been applied to the payment of debts and legacies.

13.12.4 Legal apportionment

Section 2 of the Apportionment Act 1870 requires calculations to be apportioned from day to day.

13.12.5 Apportionment and the Law Reform Committee

The Law Reform Committee in its 23rd Report stated that it agreed with the principles behind the rules of equitable apportionment but found their operation wrong. It preferred a general duty to maintain an 'even hand' or 'fair balance' between all the beneficiaries. If this recommendation is implemented, it remains to be seen whether it materialises as an obligation to fall within a margin of error of the results that would have obtained on an application of the old rules.

13.13 The incidence of debts and legacies

In the course of administering the estate, the personal representatives will have to pay debts, expenses and liabilities and also, if there are any, general legacies. The question will arise as to what funds should be used to pay the debts and legacies. Any properly drafted will should make valid provision as to what assets are to be used to pay the debts and legacies, but if it does not, then the position as to debts is governed by statute. The position as to legacies is, however, less clear.

It is important that payments of both debts and legacies are made out of the correct part of the estate because of the impact of such payments on the size of the remaining parts of the estate.

13.14 The incidence of debts, expenses and liabilities

In default of valid provision by the testator ousting the statutory provisions, the incidence of debts is governed by the Administration of Estates Act 1925.

13.14.1 Order of payment of debts out of the solvent estate – s 34(3) of the AEA 1925 and Part II of the First Schedule

Section 34(3) of the Administration of Estates Act 1925 applies where the estate is solvent. It says that where the estate is solvent the assets should be used to pay funeral, testamentary and administration expenses, debts and liabilities in the order specified in Part II of the First Schedule to that Act. It also states that this order may be varied by the will of the deceased.

The Act contains other provisions as to the incidence of debts, such as those in s 35 which relate to secured debts. Note that where a beneficiary takes a gift by will which is made expressly subject to his payment of any debt, the statutory provisions do not apply to that arrangement.

13.14.2 Part II of the First Schedule – the 'statutory order'

Part II of the First Schedule to the Administration of Estates Act sets out the order of application of assets where the estate is solvent, and reads as follows:

- Property of the deceased undisposed of by will, subject to the retention thereout of a fund sufficient to meet any pecuniary legacies.
- Property of the deceased not specifically devised or bequeathed but included (either by a specific or general description) in a residuary gift, subject to the retention out of such property of a fund sufficient to meet any pecuniary legacies, so far as not provided for as aforesaid.
- Property of the deceased specifically appropriated or devised or bequeathed (either by a specific or general description) for the payment of debts.
- Property of the deceased charged with, or devised or bequeathed (either by a specific or general description) subject to a charge for the payment of debts.
- The fund, if any, retained to meet pecuniary legacies.
- Property specifically devised or bequeathed, rateably according to value.
- Property appointed by will under a general power, including the statutory power to dispose of entailed interests, rateably according to value.

- The following provisions shall also apply:
  (a) The order of application may be varied by the will of the deceased.

  (b)... [this part repealed].

The categories referred to have been subject to some considerable case law, for much of which see 10.1. The cases also show that there are other problems with the application of the statutory order. Its ambiguities are capable of resolution in various ways. Unfortunately, the courts have not chosen to follow only one of the routes available to solve the ambiguities, which would have clarified the meaning of the Act or at least clarified how it had to be interpreted, but have oscillated between the options open to them.

13.15 Problems with the First Schedule

There are sufficient problems with the operation of the First Schedule for them to fall into particular areas.

13.15.1 Variation of the statutory order by the terms of the will

Paragraph 8 of the statutory order provides that the order itself may be varied by the terms of the will, but it is often questionable whether the terms of the will are clear enough to make an effective variation. Wills usually provide for payment out of general residue but it may not be clear when the assets out of which the debts should be paid are to be identified. Undisposed-of property and general residue are not necessarily the same thing. If the will simply directs for payment out of residue (a commonly-seen provision), and a gift of a share of the residue has failed, it may not be clear whether payment should be made out of the lapsed share or out of residue as a whole. If it is made out of the lapsed share first of all, the person who would take the lapsed share of residue under the rules of intestacy bears all the payments. If, however, it is made out of the residue before it is divided into shares, all the shares of residue bear the burden equally. (Section 35 makes it own stipulations for the variation of its provision by will, but they refer only to the secured debts to which that section applies.)

The question often arises as to whether the testator has used words in his will which are sufficient to vary the statutory order.

13.15.2 'Subject to the payment of my ... expenses ... and debts'

In *Re Harland-Peck* (1941), the testatrix left the residue of her estate 'subject to the payment of my funeral and testamentary expenses ... and debts' to A and B in equal shares. B's share lapsed, because he predeceased. The question was whether the provision in the will was sufficient to vary the statutory order. If it did not, the debts would be paid out of the lapsed share; if it did, they would be paid equally from both shares of residue. The Court of Appeal held that the words did vary the statutory order, so the debts were paid equally from A's share as well as B's lapsed share.

Re Harland-Peck (1941)

If the statutory order applied ...

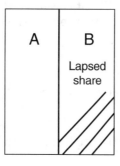

– debts payable out of lapsed share under para 1 of statutory order

... but the will varied it.

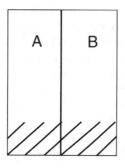

– whole residue 'subject to the payment of my funeral and testamentary expenses ... and debts'

13.15.3 Direction for payment out of residue as a whole

The case of *Re Kempthorne* (1930) resembled *Re Harland-Peck*; the testator left his residue to his brothers and sisters after payment of debts and legacies. Two of his sisters had predeceased. If the statutory order applied, their shares would be used to pay the debts. At first instance, the court held that the statutory order did apply, but the Court of Appeal reversed that decision and held that it did not. It held that the testator had clearly provided that the residue should be divided into shares 'after' the payment of debts.

13.15.4 Direction for payment from one source exonerates other

A rule had been established under the case law preceding 1926 that a testator who wished to shift the burden of debts away from personalty and onto realty had to show a definite intention to exonerate the personalty. Later cases echoed the same understanding of what was required to alter the usual order of payment, although after 1925 the distinction between realty and personalty did not apply. In *Re Meldrum* (1952), the testator by his will gave Annie Meldrum a pecuniary legacy and also gave her the contents of a deposit account 'after ... legacies debts funeral and other expenses have been liquidated'. The residue would have been primarily liable for the debts and expenses, under para 2 of the statutory order, as it would come before the deposit account which fell within para 4, unless the terms of the will had varied that order. The court held that the direction for the payment of debts and funeral and other expenses out of the deposit account necessarily involved an intention to exonerate the residue.

Upjohn J in *Re Meldrum* did not lay down any particular rules for the interpretation of whether the terms of a will are sufficient to vary the statutory order. He said it was 'essentially a matter of construction of the will in each case whether the provisions of the schedule apply, or whether they have been varied by the terms of the will.'

13.15.5 Clear intention to exonerate other funds

In *Re Gordon* (1940), the testatrix had made a specific gift and given a pecuniary legacy, being the balance of a sum after the payment of debts. She had not provided for the residue. The court held that the direction did not displace the statutory order, because no intention to exonerate residue was shown. Therefore, the debts were paid out of residue in accordance with the statutory order rather than out of the pecuniary legacy, despite the wording of the will.

13.15.6 Direction for the payment of debts and expenses 'as soon as possible'

The testator in *Re Lamb* (1929) left directions for his executors to pay his debts and expenses 'as soon as possible'. He left the residue equally between four persons. One of them predeceased, so his share lapsed and was undisposed of by the will. The court held that the statutory order applied; the testator had not varied it because he had not specified the fund or property from which the debts should be paid.

13.15.7 Assets not referred to in the schedule

Some assets which may arise in an estate are not referred to in the schedule. Although in most estates there will not be any such assets, clearly difficulty may arise if there are any, and the principle that statute, if it governs something such as the application of assets, should be clear and should be applicable to all eventualities is further offended by the omissions. The assets not referred to include money paid into the estate if the grantee of an option over property in the estate exercises that option, and property which is subject to a general power of appointment.

In *Re Eve* (1956), the testator left an option to one of the beneficiaries, which entitled him to purchase certain shares from the estate at less than market value. The question was whether the shares should be applied as specific gifts; if there is a shortfall of funds, specific gifts have priority. The court found that it was not a specific gift of the shares, but that if the money paid for the shares would render the estate capable of meeting its debts and liabilities, then the personal representatives should use the money for that rather than selling the shares to meet that beneficiary's share of the liabilities, and the property subject to the option should be the last to be available for the payment of debts. This would appear to have been a helpful compromise in the circumstances of the case, avoiding bringing the shares within para 6 of the statutory order.

The schedule is also silent as to the subject matter of *donationes mortis causa*.

13.16 Debts charged on specific property – s 35

Until the later part of the 19th century, a beneficiary who inherited realty could usually have any mortgage debt paid out of the deceased's general personalty. Now, however, s 35 of the Administration of Estates Act 1925 says that where any interest in property that belonged to the deceased is charged with a debt, and the deceased has not signified a contrary intention by any document, that interest is primarily liable to bear the charge. It also provides specifically that a contrary intention is not deemed to be signified by a general direction for the payment of debts out of the testator's personalty or out of his residuary real estate or residuary real and personal estate, or by a charge of debts on any such estate, unless the testator signifies his intention further, by words which refer either expressly or by necessary implication to the particular charge itself. The usual situation to which this section will apply is that of a mortgaged house or similar property. However, it may also apply to more unusual situations, such as a vendor's lien for unpaid purchase money, a limited company's lien over its own shares or a charging order made by the court.

The section also provides that every part of the charged interest should bear a proportionate part of the charge on the whole, in accordance with its value. This means that if a beneficiary takes only a share of the charged property, he does so subject to a share of the charge. If the beneficiaries of the other shares do not take them and pay their share of the charged debt, their shares of the debt will not (as between beneficiaries) come out of the value of the charged interest, but will fall to be paid by the estate, into which the uncharged value of the interest will also fall.

The property is only 'primarily' liable; this section does not confine a creditor whose loan is secured to looking to the mortgaged property for satisfaction of the debt. That point is particularly important in the case of 'negative equity' – where the property on which a debt is secured is of a lower value than the debt, for example where a house worth £50,000 is subject to a mortgage debt of £65,000. The £65,000 was a debt owed by the testator and the creditor may look to his estate as a whole to satisfy it, just as the deceased was liable for the whole debt when he was alive.

A charge in the sense meant by s 35 of the 1925 Act is a formal charge of the kind represented by a house mortgage to a building society. The section does not apply when the relationship between the debt and the property, though close and perhaps completely intertwined, falls short of a mortgage or formal charge.

Note that there is no obligation on a mortgagee (for example, a building society) to continue loan arrangements made by and with the deceased. It is not necessarily the case that a person who inherits a mortgaged house can keep it so long as they keep up the mortgage payments. If they cannot afford to pay off the loan secured on the house immediately, they will have to have the mortgagee agree to make the loan to them instead of the deceased – that is, they will have to remortgage it themselves with the same, or another, lender. However, in many cases the deceased will turn out to have had life assurance which will specifically repay the secured debt.

13.17 Marshalling

A creditor of the estate will not lose his claim because of the result of the rules as to the incidence of debts as between the beneficiaries. He may satisfy his claim out of any assets in the estate. Adjustments must then be made to reassert the proper position as between the beneficiaries so that the incidence rules finally prevail. Where a beneficiary's gift has been taken to pay a creditor, he may take in compensation the property which should, according to the rules of incidence of debts, have been used to pay the creditor. This process is called marshalling.

13.18 The incidence of general or pecuniary legacies

Having established where the debts and liabilities of the estate must be paid from, the personal representative must also establish what property is to be used to meet any general, or pecuniary, legacies.

13.18.1 The situation before 1926

Things were clear before the reforms of 1925, even if they were not ideal. Unless the testator altered the position by will, realty and the subject matter of specific legacies were exempt from the burden of general legacies and the general personal estate was liable *pari passu* (each part as much as another) for the legacies.

If the testator gave the residue of realty and personalty after payment of general legacies, then the rule in *Greville v Brown* (1859) meant that the legacies would be paid first out of the personalty, but that realty could be resorted to in order to meet the general legacies if the general personalty did not suffice. If the testator directed payment of the general legacies out of a mixed fund of realty and personalty, then the two parts of the fund were liable to be used for legacies in proportion to their values, in accordance with the rule in *Roberts v Walker* (1830).

13.18.2 The situation after 1925

There is no provision in the Administration of Estates Act 1925 as to what part of an estate legacies, as opposed to debts, should be paid from. In principle one would assume, therefore, that it was intended that the old law should still apply. However, given that the whole structure of the application of property was altered by the reforms of that year, the old law no longer fits well with the rest of the legal provisions. There are particular parts of the new law which are very difficult to reconcile with the continuation of the old. It seems likely that the omission of any statutory provision as to the payment of legacies from the 1925 legislation was an oversight rather than deliberate.

There are two main areas of query. First, it is unclear how the rules in *Greville v Brown* and *Roberts v Walker* operate when the testator dies partially intestate and s 33 of the Administration of Estates Act 1925 imposes a trust on the undisposed-of property. Secondly, there is potential for applying s 34(3) of the AEA 1925 and the statutory order, but it not clear whether this is appropriate. It is unclear whether s 34(3) includes legacies in any event, since it refers only to 'funeral and testamentary expenses, debts and liabilities'.

13.18.3 Legacies in a partial intestacy after 1925

Section 33 of the Administration of Estates Act 1925 deals with the administration of assets on a partial intestacy (in the case of a total intestacy, there will by definition be no general legacies). Section 33(1) provides that 'on the death of a person intestate as to any real or personal estate' such estate (if not already money) shall be held by his personal representatives upon trust for sale and conversion into money.

Section 33(2) provides: 'Out of the net money to arise from the sale and conversion ... the personal representative shall pay all such funeral, testamentary and administration expenses, debts and other liabilities as are properly payable thereout ... and out of the residue of the said money the personal representative shall set aside a fund sufficient to provide for any pecuniary legacies bequeathed by the will (if any) of the deceased.' This makes undisposed-of property primarily liable for general legacies on a partial intestacy.

It may be the case that the imposition of the statutory trust on all the property in the estate amounts to an ousting of the rule in *Greville v Brown*, as it contains no distinction between realty and personalty; this would be in keeping with the general trend of the 1925 legislation. However, the statute does not say so.

13.18.4 Section 34(3) of the AEA 1925, the statutory order and general legacies

It is possible that legacies given by the will should be treated in the same way as the debts and liabilities referred to in s 34(3) of the Administration of Estates Act 1925 (see 13.14). However, it does not refer specifically to them. If they are not to be included, then the Act fails to make any provision for how assets are to be applied to pay legacies. In that case, the old law ought logically to apply, since it was not varied by the Act. It is not clear that this is correct, as a matter of law, because the statute, again, does not mention it. Statute should be clear, and usually when a statute is changing law in a particular area then it will contain a reference to any law in a closely-related area which is not changed, specifying what related provisions are unaffected. There is no such reference in this part of the Administration of Estates Act 1925, where the related law is not merely close but potentially inconsistent. This question will be of practical importance where the estate is wholly covered by the will if, as in *Re Thompson* (1936) (below at 13.18.6), the legacies are payable out of residue but the residue is divided as to realty and personalty, and the personal representatives need to know which part of the gift will be depleted by the payment of the legacies.

The courts have no fixed view on the fundamental question of whether s 34(3) of the Administration of Estates Act 1925, which refers only to debts, includes legacies. They oscillate between the view that the old rules as to the incidence of legacies still apply, as the Administration of Estates Act 1925 made no provision changing those rules, and the view that the incidence of legacies should be regarded as analogous to that of debts and therefore dealt with in the same way. It is even possible to find the same judge apparently holding different views on the law in different cases (see the decisions of Danckwerts J, below, in *Re Beaumont* (1950) and *Re Martin* (1955)).

13.18.5 Two funds of undisposed-of property

A further question may arise in relation to the payment of legacies out of a partially intestate estate where there are two separate funds of undisposed-of property, the first being property totally undisposed of by the will and therefore covered by the statutory trust for sale under s 33 of the AEA 1925, and the second arising under a trust set up by the will, part of which does not, however, have a beneficiary. Although the statutory provisions can be varied by the will, it may not be entirely clear whether or not this has been done. If, for example, there is a will trust providing for the payment of legacies, with the residue of that property going to three beneficiaries, of whom one has predeceased without a gift over, the question will arise as to whether the shares of the beneficiaries under the trust should be ascertained before or after the payment out of legacies, or whether legacies should come out of the totally undisposed-of property, in accordance with s 33, rather than out of the property covered by the will trust.

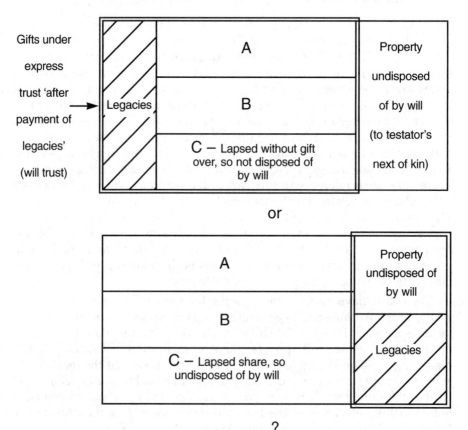

13.18.6 Courts hold that s 34(3) has no effect on legacies ...

Clauson J held in *Re Thompson* (1936) that the pre-1926 rules still applied to the incidence of general legacies. The testator gave general legacies and then left his residuary realty and personalty to charity. The court had to decide whether the legacies were payable rateably out of the residuary real and personal estate, or whether they were payable primarily out of residuary personalty in accordance with the rule in *Greville v Brown.* The court held that s 34(3) and the statutory order had not altered the old rules. Clauson J said, 'It is suggested that the effect of that provision is to alter the law ... The provision does not say so ... The provision is concerned with the way in which funeral testamentary and administration expenses, debts and liabilities are to be met. There is no indication there that there is any intention of altering the law ...' in respect of general legacies. This is, in essence, the difficulty, since an alteration is implied by the change in other rules and by the general restructuring of administration, but yet nothing is stated, either as to whether the rules remain the same or whether they should be considered analogous to those for debts and expenses.

If this is correct it means that a pecuniary legacy fund should be retained out of the testator's undisposed-of property under para 1 of the statutory order only insofar as the undisposed-of property was liable to be applied to legacies under the old rules. The same would apply in respect of retaining a pecuniary legacy fund out of residue under para 2. This would entail reading the reference to a pecuniary legacy fund in paras 1 and 2 of the statutory order as restricting the fund to being retained only insofar as it would have been liable to meet pecuniary legacies under the old rules.

Re Thompson was applied by the court in *Re Anstead* (1943), where the testator left general legacies and made a gift of residue in trust. There was no direction as to what funds should be used to pay legacies, and the question was again whether the rule in *Greville v Brown* applied. The court held that the debts and expenses were payable out of the remaining residue after setting aside a pecuniary legacy fund under para 2 of the statutory order. This meant that the pecuniary legacy fund would become liable for the debts and expenses only under para 5, which entailed that the retention of the fund was in accordance with the old rules rather than rateably out of residuary personalty and realty.

Re Thompson (1936)

If s 34(3) of the AEA 1925 and the statutory order had altered the old rules ...

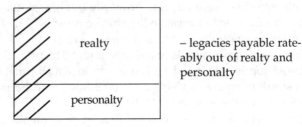

– legacies payable rateably out of realty and personalty

... but the rule in *Greville v Brown* still applied

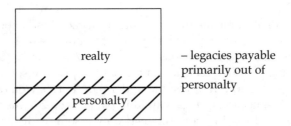

– legacies payable primarily out of personalty

Re Thompson was also applied in *Re Beaumont* (1950). The testatrix in that case gave pecuniary legacies free of duty and then left all her realty and personalty on trust for sale, after payment of her expenses and debts, to be divided amongst four persons. One of the four predeceased, so that share lapsed and went as on intestacy, falling within para 1 of the statutory order. Danckwerts J said that s 34(3) 'has in effect made no provision with regard to such things as legacies ... the position of the legacies depends on the old law'. Under the old law, the legacies were payable out of the estate before it was divided, rather than being taken first of all out of the undisposed-of share as under para 1 of the statutory order.

Re Beaumont (1950)

If s 34(3) and the statutory order applied ...

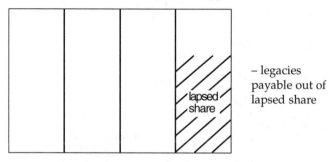

– legacies
payable out of
lapsed share

... but Danckwerts J held that the old order still applied

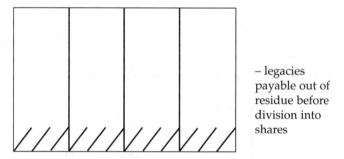

– legacies
payable out of
residue before
division into
shares

13.18.7 ... courts hold that legacies are governed by s 34(3) and the statutory order

The alternative view holds that s 34(3) and the statutory order have altered the old rules as to the incidence of general legacies, so that a pecuniary legacy fund must be retained out of the testator's undisposed-of property under para 1 (and by analogy out of residue under para 2) of the statutory order, whether or not the property referred to in that paragraph would have been applicable to legacies before 1926.

In *Re Worthington* (1933), as in *Re Lamb*, the testatrix directed for the payment of debts and expenses (which are payable anyway) and legacies without specifying what property should be used to pay them. Her residuary estate was left to two persons, of whom one predeceased. If the pre-1926 rules applied, the incidence of the legacies was governed by the rule in *Greville v Brown*, and they were payable primarily out of the residuary personalty, whether or not it went on intestacy, with residuary realty only liable in aid. The decision at first instance was the provisions of the AEA 1925 applied only insofar as the payment of debts was concerned, which were to be taken from the lapsed share of residue. In respect of the legacies, the court of first instance held that the old law applied, and they were payable out of the estate before the ascertainment of the residue. The Court of Appeal, however, held that the legacies should be treated in the same way as the debts. The lapsed share of residue should be ascertained first and the legacies then paid out of it.

Re Worthington (1933)

If the rule in Greville v Brown applied ...

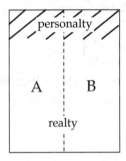

legacies from residuary personalty (whether or not lapsed), residuary realty liable in aid

... but the court held the statutory order applied

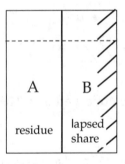

legacies paid from lapsed share under para 1 of the statutory order

The court in Re Midgley (1955) followed Re Worthington. In Re Midgley, the testatrix gave pecuniary legacies and then left her residuary estate, after payment of debts and expenses, on trust to be divided amongst six persons. She later revoked one person's gift, which was undisposed of at her death. Harman J held that para 1 of the statutory order required the legacies to be paid out of that one-sixth share, asking: 'What, then, is to be done with the fund which has been retained thereout? ... The answer, it seems to me, is that it must be used to meet the pecuniary legacies, because it has been retained for that purpose. It is, if I may say so, a tortuous way of legislating.'

The same view was taken by the court in Re Martin (1955), where the testator gave pecuniary legacies, and then left all his residuary personalty on trust, having revoked the gift of his realty, which was undisposed of at his death. There was no express trust for sale of the undisposed-of realty, so s 33(1) and (2) applied to it. Danckwerts J held that the legacies were payable out of the realty pursuant to s 33(2), construing para 1 of the statutory order without regard to the pre-1926 rules which made legacies payable out of the general personal estate. This appears to contradict the view of the law he took five years earlier in *Re Beaumont* (1950) (above).

Re Martin (1955)

If the rule in *Greville v Brown* applied ...

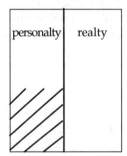

legacies payable from general personalty

... but Danckwerts J held the old rules had been altered by s 33(2) of the AEA 1925

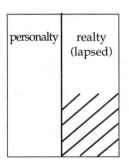

legacies payable out of lapsed share

13.18.8 Legacies and debts

In *Re Wilson* (1967), the testatrix gave such generous pecuniary legacies that there was insufficient in the estate to meet them. Notwithstanding this, she left her realty and residuary personalty to her daughter. The personal representatives needed to know whether the realty should be used to endeavour to satisfy the pecuniary legacies. The court held, on the wording of the will, that the testatrix had not intended the realty to be depleted by the legacies. However, the pecuniary legacies would exhaust the personalty, so the question also arose as to what funds should be used to meet the debts. If they were paid out of the personalty, they would reduce still further the amount available for the legacies. The court held that the realty fell within para 2 of the First Schedule to the AEA 1925 as 'property ... included ... in a residuary gift' and that the debts should be paid out of the daughter's realty.

13.19 Liability of a personal representative

A personal representative may be liable in various ways. He will be liable to the estate and its beneficiaries if he does not deal with its assets properly and he may become liable to those who deal with the estate, such as landlords or parties to contracts. In some situations he may be liable only so far as the estate is liable, and able to indemnify himself from the estate. In other cases, he will be personally liable.

13.19.1 *Devastavit*

Devastavit means 'he wasted it' – a breach of a personal representative's duty to preserve the assets of the estate and administer the estate properly and in accordance with the law which makes him liable for his failure. The personal representative is personally liable to beneficiaries and creditors of the estate, whether he has used the assets for his own purposes, failed to administer them properly without, however, any improper intention, or failed to preserve the assets.

An example of the personal representative using the assets for his own purposes might be simply pocketing money, or could be something more complex. It need not involve anything that might be considered misappropriation for his own gain. A personal representative who improperly administered the estate without appropriating any gain to his own purposes was said to have committed *devastavit* in *Shelly's Case* (1693) when he incurred funeral expenses out of keeping with the estate.

13.19.2 Breach of trust

There is, however, a distinction between breach of duty as a personal representative and breach of duty as a trustee, though some acts may constitute both. Breach of trust is, however, usually wider, so an executor who makes a profit from his office which is unauthorised by will, without causing loss to the estate, is liable to the estate for breach of trust, but not in *devastavit*.

13.19.3 Funeral expenses

The personal representative, if he arranges the funeral in that capacity, is liable for the funeral expenses to the extent that the assets in the estate meet the cost of a funeral in keeping with the deceased's position in life. If he requests a funeral which is more expensive than the estate warrants, he is personally liable to the undertaker for the full cost and will not be able to recoup the excess cost, but only the cost of what the estate warranted and its assets can bear. If another person deals with the undertaker, they will be directly liable to the undertaker for the whole cost, though they are entitled to be indemnified from the estate to the same extent as the personal representative.

13.19.4 Liability to account

The personal representative has a liability in law to keep an inventory of the assets of the estate and to keep full and accurate accounts showing both receipts and payments. He is also obliged to exhibit them on oath when the court requires. Equity provides remedies for many breaches of duty by a personal representative, including accounting.

13.19.5 Liability for co-personal representative

Generally there is no vicarious liability for the breaches of duty of a co-representative, though a personal representative must take care not to be led into involvement in bad deeds by a co-personal representative which will involve him in personal liability.

13.19.6 Limitation

Limitation is available to a personal representative as a defence in certain circumstances, the normal period being 12 years. However, it is no defence where the personal representative still holds the property in question, nor where he has committed fraud.

13.19.7 *Plene administravit*

Plene administravit means 'he has fully administered the estate'. It is a matter of procedure, and can be of great practical importance. Any personal representative who, having dealt with the estate and distributed it, finds an action being brought against him by a creditor who had a claim against the estate at the date of death should enter the plea, because if he does so he will be protected from personal liability in most cases.

If the personal representative fails to enter the plea he may find that he is liable for the full amount of judgment, even where the plea was available, as occurred in *Midland Bank v Green (No 2)* (1979). In that case, the son sued his father for breach of contract in respect of the option granted him on his property, which the father deliberately frustrated by selling the land to his wife with a clear land charges search, the son having failed to register his option. The father died in the course of the proceedings and the personal representative, having failed to plead plene administravit, was liable for the full amount of the judgment, which greatly exceeded the father's estate.

13.19.8 Relief from liability granted by court

The personal representative may be authorised to do certain things, including to be paid for administering the estate, by a clause in the will. Alternatively, he may seek authorisation from the beneficiaries, provided they are all of full age and agree.

   If instead he seeks relief from the court from liability, however, the court may grant it if it sees fit in its discretion under s 61 of the Trustee Act 1925, the onus of proving honesty and reasonableness being on the personal representative. In *Re Rosenthal* (1972), for example, the court regarded the behaviour of a professional trustee who paid estate duty on a gift from residue when the donee of the gift should have paid it much as did the residuary beneficiary; it may have been honest, but it was not reasonable or excusable, and there was no order for relief from liability.

13.20 Rights of wrongfully deprived beneficiaries

Where a beneficiary has been wrongfully deprived of his benefit under the deceased's will or intestacy, he has first of all the right to pursue the personal representatives for the wrongful distribution. However, they may not be able to satisfy his claim.

   He will have two further avenues to pursue, against the person who received the property and against the property itself. He may use his right in equity to claim a refund personally from anyone to whom money or property has been wrongfully given, or he may trace the property itself, also in equity.

13.20.1 Refund

The beneficiary may claim a refund against the recipient if the personal representative made a wrongful payment and the beneficiary has exhausted all his remedies against the personal representative, either because the personal representative is insolvent or because he is protected from liability by having complied with the advertisements provisions of s 27 of the Trustee Act 1925 or by having obtained a 'Benjamin' order before distributing the assets.

13.20.2 Tracing

A beneficiary may try to trace the money or property which has been wrongfully paid over. Tracing in equity goes further than in common law, but a claim in equity will not lie against a bona fide purchaser without notice of the wrongful payment. The beneficiary does not have to have exhausted his remedies against the personal representatives in order to trace, although if he has pursued them, then anything he has obtained from them must be set off against the property he claims to trace.

13.20.3 Example – the Diplock estate

The principle of the equitable refund was used in the case of *Ministry of Health v Simpson* (1951). This was one of the cases, with *Chichester Diocesan Fund and Board of Finance v Simpson* (1944), which concerned the estate of Caleb Diplock, who left a substantial residuary estate to such 'charitable or benevolent' object as his executors selected. Only after some £200,000 had been distributed did the next of kin bring their challenge to the validity of the wording to create a charitable gift. The House of Lords held the gift not wholly charitable and therefore it failed. The next of kin could not obtain more than £15,000 from the executors, so they claimed both a refund from the charities who had received the money and a right to trace the property. The latter claim did not succeed against the hospital which challenged the next of kin's claim, but the House of Lords held that the claim for a refund did, although the charity had notice of the wrongfulness of the payment, had changed its position as a result of the gift (it used it to commission a new building, which was why the remedy of tracing was unavailable) and the personal representatives had been under a mistake of law, not of fact, when they made the payment.

ADMINISTRATION OF ESTATES

The administration of the estate is the process whereby the personal representatives collect in the assets of the estate and then meet the debts and liabilities and pay out the legacies and devises before distributing the residue, managing the estate as necessary in the meantime.

The funds in the estate must first be applied to meet debts and liabilities. The funeral expenses come first, and then the administration expenses and the debts of the deceased at his death. Debts arising after death are next, followed by any specific gifts and then general gifts. Only after this can the residue be ascertained.

The personal representatives may be personally liable to those who suffer if they do not carry out the administration properly. There are however systems for them to protect themselves against the possibility of claims arising after they have distributed the estate.

To ascertain all the debts and liabilities, they must not only go through the deceased's papers but also advertise for creditors in accordance with s 27 of the Trustee Act 1925. If the personal representatives know of the existence of a beneficiary but cannot trace him, they may be able to seek a 'Benjamin' order enabling them to distribute the estate as though he had predeceased. In both cases the personal representatives are protected from personal liability should further claimants appear after the estate has been distributed.

The personal representatives have certain powers of administration and management of the estate under statute, but these are generally considered to be very inadequate and they are usually widened in any professionally-drawn will. Where an estate arises after 1996 and includes land, however, the powers are much wider by virtue of the Trusts of Land and Appointment of Trustees Act 1996. Certain obligations to make complex calculations as between beneficiaries entitled in succession to each other, in order to preserve equality between them, are also commonly excluded in any case where they might arise.

Where a personal representative passes land, this may be done by written assent under s 36 of the Administration of Estates Act 1925. A personal representative may also appropriate assets in satisfaction of gifts under s 41 of the AEA 1925, with certain limited obligations to obtain consents. The need to obtain those consents is often excluded by will.

The beneficiaries probably have no proprietary interest in the property in the estate, although they have the chose in action of the right to ensure due administration of the estate. A residuary beneficiary probably obtains an interest when the residue is ascertained, but not before. There is authority for saying that a specific beneficiary may obtain some form of equitable interest in the relevant property at death.

If the estate is insolvent and cannot even meet all its debts, they must be paid out in the order set out in s 34(1) of the Administration of Estates Act 1925. Debts charged on specific property are covered separately by s 35. Section 34(3) and Pt II, Sched 1 of the AEA 1925 set out the statutory order of application of assets to debts where the estate is solvent, though this statutory provision may be varied by the will. It is unclear whether this statutory order for the payment of debts may also be applied to the payment of legacies, or how the provision under the statutory order for the setting aside of a fund to meet pecuniary legacies when paying out for debts interacts with the provision under s 33 for the payment of pecuniary legacies on a partial intestacy.

A personal representative may be liable in devastavit or breach of trust for failing properly to administer the estate, but if he has acted in good faith and reasonably he may seek relief from the court under s 61 of the Trustee Act 1925.

A beneficiary who has lost out because the estate has not been properly administered may go against the personal representatives. If however they are unable to satisfy him (because they do not have enough money) he may also have rights of action in equity against the recipient of the property or may be able to trace the money or property which has been paid over. This may also apply to the subject of a Benjamin order who turns up later and cannot pursue the personal representatives.

CHAPTER 14

TAX AND TAX PLANNING

14.1 The importance of tax

The subject of taxation is relevant principally to the practice of wills and
probate rather than to the substantive law of succession. However, it is an
academic subject as well, both in itself and in what it reveals about the
priorities held by the society that imposes it on its members.

14.1.1 Principles of taxation to be applied to minimise liability

The practical aspect of dealing with taxation in the context of wills is the
minimisation of a liability to tax. To understand the principles of how the
basic rules of taxation would apply in outline to the situation of a given estate,
there is no need to perform precise mathematics. The requirement is to see
where the tax liability would fall.

The vital difference between tax avoidance and tax evasion must be borne
in mind. The former is lawful whilst the latter is fraud. To arrange one's affairs
so as to minimise liability to tax is highly respectable; to put one's property
where it will be liable to tax but undiscoverable or unattainable by the Inland
Revenue is not proper.

14.1.2 Potential liability to be minimised in advance of death

Once the areas of tax liability have been established, the ways of reducing them
should be apparent. With tax, the planning element is often vital, since many
advantages cannot be achieved unless the testator begins early. None of us
knows when we will die, so there is a constant need for anyone with any
substance to their property to keep their tax situation in mind. Even those who
have little or no property may come into some, perhaps unexpectedly. Just as a
person should keep their will up to date in order to benefit the family and
friends they consider appropriate in the event of their death, so they should
keep their tax situation under review in order to take account of changes both in
the property they own and in the law relating to taxation.

14.1.3 Structure and general rules change but slowly

The structure of the law of taxation does not change rapidly, so once that
structure is understood it becomes easier to deal with any changes in the
details. A person making a will must always be advised both as to the tax
liability their proposals may incur and as to ways of reducing it. This applies

even to a person making a will with a non-specialist 'High Street' firm of solicitors, as it is by no means uncommon for there to be a potential liability to tax which could be minimised by sensible tax planning even in a modest estate which appears to consist mainly of an interest in an ordinary family house.

14.1.4 The art of tax planning?

The art of tax planning, it has been said, is that of detaching the testator sufficiently from his property to satisfy the Inland Revenue that he has truly given it away, whilst retaining for him as much control over it as possible. The ownership of property brings with it power, and where a person is dealing with the making of a will he is dealing with his power over his family and friends, which he will usually want to retain as long as possible. This desire pulls against the desire, also usual, to let the tax man have as little of his property as possible, because the former demands the retention of control over the property and the latter demands the release of it.

The main concern in this chapter is with Inheritance Tax, but considerations of Capital Gains Tax and Income Tax may also arise in an estate. However, the former is interesting mostly because of the provisions which mean it generally does not arise, and the latter pertains mostly to continuing trusts, which are outside the scope of this book.

14.1.5 Tax avoidance and provision for the elderly

Note that avoidance of tax, however lawful, should not be allowed to become a fetish. Particularly in times when there are serious questions surrounding the state provision of care for the elderly, it may be better to risk one's successors paying tax on their inheritance than to risk giving away so much property in pursuit of tax avoidance that there is not enough to provide for one's old age.

It may be very difficult to estimate what property a person needs to keep to ensure proper provision in old age. A major factor in this difficulty is that one cannot know how long one will live. Moreover, where a person is living off the income on a capital investment, they will be affected not only by changing interest rates, which fluctuate somewhat unpredictably, but also by inflation, which may render capital permanently inadequate. There are various ways of maximising the use of property and capital for one's retirement and old age, but specialist professional advice is required. Annuities are favourably treated for tax purposes and may be advisable for someone who does not have much income but does have sufficient capital to purchase one. A person may wish to make up the resulting capital loss to his prospective estate by taking out a life policy written in trust for his children or grandchildren, which will also carry bonuses. Home equity releases, where an insurance company lends a houseowner money under a mortgage arrangement and repays itself from the proceeds of sale after death, may be appropriate and may be favourable for Income Tax purposes, but should be treated with great caution. The money advanced should be used principally to purchase an annuity exceeding the mortgage repayments, but the unpredictability of both interest rates and lifespan mean that great care should be taken in advising on such schemes. There is little risk attached, however, to advising elderly clients on the increased personal allowances for Income Tax after the ages of 65 and 75, or advising them to elect to take any interest from building society or bank account in gross, preventing the need to reclaim tax deducted at source.

14.1.6 Residential care of the elderly

A particular issue at present is that of the cost of caring for the elderly, especially when residential care is required. Changes in recent Health Service practice have meant that people are no longer kept in National Health Service hospitals unless they require medical treatment as such; long-term stays in geriatric wards for those who require only nursing care are now rare. Many elderly people are now incurring a liability to pay fees for such care which are capable of wiping out even a substantial inheritance. This results from changes in practice and circumstance more than the structure of the law.

The state provision of residential care has been means-tested ever since the inception of the welfare state under the National Assistance Act of 1948. Once Supplementary Benefit or Income Support payments began to be made towards private nursing homes, these began to be used more frequently in place of long-stay geriatric wards, so that liability transferred effectively from the NHS to local authority social services departments. The higher rate Income Support payment for these was, however, withdrawn in 1993, resulting effectively in social services departments becoming the gatekeepers for placements. At the same time, although it is estimated that there are probably six million friends and family members providing informal care to the infirm, of whom perhaps one and a half million do so for more than 20 hours a week, there has been at least a perceived increase in the absolute numbers of those requiring residential care, perhaps because of a breakdown in the sort of community responsibility that would previously have provided care, or perhaps because of an increase in longevity and its accompanying infirmity, especially for those with serious illnesses such as Alzheimer's disease. The question of individuals paying for their own care has become more relevant not only because such payments are more often required because of the shift away from NHS care (which is free) to nursing home care (which is means-tested) but also because more elderly people now have relevant means in the form of a house. The purchase of a house is often felt by someone to be provision not only of their home but also of an inheritance for their children; the effect of a period in a nursing home may be to wipe out that inheritance. Contributions of up to £20,000 a year are not considered unusual. The effect of this area of law and practice on succession matters is enormous.

There are various statutory provisions governing the state's liability to provide care for the infirm person and that person's liability to pay for himself. The criteria for eligibility for NHS care vary from one local health authority to another, and are obtainable from the authority for the relevant area. Department of Health circulars provide guidelines as to such criteria and as to how a person who feels they have been inappropriately discharged from NHS care may appeal.

Part III of the National Assistance Act (NAA) 1948, especially s 21, specifies the powers and duties of social services departments in relation to residential accommodation. If a person is assessed as requiring it, they must arrange it, provided para 3 of the NAA 1948 (Charges for Accommodation) Regulations 1992 is satisfied. The preferred accommodation must suit the person's needs, must cost what provision for those needs usually costs and must be run in accordance with the local authority's usual terms and conditions. If someone chooses accommodation which is more expensive, they may obtain it by paying the difference.

The local authority is obliged to charge for the accommodation, except in relation to a temporary stay. The person using the services will be assessed financially and is primarily liable to pay, but a spouse will be a 'liable relative' and thus may also have to pay. Children are not liable relatives, but may come under considerable pressure to pay. The service user's capital and property, as well as their income, is assessed, and that will include their house, if they have one. The value of the house may be ignored in the case of a temporary stay, or where it is still occupied by a partner or possibly a former partner, by a family member aged 60 or over or someone aged under 16 whom the service user is liable to maintain or who is incapacitated. Otherwise, in the absence of a sparingly-used overall discretion, the value of the house will be taken into account.

Sometimes, people who fear charges for nursing care are tempted to try to put their assets out of the reach of the state. This became particularly relevant with the spread of home ownership in the 1980s. Where a person has disposed of property gratuitously or at an undervalue with the intention of avoiding such charges, the transaction may be avoided under s 21 of the Health and Social Services and Social Security Adjudications Act 1983 if it took place within six months of the admission to the residential home, or after admission. The requirement of proof of the necessary intention might prove awkward; a person may very plausibly give away property to family members for other reasons. Moreover, such a disposition may not be practically reversible; for example, the donees of an elderly person's house may have sold it and dissipated its value. Regulation 25(1) of the National Assistance (Assessment of Resources) Regulations 1992 allows a person to be treated as still having resources of which he has deliberately deprived himself, but it is difficult to see how this would be implemented practically where the transactions are irreversible. Note that transactions designed to defeat creditors may be set aside under the Insolvency Act 1986, and that where charges are levied but remain unpaid they may also be enforced by bankruptcy proceedings.

The government, along with other organisations, continues to consider the question of provision of care for the elderly and infirm. In 1995, a consultative document *A New Partnership For Care In Old Age* was issued, claiming to present an 'innovative range of proposals to encourage people to make provision for long-term care', but none appeared immediately acceptable and workable.

14.2 Death and taxes

Succession law is mainly concerned with the transmission of property; inevitably, it attracts questions of whether and how that property should be taxed. The imposition of tax on a person's wealth on death might be thought to be the obvious opportunity, since the deceased can no longer make use of his wealth and will be able neither to feel the effects of the tax nor to complain. As for the deprived beneficiaries, they are obtaining a windfall anyway. The very principle of taxation is, however, described by some contemporary theorists, for example Robert Nozick, as 'theft'.

Some people believe that the inheritance of substantial wealth is wrong because it gives certain individuals an unearned head start over others for which no amount of hard work can compensate, and so is destructive of fairness, social cohesion and democratic principles. Others believe that objections to inherited wealth run contrary to the natural concern of parents to provide for their children and are based on nothing more edifying than jealousy.

In this area, those who support 'traditional family values' are usually those who are against taxation as an unjustifiable form of state interference and for the free disposition and inheritance of wealth; this may be contrasted with the situation in respect of family provision (see Chapter 15), where the minimisation of general taxation tends to call for state interference to enforce private moral obligations within the family if the deceased has failed to provide properly for his family after his death.

14.3 Inheritance tax

Estate duty preceded Inheritance Tax and was in force from 1894 to 1975. It was a charge made on wealth at death and as such was a narrow fiscal tax, easy to avoid by giving away all your property before death. When the Liberal government first introduced it, they did so with the justification that 'nature gives man no power over his earthly goods beyond the term of his life' so that the state could legitimately claim to prescribe the conditions and limitations under which the power of the dead hand to dispose of property was exercised. In the later years, the duty was widened to include gifts made immediately before death, and finally to include gifts made during the last seven years before dying.

14.3.1   Ideas for altering the system

There were proposals to change the basis of the tax on the passing on of wealth, for example, by charging it on the basis not of what the deceased passed on but on the basis of what each beneficiary received, possibly with allowances where the beneficiary was closely related to the deceased, extending the exemptions from the spouse to other family members. That indeed would have been an inheritance tax as such, but one has not yet been implemented despite the name of the current Act.

14.3.2   Recent history

The introduction of capital transfer tax in 1975 brought in a 'cradle to grave' gifts tax, to cure the perceived deficiencies of estate duty and to function as a means for the redistribution of wealth. Avoidance was to be eliminated by taxing all gifts. That principle was steadily eroded in the later 1970s, and a 10-year cumulation period was introduced in 1981. Margaret Thatcher's Conservative administration elected in 1979 had promised to repeal the tax.

14.3.3   Aim of the present tax ...

Inheritance Tax (IHT) was brought into operation by the spring Budget of 1986. The then Chancellor of the Exchequer described the old Capital Transfer Tax as two taxes, an inheritance tax and a lifetime gifts tax. He felt that the deterrence operating on lifetime giving had the effect of locking in assets, particularly the ownership of family businesses, often to the detriment of the businesses concerned. Accordingly, he proposed to abolish entirely the tax on lifetime gifts to individuals.

14.3.4   ... other views of what it achieves

Other persons interpreted the changes differently. Nigel Lawson's changes were described in the *Financial Times* as 'sham reasons for making a shabby handout to the very rich. Not only has he reverted to the old estate duty, he has falsified the label'. Inheritance Tax under the current Act is not confined to inheritances as this is popularly understood, but applies to lifetime gifts as well. It has been described as 'a welding of certain estate duty rules onto the already battered corpse of CTT ... simply a mess' (Chris Whitehouse, *Revenue Law*).

14.3.5 Justifications for the tax?

As a money-spinner for the government of the country, Inheritance Tax has always been something of a loss. It constitutes *a tiny proportion of* the total tax revenue. However, schemes and scheming to avoid Inheritance Tax may be partly responsible for this. The resulting lifetime distributions could be seen as a justification in themselves for the tax, and the whole operation certainly provides a source of revenue for lawyers and accountants.

14.4 Basic concepts

It is most useful to approach the question of the different taxes applicable in the law and practice of wills by appreciating first of all the basic structure of the tax system, the most relevant part of which in this context relates to Inheritance Tax. One should see that as a tax on the wealth the deceased had to part with at death, with particular provisions relating to gifts made in the seven years before death and some exemptions, principally for gifts to a spouse or charity.

14.4.1 Gratuitous intent

IHT is charged on the value transferred in any chargeable transfer where there is gratuitous intent. 'Gratuitous intent' means the intention to benefit the recipient by making some form of gift to them. Therefore, a deliberate sale at an undervalue is covered – if you sell your house worth £150,000 to your friend for £50,000, then assuming you were aware of the discrepancy you are making them a gift of £100,000. A poor bargain – where you unwittingly sell your house for much less than its real value – is not. In those circumstances, you will have had no gratuitous intent and there will be nothing for the Inland Revenue to charge IHT on.

14.4.2 Excluded property

Some property is excluded, such as foreign property owned by foreign domiciliaries and reversionary interests under a trust.

14.4.3 Exempt transfers – spouse and charity in life and on death

Some transfers of value are not chargeable but are exempt from the tax. Transfers between spouses (s 18 of the Inheritance Tax Act (IHTA) 1984) or to charity (s 23), or gifts for the national or public benefit or to qualifying political parties (defined in s 24(2) of the IHTA 1984) are exempt. These are the only lifetime exemptions which are reflected in the exemptions available on death.

14.4.4 The potentially exempt transfer

The potentially exempt transfer or 'PET' is the main vehicle for the encouragement of lifetime giving. The concept applies, with certain exceptions, to gifts made by individuals (that is, real persons, not those who are merely legal persons such as companies) to individuals after 17 March 1986. Some gifts into trusts are also PETs. Although the gifts are called 'potentially exempt', they might in practice be better called 'potentially chargeable', as the tax is not paid and then recouped, but is assumed not to be payable unless a later event makes it so. (For details of the operation of PETs, see below at 14.7.)

14.4.5 Taper relief (s 7(4))

The later event which makes a PET chargeable is the death of the donor within seven years of making the gift. There is a sliding scale for the amount of tax payable which means that some tax advantage will be obtained if the donor can live for three years after making the gift; the advantage then increases year by year until the full level of relief is reached at seven years from the date of the gift.

14.5 Lifetime IHT on death

The rules for IHT during lifetime and on death are intertwined, because of the rules relating to PETs in particular, and so it is necessary to appreciate the structure of the former when dealing with the latter. Some gifts made during a deceased's lifetime will have to be accounted for for IHT purposes at his death, unless they can be shown to fall within one of the various exemptions.

14.5.1 Lifetime allowances

For lifetime gifts, the IHTA 1984 has a much wider range of exemptions and allowances. There is an array of allowances which apply during a person's lifetime but which are not available on death. However, they often affect the administration of an estate and therefore need to be considered by the succession lawyer.

14.5.2 Annual allowances per donor

There is also an allowance of £3,000 in aggregate per tax year per taxpayer. This can be used as an allowance on a bigger gift and can be rolled over, if not used, for one year, so that a person who makes no gifts in one year may make £6,000 worth of gifts in the following year without their being chargeable to IHT. If, however, he leaves the making of gifts until the year after that, the first year's exemption, or whatever part of it remained unused and available, will fall out of the calculation.

14.5.3 Annual allowances per donee

Lifetime gifts of £250 per year per recipient are not chargeable and this concession can be used as well as the £3,000 allowance, but the £250 allowance cannot be severed from a bigger gift.

14.5.4 Regular gifts out of the donor's income

There is a provision that regular gifts out of income are not chargeable provided they do not reduce the donor's standard of living. This has a particular application in the area of succession law; it means that the premiums paid for a life assurance policy will not usually be chargeable to IHT. It also means, of course, that a person with a larger regular income effectively has a larger tax allowance just because he is richer; however, he can make use of it only if he gives his money away regularly. Section 11 also contains exemptions for dispositions for maintenance.

14.5.5 Marriage gifts

Section 22 provides that gifts on marriage are also exempt, although certain limits apply. These differ according to the donor's relationship with the couple. Close family relationships are the most advantageous. Parents may give £5,000, other relatives £2,500 and other persons £1,000 without a charge to IHT.

14.5.6 Business reliefs

In the business context, there are reliefs in ss 103–14 IHTA 1984 for gifts of business property and in ss 115–24 for agricultural property.

The essence of entitlement to both reliefs is that the transferor has owned and used the property for business or agriculture for the two years preceding the transfer, and is passing it on for continued use for the same purposes. Both reliefs contain provisions which equate with the provisions relating to Potentially Exempt Transfers for gifts of ordinary property, allowing the reliefs to be rescinded and reclaimed where the transferor dies within seven years, if the transferee has sold the property on or begun using it for different purposes. The detailed application of these reliefs is, however, more complicated, depending, for the level of relief in particular, on the nature of the business or agricultural property.

14.6 Exemptions on death

On death the exemptions are for gifts to spouse, charity, political parties or for the national or public benefit only. Thereafter the estate is chargeable, the first £223,000 at a nil rate ('the nil-rate band' from April 1998) and the rest at 40%. More may be payable if any 'PET' is brought into play. This occurs when the deceased dies within seven years of making a lifetime gift by death within seven years of lifetime gifts which were exempt at the time.

14.7 Potentially exempt transfers (PETs)– s 3A(1) of the IHTA 1984

PETs were brought into force by the Finance Act 1986 and refer to lifetime gifts to individuals only. If a gift is a PET, no tax is payable at the time of the gift. If the donor manages to live for seven years after the date of the gift, the gift falls out of the calculations entirely. In between, there is a sliding scale of percentage charges so that if the donor lives for three years, the amount of tax payable is reduced by 20%, and the reduction increases at 20% per year that the donor lives after the date of the gift, until the full relief is reached at seven years. This relief is known as 'taper relief'.

14.7.1 PETs and personal representatives

PETs can present a great problem to personal representatives dealing with an estate. To assess the charge on the estate to Inheritance Tax, they need full details of all the PETs the deceased made during his last seven years, of which he may or may not have kept accessible records. Although the donee is primarily liable to pay the tax on the gift, if the tax remains unpaid a year after the testator's death, the Inland Revenue may look to the personal representatives for payment of the outstanding sum. Personal representatives are personally liable for the payment of Inheritance Tax, so getting the figures wrong, even if that is because of the deceased's failure to keep clear or detailed figures, can have deeply adverse consequences for them.

14.7.2 Advantages of PETs

PETs do, however, have the advantage of attracting taper relief and, potentially, of allowing the gift to become free of tax. In times of higher inflation, they also had the considerable advantage of freezing the value of the asset chargeable to tax at the value at the date of the gift, rather than the date of death.

These days, however, particularly where house prices are concerned, there is more potential for the value of a gift to have fallen by the date of death. Section 131 of the IHTA 1984 contains provisions for relief of the liability to tax where this occurs.

14.8 Settlements for IHT

Settlements have always been a way of avoiding tax; the cases document the border fights between settlors and the Inland Revenue. There have been various approaches to the avoidance of tax by setting up trusts. Settlements for IHT purposes are defined in s 43(2) of the IHTA 1984.

Certain settlements are taxed more heavily than they were before. It is helpful to think of settlements as falling into two categories – firstly, those with an interest in possession, or fixed trusts, and, secondly, those without an interest in possession, or discretionary trusts.

14.8.1 Settlements with an interest in possession

A beneficiary with an interest in possession is treated by virtue of s 49(1) of the IHTA 1984 as beneficially entitled to the property in which the interest subsists. He will be considered to have an interest in possession if he has an immediate right to use the property, for example to live in a house, or to receive the income arising from it, for example the rent paid for the house by the tenants. Creation of, or a gift into, a settlement of this kind is immediately chargeable and cannot be a PET. Moreover, the effects of giving someone a life interest in possession include the swelling of their estate, for IHT purposes, by the capital value of the gift.

Thus, where a settlor creates a settlement under which a beneficiary is given a life interest in a house worth £200,000, he makes an immediately chargeable gift of £200,000 and the beneficiary at once has the likelihood of dying with an estate substantially chargeable to IHT even if he is otherwise of very modest means.

Note, however, that under s 55(1) of the IHTA 1984 if the settlor settles the property on himself for life, that particular part of the transaction does not give rise to a charge to tax. The charge to tax arises only where there is a change of interest in possession, so the same applies where a remainderman surrenders his interest to a life tenant.

14.8.2 Settlements without an interest in possession

If no-one has an immediate right to use or obtain income from the property in the settlement, for example, because all the payments out of the fund comprised in the settlement are to be made at the discretion of the trustees, it will be a settlement without an interest in possession. In *Pearson v Inland Revenue Commissioners* (1980), the trust fund was held for three adult beneficiaries, who were each to get one-third of the income unless the trustees exercised their power to accumulate the income or their power of appointment. The House of Lords, by a whisker, held that there was no interest in possession.

Discretionary trusts were once a good way of avoiding estate duty, but the system has been modified so that tax is chargeable. The fund is charged to tax at a rate that works out at 6% every 10 years, or more if the settlor dies within seven years of making the settlement. The settlor may fall foul of the rules relating to reservation of benefit unless he has been excluded from the trust for the seven years before death.

14.8.3 Advantageous forms of settlement

Certain kinds of settlements without an interest in possession are, however, treated favourably under the tax regulations. These are, principally, accumulation and maintenance settlements for children. A discretionary trust may also be set up by will and serve certain specific purposes including tax saving.

14.8.4 Accumulation and maintenance settlements

Accumulation and maintenance settlements (A&M trusts) are governed by s 71 of the IHTA 1984. They are tax-efficient in that creation of their interiors may be a PET, the ten year anniversary charge does not apply and no charge to tax arises when the beneficiary becomes entitled in possession at the specified age. However, they are subject to income tax. A&M trusts operate only where they satisfy all three conditions laid down by the Act:

(a) a person under the age of 25 must get the income or capital; and

(b) there is no interest in possession in the settlement and the income is applied only for the maintenance, education or benefit of a beneficiary or else it is accumulated; and

(c) either it is not more than 25 years since the trust was created or validated in conformity with (a) and (b) above; or all the beneficiaries have a common grandparent or are the children, widow, widowers of such grandchild beneficiaries who predeceased the vesting date.

An accumulation and maintenance settlement may be discretionary, but if there is an overriding power to appoint to a person over the age of 25, it is not an accumulation and maintenance settlement and will not have the tax advantages of one.

14.8.5 Discretionary trusts

Discretionary trusts may be used to maintain flexibility or to save tax.

14.8.6 Power of appointment exercisable within two years – s 144 of the IHTA 1984

Where a testator leaves any amount of property to trustees who have the widest possible class of beneficiaries amongst whom to exercise their powers of appointment, there will be no charge to tax on the making of distributions ('exit charge') within two years. The testator may leave the whole of his estate this way, giving his trustees secret instructions which are not admissible to probate; neither, however, are such instructions enforceable by the beneficiaries if breached.

14.8.7 Flexibility within the nil-rate band

A very popular use of the discretionary trust for those whose estates exceed the nil-rate band in value and who leave a spouse is to pay the nil-rate band into a discretionary trust and leave the spouse the rest. If this is all that is done in an estate, the liability to IHT will be nil. The spouse may be one of the beneficiaries to whom the trustees of the discretionary trust may pay income or capital, should she need it, but otherwise it can be held for other beneficiaries such as children. The spouse may be one of the trustees, or may be the sole trustee. Gifts to the spouse during her lifetime will not attract tax, and the balance held for and paid out to the other beneficiaries after her death is also not taxable if it is distributed within 10 years. It may be particularly advantageous for the testator to leave his severed share in the matrimonial home into the discretionary trust; the surviving spouse may continue to occupy by virtue of her own joint interest in the house whilst retaining the advantages of the deceased's severed share potentially passing straight from his estate to another ultimate beneficiary.

14.9 Gifts with a reservation (IHTA 1984, s 102 and Sched 20)

The provisions dating from estate duty days were reintroduced in s 102 of the IHTA 1984 so that a donor retaining a benefit in a 'gift' was treated for tax purposes as still owning the gift, and as giving it away on his death. Such a benefit would arise, for example, where a houseowner settled his house on himself for life with remainder to his children. If there were no rules about gifts with reservations, this would be a good way of avoiding tax on the value of your house without quite giving it away. A reservation of benefit may be something much less obvious than a life interest in property, however. The test is whether the donor is excluded from the enjoyment of the subject matter of the gift. Viscount Simonds in *Chick v Commissioner of Stamp Duties* (1958) said that where the donor had settled his property and then acquired some enjoyment of it which did not arise from an exchange related to the settlement, the question was not whether or not the non-exchange was advantageous to the donee.

14.9.1 Concession for the infirm

A houseowner who gives his house to a relative with the genuine expectation that he will not in future have any benefit from the house may, however, invoke a statutory concession, full details of which are in Sched 20, para 6(1) of the Finance Act 1986. This allows him to return there to be cared for because he has become too infirm or aged to look after himself without incurring IHT penalties relating to the reservation of benefit.

14.9.2 Interaction with other areas of financial rules and regulations?

It remains to be seen whether the new regulations for calculating the costs of the care of the elderly according to the amount of capital they own has any appreciable effect on the number of them who dispose of their capital entitlements during their lifetime. The difference that can be made to care costs can be substantial, running to thousands of pounds, whereas for many people the incidence of Inheritance Tax is irrelevant because their assets do not exceed the threshold for the payment of tax at £150,000.

14.9.3 Incidence of tax liability

Under the Finance Act 1986, Sched 19, paras 28(3) and 29, the donee is primarily liable for the tax payable on a gift with a reservation. If, however, the sum is not paid by the donee, the Inland Revenue may claim it from the personal representatives, who in turn may invoke s 204(9) of the IHTA 1984 to reclaim the tax from the donee.

14.10 Related property and associated operations

A further possible tax avoidance scheme is rendered inoperative by s 161 of the IHTA 1984. This rule applies mainly in respect of spouses, where, for example, a husband is making a gift to a third party and also makes a gift to his wife which she then passes to the third party. In the light of the exemption from IHT of gifts to spouses and the tax allowances existing per donor, this could give an unmerited tax advantage on what is essentially a gift from the husband to the third party. However, the rules of related property would mean that the value of the first gift should be added to the value of the related property and tax charged on the first gift as a proportion of the total value. This cannot therefore be used to avoid lifetime IHT and attempts to do so will inevitably affect the liabilities of the estate.

However, where items of property are concerned which are much more valuable as a group than they are as the total of separate items, and the property can be split up so that the value of it diminished, the rules may be avoided. For example, if the husband owned a collection of six antique chairs worth £25,000 together but £2,000 each individually, and he gave four to his wife, keeping the other two which he gave to the third party, the principle would not apply to the transfer to the third party of the second four because the husband no longer owned related property.

Associated operations arise where the transferor takes several steps which, taken separately, do not constitute a transfer of value but which, taken together, amount to the same result in terms of depleting the transferor's estate as if the property had simply been given direct. The Inland Revenue may view these operations together, charging tax on the whole under s 268 of the IHTA 1984. Again, this may affect the liability to lifetime IHT and thus the liabilities of the estate.

14.11 Life assurance policies

A gift by will of the benefit of a life assurance policy will not be chargeable if the donee is the spouse of the donor. It will, however, be chargeable if she is not. If the donor's nil-rate band is already used up, the donor will therefore be increasing the liability of his estate to tax by 40% of the value of the proceeds of the policy.

However, there is a real saving to tax if the policy proceeds go straight to a chargeable person without going into the deceased's estate by the policy having been written in trust for or assigned to that person. The premiums paid would be lifetime gifts but would probably fall within the exemption provisions relating to regular payments out of income.

Where a policy is assigned later, after being taken out, the chargeable value of the gift is the value of the policy when it is assigned. For IHT purposes that will be the higher sum of either the surrender value of the policy or the sum of the premiums paid.

14.12 Death

Death is the final transfer. Gratuitous intent is inferred and the estate of the deceased is treated as though the deceased had made a gift of all the property in his estate immediately before death.

14.12.1 What IHT is charged on at death

Once the date of death is known, the liability to IHT can be assessed. The personal representatives will need to know about any PETs made within the preceding seven years as well as any lifetime chargeable transfers before they can assess the amount of tax they need to reserve. Although donees of PETs are primarily liable to pay the tax on their gifts, for example, if they do not do so, the personal representatives may have to bear it.

Lifetime chargeable transfers will have been assessed to IHT at the lifetime rate (20%) assessed by cumulating the total of all the transfers, including the one in question, over the previous seven years. Liability to IHT is then reassessed on death on all the chargeable transfers, including PETs which have thus become chargeable, made within seven years of the date of death. The donor is primarily liable for the IHT on lifetime chargeable transfers, although the Inland Revenue may recover from others, including the donee.

The value of the chargeable transfers made during the seven-year period will be cumulated and the total deducted from the nil-rate band on death. Credit is given for payments made but refunds are not given. Taper relief on PETs must be allowed for. Gifts under the tax threshold may, by using up the nil-rate band, increase the rate of tax payable on the deceased's estate as a whole on death.

The full percentage rate of IHT, currently 40%, is chargeable on the value of all assets once any exempt gifts (to spouse or charity, for example) have been deducted and the nil-rate band of £150,000 has been used up.

14.12.2 The net estate on death

IHT is charged on the net estate on death. Where the deceased was domiciled in the UK, tax is charged on all his estate wherever it is situated; otherwise, it is charged only on property situated in the UK.

The 'estate' means all the property to which the deceased was beneficially entitled – that is, excluding property of which he was a trustee or administrator (s 5 of the IHTA 1984).

It includes:

(a) property subject to a reservation;

(b) non-deductible debts;

(c) settled property of which he was a life tenant;

(d) equitable joint tenancies;

(e) *donationes mortis causa*.

It does not include specifically excluded property, such as foreign property owned by foreign domiciliaries and reversionary interests under a trust. Nor will it include property which does not form part of the estate, such as life policies where the benefits go straight to another person under s 11 of the Married Women's Property Act 1882 or because they are written in trust.

14.13 *Commorientes*

The usual *commorientes* rule itself is contained in s 184 of the Law of Property Act 1925 and states that where two persons die in circumstances making it uncertain which went first, it is presumed that the elder predeceased the younger. It is subject to two exceptions; that for intestate spouses contained in s 46(3) of the Administration of Estates Act 1925 which states that, where such a spouse is the elder, his estate is to be dealt with on the basis that neither he nor his spouse survived each other, and an exception which relates solely to IHT.

14.13.1 IHTA, s 4(2), ousting LPA 1925, s 184

Purely for the purposes of IHT, when a *commorientes* situation arises, death will be presumed to have occurred at the same instant. This means that the same property cannot be taxed twice because it passes out of both estates attracting tax each time.

14.13.2 Quick succession relief – s 141 of the IHTA 1984

This is available where IHT is charged on a gift and the donee dies within five years, on a tapering basis of 20% per year. The tax on the estate is calculated and then the appropriate percentage is deducted from the tax paid on the gift to the donee. This relief is available whether or not the donee still has the gift when he dies. Rebates are available where the donee dies before the donor, who then dies within seven years of the original gift, if it was a PET.

14.14 Capital Gains Tax

Capital Gains Tax (CGT) was introduced by the Capital Gains Tax Act 1965, on the basis that there was no good reason why earned income should be subject to tax whereas the sums made by the sale of items of property should not. All the legislation is now consolidated in the Taxation of Chargeable Gains Act (TCGA) 1992.

14.14.1 Basics of assessment for capital gains tax

A liability to CGT arises when a person ordinarily resident in the UK, or that person's personal representatives, effectively make a profit on selling assets they bought at a lower price than the price at which they sell them. Assets do not include options, debts, foreign currency or property created by the owner without acquisition, for example goodwill. The tax is assessed on the difference between the two prices, save that acquisition is deemed to have taken place no earlier than 31 March 1982. Assets are all chargeable with a few exceptions such as sterling and motor cars. There is an indexation allowance to deal with gains solely due to inflation though this does not operate for periods after April 1998, and allowance for depreciation may be made in respect of wasting assets (those with a predicted useful life under 50 years).

14.14.2 Practical points

As with earned income, a person may make a certain amount before their profits become subject to the imposition of the tax. It is possible to incur a 'capital gains tax loss' on one disposal and set it off against capital gains in the same year or future years. Married couples used to have their liability to tax aggregated, reflecting the roots of the legal system of the ownership of property within marriage. However, since Britain joined the European Community, such legislation has become unlawful in terms of European law, and in 1988 the rules were changed to separate assessment.

Capital gains tax does not apply to the profits made from businesses trading in goods at a profit; such profits are regarded as income of their businesses and taxed under the rules for income tax or corporation tax. Transactions between connected persons are deemed to be at open market value (s 18). Individuals are connected to their spouses and their own and their spouse's relatives. Trustees and settlors are also connected to each other. However, husbands and wives living together may transfer between each other on a no gain, no loss basis (s 58). Joint property is held in proportion to the beneficial interests in it.

14.14.3 CGT and personal representatives

The only liability to CGT that will arrive in the hands of the personal representatives at the beginning of the administration is any liability the deceased incurred during his lifetime, for example, where he sold some antique furniture for a capital gain of £40,000 before his death, making a chargeable gain not covered by his allowance, and the tax had not been paid. Where he kept the furniture, thus swelling his estate by the gain of £40,000, no CGT will be payable on that gain. This is because there is an 'automatic uplift on death' for CGT in s 62 of the TCGA 1992.

14.14.4 Dates for calculations as to CGT liability

The result is that, when the deceased is deemed to dispose of all his property on death, the value at which he disposes of it and at which the property falls into the estate is taken to be the value at the date of death. The estate is taken to have acquired the property at the death value for Capital Gains Tax purposes, and any increase in value since the deceased obtained it is ignored. If the deceased had realised a profit from the increased value of a piece of property before death, by selling it, that realisation would have incurred a liability to CGT. If, however, the property remained unsold at death and the profit remained latent, that profit would be lost to the Inland Revenue for CGT purposes.

14.15 Interaction with inheritance tax

Obviously, however, the item would also carry its higher valuation for Inheritance Tax purposes, so the encouragement to keep property in the estate rather than realising it, for CGT purposes, would have to be offset against the encouragement built into the inheritance tax system to dispose of the property sufficiently long before death to take advantage of the system of PETs.

14.16 Liability of the estate to CGT

Capital Gains Tax is chargeable to an estate when the estate disposes of the property, and is charged on the difference between the value of property at the date of death ('probate value') and the value when it is realised for the estate.

The estate incurs a liability to CGT if it sells assets at a higher price than the probate value. The expenses of sale, including any expenses of valuation attributable to the item, can be set off against the gain (*Commissioners of the Inland Revenue v Richards* (1971)). The difference between the probate value and the sale price after deduction of expenses will be a chargeable gain.

14.16.1 Allowances against CGT

Personal representatives may make a certain amount of chargeable gains in the earlier part of the administration of the estate without having to pay CGT on them. They may set off against the chargeable gains made by the estate an allowance, at present £5,800 per year, for the three years including and following the year of death (s 3(7)). This figure represents the same level of exemption as is granted to an individual.

14.16.2 When property is transferred *in specie* to a beneficiary

Where the personal representatives transfer a piece of property to a beneficiary, rather than realising it by sale, the value at which the beneficiary receives it for Capital Gains Tax purposes is the probate value because they are deemed to have received the property at the date of the deceased's death. If the value of the property is rising rapidly, and the property is transferred at the end of the executor's year, the beneficiary may therefore receive an item carrying a huge liability to CGT. If, however, the beneficiaries become entitled not as legatees but as against trustees, there is a deemed diposal for CGT purposes and tax may be chargeable.

14.17 Valuation of the estate

In order to arrive at the amount of Inheritance Tax payable on the estate, which must be paid in order to obtain a grant of representation, the personal representatives must first ascertain what property is in the estate and then must value each item. The value of any item of property is, essentially, what it would have fetched in the open market immediately before death. Often there is no intention of selling an item in the estate, but only of passing it on to the named beneficiary, but it must still be valued.

14.17.1 Valuation is a first step in administration

Although executors can deal with property before a grant of probate is issued to them, they often will not do so, and they may in any case wish to do something for which a grant has to be produced, such as make title to property. Administrators have no power to act at all before the grant of letters of administration is issued to them.

In order to obtain the grant, the personal representatives, of whatever kind, have to submit to the Probate Registry some form of declaration or receipt to show that inheritance tax is not payable or has been paid. In the case of very small estates, they may simply state that the value of the estate is under £180,000; for those over that figure, but where no IHT is payable, a short form showing details of the assets and their values must be submitted. For estates where IHT is payable, a longer form must be completed and submitted to the Inland Revenue with the amount payable for inheritance tax before an application can be made for a grant, as that must be accompanied by the IRA duly receipted (see, also, 12.20). Therefore, valuing the estate is one of the first things the personal representatives must do.

It is also quite possible that the personal representatives' first estimate of the amount of IHT payable will turn out to be wrong, if, for example, the deceased turns out to have had property which the personal representatives discover only later. Where this happens, the personal representatives must submit a corrective account to the Inland Revenue and have the IHT adjusted accordingly.

14.17.2 Shares and other arguable items

The valuation of shares is incontrovertible only for listed shares, for which a system of precise valuation is prescribed. The figure is one quarter up between the two prices given in the Stock Exchange Daily Official List (s 272 of the IHTA 1984). The valuation of expensive individual items, such as pieces of antique furniture or jewellery, is also an art rather than a precise science.

A low valuation will be desirable if the main liability of the estate will be to inheritance tax. However, a high valuation may be better for liability to capital gains tax, since, in that context, any liability to tax arises from an asset passing out of the estate at a higher value than when it fell in. The valuation must be the same for both taxes.

14.17.3 Value altering after death (ss 178 and 190 of the IHTA 1984)

The valuation of some things may be altered after death. The legislation allows only the value of related property sold within three years quoted shares sold within one year and land sold within four years to be read back into the probate valuation (ss 177, 178 and 190 of the IHTA 1984). Again, the valuation must be the same for IHT and CGT.

14.17.4 Deductions against tax

Reasonable funeral expenses (not including a tombstone) may be deducted. If certain property is sold shortly after death (related property or land within three years, quoted shares within one year), a corrective account may be submitted to the Inland Revenue and a refund on the IHT paid on the original probate value obtained.

Debts are deductible only if they were incurred for money or money's worth; the rules are designed to restrict avoidance of tax by the creation of artificial debts. Repayment of non-deductible debts is regarded as a gift, and therefore if the deceased had, during his lifetime, incurred a debt of a non-deductible kind to an individual, his repayment of it will be treated as a PET.

14.17.5 Exemptions

The net estate may be fully exempt for Inheritance Tax purposes (if going to spouse or charity, for example) or fully taxable (if going to anyone else). It may, however, commonly be partly exempt and partly taxable. The distinction should be carefully drawn between a gift which is exempt and one which is taxable but on which no tax is payable because the taxable estate is worth less than £215,000.

That difference is between the property not being chargeable to tax and its being chargeable, but at a nil rate. Until that basic difference is appreciated, it is not possible to see how or even whether the estate will be liable to IHT in practice or how to minimise or avoid that liability. (It should also be noted again that such individual exemptions as that allowing a testator to give away £3,000 per year free of IHT are not available on death.)

There are no exemptions for capital gains tax beyond the allowances for the first three tax years of the estate.

14.18 Liability, burden and payment of IHT

It is important to know not only what IHT is payable but also who has to pay it, and when. If the donees of a lifetime gift are to pay the IHT on it, then that fact has implications for the calculation of tax payable out of the estate.

14.18.1 Lifetime gifts

The donees of potentially exempt transfers are primarily liable if the donor dies within seven years of making the PETs. However, if they have not paid the requisite tax by 12 months after the date of death, the deceased's personal representatives will be liable to pay it. Of course, this leaves them open to some risk since by the time they discover the liability, they may have distributed the property in the estate. Unfortunately, that is no defence against the demands of the Inland Revenue and the personal representatives will be liable for the tax, personally if there is not enough remaining in the estate.

14.18.2 What property is considered a gift on death for IHT purposes

Where a liability to inheritance tax arises on the death of the donor, there are three possible funds from which the tax may be payable:

(a) 'free estate';

(b) donee of property subject to retention of benefit;

(c) trustees of settled property.

The free estate is that owned absolutely by the deceased. The tax is usually paid by the personal representatives out of the free estate. Where property was included in the estate although the deceased had apparently given it away during his lifetime, because it was subject to a retention of benefit, the IHT on that gift will be payable by the donee. The ordinary personal representatives run no risks in respect of settled property, the liability for paying the tax falling on the trustees of the settlement.

14.18.3 Time for payment of tax

Interest is payable on tax not paid by six months from the date of the deceased's death, whether or not it has actually been calculated by then.

Some property, largely businesses and land, attracts the possibility of paying the tax by instalments over 10 years by written election (ss 227–28 of the IHTA 1984). This can be extremely useful to personal representatives who have insufficient money available to pay the IHT bill on the estate before the grant and therefore have to borrow in order to obtain the grant. The instalment provision means a much lower sum needs to be borrowed and therefore the amount incurred in interest payments is much lower.

14.18.4 Gifts bearing their own tax – the 'estate rate'

A testator may leave a gift specifically saying that it bears its own tax, which will then be charged at the estate rate, the remainder coming out of residue. The estate rate is the overall percentage rate of tax paid by an estate. Although the percentage at which IHT is paid is 40%, this applies only to the amount of chargeable property over £223,000. Therefore, if the chargeable estate is worth £278,750, tax will be charged on the £55,750 over the nil-rate band; 40% of £55,750 is £27,300, so the chargeable estate will share out the tax liability at £22,300 in the £223,000, or 10%.

14.18.5 Gifts left free of tax

A testator may leave a gift free of tax; the tax it should have borne will still be payable out of the rest of the estate, sometimes leading to very awkward calculations.

14.19 Tax planning between spouses

The situation for a married couple in respect of liability to inheritance tax is very special. Not only are transfers between them exempt, but they are likely (albeit not guaranteed) to want to leave as much as possible to each other. Many people would like to leave all their property to their spouse should they die first, and rely on them to do what is appropriate by way of passing it on to the next generation.

14.19.1 Why leaving everything to your spouse may be a bad idea

At first sight, the idea of leaving all one's property to a spouse might seem the obvious way of avoiding tax, since the whole gift will be exempt. However, the only advantage may well be a postponement of the liability; the process may result in a later, but much greater, liability to IHT. A surviving spouse is very likely to wish to pass on much of the deceased spouse's property, as well as her own, to the children. At that point, the disadvantages of one spouse leaving all his property to the other become apparent. The second spouse to die has an estate of perhaps double the size of the deceased's, and (unless she has remarried and leaves all her property to the new spouse rather than to her children, a situation the first spouse will probably not wish to encourage), an unnecessary liability to tax may have been incurred because the second spouse has only one allowance for her nil-rate tax band but has, effectively, the contents of two estates. The situation where the property in both estates comes together for tax purposes is called 'bunching'.

14.19.2 How to deal with bunching – *inter vivos* tax planning

Bunching can be avoided by transfering property between the spouses, so as to be as sure as possible of making the fullest use of the poorer spouse's nil-rate band. This means ensuring that she has at least £223,000 in capital when she dies, so simply giving her enough to achieve that level of capital may not suffice; she may spend it before she dies, especially if she has insufficient income and is obliged to live on capital. Transfers of capital can be carried out *inter vivos* if the richer spouse will agree, although the possible pitfalls, such as divorce, should be borne in mind when advising on this point. Equalisation of chargeable transfers and capital has lost its advantage since the rates of IHT ceased to be banded and it became chargeable at a flat rate of 40%.

14.19.3 Tax planning by will – avoid survivorship!

If the transfer of capital does not take place *inter vivos*, the tax advantages envisaged can be obtained on death if the richer spouse dies first leaving a will containing gifts which are designed to achieve the same function. In such a case, however, a survivorship clause should be avoided; the effect can be achieved only by passing the property to the other spouse and then to the estate. The object is to avoid tax by doing this, not to benefit the spouse by enjoyment of the gift as such. A survivorship clause is designed to allow the testator to keep control of the property in the event that the spouse cannot enjoy it because of her early death, not to avoid tax.

14.19.4 Using the nil-rate band wisely

On death everyone has a nil-rate band of £223,000 for IHT subject to lifetime chargeable transfers within seven years of death. Money and property up to that value can be given away to any person without incurring tax. The obvious solution to the tax dilemma of a rich spouse who also has children is to leave the amount of the nil-rate band to the children with the remainder to the spouse. If that is all that is left by will, there will be no liability to IHT.

14.19.5 Discretionary trusts

If the nil-rate band is too large an amount to leave to the children without risking hardship to the spouse, the sum can be paid into a discretionary trust for the spouse and children, The spouse may then receive such payments as she needs to, whilst the rest is still tax-free for the children because it has been passed direct to them (for tax purposes) out of the estate of the first spouse to die, chargeable to tax at a nil rate, provided the fund is distributed within 10 years. Alternatively, a two year discretionary trust can be left under s 144 of the IHTA so that rather than the property in the trust being divided by the provisions of the will, and a trustee can decide within two years what the shares for each child will be; the trustees' decisions will be read back into the will for tax purposes.

14.19.6 Possible arguments against leaving the nil-rate band to children

There are arguments against this form of tax planning, especially where the estate, though worth more than the nil-rate band, is not enormous. The spouse may need more than the remainder of the estate to live on. Also, if the spouse expected to live longer is also expected to live more than seven years after the death of the first, she may take all the property free of tax under the spouse exemption and make PETs as and when circumstances develop and make the appropriate beneficiaries of the gifts more apparent.

14.19.7 Tax planning in context

Property can be left to a beneficiary absolutely or as life tenant, but one should bear in mind that a life tenant's estate is treated as including the capital in the trust. The overall purpose of tax planning must also be borne in mind all the time. Minimising liability to tax is not an end in itself, but a way of providing more efficiently for the testator's family and friends. The spouse's expenses must be considered whenever plans are made; she may need a sum which looks inefficient for tax in order to keep a house running, for example, in which case she will be using the money for purposes the testator will approve of and the resulting depletion of the fund should mean in any case that there is no liability to tax by the date of her death.

14.20 Post-death tax planning

A will cannot be changed after the testator has died. It cannot be rewritten. If, however, the effect of its provisions is altered by a court under the Inheritance (Provision for Family and Dependants) Act 1975, the new provisions will be read back into the will for IHT purposes and a reassessment of the liability to tax may be sought or imposed.

It is also possible for the beneficiaries to rearrange the estate by agreement amongst themselves, provided they are all of full age. This may be done where the gifts are felt to be inappropriate or unfair by the beneficiaries (see, for example, *Crowden v Aldridge* (1993) at 10.5.2 above). Efficiency for tax purposes is another possible motivation, and is something to which a legal adviser must be alert for professional reasons. Provided the correct formalities are observed, the beneficiaries may rearrange the estate for tax purposes and do, effectively, what the testator should have done had he wished to minimise tax.

Note that post-death tax planning is also available to restructure an estate where the gifts are governed not by a will but by the rules of intestacy. The outcome of a variation, if it is made in writing (usually by deed) within two years of death, can be read back into the will for tax purposes provided the Inland Revenue is informed within six months of the date of the deed. This sort of arrangement is quite commonly made directly to avoid tax, although it may also serve the function of rediverting the testator's property to exactly those persons he did not intend to benefit. This may only be done once – *Russell v IRC* (1988).

14.21 Income tax

The deceased's personal representatives are liable for the income tax owed by him at the date of death, which constitutes a debt of the estate. The deceased gets his personal allowance for the year of death under s 257 of the Taxes Act 1988, and may also have the married couple's allowance under s 257A subject to election by his wife. There is a widow's bereavement allowance for the year of death and the year following, provided the widow has not remarried; any benefit under an election in respect of the married couple's allowance will be played off against this.

TAX AND TAX PLANNING

An understanding of the system of tax is necessary in practice involving succession because a good deal of the practical work in this area is aimed at minimising liability to tax. The structure of the tax system is fairly stable, although the details frequently alter.

The essence of tax planning is usually to allow the testator to retain as much control as possible over his property during his lifetime whilst still obtaining the tax advantages available from giving the property away. Care must be taken not to cross the line between tax avoidance, which is a lawful skill, and tax evasion, which is highly illegal and constitutes fraud.

Inheritance Tax is charged on transfers of property with gratuitous intent. It applies also to property transferred during a lifetime, when there is a more complex system of allowances, as well as to the final transfer of everything in the deceased's estate which is deemed to occur immediately before death.

On death, the liability to IHT is calculated by valuing the assets in the estate which will not include property passing under a joint tenancy. Gifts to a spouse or to charity are part of the estate but exempt from IHT. The rest of the estate will be chargeable to IHT, but the first £223,000 is charged at a nil rate. Some of the nil-rate band may however have been used up by chargeable lifetime transfers within seven years of the transferor's death. Transfers before that will probably have been Potentially Exempt Transfers (PETs), which are exempt from IHT provided the donor survives for seven years. A taper relief operates where he survives between three and seven years after making a PET.

Settlements without an interest in possession can be a useful form of dealing with the tax problem. Accumulation and maintenance settlements are essentially trusts for the settlor's close relatives under the age of 25 and have particular tax advantages. Discretionary trusts which will be wound up within two years of death are read as though the distribution took place at death. Having the proceeds of a life insurance policy pass outside the estate, in trust for a third party, is also tax-efficient, as the premiums paid by the deceased during his lifetime will not usually attract IHT.

Property falls into the estate for Capital Gains Tax purposes at the value it had at the date of death, and that is the CGT value at which a beneficiary receives it even if he does not actually obtain the property itself say for another year. The personal representatives therefore pay CGT only on the increase in value of property whilst it is in the estate, and during the first three years of the administration they have an allowance against CGT equivalent to an individual's personal allowance. They may also deduct expenses. The automatic uplift in CGT value on death does not exclude the obligation to pay any CGT liability the deceased had already accrued before his death.

The personal representatives must have the same valuation for property for the purposes of both IHT and CGT. Certain property such as land and shares may be revalued for IHT purposes if they are sold within a short time of death.

There is commonly a disparity between the amount of property owned by spouses which may mean that if the poorer spouse dies first she will not make full use of her nil-rate band of £150,000. It is tax-efficient to ensure she has the full sum when she dies.

It is also inefficient for a person to leave all his property to his spouse where this means not using his own nil-rate band but leaving the spouse with more than her nil-rate band on death. It is common therefore for the first £150,000 to be left to children, as gifts to them attract tax, and the rest to the spouse. However, it must be considered carefully whether this leaves the spouse with sufficient to live on.

CHAPTER 15

FAMILY PROVISION

15.1 Restrictions on testamentary freedom

Testamentary freedom may be restricted either by preventing a person from leaving their property entirely as they wish on death, or by making it possible for their dispositions to be altered after death.

15.1.1 Other jurisdictions

Other legal systems do not allow complete testamentary freedom but lay down that a certain part of a person's estate will go to his family regardless of his wishes. The idea is not new; it was found in Roman law. It occurs now, for example, in France, where between one-third and three-quarters of an estate (depending on the size of the remaining family) goes automatically to relatives, and only the rest is available to the testator to dispose of as he wishes. In Scotland too, the state requires that part of an estate must go to certain relatives, and in many parts of the US, the adoption of the Uniform Probate Code (UPC) has given the spouse the right to take one-third of the estate provided she elects to do so within six months of the grant of probate (UPC, ss 2–201–207); a share may also be claimed for infant children (UPC, s 2–403). In Ireland, during passage of the Succession Bill, the principle of freedom of testation was described as a peculiarly English phenomenon, foisted on the Irish with the first Statute of Distributions as a replacement for the ancient 'Custom of Ireland', under which only one-third of personalty could be disposed of by will.

15.1.2 Testamentary freedom in England

The English system does in theory allow complete freedom, although this has not always been the case (see Chapter 1). How individuals transfer ownership of property inevitably has social and political causes and consequences. The history of the devisability of land is fraught with the attempts of the Crown to retain control; the rise of primogeniture and the keeping together of estates by devolving them upon a single heir led to the phenomenon of the younger sons of the English nobility who had breeding but no money. Even the freedom to dispose of personalty, which today may seem the natural state of affairs, has little historical validity.

There were legal restrictions on testamentary freedom operating until the Mortmain and Charitable Uses Act of 1891 removed the restrictions on charitable gifts within a short period of death; married women only obtained full powers of disposition over their property after the Married Women's Property Act of 1893. There was therefore a very short period of full testamentary freedom between the last decade of the 19th century and the introduction of the first family provision legislation in 1938.

15.2 Challenging the will – or intestacy

A will may be challenged because it does not satisfy the criteria necessary for it to be valid in English law. For example, it may be said that the testator lacked testamentary intention, or testamentary capacity, or that there was a failure to comply with the proper formalities. Challenges to wills on the ground that the testator lacked the mental capacity to make a will have been less common since a system of challenging the effects of the will for the testator's failure to make proper provision for someone was brought in.

15.3 Reasons for family provision legislation

There are various views about whether it is right to restrict testamentary freedom in any way. There are both practical and moral considerations.

15.3.1 Freedom or responsibility?

Some people feel that a person should be able to leave his property exactly as he wishes, and that it is no business of the state or anyone else to permit or encourage interference in his private arrangements. On the other hand, others feel that, within a family in particular, there is not necessarily any merit in where the technical ownership of property falls. The wife of a rich husband, who has spent her whole life working hard to look after her husband and children may have no claim on anything as a matter of property rights. Supporters of the latter view would say that it is the business of the law to uphold and enforce obligations such as those of providing financial support for one's dependants. In the not unheard-of situation of a husband who does leave his widow without support, there is also the consideration that she must be provided for from some resources, and if those do not come from his estate, then they may well have to come from the general taxpayer.

15.3.2 Interaction with other areas of family law

England is unusual in that it has no system of matrimonial property, so that ownership of property remains with the person who acquires it under the usual rules of acquisition of property – the person who receives it as a gift or who buys it with their own money – even when they are married and the property is used for family purposes. Thus, a wife has no interest in a matrimonial home if it is in her husband's name, unless, exceptionally, she can establish one under some principle of equity. The courts have wide powers to alter the property divisions between spouses on application by either party in matrimonial proceedings (for divorce or judicial separation), but clearly these powers do not apply where a marriage is ended by death. It may be particularly important in the English jurisdiction, therefore, for a disinherited wife to be able to apply for support from the deceased's estate.

15.3.3 Practicalities or morality?

The practical and moral bases of family provision legislation are not always easily distinguished, perhaps for political reasons. Those who would object to a form of redistribution of property on the basis of some 'moral' consideration which has nothing to do with established property rights might nevertheless be quick to see the advantage of being able to refer someone who was potentially a burden on the state to a possible claim against the estate of another private individual.

15.3.4 History of family provision legislation

The first statutory provision in England allowing a family provision claim was the Inheritance (Family Provision) Act 1938. Other jurisdictions were quicker to introduce legislation of this type, especially New Zealand, where the first such provision was made in 1908. This was the culmination of attempts to introduce a system of fixed shares on the Scottish model, which led to the Testators' Family Maintenance Act of 1900. The legislation was claimed to be designed to save taxpayers' money; it was, however, more usually used in situations where state expenditure was not involved, and what was altered was the arrangement of entitlements between private individuals only.

15.3.5 Introduction of the legislation in England

The first legislation in England was introduced after pressure from various quarters, especially from women's groups. As is so often the case with property matters, legal equality between individuals almost invariably meant that, given the way legal entitlements were set up, the legal ownership of property almost always rested with men. Under a system of complete testamentary freedom, those men could disinherit their wives and children as they wished. There had been considerable debate as to whether a wife should have fixed share as of right, or have to seek entitlement at the discretion of a court. The first Bill presented to Parliament was one which would have awarded wives a fixed share; this Bill failed. It was followed by several more Bills in the next few years, which also failed, before the first Inheritance Act was passed in 1938. Spouses, infant sons, unmarried daughters or disabled adult sons or daughters could apply for maintenance or, in the case of small estates, capital payments.

15.3.6 After the 1938 Act

The 1938 Act was, on the whole, successful. It was subject to amendment by the Matrimonial Causes Acts 1958 and 1965, which brought in the possibility of applications by ex-spouses. In 1951 the Committee on the Law of Intestate Succession (the Morton Committee) reported. Its brief was principally to look at the statutory legacy for spouses on intestacy, which it recommended should be increased from £1,000 to £5,000, but it also recommended the extension of the 1938 Act to cover cases of total intestacy. It recommended that widows should be able to be awarded the whole of the income of the net estate and that the limit for lump sums should be increased. These provisions were enacted by the Intestates' Estates Act 1952.

The Family Provision Act 1966 extended the jurisdiction to allow more judicial discretion and to remove many restrictions on the amount and form of provision, as well as giving spouses a wider right to apply. Matters remained to be heard in the Chancery Division of the High Court however, save that the county courts were given a limited – and little used – jurisdiction.

15.3.7 Further need for change

By the 1960s and 1970s, a need for further change was perceived in an era of considerable social change. The Law Commission, in its Working Paper No 42 *Family Law: Family Property Law* (1971) and its Report No 61 *Family Property: Family Provision on Death* of 1974, expressed various concerns, in particular about the difference between support and property, or maintenance and capital, and the effects of divorce. When the family provision legislation was compared with that which applied on divorce, the spouse whose happy marriage was ended by death could find herself in a much worse situation than the one who was divorced; there was also a suggestion that divorce should not automatically end the spouse's right to claim maintenance. Fixed shares in the property of the deceased were suggested but not emphasised.

15.3.8 Bases of the current provisions?

There was a change during the 1970s in the views of entitlement to property, particularly where the situation of women in their traditional role was concerned. Lord Simon of Glaisdale, in the debate on the Bill that became the 1975 Act, said that the 'functional division of co-operative labour ... calls in justice for the sharing of the rewards of the labour. The breadwinner is morally bound to share the loaf he has been free to gain'. This view of matrimonial property was reflected in many court judgments during the 1970s, though the trend towards the courts regarding wives as having a share in their husband's property by virtue of their contributions to the marriage as a matter of equity has somewhat receded in more recent years. However, the rationale that a deceased husband in a traditional family, for example, should not be permitted testamentary freedom over all the property that is legally his remains, sometimes explicitly on the basis that morally he is a co-owner with his surviving wife. The changing nature of family responsibilities, especially the increasing number of women working outside the home, the spread of divorce, particularly after the Divorce Reform Act 1969, and the rise of the unmarried family all gave rise to pressure for change.

15.3.9 Law Commission Report No 61 *Family Property: Family Provision on Death*

The Law Commission undertook a Social Survey before it made its report in 1974. It found that there was support for a spouse entitlement that was wider than maintenance. It recommended that spouses should take a just share of the estate, and that conduct should not be an issue for ex-spouses save where it would be repugnant to anyone's sense of justice to ignore it, as prescribed for ancillary relief matters by Lord Denning in the matrimonial case of *Wachtel v Wachtel* (1973). It recommended that there should be no age limit on claims by children, because certain 'special circumstances' might arise in which adult children should be able to claim. It also recommended that there should be some form of basis for claiming by dependants, mentioning the Fatal Accidents Acts 1846–1959 and their provisions for establishing those who could claim for loss of dependency consequent upon a death caused by a tort. The Law Commission cited the Ontario Law Reform Committee and the Law Reform Committee of Western Australia who were reporting along the same lines.

15.3.10 Opposition to the legislation

There was some positive antipathy towards the Bill; specifically, it was said that the existence of family provision legislation encouraged disputes within families, and that the use of words such as 'fair', 'reasonable' and 'just' was unhelpful because the judge hearing a case could not know the truth of the matter and the strength of the cases would often be judged in accordance with the efficiency of the lawyers concerned (an objection which might apply to many areas!).

15.4 Who may claim now – the 1975 Act as amended

The current provisions are in the Inheritance (Provision for Family and Dependants) Act (I(PFD)A) 1975, as amended by the Law Reform (Succession) Act (LR(S)A) 1995. This allows claims by close family members, by persons who were financially dependent on the deceased when he died and by certain unmarried but quasi-marital cohabitants. The last category was added to the original provisions by the Law Reform (Succession) Act 1995. The rationale behind the statutory provisions appears to be a mixture of the moral and legal obligations the testator would have had had he lived. Certainly, ideas about moral obligations are shaped by the social mood and liable to change comparatively rapidly. The court have taken, in reality, a wide discretion in interpreting the meaning of the Act's provisions in any particular case, and the changes made by the LR(S)A 1995 to the class of those who could claim under the 1975 Act were foreshadowed not only by the theories of the Law Commission but also by the practice of the courts.

15.4.1 Details and deficiencies of the original 1975 Act

The original provisions in the I(PFD)A 1975 allowed spouses, former spouses, children, step-children and dependants of the deceased to bring a claim against his estate. The definition of 'dependant' caused particular difficulty. As strictly interpreted, it meant that an established cohabitant could not make any claim against the estate of deceased partner unless that partner had been making contributions not merely to the joint expenses but to the remaining cohabitant's share of them – that is, if the couple had shared expenses equally, no claim could lie even if the survivor could not maintain the former joint home from her own resources. This was soon felt to be inappropriate, for various reasons. One was that a cohabitant who had been paying her way was unable to found any claim against the deceased's estate, whereas one who had allowed the deceased to support her instead could found a claim on that basis. This was often regarded as failing to treat deserving family members appropriately, whilst encouraging 'sponging'. Another reason was the changing social attitude to cohabitation without marriage, and, linked to that, a widespread but mistaken perception that there is some form of legal recognition of 'family' ownership of property which applies to married and unmarried couples alike. Though the original 1975 Act mitigated the effects of this error in the case of married couples, because spouses and former spouses could claim on the basis of the married relationship, it made no provision for cohabitants unless they were also able to prove financial dependency, and thus it was arguably out of tune with the popular conception of moral obligation. The original provision of a route for those not legally related to the deceased to claim against his estate was innovative and progressive in its day, but, twenty years on, the 1975 provision seemed too restrictive.

15.4.2 Other jurisdictions' attitudes

In other jurisdictions, dependency alone is regarded as 'too broad a base' for family provision claims. At first sight this may appear to suggest that their family provision regime is more restrictive, as they require not only the establishment of dependency but also that of a personal relationship of a specified kind between the claimant and the deceased. Both the Law Reform

Commission of New South Wales, in its *Working Paper on the Testators' Family Maintenance and Guardianship of Infants Act 1916* (quoted here), and the drafters of the Uniform Act for Canada thought that there should be some other factor as well as dependency; in the latter case, there is a requirement for the claimant to be related to the deceased and to have been dependent for at least three years. However, the list of relatives includes *de facto* spouses as well as parents, grandparents and descendants, so in that respect, the regime is more inclusive, regarding a wider set of persons as constituting the deceased's close family.

15.4.3 Foreshadowing the 1995 Act – the Law Commission

In 1989, the Law Commission reported on *Distribution on Intestacy* (Report No 187). They had investigated the public's attitudes to the provisions of the existing intestacy rules. Their survey revealed that a majority of its respondents favoured some automatic provision for cohabitants on intestacy. However, the Law Commission thought that bringing cohabitants within the scheme of entitlements on intestacy would involve the sacrifice of simplicity and clarity in the intestacy rules. It recommended instead that they be more readily given *locus standi* (standing to bring a claim) under the family provision legislation.

15.4.4 ... and *Bishop v Plumley* in the Court of Appeal

By the time of the Law Commission's report on cohabitants and intestacy, the courts were also beginning to interpret the 'dependency' provisions in the 1975 Act in such a way as to include cohabitants even where, strictly speaking, they could not be brought within the legislative provisions. In *Bishop v Plumley and Another* (1991), the court was asked to consider the situation of the survivor of an unmarried couple who had cohabited for 10 years. Until January 1984, they had been largely in the same situation as each other, living in rented accommodation on a combination of casual earnings and social security. However, in 1983 the deceased's uncle had died, leaving him enough to buy a house, and since January 1984 they had both lived there, still on benefits. From 1981 onwards, the deceased had been suffering from angina, and the applicant had given him what the court described as 'exceptionally devoted care'. However, the deceased had not made any will to replace the one he had made in 1974, during a separation between him and the applicant, by which he gave his whole estate to his son and daughter and nothing to the applicant. After the deceased's death, the applicant remained in the house, living on benefits, and applied to the court for relief under the unamended 1975 Act.

The Registrar (District Judge) who heard the case held that the applicant had not been dependent on the deceased because the care she had given him had constituted full valuable consideration for the rent-free accommodation he had provided for her – that is, had she not cared for him, she might have been able to establish dependency, but as she had looked after him she could not! The applicant appealed to a judge, who dismissed her appeal. She appealed then to the Court of Appeal, who, in allowing her appeal, initiated a departure from the established interpretation of the words of the Act.

Butler-Sloss LJ said in *Bishop v Plumley* that the care given by the applicant was not to be considered in isolation from the 'mutuality of the relationship'. The deceased had provided a secure home for his partner and she had provided him with 'connubial services'. This was held to demonstrate that the deceased had made a substantial contribution towards her needs for the purposes of s 1(3) of the Act, which defines dependency for the purposes of the Act. The applicant's care of the deceased did not constitute full valuable consideration, in these circumstances, but was part of the relationship in its entirety. The case was remitted to the Registrar to be reconsidered, amidst references to the comments by Griffiths LJ in *Jelley v Iliffe* (1981) (see below at 15.14) about the need to 'use common sense'.

15.4.5 The Law Reform (Succession) Act 1995

The effect of s 2 of the Law Reform (Succession) Act 1995 was to amend s 1 of the Inheritance (Provision for Family and Dependants) Act 1975 so as to give *locus standi* under the new s 1(1)(ba) of the 1975 Act, as with dependency claims under the Fatal Accidents Act 1976, to a person who had lived as the husband or wife of the deceased for the two years immediately preceding the death. It also provided special guidelines for how claims brought on the basis of cohabitation should be treated.

15.4.6 A changing view of the family?

The decision in *Bishop v Plumley* (1991) and the effects of the Law Reform (Succession) Act 1995 involved a broadening of the view of the claims one person may have over another's property as a result of their relationship, rather than as a result of any formal contract for the buying and selling of an interest in property. In that sense, it may be regarded as an uncharacteristic departure in English law, which does not recognise a claim as of right (only at the court's discretion, albeit with rather broad and broadly-interpreted statutory guidelines) by a wife on family property in her husband's name on divorce. The changes demonstrate a wider recognition of the validity of a claim to property based not on commercial contract but on the sort of 'services' within a family relationship which do not traditionally attract compensation, in money or property terms, from an English court. Even the attitude of courts to giving traditional wives, who have cared, unpaid, for their husbands and children, financial compensation for their work where they lose the security of their husband's provision for them on divorce has been equivocal, although, in the case of a married couple, the element of bargain could be seen as considerably more explicit than with an unmarried couple, especially one where there are no children.

There are, no doubt, competing forces at work in these changes of legal attitude, including a desire to make the private individual (including the deceased private individual) responsible for the upkeep of those who might otherwise be dependent on the state and the taxpayer. This approach often entails political support for the institution of marriage. Nevertheless, the structure of the law appears to be increasingly inclusive of the unmarried family relationship. This involves a loosening of the essentially financial principles of legally valid personal relationships, including those relating to the acquisition and ownership of property, which have prevailed during the 1980s and into the 1990s. It entails a gradual extension of the original principles of the 1975 Act, which came out of a different generation. There remains, however, an unwillingness to bring the rights of unmarried cohabitants against each other so close to the rights of married parties that the principle of marriage itself seems to lose importance, and, in the English jurisdiction, the gulf between the rights of the married and of the unmarried is considerably greater than in comparable jurisdictions elsewhere.

The changes instigated by the Law Commission and the Court of Appeal and brought into force in relation to deaths after 1995 by the Law Reform (Succession) Act 1995 go a long way towards recognising the value of caring within a relationship as something other than a commercial transaction, and something that validates that relationship as such, rather than proving it to be a commercial arrangement. The moves of the last decade have brought about a complete turnaround in the way that caring fits into the structure of the family provision legislation. They have changed the courts' evaluation of caring as potentially defeating a claim by demonstrating that the potential claimant had in fact given 'full valuable consideration' for her support by the deceased, and therefore was outside the legislation. The demonstration of such caring may well now assist the claimant, provided there has been at least two years' cohabitation continuing up to the death, in establishing her right to bring the claim, rather than possibly preventing it, as before. The value of her caring will then be one of the factors in assessing reasonable provision for her.

15.4.7 Gay relationships – cohabitation or dependency?

There has been considerable social pressure recently for the recognition within English law of stable homosexual relationships. These are of necessity unmarried relationships. Other jurisdictions, such as Denmark and Holland, have instituted forms of 'registered partnership' akin to civil marriage, though without many of its privileges. There is no such legislation in England and, indeed, there is legislation in the public law context specifically directed against the recognition of such relationships as 'family' relationships.

Unmarried heterosexual cohabitants may found a claim against an estate under the family provision legislation on the existence of the cohabitation, but it is unlikely, by analogy with decisions in other areas of law, that the provisions would be found to cover cohabitants in a homosexual relationship.

Although it is unclear whether there is any scope for recognition in English law of any consequential effects in relation to the property of those who are entitled to register gay partnerships in other jurisdictions, any such effects would be unlikely to affect the family provision legislation. The 1995 amendments require a claim to be established on the basis of having lived as 'husband or wife'; in *Fitzpatrick v Sterling HA* (1998), which concerned rights of succession to a Rent Act 1977 tenancy, the court discussed analogous provisions and confirmed that the reference to the deceased's family, where it included a reference to someone living as 'husband and wife', excluded homosexual cohabitants. It should be noted, however, that a suggestion has been made that the provisions of the Fatal Accidents Act 1976, allowing claims by unmarried cohabitants, might be changed to include, amongst others, homosexual cohabitants, or merely those who can show *de facto* dependency, including that arising from sharing (see Law Commission Consultation Paper No 148 *Claims for Wrongful Death* (1997), para 3.18). This may indicate the trend of future amendments to s 1(1) of the Inheritance (Provision for Family and Dependants) Act 1975.

In order to claim against a deceased person's estate, a homosexual partner will therefore have to prove financial dependency, or use another area of law, such as proprietary estoppel, if the necessary elements can be established. Neither of these avenues makes any special provision, either advantageous or prejudicial, for a personal or sexual relationship of any kind (see, for example, *Wayling v Jones* (1996)).

15.5 How to claim – an overview

The I(PFD)A 1975 may be used to challenge the level of provision arising from intestacy as well as under a will. What is looked at is the entitlement the claimant has, however it arises, and whether it is reasonable. As with other types of action, such claims are usually settled before they reach court, but that is on the basis that the lawyers for each party believe their client has obtained something comparable to what a court would have given him. The estimate of what that would have been has to be based on the cases decided under the Act, which judges must follow in deciding how to exercise their wide discretion as to what to award, with some educated guesswork in the case of the recent amendments under the 1995 Act. The Act itself, though it gives certain guidelines, is remarkably short, and has allowed – or demanded – much interpretation.

15.6 The deceased – against whose estate can application be made?

The deceased must have died after 31 March 1976, domiciled in England and Wales. Note that being domiciled in England and Wales is not the same as living there and certainly not the same as having British nationality. For example, a person whose established permanent home is in England and who intends to stay there indefinitely will be domiciled there, whatever his nationality. A child's domicile follows that of the parent with whom the child lives. The applicant under the I(PFD)A 1975, as under the legislation it replaced, has to prove the deceased's domicile. Thus, where in *Mastaka v Midland Bank* (1941) the deceased appeared to have taken a Russian domicile from her husband on marriage (the rule whereby a married woman took her husband's domicile has since been abolished) and there was no evidence of her having changed it since, no claim could be made.

15.7 When to apply

If a person intends to claim against someone's estate, the application must be brought no more than six months from the date on which a grant of representation is taken out, save where the court gives leave for the period of time to be extended. *Re Freeman* (1984) established that if a grant is revoked and replaced with another grant, the relevant date will be that of the second, valid, grant. In that case, a grant in common form had been revoked because it was shown later that the will had not in fact been properly attested. The court held that into the word 'representation' it would imply 'effective' or 'valid' so that time ran from the later grant.

15.7.1 Extension of time

The court has a general discretion under s 4 of the I(PFD)A 1975 to extend time. In *Re Salmon* (1980), the court gave some guidelines as to how its unfettered jurisdiction to extend the time limit for bringing an application ought to be exercised. It held that the discretion ought to be exercised judicially, the onus lying on the applicant to make out a substantial case for it being just and proper for the court to exercise its discretion. The court should consider how promptly, and in what circumstances, the applicant applied to the court for an extension of time and also warned the defendant of the proposed application, and the question should be addressed as to whether negotiations were commenced within the time limit. If negotiations did begin during the time limit, this will make it very likely that the court will grant the extension, unlike the comparable situation in a personal injury action where the courts, though they have a discretion to extend time, will pay comparatively little heed to the existence of negotiations before the expiration of the limit. What is more relevant is whether the estate had been distributed before a claim under the Act was notified or made. The court should also consider the effects of refusal of an extension and whether this would leave the potential applicant without redress – an unrepresented applicant who could not sue his solicitor for missing the time limit might therefore be at an advantage for that reason.

In *Stock v Brown* (1994), a widow in her 90s had delayed six years before bringing a claim against her husband's estate. The court balanced the exceptional delay against the extenuating circumstances and the widow's needs and gave her leave to claim out of time.

In *Re C (deceased) (leave to apply for provision)* (1995), the court discussed the issues arising where the applicant is a child. There is no provision under the Inheritance (Provision for Family and Dependants) Act 1975, as there is in ordinary civil litigation, that time limits run against children only once they reach the age of majority. In this case, the applicant was a child aged eight years who lived with her mother. Her father had died suddenly when she was four, leaving a very large estate to trustees who distributed it in the two years allowed, without making any provision for her. Just before the distribution ended, the child's mother consulted solicitors but negotiations and litigation for various reasons proceeded very slowly, and the total delay was almost three and a half years. The court discussed the conflicting principles, on the one hand, that a father should maintain a child and, on the other, that beneficiaries should know where they stand within a reasonable period after the death. It accepted the argument that children often suffered from parents' mistakes (as here, where the mother had delayed) but 'to argue that it can happen is not to lessen the injustice of it'. In this case, no capital had been deployed. The argument that the beneficiaries' extensive and expensive negotiations as to their respective shares were now to be upset at even more extent was, the court suggested, somewhat exaggerated. Taking into account the size of the estate and his opinion that 'in none of the reported cases to which I have been referred, were the prospects of substantial success so clear', Wilson J granted leave for the child to apply out of time.

15.8 Who may apply

If a claimant can establish that the deceased died domiciled in England and Wales, and manages to bring his claim before a court, he will have to establish also that he is within one of the categories of persons entitled by the I(PFD)A 1975 to bring a claim. The courts will not consider anyone else and they have no power to do so, although they do have the capacity to form and revise their judgments about what the wording of the categories really mean. Showing that a person belongs in one of the categories of persons able to claim is often called establishing that person's *locus standi*. This means, literally, 'place to stand' and, in practice, that they are in a position as a matter of law to bring a claim.

There are six classes of applicant, and they are set out in s 1(1) of the Act. They are:

(a) the wife of husband of the deceased;

(b) a former wife or former husband of the deceased who has not remarried;

(ba) a cohabitant (not being the deceased's spouse, or former spouse who has not remarried) who lived as the deceased's husband or wife for the two years immediately preceding his death;

(c) a child of the deceased;

(d) any person (not being a child of the deceased) who, in the case of any marriage to which the deceased was at any time a party, was treated by the deceased as a child of the family in relation to that marriage;

(e) any person (not being a person included in the foregoing classes) who immediately before the death of the deceased was being maintained, either wholly or partly, by the deceased.

Different standards of reasonableness apply to those in s 1(1)(a) from those which apply to everyone else. Provided that there was no continuing separation under a judicial separation order, the surviving spouse must show that she does not receive from the deceased's will or intestacy such financial provision as it would be reasonable in all the circumstances of the case for her to receive, whether or not that provision is required for his or her maintenance (s 1(2)(a)). Everyone else, however, must confine themselves to maintenance (s 1(2)(b)); if they receive enough for their maintenance, they will not obtain an award from the court, and maintenance sets the level of award they will receive otherwise. However, the definition of maintenance is a moot point (see below).

15.9 Section 1(1)(a) – wife or husband of the deceased

Section 1(1)(a) of the I(PFD)A 1975 refers to the wife or husband of the deceased. Historically, it was always easier for a woman to claim against her husband than for a man to claim against his wife, for example, for maintenance where the couple separated. This was related to the different legal relationship of men and women to property – married women were unable fully to own or deal with their own property until the Married Women's Property Acts of the late 19th century; these restrictions were in turn related to the different social roles for men and women. The former were the property-owners and financial providers, and the latter performed a financially dependent domestic role.

15.9.1 Wife or husband today

In many cases, this pattern continues, but even if the perception is felt to be seriously outdated nowadays, nevertheless ideas fixed in the law often persist longer than the social perceptions which created them. Thus it is only in recent years, for example, that a husband has ceased to be responsible for his wife's tax returns, a practice which made perfect sense when what was hers was his, but which appeared odd in the 1980s. There remains, however, a grain of relevance – even after sex discrimination has been removed from the law, it may still remain in reality. Men still own more property than women; husbands who have gone out to paid work own more property than wives who have often looked after the house and family, unpaid. The 1938 Act allowed either party to a marriage to make a claim, though the tendency for husbands to die earlier owning more property than their wives would mean that claims by husbands were comparatively unusual. However, in *Re Clayton* (1966), on an application by a disabled widower for financial relief from his wife's estate, Ungoed-Thomas said, 'I certainly do not see in the Act a greater onus of proof on the surviving husband than on the surviving wife'. Undoubtedly, the same applies under the 1975 Act.

15.9.2 Proving the marriage

The burden of proof of the marriage lies on the person alleging that they are the spouse. In most cases this will not be a contentious point. If the marriage did not end in divorce then it will generally have subsisted until the death, even if there has been a judicial separation. A *prima facie* case can easily be made for this by production of a marriage certificate, and this will be sufficient for the court unless someone raises an objection.

For example, if it can be shown that the marriage was bigamous and therefore void, it may not be possible to base a claim on it. A court may therefore have to deal first of all with the preliminary issue of whether the marriage was valid. In *Re Watkins* (1953), the court had first of all to decide whether a widow could claim against the estate of her second husband when her marriage to her first husband had never been dissolved and it was not known whether he was dead at the time of the second marriage. The first husband had disappeared over 20 years before the second marriage, and neither his wife nor the rest of his family had heard anything further from him. The court presumed he had died before her second marriage, so it was valid. In *Re Peete* (1952), the wife produced a marriage certificate, but no death certificate for her previous husband. The evidence she had of his death was uncorroborated hearsay. Her application was dismissed on the basis that she had not proved she was the deceased's spouse. An applicant may, however, in certain limited circumstances, rely on a void marriage (see below).

15.9.3 Polygamous marriages

In *Re Sehota, Kaur v Kaur* (1978), the applicant's marriage to the deceased had been a polygamous marriage. The burden of proof was on her to show that she was validly married to the deceased, just as with judicially separated spouses, but the court held that it was satisfied where the marriage had not been annulled by proceedings. The court held that the ruling in *Hyde v Hyde and Woodmansee* (1866) (the case which is usually cited as providing the definition of marriage) that the divorce legislation applied only to monogamous marriages did not apply in this case. It held that polygamous marriages were generally valid in English law, and *Hyde v Hyde* had never applied to the law of succession and had been reversed by statute in matrimonial proceedings.

15.9.4 Void marriages

The 1975 Act itself does not mention voidable marriages, but it does refer to void marriages at s 25(4). Technically, a void marriage is one considered in law never to have existed, as opposed to a voidable marriage, which is considered to exist until it is annulled by a court; it is then declared never to have been valid. Thus, proceedings to annul a void marriage are technically not necessary, but may be brought because the law allows parties to both void and voidable marriages to apply to the courts for ancillary relief (orders about financial and property matters) in nullity proceedings. In the same way, there are provisions for parties to void marriages to seek relief under the 1975 Act, provided that the applicant spouse entered into the marriage in good faith and has not had the marriage dissolved or annulled by a procedure recognised under English law nor entered into a later marriage. A spouse claiming in this way will be treated as any other spouse for the purposes of the higher level of provision awarded under s 1(1)(a).

It seems likely that the recent remarkable importation into the law of ancillary relief in matrimonial causes regarding void marriages will be reflected in the law of family provision, if a relevant opportunity arises. In *Whiston v Whiston* (1995), it was held that the wife in a void marriage could not seek ancillary relief because she was herself criminally responsible for the situation that led to the marriage being void, namely that, at the date of the marriage ceremony, she was already lawfully married to someone else, as she well knew. This new rule was confirmed in the case of *J v S-T* (1997), where the applicant for ancillary relief was responsible for the marriage being void as he had falsely claimed to the Registrar of Marriages that he was a man whereas, as he knew, he had been born a woman and undergone a sex-change operation. The question of whether a person who has undergone such an operation can validly marry someone of the sex they originally were themselves was decided in the negative in the influential case of *Corbett v Corbett* (1970), which concerned a male to female transsexual who had purported to marry a man. After a considered judgment, Ormrod LJ concluded that the parties to the marriage had not been respectively male and female and that the marriage was therefore void. The wife was, however, permitted to go on to claim ancillary relief; the present restriction was discovered only in the mid-1990s with the *Whiston* case.

15.9.5 Remarriage of spouse

A spouse who can bring herself within s 1(1)(a) may pursue her claim equally if she has remarried after the deceased's death.

15.9.6 Judicial separation

It should be noted in respect of judicially separated spouses that, although their marriage is not dissolved, they will often have obtained, by consent or otherwise, an ancillary relief order from a matrimonial court in the course of the judicial separation proceedings. This will almost invariably include an order that, the court considering it just so to order under s 15 of the I(PFD)A 1975, the parties are no longer entitled to apply for provision from each other's estates under s 2. A judicially separated spouse does not, however, qualify for the higher level of spouse relief where the separation was continuing at the date of death (see below).

15.10 Section 1(1)(b) – former spouse who has not remarried

Section 1(1)(b) refers to the former wife or former husband of the deceased who has not remarried. This sub-section applies to those who have been divorced in England and Wales, and is intended more to protect those whose ancillary relief proceedings have not been completed than to provide an avenue for fresh claims.

15.10.1 Powers of divorce courts

In *Re Fullard* (1982), the applicant and the deceased had been divorced. The death of Mr Fullard released substantial capital by way of insurance policies, and his former wife applied for a share in that capital. The Court of Appeal considered the powers of a divorce court to make appropriate capital adjustments between the parties in matrimonial proceedings, and in view of those powers it stated that it was likely that there would be comparatively few cases where a divorced spouse would succeed in an application under the 1975 Act. It said that where, as in *Re Fullard,* the parties had settled their financial matters by agreement or order, an application should not succeed unless there had been a material change in circumstances.

15.10.2 Must the agreement be overt or satisfactory?

It is not clear how far this represents a change in attitude from earlier decisions, for example, that in *Re W* (1975), where a former wife succeeded under the legislation preceding the 1975 Act in obtaining a substantial capital sum from the estate of her husband from whom she had been divorced for 26 years. In that case, the court held that he had a considerable moral obligation to her because he had failed to maintain her as he should have done, and that the capital ordered to be paid to the former wife had been accumulated by the deceased as a result of making no maintenance payments.

15.10.3 Unfinished ancillary relief business

Nevertheless, the claim in *Re Farrow* (1987) succeeded. On the divorce of Mr and Mrs Farrow, an order was made within the matrimonial proceedings for Mr Farrow to pay his former wife periodical payments by way of maintenance. Less than a year later, Mr Farrow died intestate. The former wife applied to the court for financial support out of his estate, and the court gave her that relief, having regard to the fact that the periodical payments order ran for such a short time.

Section 14 of the I(PFD)A 1975 provides that where an application for family provision is made by a former spouse in respect of the death of the other party to the marriage within 12 months of a decree absolute of divorce (or a decree of judicial separation, if the separation is continuing), and there has been no order in ancillary relief proceedings, the court has power to look at what the spouse would have obtained from a matrimonial court had such an order been made.

15.10.4 Dismissal of claims in ancillary relief proceedings

As with judicial separation, it is usual for the parties to proceedings for divorce to obtain an ancillary relief order and for that to include a provision dismissing claims under the 1975 Act, pursuant to the power given to a matrimonial court to make such an order by s 15 of the 1975 Act.

The case of *Whiting v Whiting* (1988) demonstrates how the practice of the law may operate to produce a particular result. The parties were divorced in 1975, the three children going to live with the wife and the husband paying maintenance. When the wife subsequently qualified as a teacher, the maintenance order was reduced by consent to a nominal order. In 1979, the husband remarried and, in 1983, he was made redundant. In 1986 (following the insertion into the Matrimonial Causes Act 1973 of s 25A), the husband applied to the matrimonial court for a 'clean break' – the dismissal firstly of the wife's own claim for maintenance and secondly of her potential claim against his estate under the 1975 Act. The wife was at that point in a much better financial situation, from the point of view of both income and debt liabilities, than the husband, who had since remarried. The Registrar dismissed the application and the husband appealed to a judge, who upheld the dismissal. The husband then appealed to the Court of Appeal. No evidence of the new wife's situation was brought though she was known to be employed as a teacher. The Court of Appeal dismissed the appeal. It said that, though it might itself have dismissed the maintenance claim, the question was rather whether the lower court had come to an unreasonable decision. It found that the court below had been entitled to exercise its discretion as it did. The husband would have had to make out his case under s 15(1) of the 1975 Act that the dismissal of the potential I(PFD)A 1975 claim was 'just', and he had not done so.

15.11 Section 1(1)(ba) – unmarried cohabitant during two years preceding death

Section 1(1)(ba) was inserted into the 1975 Act by the Law Reform (Succession) Act 1995. It gives a right to claim to a person who had lived in the deceased's household as her or his husband or wife for the two years immediately preceding the death.

15.11.1 Meaning of cohabitation

The provision is modelled on that of the Fatal Accidents Act 1976, which gives cohabitants for the two years immediately preceding the death of the other cohabitant standing to sue the relevant tortfeasor. The definition of cohabitant does not appear to have caused too much practical difficulty, despite its apparent vagueness. The question of whether persons are spouses is usually easily answered; without the benefit of any equivalent of the marriage ceremony, the nature of a relationship may be difficult to define. The suggestion that the appropriate test is whether one party fills out the other's tax return may be frivolous but, equally, it may be as good as any other. The insertion of this sub-section is a step towards recognition of the validity of the unmarried family as a legal relationship, which is remarkable in the prevailing political climate.

15.11.2 Immediately before the death

This requirement that, for a claimant to fall within s 1(1)(ba), the qualifying cohabitation must have been 'immediately' before the death echoes not only the Fatal Accidents Act 1976 but also the requirements relating to dependency (see 15.14.6), and it is likely that the requirement would be treated analogously in practice.

15.12 Section 1(1)(c) – child of the deceased

Section 1(1)(c) refers to the child of the deceased. It is for the child applicant to prove that he is the child of the deceased. He may, however, rely on the presumption of legitimacy if he is the child of a married father.

15.12.1 Definition of children

Originally, under the 1938 Act, only unmarried or disabled daughters, or minor or disabled sons, could apply. The age at which a child ceases in English law to be dependent is in any case very variable, depending on the area of law. For much social security legislation, a child grows up at 16, though he is restricted from claiming benefits in his own right until 18 and at the full rate until 25. For educational grants under the awards regulations, his dependency ceases at 25. In the private family legislation on divorce, a child ceases childhood generally at 18 or later if he continues in full time education.

15.12.2 Adult children

Section 1(1)(c) does not refer only to infant children, but to the offspring of the deceased. Age restrictions on claims under the family provision legislation were removed in the 1975 Act, though a reading of the Law Commission's 61st Report might suggest that they did not expect large numbers of applications by adult children, and especially not by able-bodied employed children, as discussed in *Re Coventry* (1979).

15.12.3 Nature of relationship

Section 1(1)(c) includes adopted children by virtue of the general law (the provisions of the Adoption Act 1976), and illegitimate children and children *en ventre sa mère* at the date of the deceased's death by virtue of s 25(1) of the 1975 Act itself.

15.12.4 Adoption and claims under the 1975 Act

The precise words of the adoption legislation may be important; they may exclude a child from claiming from the estate of its natural parent, as well as allowing him to claim against the estate of his adoptive parent. In *Re Collins (deceased)* (1990), claims were made by the two children of the deceased, Christine Anne Collins, who died intestate in 1980. Two years before her death, she had married Mr Collins, but had started divorce proceedings against and had reached a decree nisi in divorce proceedings. She left an estate of £27,000 net which, under the intestacy rules, would all go to Mr Collins as he survived her. The first claimant, Bernice, was the illegitimate daughter of Mrs Collins; at the date of the hearing she was 19 years old, unemployed and living on social security with her boyfriend. The court held that although Mrs Collins had no liability to maintain the adult Bernice, the provision made for her on intestacy was not reasonable, and it awarded her a lump sum of £5,000. The other claimant, B, was the child of the Collins' marriage. He had been born in June 1979 and adopted away in 1987. Counsel for B addressed the court on the subject of the Adoption Act 1976, in particular ss 39(2) (which said that adopted children were to be treated as the children only of their adoptive parents) and 42(4), the 'saving sub-section' (s 39(2) avoids prejudice to interests vested in possession before the adoption), saying that the potential to make a claim under the 1975 Act was vested before the adoption and thus covered by the 'saving sub-section'.

The court held, however, that the qualifying date was that of the deceased's death. It said that the saving sub-sections of the Adoption Act could not affect law laid down by Act of Parliament such as the 1975 Act, which provided specifically that the application must be made by the deceased's child. As to the suggestion that B's right to apply under the 1975 Act subsisted as a chose in action, the court thought it was 'really no more than a hope'. The court commented on B's favourable position with his adoptive parents and dismissed his claim.

15.12.5 Relationship of blood or adoption

What is required for an applicant to have *locus standi* under this sub-section is a relationship of blood or adoption; stepchildren cannot apply under this sub-section. The relevance of earlier decisions of other courts was discussed in *Rowe v Rowe* (1980). Where there has been a finding by a court that a child is the offspring of the deceased, that will bind the child if he was a party to the proceedings by virtue of the *res judicata* (the thing has been adjudicated) rule. If, however, the child was not a party, he will not be prevented from trying to establish parenthood if the decision was not favourable to him, although if the decision was favourable to the child the estate may be prevented by that from setting up a defence on the basis that the deceased was not the child's parent. DNA testing, which has made proving parenthood much easier in the area of child maintenance, for example, is less helpful when one of the parties who would have to take part in the tests is dead.

15.13 Section 1(1)(d) – child of the family

Section 1(1)(d) refers to any person (not being a child of the deceased) who, in the case of any marriage to which the deceased was at any time a party, was treated by the deceased as a child of the family in relation to that marriage. This is the sub-section for stepchildren in particular. Before the 1975 Act, they could not claim. The Law Commission commented on this in particular. Note that the applicant not only need not be an infant at the time of application but also need not have been an infant at any time during which the relationship on which he bases his claim to *locus standi* subsisted.

15.13.1 Not an infant when the relevant family was formed

The successful applicant in *Re Callaghan* (1984) was 35 years old and living in his own home, a rented council house, with his wife when his mother married the deceased. The deceased treated the applicant as an adult child of his own by acknowledging his role as grandfather to the applicant's children, placing confidence as to his property and financial affairs in the applicant, and depending on the applicant to care for him in his last illness. He then died intestate, so that the applicant stood to inherit nothing from the £31,000 estate. Taking into account that the deceased's assets were derived from his wife, the applicant's mother, and her first husband's family, the court gave the applicant £15,000 to enable him to buy his council house.

15.13.2 Treated as a child of the family

There must have been a family as such for the applicant to have been part of, fulfilling both conditions of relation by marriage – not an unmarried family – and of living together. The child must, therefore, necessarily have been born, to have been 'treated' by the deceased (*A v A (family: unborn child)* (1974)). It was established in *W (RJ) v W (SJ)* (1971) that whether the deceased knew he was not the child's father is irrelevant to the question of whether the child has *locus standi* under this section, though it may be relevant to what the child can then claim (see below).

15.13.3 How a step-child establishes 'treatment as a child of the family'

The applicant in *Re Leach* (1985) was near retirement, and had relied her deceased stepfather's stated intention to make provision for her by will, which he failed to do. The court discussed what a step-child in particular should establish in order for a claim to be entertained. The step-child should have been treated as a child of the family by the deceased, and that treatment must amount to more than a mere display of affection, kindness or hospitality. The deceased must have assumed the position of a parent towards the applicant, with all the responsibilities and privileges of that relationship. Treatment of the applicant as a child of the family after the marriage has ended by the death of the other spouse is relevant if the treatment stems form the marriage, but such treatment, if it occurs, need not continue until the deceased dies.

15.14 Section 1(1)(e) – dependants

Section 1(1)(e) refers to any person (not being a person included in the foregoing categories) who immediately before the death of the deceased was being maintained, either wholly or partly, by the deceased. The Law Commission recommended this particular addition to the categories of potential claimants under the previous legislation, being concerned about the 'accidental or unintentional' or 'unfair' failure to provide for dependants. The Law Commission was concerned about the increasing number of 'de facto spouses', or unmarried cohabitants, who were not catered for under the previous legislation, and it is cohabitants which have proved the most fruitful source of claims. The claims of a wife under the earlier legislation had been affected by the deceased's testamentary gifts to another woman in *Re Joslin* (1941); where the law restricted testamentary freedom on either the moral or the practical basis, it was illogical to restrict that basis to members of the married family only.

The Law Commission does not appear to have given very deep thought to the question of how a person would show they were being wholly or partly maintained. It said: 'We think that these questions can be resolved by the court on common-sense lines. The principle in our view is that a person should be treated as having been maintained by the deceased, either wholly or partly, as the case may be, if the deceased was, otherwise than for full consideration, making a substantial contribution in cash or kind towards that person's reasonable needs.'

15.14.1 Whose common sense?

Unfortunately, it failed to say what constituted common sense, or perhaps whose sense was involved; in particular it failed to say what value should be placed on caring and how the problem of the interaction between financial dependency and caring should be resolved. If the applicant is required to have depended on the other on a value basis, then a person who has provided constant nursing care in return for something of comparatively little value has no claim, especially if the caring is valued at the market price of obtaining constant care. The valuation of caring is, however, not usually at market prices, whether the care is that of a nurse, in family provision proceedings, or a housekeeper in divorce proceedings; it appears to be viewed as being worth very little money, as it is often done for love. In assessing dependency for a claim under the 1975 Act the common sense of judges does not necessarily accord with the common sense of everyone. The consequences of a requirement for financial dependency often produce a result widely perceived as unfair and favouring those who 'sponged' or 'scrounged' off their providers over those whose conduct gave them a better moral claim on the estate of the deceased.

15.14.2 Other jurisdictions

Other jurisdictions or other areas of law have been looked to in the situation where a person has behaved in a particular way during their lifetime on the basis that they will be rewarded in someone's will. In New Zealand, for example, there is testamentary promises legislation which can be appealed to; in England the doctrines of constructive trust and proprietary estoppel have been used, especially during the 1970s, to rectify the inequity perceived in such situations. In *Pascoe v Turner* (1979) (not a succession case), for example, a woman badly let down by a man who broke his promises to her was awarded the fee simple of his house. The extension of proprietary estoppel to a general equitable remedy was, however, regarded as beginning to approach a remedy for those who were unable to establish more than their reasonable expectations of reward, short of a contract. Objections were often based on the perceived disproportion between the services given to the defendant in the court proceedings and the property he was ordered to make over.

15.14.3 Moral arguments less acceptable in England?

The general approach of the English courts under the family provision legislation in the past has been to reward caring at its out-of-pocket cost, for example as in *Re Cook* (1956), unless the applicant has given up employment which they already had, when the court will find a particular detriment. The courts also regard assisting in a business as showing something more than assisting in general life by caring (*Re Brownbridge* (1942)). Their general view was perhaps expressed by Oliver J, overturning an award of £2,000 to the son of the deceased who had lived with him for many years. He said in *Re Coventry* of the 1975 Act: 'It is not the purpose of the Act to provide legacies or rewards for meritorious conduct.'

15.14.4 What sort of person may claim under this category?

There has always been some doubt as to who could be included in the category, and its scope continues to be interpreted by the courts. However, the breadth of scope of the category of potential applicants, so far as the type of person who might be a potential applicant is concerned, was discussed by the court in *Re Wilkinson* (1978). It found that the category of 'dependant of the deceased' is not confined to relatives of the deceased or to members of the deceased's household, and it covers persons who during the lifetime of the deceased would have had no right to enforce a claim for maintenance against the deceased – in this case the applicant was the deceased's sister, who had been acting as a companion. The court also had to weigh up the financial circumstances of the case in order to be satisfied that the applicant was dependent on the deceased. The deceased sister had asked the applicant to live with her and she had paid all the household expenses, the two of them sharing the household tasks. The court placed a financial value on the applicant's work about the house and decided it was less than the value of the accommodation provided for her by her sister; therefore, she was financially dependent.

15.14.5 'Maintaining' and 'immediately'

The courts have not been entirely happy with having to interpret the detailed provisions of this sub-section, which have proved much more difficult to deal with than, for example, a provision which requires the courts to say whether or not a party was validly married. The courts have comparatively little experience of defining whether a person is being maintained or not, or putting a financial value on caring in order to measure it against the value of free accommodation. The two particular areas of this sub-section that have caused difficulties of interpretation are, firstly, the requirement for the deceased to have been 'maintaining' the claimant, and, secondly, the requirement for him to have been maintaining her 'immediately' before his death.

15.14.6 'Immediately'

The court in *Kourkey v Lusher* (1982) considered the question of what 'immediately' meant. The deceased had been married for 31 years, and had a chiropodist's business in which his wife had helped him. In 1953, the wife had bought the premises in which he worked and the flats above with her savings and dowry, and in 1957 she and the deceased had bought their matrimonial home in their joint names. The applicant had married an affluent Iraqi in 1945 and had two sons from that marriage. In 1963, she had met the deceased at his surgery, and in 1969 he left his wife and went to live with the applicant, who the following year divorced her husband. The deceased remained in friendly contact with his wife, paying her wages and the outgoings on the matrimonial home. In 1977, the deceased and the applicant bought a flat in their joint names, with the applicant contributing £10,000 capital and the deceased contributing £6,350 by way of mortgage. The applicant subsequently contracted to purchase a house for £39,200 with the proceeds of sale of the flat; the deceased had agreed with that but would not agree to taking on a new mortgage. In July 1979, the deceased and his wife went away on holiday together and he told her he would return to her; in August he died of a heart attack. The applicant claimed under the 1975 Act. The court held that the deceased had been reluctant to commit himself financially to the applicant during their relationship and that she had not been maintained by the deceased immediately before his death. It was also unhappy about the claimed unreasonableness of the provision for her, where she looked to her sons and her family in Iraq for support, and where the estate was in any case very small – only £1,931 net.

15.14.7 Assumption of responsibility and full valuable consideration

In 1980, in the case of *Re Beaumont*, the court held that the overt assumption by the deceased of responsibility for the applicant was essential to the success of a claim. (It was, however, subsequently overruled on this point by the Court of Appeal in *Jelley v Iliffe* (1981).) It also held that a person could claim as a 'dependant of the deceased' only – and it said the word 'only' should be implied into the Act. The court held that the Act should be construed as if s 1(3) qualified s 1(1)(e) and not as though it provided an alternative to it. Section 1(3) provides that a person shall be treated as being maintained by the deceased if the deceased, otherwise than for full valuable consideration, was making a substantial contribution in money or money's worth towards the reasonable needs of that person. As to whether 'full valuable consideration' meant 'full valuable consideration under a contract', the court thought not in both this case and *Jelley v Iliffe*.

15.14.8 Evidence and extent of assumption of responsibility

What the Court of Appeal said in *Jelley v Iliffe* about the deceased's responsibility for the applicant, as in *Re Beaumont*, was that, though some responsibility must have been assumed by the deceased while she was alive, there need be no other overt act to demonstrate the assumption of responsibility beyond actual maintenance, and it need not be shown that she had also assumed responsibility for the applicant's maintenance after her own death. The court also addressed the question of whether the category of 'dependant of the deceased' might include a 'common law husband', and held that it might, but only if he was materially dependent on the deceased.

The facts in *Jelley v Iliffe* were quite unusual. The Iliffe parents had a son and a daughter, both of whom died leaving widowed spouses. Mr Jelley, the daughter's husband, then went to live with Mrs Iliffe, the son's wife, who died eight years later leaving everything to her three children. Mr Jelley applied under the 1975 Act and the Court of Appeal considered his position on an application by the children of Mrs Iliffe to strike his claim out as showing no cause of action. It referred to the injustice done to one who has been put by a deceased person in a position of dependency being deprived of any financial support, either by accident or by design of the deceased, after his death. It held that the reference to consideration in the Act had nothing to do with the law of contract and that a broad interpretation would be put on the word 'immediately' in the sub-section – the arrangement faltered before the deceased's death, where the breakdown of the arrangement was due to the deceased being too ill in her terminal illness to maintain the regular payments previously made.

15.14.9 Burden of proof of dependency

The applicant in *Harrington v Gill* (1983) had been living with the deceased as his wife, and today would claim under the new s 1(1)(ba). The court held that when she was claiming under s 1(1)(e) as his 'dependant', the burden of proof lay upon her to show that he had been making a substantial contribution in money or money's worth towards her reasonable needs. She was successful and the court ordered a house comprised in the deceased's net estate to be settled on the claimant for life.

The insistence on the applicant establishing financial dependency echoed the decision in *Re Kirby* (1982), where the court held that the claimant, if basing the claim on having been maintained by the deceased and grounding that dependency on their having lived together and shared expenses, must establish that a substantial contribution was made to the claimant's own share of the expenses by the deceased. If the contributions were broadly equal, or the claimant's contribution was greater, the claim would not succeed. The result of this, although it is undoubtedly a reasonable reading of what the legislation says, is often felt to be completely unfair, because it means that where both parties paid their way, neither can have a claim against the other's estate, even where in practice they cannot manage alone. For instance, where they have taken on a rented flat or the mortgage on a house together and shared the expenses and the rent equally, it may well be the case that neither can afford to keep the property going alone, but still neither is dependent on the other under the sub-section, because they have not had part of their share of the expenses paid by the other party. Conversely, someone who does not work and pay their way, but allows the other person to support them will have a claim, even where the sole reason for their not working is laziness or a desire to depend solely on their partner.

15.15 What the applicant may claim – matters to which the court has regard

The court has to decide firstly whether or not the provision for the applicant under the will or intestacy of the deceased is reasonable given the circumstances at the deceased's death. The court will look at the particular circumstances of the people involved in the case – for example, even though the intestacy rules are designed with a view to giving the beneficiaries what a reasonable testator would have given them, with the spouse having first call on the estate, the court will not assume without looking at the evidence that the spouse has necessarily obtained reasonable financial provision from the operation of the intestacy rules. The Act largely leaves the calculations to the discretion of the individual court, though there are guidelines in s 3 about what level of provision is appropriate for different types of applicant. Spouses are more favourably treated.

15.15.1 Showing unreasonableness

Only if the court, looking at what the deceased's will or intestacy provides for the applicant, decides that it is unreasonable will it go on to consider what provision would be reasonable for the applicant. How this should work in practice is somewhat unclear on the face of the Act, as it does not say what the dates are for the assessment of reasonableness. The Act itself leaves open the question, for example, of whether an applicant who was unreasonably left destitute by the deceased but who subsequently came into money before the hearing of his 1975 Act action would find that his claim was thrown out because of his financial situation at date of the hearing. The court will take into account all facts known at the date of the hearing (s 3(5)).

15.15.2 Statutory directions as to unreasonableness

The court is directed by s 1(2) to the definition of reasonable provision. Reasonable provision for spouses is not confined to their maintenance (s 1(2)(a)), but for everyone else, including cohabitants, the correct standard is that of maintenance (s 1(2)(b)), as defined in the context of family provision. For the courts' definition of maintenance, and their attitude to giving capital to spouses, see below. A decision needs to be taken as to what is reasonable, first, in order to see whether or not a claimant's existing entitlement is unreasonable and, if it is, secondly, to work out what order should be made.

15.15.3 Standard of reasonableness for cohabitants

The Law Commission's proposals in their Report No 187 to extend the right to bring a claim – *locus standi* – to unmarried cohabitants specifically excluded any idea that they might claim the same level of provision as a spouse, leaving them to justify the level of their claim to the court on the same basis as any other applicant. The courts' treatment of spouses' apparent entitlement over and above maintenance is, however, questionable (see 15.23.6).

Although the special rules as to reasonable provision for spouses in s 3(2) do not apply to cohabitants, provision has been made by s 2(4) of the Law Reform (Succession) Act 1995, adding s 3(2A) to the Inheritance (Provision for Family and Dependants) Act 1975, for special rules for cohabitants which import the same provisions as those relating to spouses, save that of the hypothetical 'divorce standard' (see, further, below at 15.24). It remains to be seen how the courts treat cohabitants in practice, though it should be noted that, in the case of *Graham v Murphy* (1997), it was an important factor that there had been a long cohabitation, even though during part of it the claimant had not been financially dependent on the deceased.

15.15.4 Time for assessment of unreasonableness

Cases before the 1975 Act showed reasonableness being based on existing and reasonably foreseeable facts at the time of the deceased's death, so that in *Re Howell* (1953) where a testator left his property to his second wife on the assumption she would care for his two children, and they returned to his first wife because of their step-mother's subsequent unexpected illness, there was no claim.

The nearest relevant current statutory direction is contained in s 3(5) of the 1975 Act, which directs the court to determine what constitutes reasonable financial provision on the basis of the facts known to it at the hearing. This is not precisely on the point, as it would cover both possibilities – assessment of unreasonableness at the time of death and at the time of the hearing.

The High Court of Australia in *Coates v National Trustees Co Ltd* (1956) also took the same view as in *Re Howell* on the question of jurisdiction to hear the case, but once having decided it had jurisdiction held that it would take account of facts as at the date of the hearing when deciding on quantum. This was followed by the Privy Council in *Dun v Dun* (1959).

Later, however, the courts seemed more inclined to take account of facts at the date of the hearing in assessing whether they had jurisdiction – that is, whether the provision had not been reasonable in the first place. In *Re Clark* (1968), account was taken of the death of the principal beneficiary under the deceased's will, and in *Re Shanahan* (1971) Lord Simon said that the value of the estate would be assessed at the date of the hearing, thus necessarily implying that assessments of reasonableness would be made at that date too.

The court in *Moody v Stephenson* (1992) has now stated explicitly that the assessment of unreasonableness would be based on facts known at the date of the hearing.

15.15.5 Objective assessment of unreasonableness

The provision in s 3(5) does, however, mean that the court is not looking at whether the deceased, knowing what he knew, subjectively made reasonable provision, but at whether, objectively and in the light of all the facts shown to the court, whether or not known to the deceased, the provision was reasonable. The test is the same as under the legislation which preceded the 1975 Act and which Megarry J referred to in *Re Goodwin* (1968) when he said that the question was simply whether the will or the disposition made reasonable provision, and not whether it was unreasonable on the part of the deceased to have made no provision or no larger provision for the dependant. He said that in his view the question was not subjective but objective, and was not whether the testator stood convicted of unreasonableness, but whether the provision in fact made was reasonable. Thus, the deceased in *Re Franks* (1948) could not be said to have behaved unreasonably in failing to provide for her child, as she died only two days after giving birth, but the child was still able to bring a family provision claim based on the objective unreasonableness of the lack of provision. Note that the size of the estate will be a relevant factor in assessing what provision is reasonable; in *Re Goodwin,* the court awarded the whole of the estate to the spouse, because it was not a large estate and no-one else had a moral claim on it.

15.16 Statutory guidelines in assessing reasonableness – s 3(1)(a–g) of the I(PFD)A 1975

Guidelines as to what the court should take into account when assessing reasonable provision are laid down in s 3 of the Act. Section 3(1)(a–g) lays down seven particular points which the court is to bear in mind.

The first three provisions concern the financial situation of the applicant, other applicants and beneficiaries. Section 3(6) specifically directs that a person's financial resources in this context include their earning capacity – whether or not they are working and have any actual earnings – and their needs include their obligations – for example the maintenance of a family. There is only a finite amount of property in any estate, so there are often situations where no-one can be given their full 'reasonable' entitlement without depriving someone else of theirs. Therefore all the people who are expecting part of the estate and may be affected by whatever order the court makes have to be considered. Looking at the situations of several people and weighing it in the balance can take a great deal of work; that is why proceedings under the 1975 Act can be lengthy and expensive.

The guidelines in s 3(1) as to assessing reasonableness are as follows:

(a) the financial resources and financial needs which the applicant has or is likely to have in the foreseeable future;

(b) the financial resources and financial needs which any other applicant for an order under the Act had or is likely to have within the foreseeable future;

(c) the financial resources and financial needs which any beneficiary of the estate of the deceased has or is likely to have in the foreseeable future;

(d) any obligations and responsibilities which the deceased had towards any applicant for an order under the said s 2 or towards any beneficiary of the estate of the deceased;

(e) the size and nature of the net estate;

(f) any physical or mental disability of any applicant for an order of any beneficiary of the state of the deceased;

(g) any other matter, including the conduct of the applicant or any other person, which in the circumstances of the case the court may consider relevant.

15.17 Section 3(1)(a), (b), (c) – financial resources and needs of applicants and beneficiaries

A person's resources can include state aid. In *Re E (deceased)* (1966), the deceased left a widow, but for many years had been living with another woman, to whom he left the whole of his estate by his will. The main asset in the estate was his state death grant (the availability of these is now greatly restricted) which the court considered, holding the source of the deceased's assets to be relevant, to have been earned by him whilst he was living with the other woman. The court also held that in considering all the circumstances of any applicant for relief, including their own needs and resources, it could take into account forms of state relief, and that if the only effect of granting relief would be to relieve the state from having to pay means-tested benefits to the applicant, so the applicant was in fact financially no better off, it might be reasonable to make no provision.

The court in *Re Canderton* (1970), however, dealt with the problem by making an award which, by its careful division between income and capital, had the least possible detrimental effect on the recipient's entitlement to social security benefits.

It is questionable how far the principle of accounting for state benefits would be followed today, in a climate of different attitudes towards social security payments, when the general trend of legislation amongst other things is to avoid making or allowing people to be dependent on state resources save as a last resort, and to have them supported by other private individuals with whom they have a family relationship.

15.18 Section 3(1)(d) – deceased's obligations

Section 3(1)(d) refers to the obligations and responsibilities towards applicants and beneficiaries. The deceased's obligations and responsibilities under this section may be moral or legal. English law in this area does not refer to moral obligations, although in other jurisdictions such as New Zealand it does. In *Re Allardice* (1910), the court referred to a 'moral duty' test independent of actual dependence.

15.18.1 English courts define relevant obligations

The English courts have thus been given a fairly free hand to define what obligations and responsibilities are relevant. The court in *Re Haig* (1979) explicitly said that its decision was based on the morally reasonable thing to have done. The court in *Re Fullard* (1982), above, considered the question of actual dependency very relevant, and moral obligations to cohabitants are clearly recognised, as they were in *Re E* (1966), above, and in *Re Joslin* (1941). Both these cases involved gifts by will to cohabitants of the deceased; because they predate the 1975 Act, those persons could not themselves have claimed under the family provision legislation, because until the law was amended by the 1975 Act, it did not include any provision allowing cohabitants *locus standi*. Nevertheless, although the courts particularly in 1941 might have regarded unmarried relationships as inappropriate or even improper, in these cases they recognised not just the existence of the gift by will – which the law obliges them to – but also the deceased's moral obligation to his cohabitant.

15.18.2 Moral obligations to spouses

Moral obligations between spouses are usually clear, but where the spouses have been separated for a long time, a court may find on the facts of the case that no moral obligation existed. The case of *Re Gregory* (1971) may be contrasted with that of *Re W* (1975). In the former case, the husband deserted the wife a year after their marriage and lived with another woman for over 20 years before asking his wife to return to him on the other woman's death. She refused to do so and emigrated a few years later. After 10 years of unsuccessful appeals to her, by letter, to return to him, the husband died, leaving her nothing in his will. The Court of Appeal held that, on the facts of such a lengthy separation and the wife's independence from the husband, he owed her no moral obligation and her claim under the relevant family provision legislation failed. In *Re W*, the parties had been married for 12 years when they were divorced, and the husband failed to maintain the wife thereafter. After 26 years of divorce, the husband died and the wife successfully claimed a capital sum from his estate. The court held that the husband's capital effectively represented the maintenance payments to which his wife had been entitled but which he had not made.

15.18.3 Competing moral claims – spouse and beneficiaries

An example of competing moral claims between a spouse and another party may be seen in *Re Parkinson* (1969). The deceased left his house and contents to his widow for life, with remainder to the RSPCA. At first instance, the court refused to interfere with the deceased's testamentary freedom on the basis that the widow, who at that point wished to continue to live in the house, would be no better off. The Court of Appeal, hearing that the house would have to be sold to pay the costs of the appeal and that in any event the wife no longer wished to continue living there, held that she should receive the whole estate outright. It may be noted, however, that the strongest support in this court for the decision to give the whole estate to the wife came from Lord Denning, who at that time appeared to regard a matrimonial home very much as family property, with the wife having an enforceable moral claim to it in any event. This view gave comparatively little regard to the conception of property rights which would support the view that it was for the deceased to dispose of the house entirely as he wished. There was, however, dissent in the court from another judge, who felt that the widow, though she should obtain the whole estate, should do so only because the body with whom she was competing had no moral claim on the testator.

15.18.4 Obligations

The moral obligation of parents to their children as such, however, appears to change considerably, and perhaps to end, once the child has grown up. This does not mean the child cannot bring a claim, but just that the court will probably not find any support for it in this particular sub-section. The case of *Re Andrews* (1955) showed a court deciding that a woman who had left her father's home to live for some decades with a man who was married to someone else had ceased to be dependent on her father and become dependent on the other man. It is questionable how far a court would follow such reasoning today, since the attitude to women's dependency on men has changed, but it may be that the changes in terms of legal practice will turn out to be as much a matter of form as of substance; the courts may well come to the same decision in effect, but phrase it differently.

The Court of Appeal held in the recent case of *Re Jennings (Deceased), Harlow v National Westminster Bank* (1994), that the failure of a father to make proper provision for his son whilst still an infant child was not a basis on which to ground a finding of obligation, under this sub-section, to provide for him in adulthood on death.

15.19 Section 3(1)(e) – size and nature of estate

Section 3(1)(e) refers to the size and nature of the net estate. The courts are unhappy about applications which claim from a small estate. Where the estate is not substantial, the costs of bringing a case, particularly one which goes all the way to trial, are likely to exceed the amount the applicant is claiming. This makes such a claim self-defeating, and the courts are conscious of the inappropriateness of expensive legal actions over small estates. On the other hand, what to the Court of Appeal appears to be a small matter may to the applicant be somewhat larger, and where the courts tend not to regard a point of principle as being a valid reason for bringing a claim, applicants may not agree. The court in *Re Gregory* (1971), above, specifically stated that it would be unwilling to interfere with a testator's dispositions where, as here, the estate amounted to less than £3,000. In *Kourkey v Lusher* (1982), above, the court also criticised the bringing of a claim against an estate worth less than £2,000.

15.20 Section 3(1)(f) – disability

Section 3(1)(f) refers to any physical or mental disability of any applicant or beneficiary. The factual situation to be taken account of under this sub-section could, of course, be referred to under other headings. Any disability of an applicant or beneficiary would be very likely to affect the deceased's moral obligation to him, as well as his financial needs and probably his financial resources, such as his earning capacity as well. However, there might be situations in which having the ground spelled out were useful, for example, it might be argued that the deceased had no extra moral obligation because he was unaware of the disability or its effects, or it might be difficult to prove to the court that the disability had materially affected the applicant or beneficiary's financial situation. Putting the factor of disability in a separate category not only ensures that the courts will take account of it, but also demonstrates the importance of it to the legislature. The statutory requirement for the court to have regard to an applicant or beneficiary's disability is something to which he can draw the court's attention in support of his case.

15.20.1 Disabled applicant to rely on state support?

A disabled applicant or beneficiary may be being cared for under the National Health Service. The question of whether this would excuse the failure by a deceased to provide for such a person was answered differently in different cases. In *Re Watkins* (1953), the court thought it would be reasonable for the deceased to take into account the deceased's secure position and accordingly to make no provision. In other cases, however, the court has come to a different conclusion. For example, in *Re Pringle* (1956), the testatrix's mentally incapable son was resident in hospital and maintained by the state; he obtained £10 per week from the estate of his mother, who had left her property to two friends. In *Millward v Shenton* (1972), the Court of Appeal held that provision should have been made for the testatrix's son, who was totally incapacitated, married to a disabled wife and reliant on state benefits, even though he was in his 50s when she died. He obtained eleven-twelfths of the estate, which his mother had left to charity. Clearly, the current changes in long-term care under the NHS will have effects on cases involving this sub-section.

15.21 Section 3(1)(g) – any other matter

Section 3(1)(g) refers to any other matter including conduct. The scope of this catch-all provision is clearly potentially very wide, but the courts have so far used it only for certain particular areas. They have looked at the provenance of the assets in the estate and the deceased's own stated wishes, as well as the behaviour of an applicant or beneficiary towards the deceased.

15.21.1 Provenance of assets

The provenance of the assets in the estate may be a particularly important consideration. This was referred to in *Jelley v Iliffe* (1981), where the court said it might be material that most of the deceased's assets had been inherited by her from the father of the claimants, as well as in *Re Callaghan* (1984) (above). In *Re Canderton* (1970) (above), much of the deceased's estate had been inherited by him from a woman with whom he had lived instead of with his wife. She had provided in her will that if he predeceased her, her estate should go to a niece and a friend. The court, considering an application by the estranged wife, avoided substantial reduction of the gifts the deceased then made by will to the other woman's niece and friend.

15.21.2 Conduct of the applicant

In *Williams v Johns* (1988), the applicant had been adopted by the deceased and her husband at the age of six weeks, when their natural son was 17 years old. She had had a stormy childhood and continued into adulthood as an offender. Her adoptive parents had supported her both financially and morally. The son, on the other hand, was found to have been a 'model son'. In 1985, the mother died, leaving her entire estate by will to her son and appending to the will a statement that she had provided for her daughter during her lifetime beyond any reasonable expectation and had no response or affection from her. The applicant was very hurt by that statement and claimed the will had been made after a quarrel between them, following which they had reconciled. She based her claim on, firstly, her own impecuniosity, secondly, the fact alleged by her that the deceased had held her in continuing affection and, thirdly, that the disposition of the estate was not reasonable. At the time of the claim, she was 43 years old, unemployed, impecunious, divorced and without capital save for the houseboat in which she lived. Her claim failed, because the court held she had not established any obligation by the deceased to maintain her beyond the mere fact of the adoptive relationship. She was physically fit and capable and had been independent for many years. The court said she had taken no care of her mother but had caused her shame and distress.

15.21.3 Statements left by deceased

The court in *Williams v Johns* did not, however, say how much, if any, importance it attached to the statement left by the testatrix. It is not clear from the judgment whether the evidence on which it was making findings of fact about the applicant's behaviour included the statement or not. The deceased's statement is admissible as part of that evidence even though clearly the deceased cannot be called to be cross-examined on it, under the provisions of s 21 of the I(PFD)A 1975 and s 2 of the Civil Evidence Act 1968. However, there is no separate direction to the court to take account of it as there is of the factor of disability, for example, or indeed as there was under the original Inheritance (Family Provision) Act 1938 (s 1(7)). This leaves the court a very free hand to consider what the deceased says and ignore it or take account of it as it will, and perhaps in context that strikes a balance.

Where the deceased has left any sort of statement about his testamentary gifts, that statement is likely to explain the gifts he has made in terms of his motivation and feelings. In that sense it may be regarded as simply duplicating the terms of the deceased's will, for example, where the deceased has failed to leave anything to one child and has expanded in a separate statement, or one in the will itself, as to his reasons.

It may however, simply show that the deceased had put what the court thought was an inappropriate interpretation on his moral obligations to the applicant, or ignored them completely, whereas in considering a claim the court certainly will take account of such obligations, under s 3(1)(d) above. In such a situation, the deceased's statement will, by explaining his reasons for making the provision, have the opposite effect from that intended, since it will clarify for the court the deceased's failure to take all the necessary factors into account and show that his provision, in the court's terms, is not reasonable. In *Re Clarke* (1968), the testator, who had been aged 49 on his marriage to a woman in her thirties, stated that he had made no provision for his wife because she had deserted him; the court found as a matter of fact that her behaviour had been quite reasonable, and the deceased had rather deserted her by refusing to leave his mother's house. The deceased's statement may thus address the court's mind to, or make it aware of, facts which otherwise might have been lost, such as the applicant's treatment of the deceased, and will provide evidence to support a court's finding of fact in that area.

15.21.4 Agreement not to claim

The court in *Re Fullard* (1982) also said that an agreement between a couple on separation that they would not claim against each others estate should not be ignored simply because it was not embodied in a court order.

15.21.5 Related case failed – concealment from deceased

In *Re Goodchild (deceased)* (1997), the applicant for family provision had originally sought to have his parents' wills declared as mutual wills (see 6.9.5). When that failed, he sought provision out of the estate of his father, to whom his mother's estate had passed and who had left much of it to his second wife. At first instance, the mutual wills case failed but the court gave Gary a substantial sum, talking about how part of the father's property had come from the mother. On appeal, the second wife claimed the court had been improperly implementing the provisions of the father's revoked will as though it were a valid mutual will. She also claimed that Gary could not cite, as a relevant consideration in seeking family provision, his own indebtedness from which he would have been able to release himself had he inherited as he expected, because he had unconscionably concealed that indebtedness from his father during his lifetime when seeking loans from him. The Court of

Appeal held, however, that the existence of Gary's indebtedness did not relieve Dennis of his moral obligation towards his son, and the second wife's appeal was dismissed. It also confirmed that the agreement between the parties to an order arranged in such a way as to minimise liability to tax was valid, provided the order arrived at was one which was within the court's power to make under the Act.

15.21.6 Effect of scope of court's discretion

Because the court has a wide discretion, if it makes what a party thinks is an unfair or unreasonable order, what they will have to show if they wish to appeal is that the court exercised that discretion unreasonably. If the court is not entirely clear about its reasons, for example, if the applicant believes that a statement about his behaviour was given undue weight – the applicant will have to show not that another view of strength of the statement would have been better but that the view the court did take was unreasonable. It is not sufficient for the court hearing the appeal merely to feel that it would have taken a different view. Where there is a wide-ranging provision such as that allowing the court to take account of 'any other matter', this also inevitably gives scope for uncertainty as to the likely outcome of a case at first instance and a lesser chance of establishing unreasonableness in that decision on appeal.

15.22 Applying s 3(1) to the claimant – s 3(2)–(4)

The court is required by the terms of the 1975 Act to apply the results of its assessment of the individual applicant's position and the nature of the deceased's estate differently, depending on the basis on which the applicant claims. The special rules or guidelines for each category are set out in s 3(2) for spouses and former spouses who have not remarried, s 3(2A) for cohabitants, s 3(3) for children of the deceased and his family and s 3(4) for those claiming on the basis of financial dependency on the deceased. Spouses and former spouses are treated alike; the guidelines for cohabitants are very similar. The provisions relating to those claiming as children include aspects of the parental role such as education, and those relating to dependents require an evaluation of the extent of the dependency.

15.23 Section 3(2) – spouse and former spouse

Spouses and former spouses who have not remarried are more favourably treated in that they may reasonably expect more than others. Thus what is reasonable provision for others may not be reasonable for them. They therefore have a greater chance of establishing that provision for them was not reasonable as well as the expectation of a larger award.

15.23.1 Who these guidelines apply to

Applications in the first two categories from s 1(1) are governed not only by the guidelines in s 3(1)(a–g) above, as are all applications, but also by the specific guidelines for spouses set out in s 3(2). The cases tend to be about claims by widows against the estates of their late husbands. The same provisions apply to both spouses and former spouses. Obviously the legislation must cover not only the spouse who has the means or capacity to support herself, but the wife who has been divorced by her husband when she is too old and unqualified or inexperienced in paid work to support herself; such a wife may be reliant on maintenance payments from her husband to survive, which will come to an end on his death. The direction to the court to take into account the same factors in respect of married and divorced spouses does not mean that it will necessarily come to the same conclusion regardless of whether or not the parties are divorced, because it will bring in all the other factors, such as moral obligation, to which periods of separation and the general facts of the situation between the parties will be highly relevant. It was said in the case of *Eyre v Eyre* (1967) that a court could not guarantee a first wife equality with a widow, but that if all other things were equal they would be treated the same.

15.23.2 Substance of the extra guidelines

The court is directed to take into account the applicant's age, the duration of the marriage and the contribution made by the applicant to the welfare of the deceased's family – this specifically includes caring for the family and the family home. Where the parties were not judicially separated and still living apart at the date of the deceased's death, the court is also directed by s 14 of the I(PFD)A 1975 to take account of what the applicant would have received from a matrimonial court had the marriage been ended by divorce rather than by death (but at the same date). A difficulty with this is that English law does not properly prescribe any method of calculation for how property will be divided on divorce. The traditional 'one-third rule' has been criticised and also stated never to have been a rule; an analysis of the cases shows that the most important element in such decisions is the discretion of the court.

15.23.3 Conduct of the spouses

A particular point to note in this respect is that the principle which operates in matrimonial proceedings which says that a spouse's conduct within a marriage is unlikely to influence the award the court makes to her also applies in the context of proceedings by spouses under the 1975 Act. The irrelevance of conduct to financial applications between spouses, save where it is particularly gross, has been firmly established in matrimonial law since *Wachtel v Wachtel* (1973). In *Re Bunning* (1984), the court assessed the provision for the applicant widow on the basis of what she would have received had financial arrangements been made on a divorce at the date of the husband's death. The court took the view that, in the situation where the marriage had broken down at the date of death, it was even less relevant than it would have been on an application for financial relief within divorce to consider whose conduct might have led to the breakdown of the marriage.

15.23.4 Former spouse of wealthy testator

In *Re Besterman* (1984), Mr Besterman left an estate of over £1,400,000, most of it to the University of Oxford. To his wife he gave his personal chattels and a yearly income of £3,500 for life. The University acknowledged that this provision was inadequate for a millionaire's widow, accustomed to a high standard of living, and who after 18 years of dutiful marriage at the age of 66 years had as her only other source of income a widow's pension of £400 per year. What the court was asked was therefore to set the amount she should receive. The trial judge awarded Mrs Besterman £238,000, calculating it by reference to what was sufficient for her to buy an annuity giving her a reasonable level of maintenance. Mrs Besterman appealed to the Court of Appeal for an increase in the lump sum, and on appeal received £378,000 instead.

15.23.5 The divorce standard?

The Court of Appeal disagreed that the basis of calculation used previously had been correct – what should have been looked at was the appropriate sum for a surviving spouse, not the level of maintenance the wife might have received had there been a divorce. On divorce, after all, the calculations take into account the continued living expenses of the spouse who in a family provision claim no longer has any such expenses. In any case it felt Mrs Besterman might have expected to receive £350,000 on divorce.

The hypothetical divorce standard was discussed recently in *Re Krubert (deceased)* (1996), where a widow aged 87 sought family provision from her late husband's estate. There had been a long marriage without children. The matrimonial home had been the husband's, and he gave her a licence to remain in it as long as she wished to do so, a legacy of £10,000 and the income of the residue after payment out of some specific gifts. The deceased's brother and sister, also elderly, were to take the house subject to the wife's interest. The court gave the wife the house absolutely at first instance, as well as the residue subject to the specific gifts and legacies of £7,000 each to the brother and sister. The brother and sister appealed and the Court of Appeal replaced the original order, giving widow a life interest in the house and an absolute interest in the remainder of estate. The reasoning of Nourse LJ was: '... she needs the house to live in and, if she has to move, she will need the additional income generated by the reinvested proceeds. But no financial need for an absolute interest in the house has been made out.' Cazalet J discussed the 'divorce standard': 'One unsatisfactory aspect of placing too much emphasis on the award which would have been made on the hypothetical divorce is that ... such an approach may well, in what may be described as small asset cases produce financial provision below reasonable financial provision ... because the funds available cannot provide satisfactorily for two homes ... the court in claims under the Act is concerned with one spouse and not two.' It might be noted particularly that the legal costs in this case amounted to about £23,000 out of an estate worth about £78,000.

The legislation in this area provided originally only for the maintenance of applicants. In *Re Inns* (1947), for example, the widow was left the matrimonial home during her widowhood. Unfortunately, the deceased husband had left her insufficient income out of his large estate to run the house, which was admittedly large and expensive to maintain. The court, however, rejected her application for family provision, made on the basis that the testator had clearly intended that his widow should be able to continue living in the house. It said it would apply the same considerations in a large estate as in a small one and use its powers sparingly. It did not think the provision made by the testator for his widow was unreasonable, and refused to order more. It is suggested that the same attitude of mind continued to influence courts' decisions for a considerable period even after the passing of the 1975 Act. The court in *Moody v Stephenson* (1992) specifically warned against leaning on early authorities.

15.23.6 Maintenance or capital?

There are also other indications that the courts may be influenced by the idea of giving the widow maintenance, rather than capital, even where what they award is a lump sum. In *Re W* (1975), the registrar who originally heard the application awarded the elderly divorced wife £14,000, but this was reduced on appeal to the judge to £11,000 on the basis that, as she was aged 75, she could buy an annuity that would give her a reasonable income at a comparatively low price, and this figure would still give her some capital left over. In this situation, the spouse's age meant she received less than had she been younger, although the effect of taking into account the a spouse's age might be at least as likely to increase the potential award by drawing the court's attention to her inability, at an advanced age, to change tack and obtain employment outside the home.

The method of calculation of the wife's claim in *Re W* clearly looks at the wife's reasonable entitlement principally from the point of view of satisfying the wife's claim to be maintained, rather than regarding her as having a claim to the capital represented by the property in the estate as such; it does not allow her much by way of freedom to control such spare capital as there might be after considerations of maintenance are dealt with, but leaves that spare capital, however much of it there is, in the control of the testator to will away as he wishes. In such a scheme, the wife will, on the other hand, be left with no capital over which she has control and therefore nothing to will away as she wishes on her death.

Most recently, this conflict was exemplified in *Davis v Davis* (1993), where the applicant was the deceased's widow. He also left a sixteen year old son from a previous marriage. He had given his wife £15,000 just before his death, and left her most of his chattels and a life interest in a trust fund of £177,000, expected to increase to £267,000. The widow's claim for the house worth £70,000 which the trustees had bought for her to live in to be transferred to her absolutely was rejected by the judge. She appealed to the Court of Appeal, which agreed with the judge. He had said: '... can it be said that the disposition by will is not such as to make reasonable financial provision for the plaintiff, by which is meant such financial provision as would be reasonable in all the circumstances for her to receive whether or not the provision is required for her maintenance? I am bound to say, for my part, I regard the proposition as startling. ... In terms of what he deployed for his surviving widow, he could not have done more ... If in this case it can be said that the provision of a life interest in the entire residuary estate is not reasonable provision then I think that could be asserted in almost any case in which the testator elects to make provision for his surviving spouse by that means.' Though the court was concerned, on an appeal, not with what it would have decided itself but with whether the judge's decision was properly made, the tenor of the judgment is that it is not inappropriate to dismiss any claim that a wife may have by virtue of her marriage to the capital value of her husband's property and to regard her right as only that of maintenance.

15.23.7 A different view from the bench?

One might compare this with the decision in the ancillary relief proceedings in the matrimonial case of *Vicary v Vicary* (1992). The judge rejected the husband's contention that the wife had no claim to capital, saying: 'In the instant case should not the wife have the opportunity to feel as much independence as her husband? The opportunity to spend the remaining years she has in the knowledge that she has substantial capital which she can leave to her children or to a dogs' home as she pleases.' The Court of Appeal also refused to overturn that judgment. If matrimonial courts were to follow the spirit of *Vicary* and family provision courts that of *Davis*, that again would give rise to the spectacle of divorcing wives having a greater entitlement to property than widows of a successful marriage, despite the *dicta* in *Moody v Stephenson* (1992) as to the aim of the 1975 Act.

15.23.8 Entitlement to capital recognised by family provision courts

However, a different approach to where the claims to the capital owned within a family lie may be perceptible in the case of *Re Shanahan* (1975). In that case, the court awarded half the capital to each of the testator's current and former wives. Both had reached retirement age, but the latter was better off financially in her own right. The court may, however, have considered there was some 'fairness' in dividing the estate equally between them.

15.24 Section 3(2A) – cohabitants

The Law Reform (Succession) Act 1995 amended the 1975 Act to allow a cohabitant who had been living in the deceased's household as her or his husband or wife for the two years immediately preceding the death to claim on that basis. Such a person would claim under s 1(1)(ba) of the amended 1975 Act. That person might also be a dependant within the meaning of s 1(1)(e), but it is likely that the treatment of dependants under s 3 will be seen to be less favourable than that of cohabitants.

Where a cohabitant is concerned, the court is directed by new guidelines inserted as s 3(2A) by the 1995 Act to take account of the applicant's age, the duration of the relationship and the contribution of the applicant to the welfare of the deceased's family. These guidelines are the same as those for spouses and former spouses in s 3(2) but, as is logical, without the further direction as to a hypothetical order on divorce. Case law is awaited.

15.25 Section 3(3) – child of the deceased and child of the family

A person applying under the categories is s 1(1)(c) and (d) does not have to be a child in the sense of being young, but if he is then the court is directed by s 3(3) to take account of the manner in which he was being educated or trained, or the manner in which he might be expected to be educated or trained. It will also be relevant to whether an adult child ought to succeed if the deceased was supporting the child in the process of acquiring some educational or occupational qualification, and relevant to the question of provision for an adult applicant generally if that adult gave up work in order to care for the deceased during illness or old age. For those in the category of children of the family, s 3(3) also directs the court to consider whether the deceased made any assumption of responsibility by the deceased for the child, for how long and on what basis, whether he knew the child was not his own child, and the liability of any other person to maintain the child.

15.26 Section 3(4) – dependants

In considering an application by a claimant under s 1(1)(e), the court is directed by s 3(4) to have regard to the extent to which, and the basis upon which, the deceased assumed responsibility for the maintenance of the applicant, and how long he discharged that responsibility for. It is submitted that the general attitude suggested by the wording of s 3(4), with its emphasis on the deceased's personal relationship with the applicant, offers some support for the attitude taken by Butler-Sloss LJ in *Bishop v Plumley* (above) that what is important in considering an application by a dependant under s 1(1)(e) is the 'mutuality of the relationship'.

15.27 Any impediments to bringing a claim?

An applicant is not precluded from bringing a claim under the 1975 Act, and a court is not precluded from hearing it, by assurances given by the beneficiaries of the estate that they will not enforce their rights. In *Rajabally v Rajabally* (1987), the beneficiaries under the will had assured the applicant widow that they would not insist on their rights. Their assurances were not, however, legally enforceable by the widow, and the court held that they did not defeat the application.

15.27.1 Right to claim under the 1975 Act does not survive the applicant

The right to bring an action under the 1975 Act does not survive the applicant and cannot be carried on by their estate. It is, therefore, like an action for defamation in tort in that it is not covered by the usual rule under the Law Reform (Miscellaneous Provisions) Act 1934, which allows most actions by or against a deceased person to be carried on by their personal representatives, with particular rules relating to limitation. It is more akin to the rules in matrimonial proceedings, where actions do not subsist after death. This fits in with the nature of applications in family matters, where what the court is looking at is the situation of the parties and their respective needs and resources, rather than the enforcement of contracts and strict property rights.

15.27.2 *White v Ticehurst* (1986)

Both these points were made in the decision in *Whyte v Ticehurst and another* (1986). The couple were married in 1953, and the husband died in February 1984 after executing a will in 1982 leaving his house to charity subject to his wife's right to live there during her lifetime. The wife commenced proceedings under s 1(1) but then, in December 1984, before the final hearing, she too died. Her personal representatives applied to the Registrar of the court for leave to carry on the proceedings on behalf of her estate but he dismissed the application saying there was no cause of action. The personal representatives appealed to the Family Division saying firstly that the Matrimonial Causes Act 1973 had been extended by the 1975 Act and secondly, relying on the Law Reform (Miscellaneous Provisions) Act 1934, that the rights of a surviving spouse were not extinguished on death. It was accepted by counsel for both sides at the hearing that an ancillary relief claim does not subsist against the estate of a deceased spouse and that a claim for maintenance dies with an applicant.

The court dismissed the appeal, saying that the whole claim under the 1975 Act died with the applicant. The court also looked at the true effect of the claim; since the personal representatives' claim could not benefit the deceased wife herself, it was essentially a contest between the beneficiaries under the husband's will and those who would take under the wife's. The court commented on the inappropriateness in any event of considering such a claim, especially given the statutory direction to the court as to the factors to be taken into account in deciding any award to be made. Those factors did not fit in at all with the situation which arose once the original claimant had died.

15.27.2 Personal nature of claim confirmed

This decision was followed in *Re Bramwell, Campbell v Tobin* (1988), which concerned a potential claim by a widow against the estate of her late husband. They had married in 1975 when the wife was 65 and the husband 71; they separated four years later, and in 1986 the husband died. The wife instructed her solicitor to act in a family provision claim against her husband's estate, but no proceedings had been issued when the wife died, having survived her husband by only six months. The solicitor was then instructed by the widow's personal representative. The plaintiff in the action was the personal representative of the wife. It was argued on her behalf that the judgment in *Whyte v Ticehurst* (1986) was correct but confined to its context of a matrimonial cause. The court, however, held that the right to claim under the 1975 Act was not and did not give rise to a 'cause of action' under the Law Reform (Miscellaneous Provisions) Act 1934 unless an order was made before the death of the person entitled by virtue of the provisions of the Act to make the application. Sheldon J said, 'Until then it remains no more than a hope or contingency of no surviving value to a deceased claimant's estate.' The same phrase – 'no more than a hope' – was used in the case of *Re Collins* (1990) (above), though *Re Bramwell* was not referred to in that case.

15.28 If no claim under the 1975 Act lies

It may be possible for a person to establish that they have ownership of some of what appeared to be the deceased's property as a matter of law, so that they do not have to seek a court order for it to be given to them out of the estate.

This might be particularly important for unmarried cohabitants if they do not fall within s 1(1)(ba) – for example, if the cohabitation lasted less than two years or had ceased before the death. For example, where a person owned a property jointly with the deceased, if it could be established that they owned it as joint tenants in equity as well as at law, the deceased's share would pass to them automatically on his death in accordance with the right of survivorship (*jus accrescendi*). Even if the property was in the deceased's sole name, the potential claimant might be able to establish ownership of some or all of the property under a constructive trust or the doctrine of proprietary estoppel. There might also have been the possibility of establishing that there was a valid and enforceable contract for the property to be left to the potential claimant by the deceased.

15.28.1 Constructive trust, proprietary estoppel and contract?

In *Layton v Martin* (1986), the court was asked to consider the applicant's claim on several bases. She had first formed a relationship with the deceased in 1967, when she was 29 and single and the deceased was 50. In 1975 he asked her in a letter to live with him, offering her emotional security and financial security during his life and after his death. His wife was ill and the implication was that on her death he would marry the applicant. He paid the applicant £100 a month plus £30 a week housekeeping, but when his wife did die in 1977 he did not marry her. (She appears to have been little bothered by this.) In 1979 he made a will providing for the applicant, but in June 1980 he rescinded that provision when the couple parted, albeit on friendly terms.

In April 1982 he died and the applicant claimed under the 1975 Act. She also claimed firstly that she had relied on the representations in his letter that he would provide for her, and alleged a constructive trust in her favour. Secondly, she alleged proprietary estoppel, saying that equity should subject the estate to such beneficial rights in her favour as would give effect to the representation on which she relied. Thirdly, she said there had been a contract between herself and the deceased resulting from her acceptance of his offer – the courts are unwilling to find a contract in these circumstances. The court dismissed the application, holding that she had not been living with him until his death and did not fall within the meaning of dependant under the Act.

15.29 Orders which the court can make

Section 2 of the Act sets out the orders the court may make. The range is wide, and is increased by the court's power to attach conditions to its orders. The court may specifically order any one or more of the following, which are set out in s 2:

- maintenance;
- a lump sum;
- transfer of property to the applicant;
- settlement of property for the benefit of the applicant;
- acquisition of property and its transfer to or settlement on the applicant;
- variation of any relevant marriage settlement.

Where orders for maintenance are concerned, the court is permitted by s 2(2) to relate the order to the whole income of the estate or some smaller amount, expressing the order in terms of a fixed sum or of a proportion of the income of the estate. Alternatively, it may order the appropriation of a sum of capital within the estate for the production of the income to meet the periodical payments (s 2(3)). Maintenance is the traditional order under the family provision legislation for any dependant. There is a noticeable difference between orders for maintenance made to spouses and those made to former spouses; in the case of spouses, the order is not bound to cease if the spouse remarries, whereas in the case of former spouses, it must do so.

15.29.1 How the court applies the provisions of the law in practice

There is nothing in the 1975 Act which sets out exactly how its provisions should be applied, and in particular nothing explaining how 'maintenance' is to be defined, but the courts have laid down certain principles in the course of their decisions. Unfortunately, just as courts will disagree on the interpretation to be put on words of guidance and definition where they are laid down in statute, so, when courts have a discretion, they disagree with each other as to how that discretion should be exercised.

Under the New Zealand jurisdiction, Salmond J in *Allen v Manchester* (1942) had said that a man should provide proper and adequate support for his wife and children and that, if he did not do so, the court would imply the provisions which a just and wise father would make. The words 'wise and just' were repeated in the Australian case of *Bosch v Perpetual Trustee Co Ltd* (1935). But in Australasia there is a far stronger moral base to the family provision legislation. Courts in England have had a stronger eye to the testamentary freedom of the deceased and have tended to interfere with it as little as possible, only in so far as the legislation requires it rather than in so far as it might allow it, albeit with some exceptions.

15.30 Defining 'maintenance'

The definition of 'maintenance' has been particularly contentious. It is accepted that it is not the same as keeping someone on or even off the breadline and cannot be equated with subsistence – that was established in *Re E* (1966) (above) and *Millward v Shenton* (1972) (above). The court in *Re*

Borthwick (1949) disagreed with a suggestion that the standard of living to which a wife has become accustomed during her marriage would necessarily dictate the level of provision she might expect from her husband's estate. 'In other words it is said that the worse a man treats his wife in his lifetime the less he need leave when he is dead,' said the judge. He was unimpressed by the argument: 'I cannot accept such a cynical conclusion.' He thus confirmed the court's comments in the appeal in the New Zealand case of *Allen v Manchester* (1942), where the standard of maintenance appropriate to a widow was defined as the standard required for her 'to live with comfort and without pecuniary anxiety at such a standard as she was accustomed to in her husband's lifetime, or would have been accustomed to if her husband had then done his duty to her'.

15.30.1 *Re Christie* (1979) – maintenance and well-being

The testatrix in *Re Christie* (1979) left an estate of £13,000. Under her will, she made gifts of a share of a house in London to her adult daughter and of a house in Essex to her adult son, with the residue divided equally between them. By the time of her death, the half-share of the house in London had been made over to the daughter by deed of gift and the house in Essex referred to in the will had been sold and replaced with another. The son claimed the new Essex house worth £9,000 from her estate to replace the one which had been adeemed. The court discussed what was meant by 'reasonable financial provision' and 'maintenance'. It held that, although maintenance is not restricted to subsistence level, 'on the other hand, it does not mean anything which may be regarded as reasonably desirable for his general benefit or welfare'. Maintenance, said the court, 'refers to no more and no less than the applicant's way of life and well-being, his health, financial security and allied matters such as the well-being, health and financial security of his immediate family for whom he is responsible'. In his conclusion, however, the deputy judge appeared to rely heavily on the admission by the daughter that she had probably benefited more than her brother and stated that he would 'redress the balance' by giving the son the new Essex house.

15.30.2 Criticisms of *Re Christie*

This case has been much cited and also heavily criticised for several reasons. In particular, though the son was not very well-off and had two young children to support, he already owned a house and was in no particular need. The court did not apply an objective test of whether the provision made for him was reasonable for his maintenance; indeed it appears to have regarded the 1975 Act as indeed giving it carte blanche – an invitation to recast the provisions of the deceased's will entirely rather than to adjust them in accordance with the claim for 'maintenance'. Moreover, the court took oral evidence of the deceased's intentions and implemented them in order to avoid the effects of the ademption of the old house in Essex, thus – given that this was not really a claim for 'maintenance' – using the provisions of the 1975 Act to bypass the requirements for the formalities laid down by the Wills Act 1837.

15.30.3 *Re Coventry* (1979)

The breadth of interpretation of 'maintenance' in *Re Christie* was criticised by both the High Court and the Court of Appeal in *Re Coventry* (1979). It approved instead the Canadian case of *Re Duranceau* (1952), in which the court said that reasonable maintenance was what was sufficient to enable the dependent to live neither luxuriously nor miserably, but decently and comfortably according to his or her station in life. The deceased in *Re Coventry* had died intestate, leaving a net estate of about £7,000 consisting largely of his house. The sole beneficiary under the intestacy rules was his estranged wife, who was then 74 years old and who had lived apart from him without any maintenance for the previous 19 years. The applicant was the deceased's son, then 46 years of age, who had been living rent-free with his father for many years. It appeared that he and his father had driven out the mother many years earlier. The son had, in return for his free accommodation, provided his father's food and contributed to the household outgoings. That salary did not, however, allow him sufficient income for anything but the necessities of life, particularly once the son was faced with having to pay for his accommodation when his mother started possession proceedings against him.

The Master gave the plaintiff £2,000; he appealed to a judge for more, but Oliver J considered that requests for 'maintenance' from a young, healthy man in employment should be regarded with circumspection and, after considering whether there were any particular reasons why the plaintiff should receive anything from the estate, discharged the master's award altogether. The plaintiff appealed to the Court of Appeal, who agreed with Oliver J. It concurred in particular with his test of maintenance and his analysis of the relevant question, which was not whether the applicant needed maintenance but whether he could show that it was unreasonable that the intestacy provisions that were applicable did not provide for him. The decision was 'a qualitative decision, or what is sometimes called a 'value judgment' ... particularly difficult to disturb on appeal'. It concurred also with Oliver J's statement that the court did not have carte blanche to reform either the deceased's dispositions or those provided for him by the intestacy rules (it found there was no difference in the two cases, as the deceased might have taken a conscious decision to remain intestate, save where he left a statement explaining that he specifically desired, for example, to exclude someone). The court must decide on the basis of the facts known to it at the date of the hearing. Oliver J had been entitled to conclude that the intestacy provisions were not unreasonable to the son.

15.30.4 Courts not designed to assess what is just?

The difficulties inherent in this approach were, however, identified by Ormrod J in *Re Fullard* (1982) (above), when he said that it was impossible to consider what was 'reasonable' without considering what 'ought' to have been done, and 'ought' brought with it considerations of what was just as between the deceased and the applicant.

15.30.5 Payment of debts can be maintenance

In considering further what may constitute maintenance, the court in *Re Dennis* (1981) held that 'maintenance' connotes provision which, directly or indirectly, enables the applicant 'to discharge the cost of his daily living at whatever standard of living is appropriate to him'. The court held that although payment of an applicant's debts to enable him to carry on a profit-making profession or business could be maintenance, in this case that did not apply; the debt concerned was the tax liability consequent on the deceased's death within six years of a substantial gift to the applicant.

15.30.6 Redistributive justice?

The court in *Re Christie* referred to 'redressing the balance' between the daughter and the son of the deceased. Another example of a court regarding equality as equity where children of the deceased were concerned was that of *In the Estate of McC* (1979) (also reported as *CA v CC* (1978)), in which the younger, illegitimate child of the deceased applied for provision out of his father's estate. Though the content of the decision has not been criticised, since there was insufficient in the estate to satisfy the reasonable requirements of all the potential beneficiaries, the reasoning has been questioned. The court appeared to hold that the deceased's two children must be put on the same footing which, although it may indeed have a certain equity in the more general sense of the word, has no basis in the legislation. Both decisions have been heavily criticised because the redistribution carried out by them cannot be justified by the words of the 1975 Act and they are considered to be an abuse of the powers it confers.

15.31 How the court may carry out calculations – example

The way that a court proceeds to calculate the amount to be awarded in a fairly large estate can be seen from the example of *Malone v Harrison and Another* (1979) below. In that case, the deceased and his wife Agnes had been separated in 1939 but never divorced; he paid her maintenance voluntarily. In 1958, one Christina Milne moved in with the deceased, and she subsequently took the surname Harrison. In 1965, he met the applicant, Mavis Cynthia Malone, who at his request gave up her job, albeit it was not well paid. He gave her assurances about her future security but told her he would not be providing for her in his will; however, he sent her a newspaper clipping about the passage through Parliament of the 1975 Act.

By the time of his death in 1977, the deceased had given the applicant shares to the value of £15,000, the flat in Sutton Coldfield in which she lived and a flat in Malta valued at £10,000. The deceased had been giving Miss Malone about £4,000 a year, but had continued to live with Christina Milne. He had told Christina Milne that he no longer had any relationship with the applicant; he had told the applicant that Christina Milne was no more than his housekeeper, but very possessive of him. The deceased left a substantial estate. Provision was made in the will for the deceased's wife, for Christina Milne and her son and for the deceased's brother Mr Harrison. The applicant was earning £23 per week and had no greater earning capacity; her shares less her overdraft were worth about £13,000. She was 38 years old, with an actuarial life expectancy of 38 years.

It was agreed that she should get, if anything at all, a lump sum. The court (commenting that 'the deceased worked hard and for long hours, but he also allowed himself considerable relaxation') held:

(a) The deceased had maintained the applicant on the basis of a promise that she would be provided for by him after his death; if the provision in his will was not reasonable, the court would alter it.

(b) The court would balance the plaintiff's needs with the deceased's obligations to the beneficiaries. The plaintiff would have to resort to capital during her lifetime but the value of her home was not expendable.

(c) The plaintiff reasonably needed £4,000 a year, to which figure the court would apply a multiplier of 11 (a multiplier represents the number of years for which a person will be compensated for a loss which is expected to continue; it is invariably considerably less than the number of years they are expected to live, because they obtain the capital early and can invest it). She was already earning £2,000 so she would get £22,000 by way of capitalised maintenance. She should get capital of £4,000 with a multiplier of 5. From the total of £42,000 they court deducted her free capital of £13,000 and the value of the flat in Malta, so she got £19,000, which the court directed to be paid from the deceased's brother's share of the estate. It is perhaps interesting that the court rejected the argument that the applicant's award should be put in trust so that it reverted to the brother after her death. It allowed her to take the capital and the independence and control it represented, saying the brother had already had enough.

15.32 Property available for provision

All of the deceased's net estate is available to satisfy any order the court may make. The net estate is all the property the deceased had power to dispose of by will (other than by virtue of special power of appointment), less funeral, testamentary and administration expenses, debts, liabilities, and Inheritance Tax. It includes property in respect of which the deceased held a general power of appointment not exercisable by will and not exercised, money or property passing by statutory nomination or *donatio mortis causa* (less the Inheritance Tax referable to it (s 8)), the value of the deceased's severable share of property held on joint tenancy and money made available by the court exercising anti-avoidance powers in relation to family provision.

15.32.1 Joint tenancies

Section 9 of the I(PFD)A 1975 states that the deceased's share of a severable joint tenancy may be ordered to be included in the net estate provided that an application under s 2 of the Act is taken out within six months of the grant of representation to the estate, with a provision that anyone who does anything before such an order is made is not rendered liable by the section for anything he did prior to the making of the order. Thus, a bank paying out the proceeds of a joint account or a survivor of joint tenants dissipating assets may be rendered not liable by this provision. The section is not restricted to holdings of land; it specifically states that a chose in action may be held on a joint tenancy. In *Re Crawford* (1983), the court was considering a claim by the deceased's first wife against money held in building society and bank accounts held jointly by the deceased and his second wife. It held that the net estate of the deceased against which the first wife could claim included his share of that money.

15.32.2 Insurance policies

It has long appeared that the proceeds of insurance policies written in trust were not available, the report of the Law Commission having apparently assumed that the act of creating a trust of a policy did not amount to a disposition of property. Given the breadth of the categories of property which are included in the net estate, this was surprising. In *Re Cairnes* (1983), the court considered whether occupational pension benefits formed part of the net estate for the purposes of family provision orders, and held that they were an example of property which is not included in the net estate of the deceased, if they were payable direct to a beneficiary and not to the deceased's estate.

Section 9 provides that the deceased's severable share of joint property should be valued immediately before his death. In *Powell v Osbourne* (1993) the court considered a case in which the deceased had been in the process of getting divorced when he died leaving a share of a house, jointly owned with a cohabitant and subject to a mortgage, with insufficient other assets to cover debts. There was about £6,000 equity in the house, until the mortgage of £85,000 was paid off by the proceeds of an insurance policy (not available for the payment of debts) on the husband's death.

The recorder in the county court had made an order giving the widow £5,750 – most of the equity of redemption – but indicated that he would have given her £15,000 had the house been free of mortgage. The widow appealed. Dillon J in the Court of Appeal, however, disagreed that the insurance policy had to be valued immediately before the deceased's death, when it had a surrender value of nil. He analysed the object of the section as being to bring in what could have been severed immediately before the date of death; if the joint tenancy of the house had then been severed, the deceased would have become entitled to half the property, subject to the mortgage but with the benefit of a half-share of the policy proceeds, so that on his death his estate would have benefited by half the value of the house (£45,500), with the debt represented by the obligation of half the mortgage being cancelled out by the benefit of half the proceeds of the insurance. Holding that regard must be made to the deceased's imminent death, he found the widow should be awarded the £15,000 she claimed. Simon Brown LJ concurred, saying that Parliament did not intend by its direction in s 9 to require the court to ignore both the fact and the imminence of death, and that when the value of property depends on death, the value immediately before death will be effectively the same as the value upon death. Endowment mortgages are quite common and *Powell v Osbourne* is potentially of very wide application.

15.33 Burden of orders

Once the nature of the net estate has been established, the court may order where the burden of its provisions should fall, under its powers in s 2(4). It may, for example, order one particular beneficiary under the will to transfer part of his property to the successful applicant, rather than dividing the burden amongst all the beneficiaries, if it sees fit. If any trust is created or affected by the order the court makes on an application under the 1975 Act, it may confer on the trustees such powers as appear to it to be necessary or expedient.

15.34 Anti-avoidance

Avoidance of the family provision legislation was a particular problem under the 1938 Act. A person who wished to ensure that some particular person benefited from his estate, to the detriment of a potential applicant with a valid claim under the Act, could avoid the consequences of the act by selling at an undervalue or giving away the property before his death. Where the recipient provides full consideration for the property, it is not regarded as falling within the anti-avoidance provisions and cannot be recalled into the deceased's estate by the hopeful applicant under the Act.

Anti-avoidance is dealt with in ss 10–13 of the I(PFD)A 1975. Section 10 relates to dispositions (the giving away or selling of property) less than six years before death and s 11 to contracts to leave property by will. In either case, the transaction must have been at an undervalue; where the property has been effectively sold for its full market value, it will not be available to be pulled back into the estate under these provisions so as to be used to satisfy a claim under the 1975 Act.

15.34.1 Powers and guidelines

Section 10 sets out the court's powers in relation to avoidance. It provides that it is for the applicant for financial provision to show that the disposition was made less than six years before the date of the deceased's death, with the intention of defeating an application under the 1975 Act, that full valuable consideration was not given and that the exercise of the court's powers under s 10 would allow the court to make financial provision for the applicant, or allow it to be made more easily than otherwise. In considering whether and how it will exercise its powers under this section, the court is directed to have regard to the circumstances in which any disposition was made and any valuable consideration that was given for it, as well as any relationship between the donee and the deceased and his conduct and financial resources. The court is also directed to have regard to 'all the other circumstances of the case'. This means that the court may well find a situation in which the deceased undoubtedly made a transaction at an undervalue, or a gift, within six years of his death, intending to put the property beyond the reach of a potential applicant for family provision – but that it was reasonable for him to do so in the circumstances, because of his relationship to the donee, and that it is not a disposition that should be disturbed by the court.

Section 11 refers to contracts made by the deceased to leave property by will. This is essentially the same provision as in s 10, but referable to cases where the deceased has held on to the property until death rather than disposing of it beforehand. Again, an intention to defeat the operation of the 1975 Act must be shown, as well as a lack of full valuable consideration. There is no time limit on when the contract may have been made save the commencement of the 1975 Act.

Section 12 provides for how the court will decide whether or not the relevant disposition was made by the deceased with the intention of defeating an application for family provision. It allows the court to base its decision on the opinion on the balance of probabilities that this was, in whole or in part, the deceased's intention. This may be presumed where a contract is alleged but no valuable consideration was given for it. The court is also empowered to make directions so as to obtain property for the applicant whilst treating the lifetime recipient of the property fairly.

Section 13 deals with applications made about property given to persons as trustees; the court may not order the trustee to provide more than the trustee has in his hands at the date of the order in respect of the property involved in the claim.

15.34.2 Joining the lifetime recipient

If an applicant wishes to ask the court to make an order against a donee under these sections, then procedurally that person has to be joined in the proceedings. This means making them a party to the court proceedings by issuing an application against them and making them one of the named people against whom the applicant is making his claim under the 1975 Act.

15.34.3 Disposition cannot be set aside as such

The court does not have the power to set aside dispositions and contracts directly, but to order a person who has benefited to help to provide the resources from which a family provision claim can be satisfied. This is different from the powers a bankruptcy court has to set aside transactions at an undervalue within certain periods of the bankruptcy – those powers have caused grave problems particularly where land is concerned, because they mean that a court may come back at a later date and effectively wipe out retrospectively the good title to property obtained by a third party, with no connection with the bankrupt, who bought for full consideration from the bankrupt's donee. The provisions under the 1975 Act allow the court to order the donee, or recipient at an undervalue, to provide a sum of money representing the property given to him by the deceased. Section 10 provides that it may order a donee to provide money representing no more than the value of the property given to him, after deducting any inheritance tax he had to pay on it as a result of the deceased's death. Section 11 makes the same provision in relation to the money paid under a contract, but additionally provides that, if the contract has not been carried out, the court can order it not to be fulfilled.

15.34.4 Order to provide funds

In the case of *Re Dawkins (deceased)* (1986), the deceased's estate was insolvent. Fifteen months before he died, he had sold his house, worth £27,000, to his daughter for £100 with the intention of defeating an application under the family provision legislation. His second wife applied under the 1975 Act. The court was satisfied that an anti-evasion order was appropriate and it ordered the daughter to provide £10,000 for the purpose of providing the applicant with a lump sum.

15.35 Family provision and contracts to leave by will

A person may make a valid contract to leave property by will (see *Hammersley v De Biel* (1845) and *Synge v Synge* (1894) at 2.5). If the deceased concluded a valid contract to leave his property by will in respect of which the applicant cannot show that there was an intention to defeat family provision claims and that there was a lack of full consideration, the property or the value it represents will not be available to the court to satisfy claims under the 1975 Act.

15.35.1 A valid contract to leave by will

The most helpful case may be one under the relevant Australian legislation, *Schaefer v Schuhmann* (1972), which came to the Privy Council from New South Wales. The deceased had made a will in 1962 leaving his four daughters $2,000 each, the residue to be divided between his three sons. In 1966 he bought a house and engaged a housekeeper at $12 a week. In May of that year, he made a codicil, which he asked the housekeeper to read to him, giving his house and its contents to her if she should 'still be employed by me as a housekeeper at the date of my death'. He then told her she would have no more wages because of the provision in the codicil. In November 1966, when the testator died, she was still his housekeeper. The estate was valued at $68,700 net, of which the house and content were valued at $14,500. The daughters applied under the relevant New South Wales legislation for extra provision.

15.35.2 Valid contract but could the family provision court overrule it?

The court of first instance found that the testator and his housekeeper had a contract but that the court had jurisdiction to throw the burden of the daughters' additional provision onto the housekeeper's part of the estate, putting a charge on the house except as to $2,300, thereafter the burden to fall on the residue of the estate. The housekeeper appealed saying the court had no power to make such an order and that all the extra provision should come from residue.

The court allowed the housekeeper's appeal, upholding the contractual arrangements as genuine and declaring that there was no basis for the contention that the rights of a party to a contract became simply the rights of a legatee. Property over which someone had rights of ownership under a contract did not form part of the net estate available for distribution.

15.35.3 Would that case be followed in England today?

If a case were brought in England today on the same facts, the housekeeper might have greater difficulty in establishing her right to the house, because of the effects of s 2 of the Law Reform (Miscellaneous Provisions) Act 1989. The enforceability of her contract with the deceased was based on the doctrine of part performance, which is no longer applicable. Someone in a similar position might instead seek to rely on establishing a constructive trust or might base her claim on proprietary estoppel.

15.35.4 Should that case be followed in principle?

Lord Simon of Glaisdale was cited by the Law Commission in its 61st Report as having made a particular objection to the exclusion of property passing under a contract to leave by will from being available for family provision. He suggested the situation in which a widower with two infant children proposes marriage to another woman, promising her all his estate if she will accept his proposal. She does accept him on those terms. He then dies, leaving the court powerless to award any provision for the infant children. Although the Law Commission suggested only contracts for which full valuable consideration was not given or promised by the proposed donee (marriage not being valuable consideration for these purposes) should be upheld, there is no specific reference to marriage consideration in s 11 of the I(PFD)A 1975, which deals with contracts to leave property by will. Moreover, the courts are not quick to find that a contract is invalid for being designed to defeat a claim (*Midland Bank v Green* (1981) is a case in point).

15.36 How to apply – jurisdiction and procedure

Applications for orders under the 1975 Act can be made in the county court, or in the Chancery or Family Divisions of the High Court. The county courts' jurisdiction is now unlimited, but some cases will still be suitable for transfer to the High Court, for example where there is a great deal of money or property involved or the action is particularly important or raises any questions of general public interest. Where there is a problem of construing the will, the Chancery Division may be thought more appropriate than the Family Division, although the Law Commission had proposed that all cases under the 1975 Act should be heard in the Family Division. Where there has already been an order in matrimonial proceedings, the Family Division will be the appropriate choice. Persons under a disability may be parties in the usual way and proceedings may be compromised (settled between the parties rather than decided by a judge), although the Act does not provide specifically for this. Costs can be awarded out of the estate and usually are. Procedure in the county court is essentially the same as in the High Court, though every defendant, not just the personal representatives, must file an answer to the action.

15.37 Costs

The question of costs, whilst essentially one of practice, does impinge on the substantive law, especially in the area of family provision. The courts have comments to make on the subject of costs in many of their judgments, and they are very ready to condemn the bringing of cases about small estates, since the legal costs will exhaust the estate and the net effect is often simply to deprive anyone, save perhaps the lawyers involved, of any benefit at all. One might bear in mind, however, that what a judge considers to be a small estate is not always seen as such by the aggrieved claimant, and that a prohibition on 'small' cases being brought to a court might mean that a good claim, to which any reasonable beneficiary would accede by agreement, could be defeated by any unreasonable beneficiary without fear of the consequences.

The rules about the payment of other parties' costs are based on the person whose case is better not suffering, and on the prevention of unreasonableness by deterrence; in family provision claims, however, costs usually come out of the estate, on the basis that the deceased was responsible for not having made proper provision. That is no comfort to the person who succeeds in a very reasonable claim against an estate that has been totally depleted by legal fees.

The operation of costs can have a very material effect on a case and has to be borne in mind by practitioners at all times. In *Re a firm of Solicitors* (1982), the court heavily criticised the solicitors acting for the widow of the deceased Mr Coventry for incurring the costs of Queen's Counsel. Even though the legal aid authorities had authorised the instruction of a leader, and the case was one of great public interest, the expense of using such a senior barrister meant that the widow gained no benefit from the action, even though she had been reasonable throughout the case, willing to accept the original order of the Master giving the son provision, and indeed had become involved in further litigation only when the son appealed, disastrously, to Oliver J and the Court of Appeal.

In *Powell v Osbourne* (1993) (above), both parties had obtained legal aid, and the court made an order for costs so that the losing cohabitant should have paid the costs of the winning widow. However, the order was not to be enforced without leave (as is usual against a legally aided party), so the widow would have had to bear her own legal costs of the case, including a hearing before the Court of Appeal, out of her award of £15,000.

The details of legal aid provision may have a substantial effect on the course or outcome of a case. In *Moody v Stephenson* (1992), for example, the effect of the court's careful consideration of the appropriate order was thrown into some disarray by the revelations about the plaintiff's legal aid contribution of £3,700 and the revocation of his certificate during the judgment. It is likely that the current changes in legal aid provision may have some effect on the operation of the substantive law, by changing the way cases are decided as well as the way they are brought to the courts in the first place.

FAMILY PROVISION

Although testamentary freedom as such has a comparatively short history, the possibility of bringing an action against a person's estate after his death on the basis that he has failed to make reasonable and proper provision is very recent in succession terms, and is entirely a creature of statute. The first legislation was passed in 1938. The current Act is the Inheritance (Provision for Family and Dependants) Act 1975.

Section 1(1) of the 1975 Act as amended gives six categories of persons who have the right to apply:

- the wife or husband of the deceased;
- a former wife or husband who has not remarried;
- a cohabitant for the two years preceding death;
- a child of the deceased;
- a person treated as child of the family in relation to a marriage of the deceased;
- a person not in the above categories who was being maintained by the deceased immediately before his death.

The applicant must first show that he falls within one of the above categories before he can bring a claim. He must then show that what he receives under the deceased's will or intestacy is not reasonable. The court will then assess what award to make. The assessment of both unreasonableness and what would be a reasonable order is made on the basis of the facts known to the court at the date of the hearing, thus taking into account changes in people's situations since the date of death as well as earlier facts unknown to the deceased.

The statutory guidelines to assessing reasonableness under s 3(1) have a very wide scope and allow the court to consider anything it wishes, though it is specifically directed to look at the financial situation of anyone who might benefit from the estate, the size of the estate, the obligations the deceased had towards them and any disability of any beneficiaries.

The standard of reasonableness under s 3(2) is different for spouses and former spouses. Their claim, unlike that of persons in the other categories, is not limited to reasonable maintenance. However, the definition of reasonable maintenance is not to be equated with subsistence and has sometimes been interpreted very liberally.

Actions should be brought within six months of a grant of representation to an estate, but the courts are fairly liberal with leave to apply out of time. They discourage applications about small estates, which can be rendered useless by the legal costs involved. The right to claim is personal and does not survive the applicant, so cannot be continued by his estate if no order has been obtained by the date of his death.

The court may order maintenance, a lump sum, transfer, acquisition or settlement of property or the variation of a marriage settlement. This is much wider than the original provisions under the 1938 legislation, which allowed maintenance only. It has sometimes been suggested that the courts, in particular cases, have used the provisions of the 1975 Act to provide for a general distribution of property for which it was not intended.

FURTHER READING

General and textbooks

Miller, J Gareth, *The Machinery of Succession*, 2nd edn, 1996, Aldershot: Dartmouth

Mellows, AR, *The Law of Succession*, 1993, London: Butterworths

Kerridge, R, *Parry & Clark's Law of Succession*, 10th edn, 1995, London: Sweet & Maxwell

Clark, JB and Martyn, JGR, *Theobald on Wills*, 1993, London: Stevens

Oughton, RD, *Tyler's Family Provision*, 1984, London: Butterworths

Finch, J, Hayes, M, Masson, J, Mason, J and Wallis, L, *Wills, Inheritance and Families*, 1996, London: Sweet & Maxwell

Yeldham, RF, *Tristram and Coote's Probate Practice*, 1995, London: Butterworths

Barlow, JS, King, LC and King, AG, *Wills, Administration and Taxation*, 5th edn, 1992, London: Sweet & Maxwell

Biggs, AK and Rogers, AP, *Probate Practice and Procedure*, 1995, Croydon: Tolley

Masson, J, 'Making wills, making clients' (1994) 58 Conveyancer 267, p 360

Chapter 1   History

Baker, JH, *An Introduction to Legal History*, 3rd edn, 1990, London: Butterworths, esp Chaps 15–16.

Barton, JL, 'The Statute of Uses and the trust of freeholds' (1966) 82 LQR 215

Baker, JH, 'Uses and wills' (1978) 94 Selden Society 192

Drobac, J, 'The "perfect" jointure: its formulation after the Statute of Uses' (1988) 19 Cambrian L Rev 26

Virgoe, R, 'Inheritance and litigation in the fifteenth century: the Buckenham disputes' (1994) 15 Journal of Legal History 23

Spring, E, 'The heiress-at-law: English real property law from a new point of view' (1990) 8 Law and History Rev 273

Brooke-Taylor, JDA, 'Section 3 of the Inheritance Act 1833 and *Shelley's Case*, a forgotten piece of learning' (1979) 43 Conveyancer 164

Cretney, S, 'Reform of inheritance: the best we can do?' (1995) 111 LQR 77

Chapter 2   Will substitutes

Deeds

Law Commission Working Paper No 93 *Transfers of Land: Formalities for Deeds and Escrows* (1985)

Nominations

Chappenden, WJ, 'Nominations and the law of succession' (1982) 56 ALJ 270

Nunan, WF, 'The application of the Wills Acts to nomination of beneficiaries under superannuation or pension schemes and insurance policies' (1966) 40 ALJ 13

Rule in *Strong v Bird*

Kodilinye, G, 'A fresh look at the rule in *Strong v Bird*' (1982) 46 Conveyancer 14

Donationes mortis causa

Bonfield, L and Poos, LR, 'The development of the deathbed transfer in medieval English manor courts' (1988) 47 CLJ 403

Samuels, A, '*Donatio mortis causa* of a share certificate' (1966) 30 Conveyancer 189

Warnock-Smith, S, '"*Donationes mortis causa*" and the payment of debts' (1978) 42 Conveyancer 130

Joint tenancies

Brady, JC, 'Succession – the adequacy of joint deposit accounts as will substitutes' (1990) 12 Dublin ULJ 155

Bandali, SM, 'Injustice and problems of beneficial joint tenancy' (1977) 41 Conveyancer 243

Garner, JF, 'Severance of a joint tenancy' (1976) 40 Conveyancer 77

Hayton, DJ, 'Joint tenancies – severance' (1976) 35 CLJ 20

Contracts/Estoppel

Lee, WA, 'Contracts to make wills' (1971) 87 LQR 358

Davey, M, 'Testamentary promises' (1988) 8 LS 92

Secret trusts

Andrews, JA, 'Creating secret trusts' (1963) 27 Conveyancer 92

Burgess, R, 'Secret trust property' (1972) 36 Conveyancer 113

Statutory succession

Samuels, A, 'Succession to residential tenancies: a plain man's guide' (1990) 134 SJ 530

Slatter, M, '"Only": a four-letter word? Statutory succession and agricultural holdings' (1986) 50 Conveyancer 320

Chapter 4   Capacity to make a will

Turing, J, 'Testators – vicious and capricious' (1982) 79 Law Society Gazette 1361

British Medical Association and Law Society, *Assessment of Mental Capacity: Guidance for Doctors and Lawyers*, 1996

Furia, JW de, 'Testamentary gifts from client to attorney-draftsman' (1987) 66 Nebraska L Rev 695

Chapter 5   Formalities for the execution of wills

Real Property Commissioners, *Fourth Report* (1833)

Law Reform Committee, 22nd Report, *The Making and Revocation of Wills*, Cmnd 7902, 1980, London: HMSO

Law Reform Committee, 19th Report, *Interpretation of Wills*, Cmnd 5301, 1973, London: HMSO

Langbein, JH, 'Substantial compliance with the Wills Act' (1975) 88 Harv L Rev 489

Sherrin, C, 'Correcting errors: rectification of documents' (1980) 124 SJ 229

Ormiston, WF, 'Formalities and wills: a plea for caution' (1980) 54 ALJ 451

Mithani, A, 'Rectification of wills' (1983) 80 Law Society Gazette 2589

Samuels, A, 'The new law on wills' (1983) 47 Conveyancer 21

Langbein, JH, 'Excusing harmless errors in the execution of wills – a report on Australia's tranquil revolution in probate law' (1987) 87 Columbia L Rev 1

Clark, JB, 'Darning the law of succession – the wills provisions of the Administration of Justice Act 1982' (1984) 37 CLP 115

Chapter 6   Special wills

Soldiers and sailors

Megarry, RE, '"Actual military service" and soldiers' privileged wills' (1941) 57 LQR 481

Potter, DC, 'Soldiers' wills' (1949) 12 MLR 183

Palk, SNL, 'Informal wills: from soldiers to citizens' (1976) 5 Adelaide L Rev 382

Cole, G, 'How active is actual military service?' (1982) 46 Conveyancer 185

Mental incapacity

Whitehorn, NA, *Court of Protection Handbook*, 8th edn, 1988, London: Longman

Whitehorn, NA and Ingham, J, *Heywood and Massey's Court of Protection Practice*, 12th edn, 1991, London: Stevens

Macfarlane, AB, 'The Court of Protection and its work' (1984) 128 SJ 571

Hunt, DG and Reed, ME, 'Statutory wills for mentally disordered persons' (1970) 34 Conveyancer 150

Thurston, JMR, 'Wills for mentally disordered persons' (1985) 82 Law Society Gazette 1617

Law Commission Report No 122, *The Incapacitated Principal*, Cmnd 8977, 1983, London: HMSO

Law Commission Consultation Paper No 119, *Mentally Incapacitated Adults and Decision Making* (1991)

Law Commission Consultation Papers Nos 128, 129, *Mentally Incapacitated Adults and Decision Making* (1993)

Law Commission Report No 231, *Mental Incapacity*, HC 189 (1994–95)

Lord Chancellor's Department Consultation Paper, *Who Decides? Making Decisions on Behalf of Mentally Incapacitated Adults*, Cm 3803, 1997, London: The Stationary Office

Mutual wills

Burgess, R, 'A fresh look at mutual wills' (1970) 34 Conveyancer 230

Youdan, TG, 'The mutual wills doctrine' (1979) 29 Toronto ULJ 390

Law Commission Report No 242, *Privity of Contract: Contracts for the Benefit of Third Parties*, Cm 3329, 1993, London: HMSO

Enduring powers of attorney

Law Commission Report No 220, *Law of Trusts: Delegation by Individual Trustees*, HC 110 (1993–94)

International questions

Scoles, EF, 'The Hague Convention on Succession' (1994) 42 AJCL 85

Depositing wills

Law Commission Working Paper No 4, *Should English Wills be Registrable?* (1966)

Gillis, I, 'Missing wills, a solution to the problem' (1975) 72 Law Society Gazette 4

Chapter 7   Revocation of wills

Warren, J, 'Dependent relative revocation' (1920) 33 Harv L Rev 331

Newark, FH, 'Dependent relative revocation' (1955) 71 LQR 374

Kiralfy, A, 'Partial revocation of wills' (1959) 23 Conveyancer 103

Edwards, RH and Langstaff, BFJ, 'The will to survive marriage' (1975) 39 Conveyancer 121

Bagwell Purefoy, PR, 'Have you revoked your privileged will?' (1982) 79 Law Society Gazette 570

Chapter 8   Alteration, republication and revival

Mitchell, JAB, 'The present state of testamentary republication' (1954) 70 LQR 353

Chapter 9   Intestate succession

Sherrin, C and Bonehill, RC, *The Law and Practice of Intestate Succession*, 2nd edn, 1994, London: Sweet & Maxwell

Ing, ND, *Bona Vacantia*, 1971, London: Butterworths

Morton Committee, *Report of the Committee on the Law of Intestate Succession*, Cmd 8310, 1951, London: HMSO

Cretney, S, 'Intestacy reform – the way things were, 1952' [1994] Denning LJ 35

Graham, GB, 'Intestates' Estates Act 1952' (1952) 16 Conveyancer 402

Ryder, EC, 'Hotchpot on partial intestacy' (1973) 26 CLP 208

Palk, SNL, 'Hotchpot – or hotchpotch?' (1981) 7 Adelaide L Rev 506

Law Commission Working Paper No 108, *Distribution on Intestacy* (1989)

Law Commission Report No 187, *Distribution on Intestacy*, HC 60 (1989–90)

Kerridge, R, 'Distribution on intestacy, the Law Commission's Report (1989)' (1990) 54 Conveyancer 358

Law Commission Report No 184, *Title on Death*, Cm 777, 1989, London: HMSO

Miller, J Gareth, 'International aspects of intestate succession, (1988) 52 Conveyancer 30

Chapter 10   The classification and failure of gifts

Illegality and public policy

Cretney, S, 'The Forfeiture Act 1982: the Private Member's Bill as an instrument of law reform' (1990) 10 OJLS 289

Tarnow, NM, 'Unworthy heirs: the application of the public policy rule in the administration of estates' (1980) 58 Canadian Bar Rev 582

Youdan, YG, 'Acquisition of property by killing' (1973) 89 LQR 235

Mackie, K, 'Manslaughter and succession' (1988) 62 ALJ 616

Reed, P, 'Does crime pay?' (1982) 132 SL 238

Disclaimer

Goodhart, W, 'Disclaimer of interests on intestacy?' (1976) 40 Conveyancer 292

Oughton, RD, 'Disclaimer on intestacy – an American viewpoint' (1977) 41 Conveyancer 260

Pinkerton, JL, 'Disclaimer of interests on intestacy – some thoughts from Northern Ireland' (1978) 42 Conveyancer 213

Martyn, JG, 'Variation of wills' (1994) 58 Conveyancer 446

Divorce

Law Commission Report No 217, *Family Law: The Effects of Divorce on Wills,* Cm 2322, 1993, London: HMSO

Kerridge, R, 'The effect of divorce on wills' (1995) 59 Conveyancer 12

Mitchell, RJ, 'Will drafting after the Succession Act – divorce, survivorship and second death legacies' (1996) 60 Conveyancer 112

Witnessing

Yale, DEC, 'Witnessing wills and losing legacies' (1984) 100 LQR 453

Lapse

Maurice, SG, 'Distribution of interests saved from lapse by the Wills Act' (1954) 18 Conveyancer 341

Chapter 11   The construction of wills

Morris, JHC, 'Palm-tree justice in the Court of Appeal' (1966) 82 LQR 196

Adams, J, 'The doctrine of very heir' (1973) 37 Conveyancer 113

Sherrin, C, 'The wind of change in the law of wills' (1976) 40 Conveyancer 66

Sparkes, P and Snape, R, 'Class closing and the wait and see rule' (1988) 52 Conveyancer 339

Crago, N, 'Mistakes in wills and election in equity' (1990) 106 LQR 487

Stone, D, 'The presumption of death: a redundant concept?' (1981) 44 MLR 516

Report of the Russell Committee, *The Law of Succession in Relation to Illegitimate Persons,* Cmnd 3051, 1966, London: HMSO

Ryder, EC, 'Property law aspects of the Family Law Reform Act 1969' (1971) 24 CLP 157

Samuels, A, 'Succession and the Family Law Reform Act 1969' (1970) 34 Conveyancer 247

Law Commission Working Paper No 118, *Illegitimacy* (1982)

Miller, J Gareth, 'The Family Law Reform Act 1987 and the law of succession' (1988) 52 Conveyancer 410

Latey Committee, *Report of the Committee on the Age of Majority,* Cmnd 3342, 1967, London: HMSO

Chapter 12   Personal representatives

The Law Society, *The Probate Practitioner's Handbook,* 1995

Oerton, RT, 'Solicitors as executors' (1967) 64 Law Society Gazette 244

Harris, JW, 'Ten years of variation of trusts' (1969) 33 Conveyancer 113 and 183

Ker, BS, 'Personal representative or trustee?' (1955) 19 Conveyancer 199

Ryder, EC, '*Re King's Wills Trusts*: a reassessment' (1976) 29 CLP 60

Walker, RRA, 'Personal representatives assenting to themselves' (1964) 80 LQR 328

Garner, JF, 'Assents today' (1964) 28 Conveyancer 298

Chapter 13   Administration of estates

Law Reform Committee 23rd Report, *The Powers and Duties of Trustees,* Cmnd 8733, 1982, London: HMSO

Graham, GB, 'The remuneration of trustees' (1952) 16 Conveyancer 13

Parry, NDM, 'Remuneration of trustees' (1984) 48 Conveyancer 275

Bartlett, RT, 'The Law Reform Committee's trust investment recommendations – 10 years on' (1992) 56 Conveyancer 425

Ker, BS, 'Trustees' powers of maintenance' (1953) 17 Conveyancer 273

Graham, GB, 'The order of application of assets' (1952) 16 Conveyancer 257

Maxton, J, 'The nature of a beneficiary's interest pending the administration of the estate' (1992) 56 Conveyancer 92

Ganz, G, 'Heirs without assets – assets without heirs: recovering and reclaiming dormant Swiss bank accounts' (1997) 20 Fordham International LJ 1306

Law Commission Consultation Paper No 146, *Trustees' Powers and Duties* (1997)

HM Treasury, *Investment Powers of Trustees: A Consultation Document,* 1996, London: HMSO

Law Commission Consultation Paper No 148, *Claims for Wrongful Death* (1997)

Capper, D, 'The heir-locator's lost inheritance' (1997) 60 MLR 286

Clements, L, 'Problems arising on the death of a property owner: Law of Property (Miscellaneous Provisions) Act 1994 Part II' (1995) 59 Conveyancer 476

Chapter 14 Tax and tax planning

Law Society, *Gifts of Property: Implications for Future Liability to Pay for Long Term Care*, 1995

Laidlow, P, 'Deeds of variation' (1990) 134 SJ 595

Rodgers, CP, 'Troubled inheritance down on the farm' (1987) 51 Conveyancer 387

Government Consultative Document, *A New Partnership for Care in Old Age*, Cm 3242, 1996, London: HMSO

Dept of Health, PO Box 4120, Wetherby LS23 7LN, *Dept of Health Circular LAC (95) CRAG (Charging of Residential Accommodation Guide)*

Chapter 15 Family provision

Rathbone, E, *The Disinherited Family, a Plea for the Endowment of the Family*, 1977, London: Allen & Unwin

Breslauer, W *et al*, 'Freedom of testation: the Inheritance (Family Provision) Bill (1938) 1 MLR 296

Unger, J, 'The Inheritance Act and the family' (1943) 6 MLR 215

Tolstoy, D, 'The Family Provision Act 1966' (1967) 31 Conveyancer 13

Law Commission Report No 61, *Second Report on Family Property: Family Provision on Death*, HC 324 (1974)

Cretney, S, 'Succession – discretion or whim, freedom of choice or caprice?' (1986) 6 OJLS 299

Glendon, MA, 'Fixed rules and discretion in contemporary family law and succession law' (1996) 60 Tulane L Rev 1165

Green, K, 'The Englishwoman's castle – inheritance and private property today' (1985) 51 MLR 187

Time limits

Prime, T, 'Time limits on dependants' applications for family provision' (1982) 31 ICLQ 862

Eligible applicants

Tobin, B, 'The Family Protection Act 1955: expanding the categories of eligible applicant' (1994) 16 New Zealand UL Rev 1

Spouse

Sherrin, C, 'Disinheritance of a spouse: a comparative study of the law in the United Kingdom and the Republic of Ireland' (1980) 31 Northern Ireland Legal Quarterly 21

Miller, J Gareth, 'Provision for a Surviving Spouse' (1986) 102 LQR 445

Miller, J Gareth, 'Provision for a Surviving Spouse' (1997) 61 Conveyancer 442

Interaction with divorce

Miller, J Gareth, 'Gifts, inheritances and the allocation of property on divorce' (1995) 24 Anglo-American L Rev 31

Adult children

Miller, J Gareth, 'Provision for adult children under the Inheritance (Provision for Family and Dependants) Act 1975' (1995) 59 Conveyancer 22

Dependants

Sherrin, C, 'Defeating the dependants' (1978) 42 Conveyancer 13

Naresh, S, 'Dependants' applications under the Inheritance (Provision for Family and Dependants) Act 1975' (1980) 96 LQR 534

Cadwallader, CF, 'A Mistresses' Charter?' (1980) 44 Conveyancer 46

Welstead, M, 'Truly a charter for mistresses' (1990) Denning LJ 117

Bates, F, 'Housekeepers, companions and family provision – a comparative interlude' (1993) 57 Conveyancer 270

Comparative/conflicts

Uniform Probate Code and Uniform State Laws (United States of America) (1983)

Macdonald, D, *An Introduction to the Scots Law of Succession*, 1990, Edinburgh: Green

Dyson, H, *French Real Property and Succession Law: a Handbook*, 1988, London: Robert Hale

Guest, AG, 'Family Provision and the *legitima portio*' (1957) 73 LQR 74

Dodds, J, 'The impact of the Roman law of succession and marriage on women's property and independence' (1992) 18 Melbourne UL Rev 899

Hayton, DJ, *European Succession Laws*, 1991, London: Chancery Wiley Law

Foster-Simons, F, 'The development of inheritance law in the Soviet Union and the People's Republic of China' (1985) 33 AJCL 33

Brady, JC, *Succession Law in Ireland*, 2nd edn, 1995, Dublin: Butterworths

Soul, M, 'Spanish succession law' (1991) 135 SJ 1056

Hudson, AM and Barbalich, R, 'Succession law in France and Italy' (1991) 135 SJ 1032

MacDonald Allen, DJ, 'Dying intestate in France' (1983) 127 SJ 850

Dyson, H, 'The tontine in French law, with some English comparisons' (1993) 57 Conveyancer 446

Anibaldi, A, 'International inheritance' (1989) 63 Law Institute Journal 842

Uzodike, E, 'Nigeria: defining the ambit of custom' (1990/91) 29 Journal of Family Law 399

Bradley, D, 'Marriage, family, property and inheritance in Swedish law' (1990) 39 ICLQ 370

Cushman, B, 'Intestate succession in a polygamous society' (1991) 23 Connecticut L Rev 281

Shammas, C, 'English inheritance law and its transfer to the colonies' (1987) 31 American Journal of Legal History 145

Miller, J Gareth, 'Family provision on death – the international dimension' (1990) 39 ICLQ 261

Morris, JHC, 'Intestate succession to land in the conflict of laws' (1969) 85 LQR 339

INDEX